Producing Beauty Pageants

A Director's Guide

2nd Edition

Anna Stanley

BOX OF IDEAS PUBLISHING
SAN DIEGO

BOX OF IDEAS PUBLISHING
P.O. Box 181218
Coronado, California 92178

Producing Beauty Pageants
A Director's Guide, 2nd Edition

Anna Stanley

Published in the United States by
Box of Ideas Publishing
www.boxofideaspublishing.com
ISBN 978-0-9621972-3-9 (paperback edition)
ISBN 978-0-9621972-4-6 (e-book edition)
Library of Congress Control Number: 2016900564

Cover Credits

Cover Design — *Photo Retouching by Courtney*
photoretouchingbycourtney.com

Photographer — *Robert Goold Photography*
facebook.com/RobertGooldPhotography

Photography Studio — *Right Light Studios*
rightlightstudios.com

Gown — *Dazzles Pageant & Prom*
shopdazzles.com

Crown Designer/Manufacturer — *Rhinestone Jewelry Corp.*
rhinestonejewelry.com

Scepter — *Shindigz*
shindigz.com

Sash Designer — *From Wishes to Stitches Embroidery*
cinderellagrammy@swbell.net

Cover Makeup Artist — Aleesandra Jones
Maquillage the Makeup Academy
maquillagemakeupacademy.com

Cover Hair Stylist — Brianna Tait
briannatait@yahoo.com

Cover Model — Mia Stanley

Contents

Preface

Anna Stanley, a pageant director (since 1983) and the author of *The Crowning Touch: Preparing for Beauty Pageant Competition* (1989), also wrote the first edition of *Producing Beauty Pageants: A Director's Guide* (1989). In the '90s, this first edition was used in the production of *The Secret World of...* series for The Learning Channel. Twenty-five years later, Anna has written *Producing Beauty Pageants: A Director's Guide, 2nd Edition*. Nine years in the making, not only does it feature entirely *NEW* pageant trade information, *Producing Beauty Pageants* has also been expanded into a series.

The *Producing Beauty Pageants* series includes:

A Director's Guide, 2nd Ed.
Creating a Synergized National Pageant System
Brokering a Pageant through Barter
Contestant Handbook
Sponsorship Fee
Optionals
Open Call
Directing a Fundraiser Pageant
A Guide to Pageant Terminology (FREE e-book)

If you want the convenience of interactive hyperlinks to the references in this book, you will need to purchase the e-book version of the same title.

Respectfully Yours,

Anna Stanley

Acknowledgments

Courtney Coleman, owner of *Photo Retouching by Courtney*, designed my PBP series' covers. Her graphic expertise resulted in the red gown being changed into a sequence of colors for each PBP title. Courtney, who also possesses an English degree, is the editor of the *Producing Beauty Pageants* series.

Gregg Schudel, my tech specialist, taught me that there is more to cookies than just eating them.

Carol Schudel, equipped with piercing wit and a love of cookies, sharpened my Introduction.

Melanie Brittingham, my dear friend, had the arduous task of marking a partial draft of this book, which became spread out within the series.

Maryke Davis, a bookworm, read the first six chapters of this book and made helpful suggestions.

Mia Stanley, who took time away from her studies prior to graduating from UC Irvine, modeled for the cover of my PBP series. Thank you, my daughter, for your support.

Henry "Turner" Stanley, equipped with a Stanford math degree, was my numbers expert. Thank you, my son, for being my PBP series' math whiz while serving our country as a Navy pilot.

Robert Goold, expert photographer, spent quality time with Mia capturing the perfect pose for my PBP series.

Jill Rowland, owner of *Dazzles Pageant and Prom*, selected a beautiful red gown for the cover.

Aleesandra Jones, a graduate of *Maquillage the Makeup Academy*, was Mia's makeup artist.

Jason Kirby, owner of *Togally* and *Right Light Studios*, hosted the PBP cover shoot.

Cyndi Neely, owner of *From Wishes to Stitches Embroidery*, created the sash featured on my PBP series' cover.

Brianna Tait, professional hair stylist, made a three-hour drive from the mountains to be at Mia's 8 a.m. hair call.

Henry Stanley, my husband, gave me his unwavering support for the nine years that it took for me to write this series.

Carl Dunn, CEO of *Pageantry/Prom Time Magazine*, marketed the first edition of this book for over 20 years!

Laureen Oglesby, also with *Pageantry/Prom Time Magazine*, hunted me down even when I tried to stop selling the 1st edition after twenty years. Your belief in my 1st edition led me to write an entirely new 2nd edition and turn it into a series.

Introduction

Today's pageant industry is monopolized by a handful of pageant systems. These few pageant systems expertly draw in huge contestant entries while the rest struggle to make production ends meet, or worse, fold with massive debt.

Twenty-five years ago, I wrote *Producing Beauty Pageants: A Director's Guide*, 1st Ed., which continues to receive five-star ratings on *Amazon*. In the early '90s, *Producing Beauty Pageants: A Director's Guide* was used in creating a respectable documentary about pageantry. It was produced by *Film Garden Entertainment* for The Learning Channel.

The second edition of my book (and the books within the *Producing Beauty Pageants* series) brings to light a pageant industry that no longer operates on a level playing field and has become dominated and controlled by a few heavy hitters who won't lose power or speed...*unless you know the intricacies of their game plan and develop your own game-changing plans*.

A handful of pageant directors control the largest percentage of contestant entries and *annually rake in double-digit millions of dollars*. They successfully manage to lure a huge number of repeat contestants (alumnae) into their labyrinth for as long as nine or ten years and counting.

They also earn considerable sums of "silent income" from girls who don't end up participating in their pageants (drop-offs). The silent income that they generate from drop-offs is more than what most pageant systems gain from basic entries.

The books in this series provide breakthrough information about the pageant world's heavy hitters and the elaborate barriers that they have constructed to create a vastly uneven, and often unethical, playing field.

If you are financially involved in the pageant industry *in any fashion*, what you don't know will hurt you. *Producing Beauty Pageants: A Director's Guide, 2nd Edition* (and the other books in the series) provide the foundation for a pageant industry in which everyone has a fair and equal chance of succeeding. This book aims to: provide guidance to help keep new pageant systems from faltering; help already established pageant systems formulate sound, game-changing strategies in light of this new pageant knowledge; and assist top-producing, ethical pageant systems in how to maintain their competitive edge.

Chapter 1

Starting My First Pageant with $100

I enjoyed competing in pageants, though I never imagined that I would become a pageant director, much less direct one starting with only $100. During the summer, in 1983, at the age of twenty-three, I became a pageant director. The transition from competitor to director was a natural one, and it allowed me to remain in a field that I truly enjoyed.

With the business knowledge that I had, having two years of experience being self-employed with an exercise business, I became a pageant director while remaining an exercise instructor. Interlacing the two businesses so that each would complement and promote the other was my goal. This joint effort could promote female participation in my exercise business and vice versa. Pageant contestants who joined my exercise classes could learn about weight control; fitness students could participate in the pageant. However, because of the tremendous success of my first pageant, I immediately began promoting my second pageant and discontinued my exercise business due to a lack of time.

It was easy for me to relate to pageant girls because I was twenty-three when I directed my first pageant, and I was familiar with the type of music, fashion, and movies that they liked. This was one advantage that I had over older pageant directors. Now, I'm not saying that you have to be twenty-three or twenty-five years old, or be a female, for that matter, to become a successful pageant director. You just have to be honest with yourself and honest with contestants, and everything else has a way of falling into place.

Until I decided to direct a pageant, competition was my only pageant experience. I had no other experience or knowledge in producing pageants, and I never had paid much attention to what was going on behind the scenes. I didn't know that I would soon be producing pageants on a full-time basis, or I might have paid closer attention.

And what about cost-saving measures? Wouldn't it be nice to start off as a pageant director knowing all of the cost-saving measures that would help your first pageant be even more profitable? It could be your pageant's surviving difference! For example, *United America Pageant* system's (Denton County Preliminary) biggest cost-saving measure was booking a venue on a Sunday (at a cheaper rate than on a Friday or Saturday) and sharing it with a Princess pageant. That meant that time would be tight, and things would be a bit more hectic on pageant day; however, it kept both pageant systems out of the red. Had I known this, I would have invited another non-competing pageant director to share and split venue costs, allowing him/her to use the morning part of the day while my Teen and Miss Divisions competed in the evening. Better yet, I would have bartered for the venue! Learn more about bartering for your FREE venue by reading my book *Producing Beauty Pageants: Brokering a Pageant through Barter*, Chapter 5, "Pageant Venue Bartered."

At the time I decided to produce my first pageant, I only had $100 and no other means to financially support a pageant. I had no idea of what the cost of producing a pageant would be. In fact, one pageant director tried to scare me away from becoming a pageant director in her area by saying that her prize package alone cost her $5,000 (all were donated by merchants). I knew that I could produce a pageant. Learn more about bartering for your FREE prizes by reading my book *Producing Beauty Pageants: Brokering a Pageant through Barter*, Chapter 7, "Barter Your Prize Package."

I knew that I could obtain financial support through sponsorship entry fees. The only problem with this was that the fees would not be turned in to me until after I had my brochures, applications, sponsorship forms, and other pageant marketing materials printed. This would come after I secured my pageant location — all of which costs money, and certainly more than $100! What I did was find a pageant location that would allow me to pay the rental deposit at a later time, *after* I obtained sponsorship entry fees from official contestants. I secured that location.

During my first pageant, I was not aware of the financial impact bartering has on businesses who actively participate. Consequently, I only approached a local cable TV company for Official Sponsorship support. Not only did I want our community cable station to promote contestant entries, I wanted my pageant to air on television. I asked the cable station manager if he would 1) tape and air pageant promotional spots and 2) tape and air my pageant on its public access cable. The cable station needed my pageant promotion for its slow season. Without other Official Sponsors, the cable TV general manager agreed to sponsorship. Learn more about bartering for free TV promotion by reading my book *Producing Beauty Pageants: Brokering a Pageant through Barter*, Chapter 6, "Media Partners," under "Television Official Sponsor."

All I could think of at this time was how I was going to distribute my $100. I enlisted a professional printing company as an Official Sponsor. Through barter, I obtained various pageant marketing materials: flyers, admission tickets, and a Pageant Program Book (PPB). Learn more about bartering for your printing needs by reading my book *Producing Beauty Pageants: Brokering a Pageant through Barter*, Chapter 9, "In-Kind Sponsors" under "Printing Company," "Graphic Company," "Logo Designer," and "Pageant Program Book."

After my flyers were printed, I posted them on grocery store bulletin boards, church bulletin boards, and at colleges and high schools (my pageant ages ranged between thirteen and twenty-five). Remember, this was during a time when we didn't have social media. In fact, I would post flyers inside and outside of high school bathroom stalls so that girls would see the pageant information on their way in or out! How to Create a Beauty Pageant Flyer can be found on *eHow*. Fortunately, I was aware of (and took advantage of) free advertising through press releases and public service announcements, and I had cable TV promotion.

In today's Internet age, pageants can be promoted on various sites including *Facebook*, *Twitter*, and *YouTube*. They can also be promoted on free pageant listing sites such as *The Pageant Center*, *Pageant Emporium*, and *Beauty Pageant News*. Want national exposure for your pageant? *Pageantry Magazine* has been covering all aspects of pageantry for over thirty years. It is an ideal vehicle to advertise a National pageant system. You can even link your pageant to the Georgia-based blog *Glitzy Crown Pageant Pages*. Not to be confused with the *Glitzy Crown Pageant Pages* blog, *Glitzy Girl Magazine*, based out of New York, is a pageant community-driven publication, sold in 11 countries, reaching over 11,000 readers with each issue. Since 2009, *Glitzy Girl Magazine's* base has grown since the popularity of pageantry has grown in Europe. UK's January 2016, 32-page pageant magazine, *Miss Pageant*, can be found on *issuu*. And new to the scene, in 2016, and posted for your viewing on *issuu*, is January 2016's, 64-page issue of *Pageant Girl Magazine*.

Remember to advertise your pageant on your own pageant website and form a co-op with other pageant producers to trade website links and PPB ads to promote each other's pageants.

Prior to meeting prospective contestants at my Open Call, in 1983, I began gathering prizes for the Queen and Runners-Up. A beauty college was the first Official Sponsor I approached for a beauty college scholarship donation. My next target, a nursing school, was receptive to my pageant and sponsored a non-transferrable $1,000 nursing scholarship ($2,500 in today's dollars). Unfortunately, the winner of the pageant did not want a nursing career, so the prize was cancelled. On the other hand, approximately fifteen percent of the candidates registered into my pageant *because* I offered a nursing scholarship. Other prizes I obtained included, but were not limited to, a modeling school scholarship, a modeling/photo portfolio, a dance scholarship, a commercial workshop, a moped, a 14k gold and diamond crown ring, a one year athletic club membership, and a $500 cash award. (Five hundred dollars, in 1983, had the same purchasing power as $1,186.21 in 2014.) Except for the cash, all of these prizes were donated by Official Sponsors and In-Kind sponsors.

Creating categories of competition was my next step. Each category, or area of competition, is some specific quality, trait, or action upon which the judges will give a graded score. The three categories that I decided on were Personal Interview, Sportswear, and Evening Gown. I didn't include a Swimsuit competition because I felt that girls would be more comfortable about participating in a pageant if one was not included.

There are many other categories that you can incorporate into your pageant. You can include aerobic wear, western wear, leadership, essays, community involvement, etc. Many teen pageants stress scholarship achievement. In fact, many teen pageants require candidates to take a written test that covers academic subjects. In the _San Antonio Stock Show and Rodeo Queen_ pageant, candidates are expected to demonstrate their horsemanship abilities. Although no longer a prerequisite, official contestants at San Francisco's *Miss Chinatown USA* were once required to answer on-stage questions in Chinese, even though some of them could barely muster more than a few words in their language. Audiences did not hesitate to laugh when a contestant's Chinese was not up to par. *Miss Northern Navajo Nation Pageant*, on the other hand, states that "Contestants must be able to speak both Navajo and English."

Throughout my first pageant, I personally interviewed prospective contestants in large group gatherings. First, my budget did not allow me to purchase many stamps. Second, I felt that if these girls wanted information about the pageant, they would be interested in meeting me, so I would set up various dates to have these "information sessions." Years later I "discovered" that these sessions were the absolute pageant bible secret — Open Call — to the success of my pageant. Look at *National American Miss*, currently the number one youth pageant system. NAM is a perfect example of a pageant system that, for years, didn't present Open Call sessions. NAM began its pageant system, in 2003, at the heels of leaving its State directorship at *Miss American Coed*. It wouldn't be until five years later, in 2008, when NAM changed its business model and incorporated Open Call, that it took the pageant industry lead. More information on how NAM made the leap from a non-Open Call pageant to an Open Call pageant can be found in my book *Producing Beauty Pageants: Open Call.*

To motivate prospective contestants to pay their first sponsorship installment, about three weeks out I scheduled a group photoshoot, which doubled as registration, at a local boutique. Immediately after registration, the now-official contestants began choosing outfits that they would model for the publicity photoshoot. After the photoshoot, I mailed the pictures and press releases to area newspapers. Although there was no guarantee that the pictures and press releases would be published, many were. Hone your sponsorship-raising knowledge so that you can relay these razor-sharp skills to prospective contestants by reading my book *Producing Beauty Pageants: Sponsorship Fee.*

Many pageant promoters who go all out in their National pageant lose several thousand dollars on their inaugural event. On the other hand, pageant promoters who employ the "industry secret" — Open Call — almost always make a huge profit on their first pageant. Pepper that with a bartered host hotel, stunning prize package, and other business freebies to keep your pageant system in the black, and you're sure to be a floating success. To give you an idea of the amount that you can make on a Local or Preliminary pageant, below is a simple balance sheet for my first pageant.

Income and Disbursement

Income	
Sponsorship entry fees	$ 36,000
(120 official contestants at $300 each)	
Drop-Off Income	$ 6,300
(42 ex-official contestants at $150 each)	
Ticket Sales	$ 11,500
(840 at $10 each; 155 at $20 door price)	
Photogenic fees	$ 4,650
(186 at $25 each)	
Total Income	**$58,450**

Disbursement	
Pageant Program Booklets (400 books)	(bartered)
Admission tickets (1000 tickets)	(bartered)
Business cards (500)	(bartered)
Flyers (600)	(bartered)
Stationery printing (custom envelopes and paper)	$ 150
Auditorium rental (Scottish Rite Temple theater)	$ 385
Insurance	$ 150
Postage	$ 30
Cash Prize	$500
Total Disbursements	**$ 1,215**

Subtracting my total disbursements from my total income gave me a net income of $57,235 — a great return for a three-month period on my original investment of $100 — during the summer, in 1983, and during a recession. If you factor in inflation, the net income in today's dollars would be about $134,000! Learn how I bartered for nearly everything — including a host hotel's "the bottom floor" — for ALL subsequent pageants by reading my book *Producing Beauty Pageants: Brokering a Pageant through Barter*, Chapter 5, "Pageant Venue Bartered" under "The Bottom Floor."

Chapter 2

Start Your Own Pageant Business

If you're new to the pageant industry, you might be surprised at all of the different types of pageants there are and the different rules governing each sort. There are glitz pageants, semi-glitz pageants, natural pageants, face pageants, online pageants, scholarship pageants, married women pageants, and plus-size pageants, just to name a few. There are even FFI (for female impersonators) pageants! If you visit *Habee's HubPages*, the article "Beauty Pageant Rules" will provide you with a description of many of these types of pageants. Once you figure out what type of pageant you will produce, then you will be on a path to starting your own pageant business.

This chapter will guide you through the administrative aspects of the pageant business — from registering your pageant business to getting bonded to setting up shop. Whether you are starting your own beauty pageant business from scratch, or you have been producing pageants for years, this chapter will help you to focus on areas which will expand your pageant, make your system easier to operate, and save you time and money.

Partnership

What will be your business entity: sole proprietorship or partnership? If you are afraid to start a pageant business alone, if you think that you're not tech-savvy enough to run a pageant business alone, or if you believe that you will need financial backing to run your pageant business, think long and hard about bringing a co-founder into your new pageant system. If you must have a co-founder, hire one. Give him/her a large sum of equity — between 20 and 40 percent — vested over, say, four years. If by the end of four years the relationship isn't stable, you have an operating agreement in place that allows for a divorce.

If you do bring in a permanent co-founder, and things don't work out, breaking up is hard to do. The best way to handle a business breakup is to prepare for the possibility of a divorce happening when you're just starting out. You can do this by including a set of instructions in your Operating Agreement covering how a split would happen. For example, there should be a requirement that the exiting founder sign a non-solicitation agreement should s/he decide to launch a similar business after leaving. If the new partner that you have in mind can't talk about the potential bad times, chances are s/he won't be able to reach a consensus when it comes to breaking up.

If you and your co-founder decide to team up on a pageant business, make sure that you obtain a third-party arbitrator, such as an attorney, so that you can ensure that both of you trust this person and that there are no issues afterward. Legal removal of a co-founder, and how you go about it, depends on if your pageant business is a partnership, limited liability company, or corporation, as well as the state in which you set it up. Before you decide on bringing in a co-founder, take a look at Mark Suster's video *The Co-Founder Mythology*. Mark spoke at Stanford, in 2010, about starting a tech company. Stanford heads cleverly chopped the video up into small, bite-sized segments — each nearly four minutes long. My son, Henry "Turner" Stanley, a 2012 Stanford graduate, believes that viewing Mark Suster's video could keep you from making a huge, drawn-out, and painful financial mistake.

Limited Liability Company (LLC)

A LLC is an abbreviation that (in the U.S.) most commonly refers to a limited liability company. Often incorrectly called a "limited liability *corporation*" (instead of *company*), it's a hybrid business structure. It's also allowed by state statute to have certain characteristics of both a corporation and a partnership or sole proprietorship (depending on how many owners [members] there are). A LLC, although a business entity, is a type of unincorporated association and is *not* a corporation. The primary characteristic that a LLC shares with a corporation is limited personal liability for the debts and actions of the LLC, meaning, the liability of the owners of a LLC for debts and obligations is limited by the financial investment of the owner(s). Basically, if you do form a home-based LLC, this would ensure that you don't have personal liability for debts and civil liability arising from your pageant business dealings.

The primary characteristic a LLC shares with a partnership is that it provides management flexibility and the benefit of pass-through income taxation. LLC income is not taxed at the corporate level. It is only taxed at the individual owner's level. A LLC is often more flexible than a corporation, and it is well-suited for companies with a single owner. Start customizing your LLC by visiting _legalzoom_, _Nolo Law for All_, or _BizFilings_.

Tax Identification Numbers

A new pageant owner will need to secure a tax identification number: EIN (employer identification number) or TIN (tax identification number). Proprietors and partners often choose to get a TIN for their business operations even though taxes from the businesses may pass on to the owners. Individual states issue tax identification numbers so that business owners can submit state income tax. Corporations, limited liability companies (LLCs), and limited liability partnerships (LLPs), which are business entities registered with states, usually get EINs for tax identification purposes. Whichever form of identification number your pageant business gets, you must have one to operate and comply with federal and state tax laws. Some states and localities also require new business owners to get a sales tax ID number so that the business can collect sales tax from customers — most common in the case of a pageant that sells tangible goods. In many cases, when someone asks for your business tax ID, they are referring to your EIN.

When you organize your pageant business, you must file a Form SS-4 or Form SS-5 to get an EIN or TIN from the IRS. The form is available as a free download from the IRS website. Moreover, it costs nothing to file. Most states and municipalities require a TIN or EIN to issue a business license or permit for state-regulated industries.

Better Business Bureau

Businesses are under no obligation to seek _Better Business Bureau_ accreditation, and some businesses are not accredited because they have not sought BBB accreditation. However, to be accredited by BBB, a business must apply for accreditation. The BBB will then determine if the business meets BBB Accreditation Standards, which includes a commitment to make a good faith effort to resolve any consumer complaints. BBB accredited businesses must pay a fee for accreditation review/monitoring and for support of BBB services to the public.

Accreditation in BBB is by invitation to companies that, at minimum, have been in business for at least one year, have demonstrated sound business practices, and meet BBB's Accreditation Standards. National pageants which are BBB Accredited include, but are not limited to, *American Coed Pageants*, *America's Homecoming Queen*, and *Miss Teen of America*.

Licenses and Permits

Some states require different types of licenses. Some require that you obtain a solicitor's license if you will be selling food at a concession stand. Before buying a property or signing a lease, contact the city or town clerk where the business will be located to ensure that your plans conform to local restrictions and to obtain the necessary permits for building types and signs. Be sure that you have all of the proper permits and licenses before you operate. To find out what you will need, contact your local *Better Business Bureau*, Small Business Administration, or City Hall.

If you were to operate a pageant business in Paragould, Arkansas, for example, you would need at least a Paragould, Arkansas Pageant System occupational business license or a home occupation permit. You would also need a Paragould, Arkansas fictitious business name A.K.A. (also known as) or DBA (doing business as) filing for your business. If you employ workers, you will need a federal EIN and a State EIN tax ID number. LLCs (as well as partnerships and corporations) are required to get a federal tax ID number, a state employer tax ID number, and a sales tax ID number (seller's permit). Check with your City Hall to see what licenses and permits you will need in order to operate your pageant system.

Bonded

According to the *Bureau of Labor Statistics*, in 2010, there were over 83,000 directors employed nationally? And, in 2010, the *Better Business Bureau* received nearly 10,000 inquiries from consumers about beauty pageant promoters, up from nearly 6,000, in 2009, and nearly 6,200, in 2008. With so many unscrupulous pageant promoters, it is to your advantage to get licensed and bonded, as did *Little Miss Arkansas*. Several states have enacted a bonding law requiring that new pageant organizers entering the industry place a deposit to guarantee the safety and security of pageant contestants and their sponsors. National pageant directors will need to secure bonds in the states of Tennessee, Georgia, and Arkansas if they hold a State pageant in any of these states. Registration in another state as a National pageant producer will not be effective for Tennessee, Georgia, and Arkansas.

Tennessee now requires that pageants be registered and bonded so that an unscrupulous promoter can't make off with entry fees before the contestants show up. The Beauty Pageant Operator Surety Bond — in the amount of $10,000 — is required by The Tennessee Division of Consumer Affairs. An unregistered pageant operator is subject to a $5,000 civil penalty for violation of Tennessee's Beauty Pageant Law in addition to potential sanctions under the Tennessee Consumer Protection Act of 1977, as amended, codified at TENN. CODE ANN. § 47-18-101 *et seq.* Pageant operators who have any questions regarding this state's Beauty Pageant registration process should contact the Consumer Affairs Division of the Tennessee Department of Commerce and Insurance.

If you produce a pageant in Arkansas, you will be required to possess an Arkansas Beauty Pageant Operator Surety Bond, also in the amount of $10,000, and you will be required to be licensed. Only pageant producers that can prove that they have been producing beauty pageants for at least twenty-five years can be exempt from bonding in the state of Arkansas. Before you can obtain your license, you need to be bonded first. This bond is payable to the State of Arkansas for the use of the pageant director and any person(s) who may have a cause of action against the obligor on the bond for any losses caused by failure to conduct a beauty pageant. Though not all states have this requirement, it is to your advantage to do everything possible to emphasize the quality and legitimacy of your pageant. Quality pageant promoters who are licensed and bonded will list this on their paperwork. The law also states that they will have a copy of both at registration and are required to show it if official contestants and parents ask. Both Tennessee and Arkansas offer bonds without credit checks. "Sometimes people worry about their credit score being [dinged] when we do a check credit," says Ralf Rigo of *BondsExpress.com*. "Since no money is being borrowed, it doesn't affect the score."

Georgia law has a specific provision regulating pageants. Therefore, it also requires pageant companies to post a $10,000 cash bond. Under the Georgia law, the pageant operator must provide official contestants with the following information: 1) the operator's name, address, and telephone number; 2) the name, address, and telephone number of the organization or individual conducting the pageant; 3) the names of the pageants that the operator usually promotes; 4) the name and address of the authorized business representative; 5) the name, address, and telephone number of the company holding the bond; and 6) the statement:

> The State of Georgia requires bonding or escrow of
> pageants conducted for the profit of the operators.

A surety bond is a promise with a finite term to an obligee. A surety bond, unlike an insurance policy, has no refund value after issued. A surety bond protects the party requesting the bond, the obligee, against any financial losses as a result of poor financial decisions, damages, unethical decisions, or failure to follow state and local laws on the part of you, the pageant promoter. A surety bond holds the pageant director accountable for his/her business decisions, and the price is the same for one day or the full term. Ralf Rigo of *BondExpress.com* added,

> A surety bond is also different from insurance in that
> whatever the bond is asked to pay out has to be paid
> back. It's like a loan in that respect. If it's used, you
> have to pay it back no matter what. These debts
> cannot even be eliminated by bankruptcy. A surety
> can even take the client's property to collect the debt.
> Once a bond is asked to pay, and the funds are not
> returned, it's doubtful that the person can ever be
> bonded again. Moreover, a bond requires the client
> to sign an indemnity agreement that spells out the
> terms for re-payment. This agreement is usually
> signed by all owners, partners, and spouses, unless
> it's a publicly traded company.

Depending on several factors, a surety company may issue a bond to an individual based on satisfactory credit. Some companies have variable rates based on credit, and others will issue a bond without credit approval. This varies by state and bond terms.

BondExpress.com sells Beauty Pageant Operator Surety Bonds. No pageant director is turned down. Your Social Security isn't needed, and there isn't a credit check. Surety bonds in the amount of $10,000 cost $100. They expire on the last day of each year and need to be serviced annually. Access *BondExpress.com's* Bond Information application, or call (800) 331-5453.

Trademarks

You may also protect your company name and pageant titles with a trademark. A trademark, also known as a service mark, is a brand name distinguishing you from others in the pageant industry. To register your trademark in your state, call or write to the Secretary of State in your state's capitol for a trademark application form. The Patent and Trademark Office in Washington, D.C. can help you register your trademark federally. The best available source for learning about trademarks is the *Trademark Law Handbook*, published by the U.S. Trademark Association. It is interesting to see the searches that go into such trademarks. An example of *Crowned Princess Charm Pageant's* trademark can be found at Justia.com Trademarks.

Ms. America applied for various trademark variations, in 2000, under its main trademark. Some of the variations of trademarks that were applied to its brand include "*Ms. America Beauty*," "*Ms. America Fitness*," and "*Ms. America's Beautiful Baby*." Scroll down, and you will find protections on over a dozen statements, including "Empowering Women Across America," "Empowering Teens Across America," and "Dream it! Believe it! Live it!"

Spirit Productions, Inc., filed for a U.S. federal trademark for *National American Miss* on November 22, 2002, and on June 15, 2007, at *LegalForce Trademarks*. Annette Hill, producer of *Universal Royalty Beauty Pageant*, filed a Trademark at Justia.com on April 18th, 2012. However, a U.S. federal trademark on *Logos Database* and *LegalForce* shows Annette as having filed with them on February 25th, 2010. All trademark sites show Annette as having started her pageant business on June 1, 1995. *LegalForce* appears to be an ideal place to have your pageant trademark posted. Annette's legal posting reads in part:

> [Contact] the owner Hill, Annette of the Universal Royalty Beauty Pageant trademark by filing a request to communicate with the Legal Correspondent for licensing, use, and/or questions related to the Universal Royalty Beauty Pageant trademark.

It's no wonder that Annette's pageants were often filmed for *Toddlers & Tiaras*! This statement announces that licensing and use of her pageant are welcome for consideration.

Parent Company Name and Pageant Title(s)

The first task in setting up shop is naming your business and your pageant(s). Some pageants choose a parent company name and then list various businesses under that name, including its pageant system. Do extensive research to see if your chosen company name is already in use, in the event that you don't want a name that is already out there.

Let's look at *National American Miss* as an example. Steve and Kathleen Mayes, in 1985, became State directors for *Miss American Coed*. In 2003, they became the National directors of *National American Miss* pageant system. Steve established and incorporated (in Texas) the parent company *Spirit Productions, Inc.* This is, of course, not to be confused with *American Spirit Pageants* whose parent company name is similar: *American Spirit Pageants, Inc.* There doesn't appear to be a website for Steve Mayes' *Spirit Productions, Inc.*, at least not one related or connecting to NAM. There are, among others, *Spirit Productions, Inc.* — producers of outdoor community events and indoor corporate events; *Spirit Productions* — a resource center for Theater, Speech, and Forensics; and *Spirit Productions* — creator of films that celebrate the strength of the human spirit.

As a former pageant director in Texas, I used *South Texas Pageants, Inc.* In California, I used *Pageants of California, Inc.* It is not necessary to use the words "pageant" or "system(s)" in your company name. Many directors have creative names for their pageant programs that don't use either word, including *Our*

Diamond Miss. Additionally, you can create one with initials. In the name _World of IBC_, for instance, the IBC stands for intelligence, beauty, and charm. Combining initials to create an acronym is another idea. _P.E.A.R.L. Girls_ stands for "Poised, Elegant, And Responsible Leaders."

Look at your existing pageant title and expand on it. When _Southern California Rose of Tralee_ pageant officials developed their Princess Program, a distant time after the inception of their Miss division, they plucked the "Rose" and fashioned their 5–12 age division "Rosebuds."

Be careful with your chosen names. Girls ages 13–17 would rather _not_ have a _"Miss Pretty Pretty_ (yes, two-in-one)" title division, as does _Boz Pageants California_. They would prefer _Miss Ultimate Teen_ (to complement the _Miss Ultra Beauty_ title of the 18–35 age division) because it is more regal. Moreover, although _Our Little Miss_ is no longer just a children's pageant, as was intended when it was created, in 1962, the title _still_ suggests it.

Is the company name and pageant title that you want to use available? Research is needed to make sure that both the company name and pageant title that you want to use are legally available. It's best to find this out before you begin your pageant business. It is the pageant director's responsibility to ensure that the name(s) used doesn't infringe upon another company's name(s). Ensuring that your name is legally available means that people who choose to do business with you will not confuse your products/services with another pageant director's products/services. Moreover, when customers look for your pageant system, they are finding you and not your competitor.

You can start your company name and pageant title search by performing a free corporate name search on _Direct Incorporation_. Then, visit your County Clerk. S/he may have an online searchable database to help with your initial search. Next, contact your Secretary of State. Check the online searchable database. After all, the Secretary of State is responsible for issuing name registrations. Your next step would be the USPTO (United States Patent and Trademark Office), going right to the TRADEMARKS section. Finally, your last efforts can include search engines, online Yellow Pages listings, and domain name databases. While it is best to have comprehensive research performed by professional firms or attorneys, it is more economical to first take advantage of the free resources available. Then, if your chosen name appears to be available, you can conclude your research by having comprehensive research performed, and you can decide if you want to file for a Federal or State Trademark.

I produced a pageant, in 1987, in which the winner won a trip to compete in the *Miss Hawaiian Tropic* pageant in Daytona Beach, Florida. Because my Preliminary took place in Texas, I named the pageant *Miss Texas Tropical*. If the name of your county is not already in use, you can use it for a pageant title. If your state is known for a particular industry or product, use that to create a title for a pageant. For example, Florida produces oranges; Texas is known for armadillos. If you live in Idaho, hold a potato Queen contest. The bayou country of Mansura, Louisiana, has been christened La Capitale du Cochon de Lait (The Suckling Pig Capital). Every year Mansura holds a *Cochon de Lait Festival*, at which a Queen is chosen and given the title of *Miss Cochon de Lait*. If your chosen names are spoken for, add a word to differentiate the title, such as *Miss Greater...*, *Miss Western...*, or *...'s Most Beautiful....* The possibilities are endless.

Titles can refer to a civic organization, such as *Miss Knights of Columbus*. Urban areas can be named in pageant titles, for example, *Miss Dallas* or *Miss Metroplex*. Another idea for creating a title is through a community event, such as Corpus Christi's *Miss Buccaneer Days*.

When thinking of pageant title names, think of its expandability, i.e., room for growth. When *America's Perfect Preteen, Junior Teen, Teen, Miss, and Woman Pageants* named its pageant system, in 2009, little did pageant officials know that six years later they would be changing the name to reflect the pageant's international participation: *World's Perfect Preteen, Junior Teen, Teen, Miss,* and *Woman Pageants*. Also known as the International Pageant/Model Search, *World's Perfect Pageant* now recruits from eleven countries, and the list continues to grow — already including USA, Bahamas, Puerto Rico, Europe, Canada, China, North America, and France — with additional countries who love the runway feel of the pageant. *World's Perfect Pageant* feels very modern, hip, and progressive. The young ladies are able to showcase their personal style and expression on nearly sixty feet of runway! *World's Perfect Pageant* is one of the world's premiere beauty celebrations. The title change certainly reflects this message.

Once you create your pageant company name, you will have pageant titles under that name. Then, you might have subtitles under your pageant titles. Let's take a look at pageant company *Coastal Georgia Pageant Productions*. It hosts the *Coastal Georgia Beach Beauties Pageant*, and under that title, CGPP has various subtitles, including "Living Doll," "Beauty Supreme," "Princess Supreme," etc. To help pageant candidates understand the differences of each subtitle, pageant promoters often provide an explanation of all pageant subtitles in their "Rules & Regulations."

Overlapping Titles

Titles do overlap, especially in urban areas. For instance, when *Miss Texas USA* former pageant Contestant Recruiter Joe Rinelli found Christy Fichtner, in 1984, he didn't name her *Miss Dallas*. He had already given that title to someone else. Instead, he named her *Miss Dallas County*. If that title had been taken, he would have named her *Miss Metroplex*.

Titling Runner-Up Positions

In an effort to showcase as many amazing young women as possible at its National pageant, pageant officials at *World's Perfect Pageants* do not simply announce Runner-Up positions; instead, they award prestigious state titles! For example, the Florida winner is announced as *Florida's Perfect Teen*. The First Runner-Up is announced as the state nickname, *Sunshine State's Perfect Teen*; the Second Runner-Up is announced as the state's capital, *Tallahassee's Perfect Teen*; the Third Runner-Up is announced as the largest city in its state, *Miami's Perfect Teen*; and the Fourth Runner-Up is announced as the state flower title, *Orange Blossom's Perfect Teen*. If the state is selecting young ladies through the National Office without holding a state pageant, title assignment will be on a first come, first serve basis. Imagine all of the promoting that these "titled Queens," i.e., Runners-Up, will do for WPP!

Open/Closed Pageants

When creating your pageant title(s), keep in mind if your pageant is to be an open or closed pageant. If you want an open pageant, it's best to create a title that is general, allowing a greater number of entrants from a larger area to participate. *Miss Archdale-Trinity Pageant* is an open pageant. Candidates from all areas of North Carolina are able to participate. *Creative Princess Beauty Pageants* is also an open beauty pageant. Participants don't have to live only in Las Vegas, Nevada. A candidate doesn't need to hail from Pickens County to enter the *Miss Pickens County* pageant because it, too, is an open pageant. *Miss Gardendale Pageant* makes it clear that you don't have to be from Gardendale: "No residency restrictions! You do not have to live in the area to compete!" *America's Perfect Teen* is also an open pageant. *America's Perfect Teen* 2010 was UK's Anysha Panesar! (Since this crowning, *America's Perfect Teen* changed the title to *World's Perfect Teen* in order to reflect its international growth.) *Angels Pageant System* is not only an open pageant, it also accepts any boy or girl with a special need, newborn to 105! *Junior Miss Cherry Festival Pageant* is open to Gem County residents and children or grandchildren of Gem County residents.

Little Miss Texarkana is a closed pageant. In order to participate in this pageant, a candidate must live in Bowie, Red River, Cass, Morris, Titus, or Marion Counties; in Arkansas she must live in Howard, Pile, Nevada, Sevier, Miller, Hempstead, Little River, Columbia, or Lafayette counties — hence, the title name "Texarkana." To participate in the *Miss Gurnee Pageant*, a candidate must live within the 60031 zip code and must be a Gurnee resident. Candidates may be asked to show proof.

Registering Your Pageant Name and Pageant Title(s)

Begin by registering your pageant name, pageant title(s), and pageant subtitles(s) at your county clerk's office. If your chosen names are not already in use, a county clerk will issue you a certificate of ownership. The certificate — DBA (doing business as) — states the number of years that your pageant name(s) will be reserved for you. Choose the maximum number of years (usually ten) that you want to protect your chosen name(s).

When you are cleared to use the assumed name(s), a notary public will date, sign, and notarize the certificate of ownership. The original certificate is yours to keep for your files, and a copy will be placed in the county clerk's files. You will need to pay the county clerk a small fee for registering the title. The notary public will charge an additional fee to notarize the original. Registration fees vary from state to state.

When I first started my pageant business, I created and registered a variety of titles and subtitles. To date, I have not used them all. Still, it is good to have them registered for a potential future use. One San Diego pageant director registered a dozen titles and permitted her Finalists to use them at the _Miss California USA_ pageant, even though most are Delegate-At-Large candidates.

Inaugurating Your First Year

If your pageant is a first annual, don't announce it as the "First Annual." Instead, use the word "inaugural" in your first set of pageant marketing materials. Two pageants that did just that include: _"Celery City Charm Pageant's_ inaugural event, March 24th, 2012, in beautiful Historic Sanford, Florida..." and _American Glamour Pageant_: "Join us in our AMAZING Inaugural Year! This is what we've all been waiting for, a pageant showcasing Glamour and Elegance!" The following year you can announce your pageant as a second annual because, by now, you _are_ an annual event. _U.S. Universal Pageant_ presented its inaugural pageant in June 2013. Even after twenty-five years in the pageant industry, _Pageants of New Zealand_ held its inaugural _International_ Pageant — _Southern Star_. Leaving a pageant system to start your own? Don't tack the years you directed for a previous pageant system onto your inaugural pageant. Separate the two, start over, and be proud of your inaugural event as you roll out your own red carpet.

Refund Policy

Before you print your pageant paperwork, have your Refund Policy in place. Discover how successful pageant systems set up their refund policies by reading my book _Producing Beauty Pageants: Creating a Synergized National Pageant System_, Chapter 15, "Refund Policy." Present your Refund Policy, complete financial disclosures, and supporting pageant materials, in writing, to prospective contestants before requiring a legally-binding signature on your Official Application (contract).

Pageant Insurance

Many National pageants charge an insurance fee to each of its State/Regional/Preliminary directors, thus blanketing them all with insurance coverage. The fee is relatively inexpensive and provides coverage for all directors who purchase coverage. This alleviates them from having to obtain insurance on their own. For the *Cinderella International Scholarship Pageant*, all official participants, chaperones, and staff members must be covered by the *Cinderella Pageant System Registration & Insurance Program*. Cinderella insurance coverage includes twenty-four-hour coverage during the pageant for accidents. Participants who have registered with the *Cinderella Pageant System Registration & Insurance Program* at an official Local or District pageant during the current year are not required to register again. Their prior insurance coverage extends through the International Finals. Their chaperone, on the other hand, must register. All entrants and chaperones who have not previously registered will be required to register to participate in the State Finals AND must pay the Registration & Insurance Fee. As of this writing, the participant fee is $4; the chaperone fee is $8. Insurance benefits include a $5,000 accidental death and dismemberment policy and a $1,000 blanket accident medical expense. The insurance fee is not included in the entry fee.

On January 8, 2014, plaintiff Lindee Wilson filed what appeared to be "an amount that exceeds $75,000,"[1] against *Spirit Productions, Inc.*, *National American Miss*, Steve Mayes, Kathleen Mayes, Tiffany Hague, and Jane and John Does 1–100, at the Mississippi Southern District Court. The case involved a State Finalist (official contestant) who sustained personal injuries while participating in the 2010 *National American Miss* pageant held at the Jackson, Mississippi Marriot. It wasn't clear if any of the defendants had insurance coverage for accidents.

When you set up a National pageant system, check into a group insurance rate that would cover not only the National pageant, but your State and Regional pageants as well. You can offset the cost by charging State/Regional directors a small premium. In turn, the State and Regional directors can incorporate this expense in their sponsorship entry fee or charge a separate insurance fee, as does *Cinderella International Scholarship Pageant*. Miss America incorporates insurance costs into its franchise fee. State directors just need to fax over their

---

[1] Lindee Wilson vs. Spirit Productions, Inc., National American Miss, Steve Mayes, Kathleen Mayes, Tiffany Hague, Jane and John Does 1–100. Civil Action No. 3:14cv13DPJ-FKB, Document 1, Case1:14-cv-00033-HSO-RHW, filed January 8, 2014,
http://dockets.justia.com/docket/mississippi/mssdce/1:2014cv00033/84994.

filled-out Certificate of Insurance Order Form to the National headquarters *before each pageant. eSportsInsurance.com* can provide accident and liability insurance specifically for your pageant event. Ask your insurance company if it will insure your National, State, Regional, and/or Preliminary pageants (under its Special Event Liability Insurance), at a discounted rate. For an even better rate, check into a package discount tied to a number of pageants per year. Look into this soon because many hotels and auditoriums will not rent or barter its venue without proof of liability insurance.

Will your insurance policy cover candidates in your pageant during their travels? While *Face of Europe* pays its area final winners' expenses and accommodations to the National pageant, those girls are responsible for their own personal travel insurance.

Setting up Shop

While every pageant director dreams of having a business office in an office building suite like *Miss Mundo Latina*, located in front of *Universal Studios* in Orlando, Florida, this is also the most expensive way to go. Instead, make an office out of a spare bedroom or corner of a room. If you have a spare room that you can convert into an office, you may be able to deduct a portion of the expenses of maintaining your home from your taxes as a business expense. If you are considering purchasing a building or office condo to house your pageant business, negotiate a one year lease with an option to purchase. You will be able to see in a year's time if the property suits your pageant needs.

Several pieces of equipment are absolutely essential to running your business. A list of these items are below:

Vision Board

Keep a vision board handy where you can keep postings of your short- and long-term pageant goals. A vision board is any sort of board on which you display images that represent whatever you want to be, do, or have in your business. It will help you keep your attention on your intentions. In addition to images, a vision board can include words, phrases, or sentences that affirm your intentions. Most importantly, a vision board will help keep you focused on all aspects of your pageant. If you really want to stay focused, vision board software allows you to create vision boards from your computer screen, cell phone, or other mobile devices — even on your pageant website. Digital vision boards can be with you anywhere you go. *StepOne Vision Boards* and *Visualize Your Goals* can help get you started.

Telephone Lines

When you get a business line, get a number that is easy to remember. Customers like easy-to-remember, easy-to-dial numbers. Your phone company will assist you in selecting such a number. Choose numbers that end in hundred or thousand figures, such as 000-5700 or 000-4000, or choose code words for numbers. For example, *Miss American Coed* pageant's phone numbers (at one time) were 1-904-432-TEEN and 1-800-346-COED. *U.S. Man of the Year*'s number was 1-800-USAS-MEN. *US Crowning Pageants*' toll-free number is 1-866-431-PGNT. *Blue Crab Festival Beauty Pageant* notes to prospective contestants, in pageant marketing materials,

> Any questions, contact Holly Bellamy, Pageant Director, at 1-386-882-1993 (must dial the 1).

When you request a number, either for a personal or business line, you are requesting a personalized number. In most areas, you will pay a one-time fee in addition to a monthly charge throughout the time you use the personalized number. The charges are relatively inexpensive and well worth the added cost of a personalized number.

Custom Calling Services

There are several custom calling services available to you and your business. Some of the features include call waiting, call forwarding, three-way calling, and speed calling. Find out the cost of a personalized number, a second line, a business line, and other special features by contacting your phone company.

Essence Pageants provides a Conference Call Schedule on its website. All conference calls are conducted at 7 p.m. Eastern Standard Time/6 p.m. Central Standard Time/4 p.m. Pacific Time. Prospective or official contestants who need some general information about the pageant have the opportunity to call 1-800-

662-6992 or 1-917-210-2631 to speak with the Executive Director and learn more about *Essence Pageants*.

Purchasing a business telephone line ensures a free listing in The Yellow Pages. Additional advertising may also be purchased. Independent companies that publish their own directories may be receptive to a promotional trade. Directories are generally published annually (and some semi-annually), so put your bid in early. Good planning makes for a great marketing campaign. Contact your local phone company for details. Remember to include your company name in online *yellow pages*.

Once your business is up and running, create office hours and post them on your website, as does *From My Crown to Yours*. The pageant's office hours are Monday through Friday, 9 a.m. until 5 p.m.; Saturday from 11 a.m. until 3 p.m.; and Sundays they are closed.

Blocking Your Caller ID

Normally, telephone calls are accompanied by the identifying telephone number of the originating caller. People who have subscribed to Caller ID with their phone service will normally be able to see the number of the party calling them. If, for whatever reason, you don't want the party you are calling to see the number of the phone you are calling from, then use *67 to block the transmission of your phone number before placing a call. You would need to enter *67 on a per call basis. According to the tech how-to site *How to Do Things*, you won't have any way to tell if this is working (it does), but if you want to reassure yourself, just call another phone number that has caller ID to double-check that your number is, indeed, blocked.

According to *How to Do Things*, you have two options: you can permanently block your phone number, or you can block your number on a call-by-call basis. There's no need for an expensive cell phone blocker. The most permanent solution is to request a "line block" from your cell carrier. Please note that this will not block your number from being visible to emergency services or any toll-free number. It only works when you call businesses and individuals.

Answering Machine

Investing in an answering machine can save you time and money. Most prospective contestants who want information about your pageant will leave their name and number on your machine. Having an answering machine to receive incoming calls allows you the option to return calls at your convenience. It can also help your business to expand by not letting you miss important calls from Official Sponsors (explained later in this chapter), sponsors, media, or prospective contestants. Your phone center (or most electrical appliance stores) can help you select the right answering machine to fit your business needs. *Iris Festival Beauty Pageant* reminds prospective contestants that when they leave a message on its answering machine to "leave a phone number and speak *slowly*."

Answering Service

It is smart to have an answering service to take your incoming calls when you are out of the office for an extended period. People are more likely to leave a name and number with a real person than with a machine. Answering services can be expensive, so shop around for the best prices and features before you decide. A good answering service can enhance your appearance as a professional. *American Royalty Supreme Pageants* reminds prospective contestants, "If you call the 1-800 number, please leave a message with the service, and someone will return your call. Thank you!"

When looking for a phone answering service that will abide by your trade needs, in addition to a live person, there are other options to choose from:

- *Virtual Live Call Answering Service* — This service enables the pageant company to forward the call to another number that can be answered immediately. Some phone answering services give customers the alternative to have their calls answered live or be directed to the company's computer. This is perfect for a small pageant system.

- *Online Answering Service* — Companies who use this service are able to track all incoming calls through downloadable software on their computer. A company representative is able to listen back to the messages or listen to them while they are recorded. The downside to this is that customers employing the service will need to leave their computer on all of the time.

- *Interactive Voice Response* — This is a useful service for large pageants that need to pick up multiple calls at once. This is a digital phone answering service which will have a computerized voice wanting to know your queries that can point the caller to the fitting line. The computer will ask for a word-of-mouth response, and it has to know what the caller is communicating.

Obviously, the preferred phone answering service a pageant system can use is a live, kind phone operator. But if such a service doesn't fit in a pageant's operating budget, an answering machine will also work. In this case, ask prospective and official contestants to leave a detailed message for a fast response, but to speak *slowly*.

Personal Computers

Computers allow businesses to be organized and efficient. They can also greatly streamline the work pageant promoters do in finding prospective contestants and converting them into official contestants. Computers allow pageant directors to efficiently keep a mailing list for prospective and official contestants. Completed Official Applications can also be kept on file in the computer. Thus, prior to the pageant evening, directors can pull out biographies on every official contestant to prepare Master of Ceremony cue cards. Business transactions, from daily notes to letters, can be stored and updated using computers. Last, but not least, quarterly business records can be updated weekly or monthly. When quarterly tax periods arrive, pageant promoters will have a legible report ready for their accountants.

If you do not know much about computers, take a computer course at your community college. A beginner's course is fairly simple, and many can be applied to your business. Besides, the money you spend on this course may be deductible as a business expense. Being able to deduct your courses through your business is one great way to take advantage of a college education.

A computer can help your business expand and make it much more efficient. The computer you get should be determined by the software that you need. For a pageant business, three main pieces of software are recommended (when purchasing your computer, these may come already installed):

- A *Word Processing* program is best for business letters, newsletters, and information forms.

- A *Database* program is best for compiling lists of prospective contestants for mailshot. A database program can automatically sort by zip code (for cheaper bulk mailings) and print address labels.

- A *Spreadsheet* or *Accounting* program is best to keep track of business finances (and can also be used for score tabulation).

Inexpensive versions of each type of these programs are available. The more popular expensive programs are great, but you probably don't need all of the features. Find someone who understands computers to help you learn to choose software and equipment.

Computer Printer

Computer printers come in a variety of styles and with a host of features. A laser printer — which prints using the same mechanism as office copiers — can cut out typesetting costs because you can typeset most (if not all) of the work. Visit your local computer center to obtain information about the printer that would best suit your needs. Caution: Several replacement inkjet cartridges may cost more than an actual printer.

Website

You cannot set up shop without a pageant website. You can create your own with the help of online tutorials, or you can hire professionals to develop one. Chapter 8, "The Internet," will guide you with either choice you make.

Self-Inking Stamps

In addition to your self-inking business checking account stamp, add to your order self-inking stamps that say "PSA Dept." (Public Service Announcement), "P.R. Dept." (Public Relations), and

"Journalism Dept." to your order. If you don't send your news release to the proper department, it may take days to arrive, or sometimes not arrive at all. In either event, you'll miss a printing deadline, and writing each by hand can take forever *and* may not be legible by the company's mail department. If you mail press releases to high schools, be certain you include "Journalism Dept." on the outside of the envelope, otherwise, your press release may not make it to the proper location. *NEBS Business Forms & Supplies* carries a line of self-inking stamps that can be customized to print any special wording.

Post Office Box/Mail Box

If you don't want to use your personal address for your business, see your postmaster about renting a post office box. Prices of the boxes vary according to the size that you rent. An alternative to a post office box is to rent a specialized mailbox that allows you to use its street address as "your business address," and the box number as your "suite" number. Companies such as *Mail Boxes, Etc.* and *The UPS Store* rent such boxes, but rental costs vary from franchise to franchise.

Camera

Even if you have a personal photographer for your pageant, if your phone doesn't have a built-in camera, carry one with you at all times. You never know when you may come across someone famous who may grant you and your official contestants a publicity picture. The teen musical group *Menudo*, in the mid '80s, made an appearance at a mall in Corpus Christi, Texas. I invited official contestants to meet me at the mall for a (possible) publicity picture with *Menudo* group members. Although not famous at the time, my pageant candidates certainly loved being photographed with group member Ricky Martin, before he was *Livin' La Vida Loca*! Always carry a camera for such unexpected moments; use your cell phone camera as a backup.

Budget

Although only a guideline, a budget is the most important tool in establishing a financially sound pageant. Project your anticipated income, as well as your disbursements, early in your planning.

Continually improve upon and update your budget as time goes on. Once a projected pageant production cost has been determined, wise directors will set aside this amount prior to getting the initial promotions and advertising underway for their next event. When the pageant has been completed, they can easily determine what profit has been made, where future costs can be eliminated (or lowered), and where operational changes need to take place. There are many ways to set up a budget. Regardless of which way you choose, the point is to do it. Be conservative in projecting income and realistic in projecting costs.

Income Streams Never to Give Away

There is one thing that you should never offer for "free" in your promotions: an income stream, but if you do, be critically selective. *National American Miss* waives the $20 application fee for girls who attend Open Call. If 500 official contestants (State Finalists) had their $20 application fee waived because they attended Open Call, this represents a $10,000 income stream loss for NAM. While NAM will probably gain a portion of it back through a tax write-off, it was wise of NAM to give away this income stream for "free." (This example doesn't factor in nearly as many prospective contestants who attended a NAM Open Call, paid the first sponsorship installment, but then became drop-offs.) Learn about NAM's BEST KEPT SECRET, in my opinion, by reading my book *Producing Beauty Pageants: Open Call*, Chapter 10, "Drop-Off."

Think twice before you give away any income stream — application fee, Optionals fee, or admission tickets — that supports your pageant. Use "free," but use it wisely and sparingly. *Miss Royalty International* gives every candidate two complementary tickets to the pageant event — a $52 value. If there are 600 official contestants, the pageant will be giving away a $31,200 income stream!

If you think trophies cannot generate an income stream, think again before you give them away for free. Girls who enter a *National American Miss* State or National pageant can EARN a trophy IF they sell a half-page of advertisements in the Pageant Program Book (PPB). Imagine your multi-age State OR National pageant with 500 official contestants, and each candidate sells the required half page, $375 ad in PPB advertisements to *earn* a small trophy. That's an income stream of $187,500 generated from 500 trophies from one State pageant alone! Most parents want a guarantee that their daughters will earn a trophy, so many will rally family and friends to purchase a half-page, $375 ad congratulating their daughters on becoming a "State Finalist" in a NAM State pageant (or pay it themselves).

Another opportunity for an official contestant to take home a trophy from any NAM pageant is to earn it through five or more "credits." Candidates can earn those five credits by participating in any of its Optionals contests. Each Optionals contest earns them one credit (five Optionals at National costs $875). Candidates will also earn a single credit by selling fifteen admission tickets ($15 per ticket; $75 for 15 tickets). Let's say that 500 out of the nearly 700 official contestants at the 2012 NAM National pageant took home the Spirit trophy for entering five Optionals. That would be an income stream, via paid Optionals alone, of nearly a *half million dollars* for NAM — from one pageant alone! Imagine receiving *a half million dollars* for a few trophies that cost pennies to produce *en masse*! Candidates EARN these guaranteed trophies by handing Optionals monies, PPB ad monies, etc., over to NAM. As you can see, NAM doesn't just give trophies away for free (unless you count the few free Optionals contest winners noted below).

NAM hands out very few free trophies to the winners and sometimes to the 1st Runner-Up in the following Optionals: Best Thank You Note, Art Contest, Miss Spirit, Academic Achievement, Miss Personality, Most Ticket Sales, Most Recommendations, Volunteer Service, Best Résumé, and Scrapbook (at least at the National pageant). Many of those "free" Optionals contests have direct agendas — particularly its cleverly-designed Scrapbook contest. Learn about NAM's ingenious FREE Scrapbook Optionals by reading my book *Producing Beauty Pageants: Optionals*.

An Income Stream to Give Away

Many pageant systems charge a fee if official contestants want their scores and judges' comments. This is the most shortsighted move a pageant director/producer can make. Consequently, in an effort to create an additional income stream, most official contestants won't pay a fee to retain their scores because many are "over it" by now. As a result, the pageant misses a HUGE opportunity to resell those girls into its *next* pageant by inviting them as "returning" alumnae — with a discount offer to boot!

Never one to miss a promotional opportunity, *National American Miss* pageant officials distribute official contestants' scores for *free*. They present official contestants with their "outstanding" scores and comments, along with their placement in comparison to how other official contestants and winners fared. In retrospect, those girls are thrilled to find that they performed so well. Moreover, NAM pageant officials also take this opportunity to offer those girls an alumnae discount if they enter the next pageant by a certain deadline day! And, at least at the NAM California South State pageant, in 2013, every official contestant received a free group photo of their age division to accompany their scores and alumnae discount. To learn what specific income streams that NAM gives away to prospective contestants, read my book *Producing Beauty Pageants: Creating a Synergized National Pageant System*, Chapter 4, "Pricing a Pageant" under "Upcharge Revenue: Building Upcharge Revenue on 'Free' Products via Prospective Contestants." To learn what specific income streams that NAM gives away to official contestants, read my book *Producing Beauty Pageants: Creating a Synergized National Pageant System*, Chapter 4, "Pricing a Pageant" under "Upcharge Revenue: Building Revenue on 'Free' Products via Official Contestants."

Pageant Season

Before you set up your pageant schedule, determine what your pageant season will be. For example, the *International Junior Miss'* 2013 Season began August 1, 2013, and lasted through July 30, 2014. *Miss American Coed* and *National American Miss'* pageant season beings in January and ends in November. *America's Natural Supreme Beauties'* pageant season goes from February to December.

Areas of Competition

Before you create your pageant marketing materials, know your areas of competition. Before you develop your pageant's areas of competition, read my book *Producing Beauty Pageants: Creating a Synergized National Pageant System*, Chapter 5, "Areas of Competition." This chapter will help guide you in developing (or polishing) your areas of competition.

Sponsorship Fee

Once you set your sponsorship fee in writing, you are ready to teach prospective contestants how to find and secure sponsorship support. Extensively researched, *Producing Beauty Pageants: Sponsorship Fee* was written for pageant directors who want to stay abreast of the MANY ways that successful candidates retain their sponsorship fee. Once they learn of this helpful data, they can cultivate what information they think will work best for their pageant system. Then, they can present that sponsorship sales information to their prospective contestants. In doing so, they stand a better chance at converting them into official contestants. After all, if prospective contestants are not aware of the most current sponsorship sales strategies, they might not become official contestants. Or, they might not become *complete* official contestants if they personally paid the first sponsorship installment and then became drop-offs because they didn't really know how to find sponsors! What director wants to convert half of a sponsorship fee into silent income when s/he can at least double it with a full sponsorship income — if not income gained from Optionals, Pageant Program Book ad sales, admission ticket sales — the list does go on. It is your place to educate prospective contestants on the finer selling points of securing sponsorship support.

Pageant Paperwork

At some point, you will be creating your pageant paperwork. My book *Producing Beauty Pageants: Creating a Synergized National Pageant System*, Chapter 12, "Pageant Paperwork and Forms" includes a vast number of descriptions for pageant paperwork and forms that will likely aid your pageant system in developing your own.

Graphic Designers

There are a number of graphic (and web) designers who have experience producing excellent pageant-related graphics but who don't rise to the top of a Google or Bing search, at least not *yet*. One of them, Richard E. Bernico of *Hawaii Profiles*, is known for his professional services in the area of graphic design and website services for the *Miss Hawaii USA* pageant. Richard is an expert at

Pageant Program Book (PPB) layout and design. Additionally, he offers graphic services in the creation of admission tickets, flyers, posters, banners, *Facebook* updates, and last, but not least, contestant and sponsor ad page layout. To view a sample advertisement that Richard created for Aureana Tseu, *Miss Hawaii USA* 2009, scroll to the bottom of his Program Book Ad Page Requirements Including Tips guide. Have a question for Richard? Email him at rick@hawaiiprofiles.com.

If Richard wanted his pageant graphic design services to appear at the top of a Google or Bing search, he would be sure to submit his site information to Google through this link: Submit site to Google and to Bing through this link. By resubmitting your site information every time you make a change, you inform these search engines to make sure that the latest version of your site is indexed. If you want your graphic design services to rank at the top, be CERTAIN to include in your SEO (search engine optimization) list of keywords: graphic, pageant, program book ads, PPB cover, solutions, design, paperwork, paperwork cover designs, PPW (pageant paperwork), brochure, flyer, pageant *Facebook* timeline covers, pageant website design, pageant blog design, comp cards, centerfold spread, branding, website designer, director, delegate, contestant, coach, score sheets, scoring systems, digital ports, portfolio, composites, series, special effects, banners, web banner, social media banner, posters, mailers, pageant e-marketing designs, pageant platform pages, pageant postcard, pageant ports, photo backers, and photo borders. If you need an SEO expert in the field of pageantry, look no further than *PageantReady*'s website developer and SEO expert Charlie Hoff. Learn more by visiting *PageantReady*'s *Facebook* page, or call 877-2-PAGEANT (877-272-4326). A SEO expert is one thing your graphic (or pageant) business cannot afford NOT to hire.

Regarding an image search, if Richard (of *Hawaii Profiles*) wanted his PPB ad designs highly visible to the Internet public, instead of burying his PPB ad examples in his Program Book Ad Page Requirements Including Tips guide, or worse, only featuring them in the *Miss Hawaii USA* souvenir PPB, Richard would be sure to Add an image to Google to make his images findable in search results. It is smart to add completed images to a website, along with a description, so that the pageant industry can see various graphic designers' creative differences. While you can't directly upload images into search results, searchable images posted on a website can show up in Google's search results. *So, if you'd like your photograph or image to appear at the top of Google search results, you'll need to post the image on your website.* Other free content hosting services that you can use include Google+ and Blogger. To help your image appear in Google search results, follow these image publishing guidelines. Since ranking on image search requires both the optimization of images and page elements, you will need to get everything you visually want with the least amount of code and the smallest size. Image Optimization: How to Rank on Image Search is a must-read to learn how to do this.

Photo Retouching by Courtney A stickler for details and deadlines, Courtney has extensive experience in all forms of photo retouching, photo restoration, and graphic design. Her mission is to deliver clean, elegant, high-quality results for all of her services, which is evident in her work as the cover designer of my *Producing Beauty Pageants* series. Courtney can provide various sizes of advertisements, in black and white or color, ranging from 1/8th page to a full page, as well as a centerfold spread. She also creates designs for the following: pageant banners, brochures, flyers, business cards, *Facebook* timeline covers, gift cards, logos, magnets, postcards, posters, signs, t-shirts, and more. Courtney also offers natural, semi-glitz, glamour, and full-glitz retouching of photographs — perfect for photogenic entries. Additionally, her graphic design skills lend beautifully to comp cards, digital ports, pageant ads, photo backers, series, and special effects.

Imagine promoting your pageant on magnets, and then having official contestants display them in their school lockers. Let's also not forget about the car door magnets to present to each of your State or National winners, which they will place on their cars, and as a result, advertise your pageant during their year of reign. Courtney can produce car magnet designs for any size magnet that you would like.

More importantly, having a graphic designer like Courtney on your team — someone who can design your Pageant Program Book (PPB) cover, pageant paperwork, PPB ads, and/or design a full PPB layout — rather than sourcing these jobs out to multiple graphic designers (or worse, doing it yourself), lends to exclusive branding of your pageant business. With such unique branding, Courtney can synergize your pageant marketing materials to any of your social media platforms.

Courtney's prices are among the most reasonable, and for most services, her Standard turnaround time is within 48 hours of receiving payment; 24 hour and Same Day Rush Orders are available for an extra fee (Same Day must be placed by noon

Eastern Time in order to be eligible). Courtney's advertising and graphic design rates provide the sizes and costs for most graphic design services noted above. If you have any questions regarding Courtney's services, including those not listed here, please contact *Photo Retouching by Courtney* via email at photoretouchingbycourtney@yahoo.com; *Facebook*: *Photo Retouching by Courtney*; or at her website portal.

 Pageant Program Books — Design Your Way... to the Crown *Pageant Program Books* is a successful online graphic design company specializing in creating contestant ad pages for pageants across the United States and internationally. Graphic designers at *Pageant Program Books* have worked with Mrs. contestants, Miss contestants, Teen contestants, and Junior contestants at the State, National, and International levels. If you or your official contestants need PPB ads, custom ad page(s) are designed at pageantprogrambooks.com!

 Pageant Program Books has developed unique partnerships with pageants across the United States, offering exclusive discounts for their pageants. For candidates to take advantage of these exclusive codes supplied by pageant directors, the process is simple. If their pageant director doesn't have a code, candidates can send *Pageant Program Books* a message on their contact page with the director's contact information. The director will be notified and provide them with their own exclusive code. The discounts that *Pageant Program Books* offers with each code are unique to the partnership that it develops with each pageant. Better yet, pageant directors should contact *Pageant Program Books* to set up the discount code prior to putting out their pageant paperwork, so that they can include the code on this information. If the majority of your official contestants take advantage of the unique discount, your Pageant Program Book (PPB) will be graphically uniform — ideal when one graphic designer designs all of the ads. Along with its contestant services, *Pageant Program Books* also offer services for pageant directors. These services include full PPB layout, logo design, and website development. Moreover, it provides brand development with business cards, pamphlets, and brochures. To inquire about any of *Pageant Program Books'* services, or to inquire about ones that you don't see, visit its website contact portal, or its *Facebook* page: Pageant Program Books — Design Your Way...to the Crown.

 Kelly Johnson Designs Whether you are a director or contestant, when it comes to pageants, you can become a little overwhelmed. Kelly Johnson can lighten your load by providing you with many of your pageant graphic needs. Kelly has created several complete Pageant Program Books (PPBs), so she knows about PPB layout. Kelly is also an expert at designing score sheets AND scoring systems. All you would need to do is tell her the percentages you'd like to base a winner on, and she can produce the paperwork that you would need. Kelly also creates pageant blog designs, logo designs, professional PPB ads, contestant platform page designs, contestant portfolio designs, contestant paperwork, pageant paperwork, contestant blog designs, sign/comp cards, buttons, banners, t-shirt designs, and last, but not least, business cards. If you need a graphic design solution for something that you don't see here, contact *Kelly Johnson Designs*, or visit her *Facebook* page: Kelly Johnson Designs.

Gratzer Graphics Founded in 2003, *Gratzer Graphics LLC* is an award-winning, woman-owned graphic design/visual communications studio in Boonsboro, Maryland. Colleen Gratzer, principal/Graphic Designer (and Pack Leader), provides professional graphic design for a number of pageants, including *Miss USA* state pageants. One of *Gratzer Graphics'* recent jobs was the *Miss Maryland USA* Pageant Program Book (PPB) layout, featuring 92 pages, black text, and an incorporated cover. The work done (except for the predesigned and pre-printed cover) included layout, proofreading, and placement of ads. *Gratzer Graphics'* conscientious attention to detail, along with the team's talent and skills as designers — not to mention lightning speed of production — culminated into a successful PPB. Contact *Gratzer Graphics* at its website portal, or visit its *Facebook* page: Gratzer Graphics LLC.

Atlanta Glitter Girls Graphics The creative staff that only worked for *Glitter Girls Pageants* is now available to make your pageant stage shine, now that its exclusivity contract with GGP has ended. If you need pop-out lettering for your stage — similar to what *Atlanta Glitter Girls Graphics* created for the *Toddlers & Tiaras* episode: *Glitter Girls Bollywood* — it can be created. If you already have your own fonts and colors, *Atlanta Glitter Girls Graphics* can customize your own very large airbrushed backdrop lettering to cover-sit on your 18' x 8' airbrushed backdrop. *Atlanta Glitter Girls Graphics* will even supply the tools to hang your custom backdrop, which takes about a month to design. For a reasonable price plus travel fees, *Atlanta Glitter Girls Graphics* will set up your entire stage — gigantic logos and lighting — and break it down. Audio can be provided at an additional cost. A $250 deposit will secure the job, and your customized set will immediately be created. Last-minute sets (three weeks or fewer) can be arranged for an extra fee. And although it will be striking, it will not be 100% customized, as custom staging takes about a month to design. Additionally, *Atlanta Glitter Girls Graphics* can create high-quality banner ads to help you promote your pageant to the masses. A collage of its images can be see online. View *Atlanta Glitter Girls Graphics'* à la carte prices plus shipping costs. Contact *Atlanta Glitter Girls Graphics* at atlglittergirls@yahoo.com and type: "make me a banner" on the subject line of the email. Should you be in a bind for crowns, tiaras, trophies, custom OOC music, lights, etc., *Atlanta Glitter Girls Graphics* also provide these items for sale at great rates.

Vive Designs (UK) Pageant producers who are looking for a website design, logo design, or social media marketing services can find these solutions at *Vive Designs*. No matter how big or small, *Vive Designs* can meet your demands with excellent graphic design. If your pageant system is opening an online store, *Vive Designs* can let the world see what amazing products you have to offer with a great eCommerce web design. *Vive Designs* designed United Nations Pageants' logo. Ten logo concepts — using a mixture of color and text — were created for UNP to choose from. The logo UNP chose proved successful. Just check out UNP's website to see how the *Vive Designs'* logo fits! When Miss Congo Ireland needed a smart and beautiful website, pageant officials enlisted *Vive Designs* to create their website, blog, and website flyer. The website flyer that *Vive Designs* designed can be found here, and its blog can be found here. Contact *Vive Designs* via email at: info@vivedesigns.com, via *Facebook*: Vive Designs Creating Visions, or at its website portal.

Pageant Ready To be *PageantReady*™ is to feel empowered. For pageant producers, it's making sure that you have all of your pageant marketing materials in tip-top shape — pageant paperwork/bio/application, graphic design/program ads, sponsorship tools, and website development. Moreover, if you or your official contestants need assistance with the development of your/their Public Relations campaign to include press releases, media alerts, and one-on-one media interviews, Jules Meyer, *PageantReady* Co-Founder, can provide you with excellent Public Relations services. With clients such as *Henri Bendel, Tiffany & Co.*, and last, but not least, *Gucci*, Jules secured media for her clients on both the Local and National level. This included, but wasn't limited to, every major television network, local newspaper outlets, and a variety of news and fashion publications. For your pageant graphic design needs, Scott Allbee of *Allbee Creative* — equipped with a BFA in Illustration from *Northern Illinois University* — leads the *PageantReady* design team with over 25 years in the field of graphic design, digital artistry, and illustration. Scott's expertise includes graphic design, illustration, direct marketing, advertising, and social media. He is truly experienced in the preparation and production of all print media. If it's a website you need developed, or official contestants need a webpage, *PageantReady's* website developer and SEO expert, Charlie Hoff, can assist in the development of either. Learn more by visiting *PageantReady's Facebook* page, or call 877-2-PAGEANT (877-272-4326).

Glitz N' Glitter Graphics Specializing in website, comp card, banner, ad, and e-marketing designs that have a glitzy flair, *Glitz n' Glitter Graphics* is the place to be if you want your pageant to STAND OUT in the pageant and beauty industry. Custom banner ads designed by *Glitz N' Glitter Graphics* is one of the most effective ways to advertise on the web. Every day, thousands of prospective contestants are scanning message boards to help them gain the information they need to choose a pageant. If you're a glitz pageant, you need to "WOW 'em" with flashy graphic designs. *Glitz N' Glitter Graphics* knows just how to do this with even MORE design options available than ever before. If it's a stunning, eye-catching website that you need, *Glitz N' Glitter Graphics* offers complete business packages starting at just $120. Website design, homepages, Pageant Program Book cover design, and paperwork cover designs are also offered. Pageant websites glitzed by *Glitz N' Glitter Graphics* include *NES Pageants*, *America's Baby Doll Beauty*, *Elite Beauty USA Pageant*, *Angelic Beauty Pageant System*, *Miss Beautiful Model*, Model Beauty USA, *Kings & Queens Awards Pageant*, *MailinPageants.com*, and *Pageant Emporium*. Contact *Glitz N' Glitter Graphics* via email at pilatoproduction@aol.com, or visit their website.

99designs When a *Mrs. Arizona America Pageant* candidate needed a high-quality, affordable, full page pageant ad design, she visited *99designs*. First, she told the design team what she wanted in her design by filling out a brief. Next, she chose one of four design packages: Bronze; Silver; Gold; or Platinum. Then, the design contest would be launched in the *99designs* marketplace to its community of more than one million graphic designers. From Berlin to Bombay, professional creatives would read the customer's brief and begin to brainstorm ideas for the project. Interested designers submitted designs to the design contest. After this process, the *Mrs. Arizona America Pageant* representative gave feedback to help designers shape their ideas to fit the customer's needs. After seven days, and having to sift through sixteen designs offered by five graphic designers, it was time for the *Mrs. Arizona America Pageant* representative to pick the winner, sign the copyright agreement (a.k.a. Design Transfer Agreement), and pay $195. Once *99designs* transfers the prize money ($195 payment) to the designer, the pageant representative then downloads the winning Mrs. Arizona America Pageant Ad Page design.

PR Inc. was the graphic designer for *Miss Texas'* Media Kit, Local Directors Forms, People's Choice voting site (be sure to click on the "Miss" or "Teen" to be brought to the vote-casting page), and last, but not least, Pageant Program Book layout and contestant ads.

Acceptance Package

How will you present your pageant's acceptance package? Produce a large pocket folder to house your Contestant Handbook and other pageant marketing materials, or you can use an 11" x 13" (or larger) envelope — large enough to include whatever pageant materials a candidate would need in order to be a part of the program. A large, sturdy envelope will allow room for a number of loose items including lanyards, receipt books, admission tickets, and a Contestant Handbook. An 11" x 13" (or larger) envelope can be purchased at an office supply store, and so can pocketed folders. A printing company can also provide both and customize them.

Tagline

Create an awesome pageant tagline. A tagline is a variant of branding slogan typically used in pageant marketing materials, pageant paperwork, and pageant advertising. Pageant taglines could include: Wouldn't You Like to be Miss...; How You Can Become Miss ...; and You Could Be Our Next Miss...! Do not state, "We Can't Wait to Crown You!" as does *California Kisses Beauty Pageant* — unless you DO crown every participating candidate, as does The Ultimate Pageants at its National event. Then it would be a perfect tagline! All American Miss' tagline is: "Will You Take Home the Crown?" Miss Utopia's tagline is: "A Legacy of Love and Acceptance." National American Miss' tagline is: "[The] search is on for the next National American Miss...are you her???" America's Girls & Gents Pageants' tagline is: "Celebrating Today's Youth and Tomorrow's Leaders." Miss Georgia Girl's tagline is: "Use the crown to make a difference." Pageant Associates' (directors of *Miss Connecticut USA, Miss Indiana USA, Miss Pennsylvania USA, Miss Vermont USA,* and *Miss West Virginia USA*) tagline is, "Your journey to the crown begins here!" And, a national favorite, <u>*USA National Miss*</u>' tagline is: "Put a crown on it!"

Logo

If a picture is worth a thousand words, is a pageant logo worth a thousand official contestants? It sure appears to be for <u>*National American Miss*</u>, at nearly each of its State and National pageants! NAM officials prides themselves in being a fresh and fun modern program, and they aren't afraid to change with the times. NAM unveiled, in 2009, its new official logo coast-to-coast — from its Open Call invitations to souvenir hoodies — at its approximately 40 State pageants! This logo unveiling occurred the year after NAM changed its MO (method of operation) and introduced Open Call into its pageant system. To see what earlier NAM logos looked like, Google "images for National American Miss logos."

If you're on a limited budget, <u>*Logo Garden*</u> is where you can make a FREE logo. Simply follow the prompts. At the search bar, type in "crown," and you'll be delivered to, as of this writing, 28 crown designs. Once you choose a crown symbol, you'll be taken to a portal that will give you the opportunity to choose various symbol and text effects. Moreover, you can choose an advanced layout by clicking on the video icon right below the Symbol & Text Effects. Then, choose from various fonts and font sizes, text, and even shape the text. Note that *Logo Garden's* symbol database is updated regularly, so some symbols that are available today might not be made available in the future. Once you decide on the symbol, you'll be brought to the "Select Color" page. Then you are asked to add your tagline. Next, you will be asked to create a free account by filling in your first name, email address, password, and telephone number (optional). Within moments, *Logo Garden* will provide your self-designed logo — graphics and text included! While the free logo is design-limited, if you're on a tight budget, a *Logo Garden* logo can tide you over until you have a looser budget to incorporate a professional graphic designer.

When to Schedule Your Pageant

Determine the amount of time you need to devote to your pageant in order to reach your pageant goal. How much time will you need to structure and secure your prize package? How many official contestants do you expect to have? Consider that a souvenir Pageant Program Book (PPB), including roster pictures of candidates and advertisements, will take more time to produce than a simple leaflet PPB. If you are an Open Call pageant, what will be your Open Call schedule? A thorough understanding of Open Call can be found in my book *Producing Beauty Pageants: Open Call*, Chapter 4, "How Open Call Works"; Chapter 8, "Behind Open Call Scenes"; and Chapter 13, "NAM Open Call in Session."

Figure out all of the above details (and your own personal extras), and back that into your chosen day. Then, set your pageant date. Roughly, directors plan for a Local, Regional, or State pageant three to four months in advance and nine or ten months in advance for a National. (Highly organized National pageants run multiple State pageants practically simultaneously.) Whatever days you choose to present your State (and National) pageants, don't change your date. If your pageant is to take place on a Saturday and a Sunday, don't, at the last minute, change it to Sunday and Monday. Parents who work on Monday will either miss the pageant or need to take the day off — often without pay. Moreover, last-minute travel rescheduling is expensive, if not impossible.

How Many People You Expect to Attend

For every candidate who participates in a pageant, approximately seven people will purchase an admission ticket. But, not all ticket buyers will attend. I base this figure on an average of the total number of tickets that have been sold (at previous pageants that I have held) divided by the number of official contestants. Your average may differ depending on incentives offered to candidates selling tickets and if your pageant is a Local, State, or National. Pageants often oversell tickets, much as airlines overbook. Pageant officials count on no-shows, and, consequently, provide fewer seats than tickets sold — much like an airline! But, unlike an airline's accounting, there is no "accounting" for those unused, sold admission tickets. Money generated from unused admission tickets becomes non-refundable, silent income for pageant officials. Learn more about various silent income streams by reading my book *Producing Beauty Pageants: Open Call*, Chapter 10, "Drop-Off" under "Silent Income from All State Pageants Combined" and "How Silent Income is Split."

While a candidate may have sold dozens of admission tickets, pageants that are a good distance away from an official contestant's hometown (generally) don't fare well for their non-traveling ticket buyers. *National American Miss* (National) official contestants sold over 5,700 admission tickets for the 2012 National pageant. It's not clear how many people actually attended, but it was nowhere near 5,700! Having nearly 700 official contestants in the National pageant that year averaged to each candidate selling 10.5 tickets.

Now, imagine if half of those tickets sold for the basic NAM admission of $20 — you'd gain $57,000, and if the other half sold at the upgraded NAM admission price of $45 — you'd gain $128,250 — a combined total of $185,250! (You would still earn over $100k in admission tickets even if you didn't sell any upgraded admission tickets.) These are the kinds of numbers you can expect from your admission tickets *alone* if you operate in a NAM-like fashion. This only represents the National pageant. There are nearly forty NAM State pageants averaging similar numbers. For additional information on ticket upgrading, read Chapter 5, "Admission Tickets," under "Admission Ticket Upgrade."

Venues to Present Your Pageant

There are several factors to consider when choosing a venue to present your pageant. The time of year in which you present your pageant, the number of people attending your pageant, and your pageant budget are just a few. Venues can range from school gymnasiums to hotel banquet rooms to coliseums. For venue options available to you, read Chapter 3, "Pageant Venues." Learn how to barter for a FREE venue by reading my book *Producing Beauty Pageants: Brokering a Pageant through Barter*, Chapter 5, "Pageant Venue Bartered."

Housing for Overnight Candidates

Pageant facilities and sleeping accommodations can range from private hotel rooms to college dormitories. The late Texas pageant producer Jimmy Goodman, Jr., whose story is featured in my book *Producing Beauty Pageants: Open Call*, Chapter 15, "Have Open Call, Will Travel," arranged for local families to host official contestants in their homes over an entire pageant weekend — for nearly every pageant he produced. At no cost to Jimmy, each host family hosted their respective candidate for the weekend, feeding her meals and giving her emotional support. For most candidates, host families become second families, and lasting friendships are established. Pageant producers can also make arrangements with community colleges and universities to rent out its summer dorms for a summer pageant. Many campuses have available dorm rooms during summer months and will gladly rent them out. They are often cheaper than hotel rooms, so it may be worth it to check out this possible option. *Miss New York USA* housed its candidates in dorm rooms, as did *Miss Georgia*. If you house official contestants in hotel rooms, don't even think to put *three* candidates in one bed, as did one National pageant system!

Official Sponsors

Many Official Sponsors feel that the most effective sales lure is a bundle about five-and-a-half feet tall, measuring around 36-25-36: the American girl. A beauty Queen typifies the American girl. She makes a logical, believable image for products. Businesses feel that a beauty Queen reinforces the quality representative of its products and/or services. Because a beauty Queen is believable, she will enhance its product. Apparently loveliness sells, because Official Sponsors who have backed beauty pageants in the past continue to do so today. The success Official Sponsors receive from pageants has newcomers wanting to jump on the band wagon. It's clear that beauty pageants do line up plenty of Official Sponsors. *Cinderella Scholarship Pageant* recommends that pageant directors who want donors for entry fees to the next level pageant, flowers, stage decorations, travel expenses for the winners, wardrobe gifts, scholarships, etc., should seek these Official Sponsors before information is released to the general public and the official contestants begin looking for their own sponsors. Make arrangements with Official Sponsors early. Learn more about securing Official Sponsors, such as how to approach a prospective Official Sponsor, what to put into an Official Sponsorship Kit, and how to keep Official Sponsors wanting to sponsor your next pageant by reading my book *Producing Beauty Pageants: Brokering a Pageant through Barter*, Chapter 1, "A Bartered Pageant Production" under "Secure National Product Official Sponsors," "Fab Five Official Sponsors," and last, but not least, "Official Sponsor Exclusivity." Learn what ammunition you need to use in securing Official Sponsors by reading the same book, Chapter 2, "Benefits Package" under "What Not to Offer in a Sponsorship Benefit Package" and "Putting Together a Sponsorship Proposal." But, before you do seek out Official Sponsors, know how to rank them and to calculate their value by reading the same book, Chapter 4, "Official Sponsor Ranking."

Canceling a Pageant

First and foremost, you should never cancel your pageant. If conditions force you to cancel, then you have no choice, but if at all possible, do not cancel or postpone the pageant. It is best to see it through. If you need to cancel due to lack of official contestants, do not wait until the last minute to do so. Candidates put a lot of time and money into the pageant, and waiting until the last minute to cancel is unfair to them. If you cancel a pageant, return 100% of the entry fees. Explain why you had to cancel, making sure official contestants understand that circumstances forced the cancellation. Being frank about the situation builds integrity into your pageant system.

Postponing is a fancy way of telling official contestants that you have canceled your pageant without giving reason. If a postponement is necessary, then give candidates all the particulars — the new date(s) and time(s) regarding the rescheduled competition — and give the reason why you're cancelling the pageant event. It is better to cancel than to postpone to an indefinite future date. An indefinite future date makes any pageant system look shady. Once cancelled, you can try for a later date, under better circumstances. In the meantime, return all entry fees. Chances are that your "now former" official contestants will not have lost interest in your pageant. After all, candidates signed up for the previous pageant date, *not the postponed pageant date*.

Enforce and Abide By Your Rules and Regulations

Set a good example by enforcing and abiding by your own rules and regulations. If you say you are going to choose twelve girls as Semifinalists, then do so. Don't, at the last minute, change it to ten. If you say up to sixty girls will participate in each pageant division, don't permit more. If you say twenty-five girls have made it to the Semi-finals to be judged, then don't judge only five girls with the highest preliminary scores. This is misleading pageant marketing information. Moreover, it isn't fair to the other twenty "Semifinalists" who are not being judged when they were led to believe that they would be. Change the rules of your pageant game before or after a pageant, but not *during* a pageant. And don't ask prospective contestants to sign to your R&Rs and legally-binding clauses before presenting them in their entirety, in writing, preceding the Official Application and consenting signature line.

If your rules and regulations state the Queen will reign for a year, do not cut her reign short. According to an article in the *New York Times*, *Miss Arlington*, Julie Ann Willschleger, had her reign shortened so that she had only twelve days to go in on her reign, rather than three months, all because the city switched dates so its new Queen could have more time to get ready for the *Miss Texas* pageant. Julie sued the City of Arlington for $60,000 in damages. Premature dethronement, she said, "will hurt her budding modeling and acting career."[2] Such lawsuits take time out of a pageant promoter's promotional efforts for future pageants — not to mention money — because they often drag in court for years.

Present a Clean Image

In the report "Five Signs of a Rip-Off Beauty Pageant," the _Better Business Bureau_ and Lori Lee, former director for the *Miss North Carolina Sweetheart Pageants*, offers some tips to prospective contestants and parents when considering a pageant:

1. Find out how long the pageant company has been operating, and who the directors are.

---

[2] *The New York Times*, January 2, 1979

2. Be aware of a pageant's total participation costs.
3. Verify the location of the pageant.
4. Check up on the details.
5. Question ridiculous winnings and know that some prizes are not worth anything.

To view answers to these questions — and I recommend that you do — visit _CreditCards.com_. Above all, provide answers to these questions to any caller. When Michelle, from Wallingford, Connecticut, whose daughter received an unsolicited pageant Open Call invitation in the mail, in 2014, wanted to avoid wasting time and money, she followed BBB's advice. She called the number on the invitation. When she politely began asking the Five Signs of a Rip-Off Beauty Pageant questions, the pageant representative hung up on her. Michelle called back and got a recorded message that the office was closed. It shouldn't have been; she called well within the office hours noted on the pageant Open Call invitation that her daughter received! This prompted Michelle to file a complaint with _Ripoff Report_. You can read her permanently-filed report here.

This polite and concerned mother didn't deserve to be hung up on. Her daughter _wanted_ to be a part of the pageant. After all, the pageant system sent _her_ an unsolicited invitation! Michelle was following BBB's advice. How can prospective contestants or parents find answers to BBB's questions if a pageant representative won't respond? Had the pageant representative answered her questions, or took her name and gave it to someone who _could_, Michelle wouldn't have filed this national complaint that will permanently remain in the "Unusual Rip-Off" category file for wise prospective contestants to find. Isn't that who you want invested into your pageant system — _wise_ official contestants?

Chapter 3

Pageant Venues

By now you are ready to locate and secure your pageant venue. Armed with proof of insurance, arrange to speak with the venue's General Manager or rental manager to get a feel for what dates are best and how much lead time is needed to secure those dates for any venue listed below. Just be thankful that your pageant is not taking place in Ireland, at least for the time being. Many Irish hotel venues have refused to host American style child beauty pageants, despite there being a demand for them. _Universal Royalty Beauty Pageant_ producer Annette Hill discovered this when, in 2012, she attempted to have her first ever beauty pageant in Ireland. Annette ended up having difficulty finding a hotel venue that would host her pageant because Irish hotels were concerned that protestors might interrupt the events. As of this writing, Annette may or may not have found a location in Ireland for her pageant, but when she does, she "[intends] to keep the venue location top secret and is planning on hiring a security team."[3] Fortunately, U.S. hotels will gladly host a pageant — many even bartering 100% of your venue needs. They certainly did for _every single pageant I ever held_ except for the first one, because I didn't know to ask! This is a perfect example of what you don't know _can_ hurt you. Learn how to barter for a free hotel venue — "the bottom floor" — by reading my book _Producing Beauty Pageants: Brokering a Pageant through Barter_, Chapter 5, "Pageant Venue Bartered" under "Hotel/Venue Official Sponsor Promotion." Regardless of where your pageant venue is, be certain to include in your pageant paperwork, as does _U.S. Sophisticate Pageants_,

> [the venue] and the pageant are not responsible for lost, stolen, or misplaced items. [Neither] the

---

[3] Higgins, Hilda. "Irish Hotels Refuse to Host 'Toddlers and Tiaras' Style Child Beauty Pageant." _Irish Central_, July 11, 2012. http://www.irishcentral.com/news/Irish-hotels-refuse-to-host-Toddlers-and-Tiaras-style-child-beauty-pageants--VIDEO-162046015.html.

pageant nor the [venue] are responsible for injury before, during, or after the pageant.

High School/College/Technical School Gymnasiums, Cafeterias, Multi-Purpose Rooms, and Auditoriums

High school/college/technical school gymnasiums, cafeterias, multi-purpose rooms, and auditoriums are ideal venues to present pageants. Although the arrangement is less formal than a town theater, any of these venues may be suitable for your pageant needs. For rental information, contact the school's officials. Gymnasiums, cafeterias, and multi-purpose rooms can even be turned into a reception ballroom after the pageant.

If you were to present your pageant at Astoria High School auditorium in Astoria, Oregon, the maximum seating is 880. In the cafeteria, the maximum seating is 200, and in the gymnasium, the maximum seating is 2,000. If you wanted a smaller venue, you could rent the Astoria Middle School cafeteria, which seats 200, and their gymnasium seats 600.

- The *Miss Georgia National Teenager Pageant* took place at Mountain View High School Theater.

- The *Miss Amazing Pageant* took place at the Kuna High School Commons.

- *Coastal Pageant Productions* held the *Little Miss & Teen Miss St. Patrick's Day* pageant at the Savannah County Day School. The cafeteria doubled as the dressing room area. Because there is NO covered walkway between the cafeteria and backstage, pageant officials noted,

  Official contestants should come prepared for any type of weather, including wind, drizzle, and rain. Please do not arrive expecting to have access to the dressing area before 8:30 a.m.

- *American Superstarz Pageants* presented its *Georgia Superstarz Pageant* at Middle Georgia College.

- *Beehive Beauties* was presented at the Weber State University Wild Cat Theater.

- *Miss United States Woodlands Scholarship Program* was presented at Southeastern Technical College.

Town Theater/Civic Auditorium/Performing Arts Center

A town theater/civic auditorium/performing arts center is ideal for presenting pageants. The facilities cannot be beat. To secure the best date possible, plan on booking at least three months in advance.

- The *Texas United America Pageant* was presented at the Josephine Theater in San Antonio, Texas.

- *Mrs. Texas International* was held at the Selena Auditorium in Corpus Christi, Texas.

- *Crowned One Productions* presented its *Miss California U.S. International* pageant at the Curtis Theatre in Brea, California.

- *Southern Pageant Productions* presented its *Springtime Sweet Peas Pageant* at the Loxley Civic Center in Loxley, Alabama.

Hotel Ballroom

Hotels have ballrooms (as well as small and large meeting rooms) available for lease. Hotel ballrooms are one of the most common venues for a pageant. Many of the larger hotels have partitioned rooms that, together, make one huge ballroom. If you need to use only two of the four petitioned rooms, for example, note that to the leasing manager. Be careful how you present your request. You don't want to sign up for an entire ballroom if half is all you need. Speak to the General Manager for information on leasing hotel ballrooms. If your plans are for a summer pageant, take into consideration that many hotel ballrooms will be reserved for summer weddings and receptions. Although graduations take place at the beginning of summer and are commonly held in theaters, receptions usually follow in hotel ballrooms. This might be a good time of year to *avoid*. Remember to look into Inns and Suites, such as the *Terre Haute Comfort Suites, Candlewood Suites, Quality Inn*, and the *Hampton Inn*, about their banquet and ballroom capacity and rates, and remember to ask about barter. Learn how to barter with a true host hotel — "the bottom floor" — by reading my book *Producing Beauty Pageants: Brokering a Pageant through Barter*, Chapter 5, "Pageant Venue Bartered," under "The Bottom Floor."

When securing a hotel for your pageant, choose one that features a pool. Keeping in line with its "Pageants of the Caribbean" theme, *Storybook Pageants* booked its pageant at the *Clarion Hotel Batavia* in New York. The hotel is connected to the *Palm Island Indoor Water Park*, a lovely convenience for official contestants and their families. Two options were made available. Option one included: a one night hotel stay plus four (two-day) water park passes, a $25 breakfast voucher for the hotel buffet, and a $25 free play voucher to *Batavia Downs Casino*. The cost of this package was $154 per night plus tax. Option two included: a room rate of $88 per night plus tax and water park pass prices at $15 per day per person.

Lodges/Resorts

Lodges, Resorts, and other private clubs (such as the *Shriners*) will often lease its banquet space. Such venues are typically less expensive than hotels, but you will be required to do more of the set-up. *Fleet Reserve Association, Knights of Columbus, Lions Club Den, Loyal Order of Moose, Eagles Hall, American Legion*, and *Elks Lodge* are other options. Locate Lodges and Clubs in The Yellow Pages under Lodges, Clubs, or Organizations. A *Masonic Lodge* was the site for *Pretty in Pink Pageants'* Colorado pageant.

Storybook Pageants booked its summer Nationals, in 2012, at the *Holiday Valley Resort* in Ellicottville, NY. This four-season resort, nestled in the Alleghany Mountains, included five swimming pools — one being a fun pool with an awesome slide! (The location doubles as a ski resort in the winter.) *Storybook Pageants* was able to secure a competitive block rate price for the pageant — which also included a continental breakfast. The competition part of the weekend pageant was held in the

Tannenbaum Lodge — a beautiful, two-level facility that featured the top floor for the competition and the bottom floor for complete outfit changes and hair and makeup. This facility is, of course, at the top of the mountain — a truly amazing place. After the competition, candidates and their families roamed the quaint resort town of Ellicottville, where unique dining and boutique-style stores lined the streets. A pageant weekend like this is the ultimate mini vacation families are seeking.

Banquet/Reception Halls

Banquet/reception halls are designed to be generic. Many banquet/reception halls have generic space available for lease. Large apartment complexes often have banquet halls/clubrooms for rent. Yacht clubs, country clubs, senior centers, and County Fair Associations also have banquet/reception halls to lease, even to non-members. But, that's not the only place you'll find a banquet room.

- *Miss Salt City Royalty Pageant* held a pageant in the banquet facilities at the *Rosamond Gifford Zoo* at Burnet Park in Syracuse, New York. Additionally, pageant officials secured zoo passes for every candidate.

- *Little Miss Johnson County* held a pageant at the *Buffalo Senior Center.*

Women's Clubs

The *San Diego Woman's Club* banquet hall can be leased for a variety of functions, *including* beauty pageants. It includes a built-in stage with curtains — perfect for a pageant. There is an extensive inventory on site, including 25' dinner tables, over two dozen 8' banquet tables, three deejay and gift tables, one sign-in desk, 300 cushioned seat and back chairs, a PA (public address) system, in-house speakers, stage lighting, and a projection screen. The location seats 357 people and has theater seating. Curfew is 11 p.m.; music to be off at 10 p.m. The *San Diego Woman's Club* also features additional rooms available for rent.

Churches

Many religious organizations have space available for a donation/fee, including a church (sanctuary) and Fellowship Hall. Since size varies from church to church, ask about seating capacity. Some churches don't rent out the sanctuary, but *do* rent out its Fellowship Hall. Fellowship Halls are sometimes divided into sections, with one section renting for, say, $200; $350 for two sections; and $450 for the full Fellowship Hall. Additionally, there is often a cleaning fee of, say, $75; some charge a flat custodial fee of $10/hour with a $50 minimum. Need to rent Sunday school (or common) rooms for your official contestant interviews or Pageant Workshops? *St. James Presbyterian* in Littleton, Colorado, rents Sunday school rooms. Non-profit pageants would receive a fifty percent discount. Learn more about non-profit pageants by reading my book *Producing Beauty Pageants: Directing a Fundraiser Pageant*. Remember to look into chapels on college and university campuses.

- *Social Butterfly Pageants* and *The Best Shining Stars Pageants* presented a Double-Header natural/semi-glitz pageant at the *Grace Covenant Church* in Austin, Indiana. Learn more about Double Header pageants by reading my FREE e-book *Producing Beauty Pageants: A Guide to Pageant Terminology*.

- *Baker Pageants* presented its pageant at the *Pleasant Ridge Baptist Church* in Hueytown, Alabama.

- *Fairytale Pageant Productions* held its *Miss Lake Martin* pageant at the *First United Methodist Church* in Alexander City, Alabama.

- *Elite Pageant Productions* presented the *Miss Gardendale* pageant at *The Church Revived* in Gardendale, Alabama (in the auditorium); interviews took place in the Fellowship Hall.

- *West Coast All Canadian Girl Pageant* presented its pageant at the *Sharon United Church Hall* in Langley, BC, Canada.

- *Southern Beauties and Beaus* doesn't present pageants in a church; however, pageant officials provide an 8 a.m.

church service for anyone who wants to attend, followed by a 9:30 a.m. crowning ceremony.

Public Library

Community libraries have large, generic rooms for rent. Think all library rooms are too small? The *Ronald Regan Presidential Library* auditorium is 4,000 square feet! *Sealed With A Kiss Pageants* presented its pageant at the *Grace Dow Library Auditorium*. When you arrive at the library's site, click on "Rooms for Rent." Here you will find an auditorium, lounge, and conference rooms for rent — a perfect mix for pageants. Judges' interviews can take place in the conference rooms while the pageant occurs in the auditorium — which includes a Video Projection System and a piano. Your after-pageant party can take place in the lounge. *Indiana Elite Pageants* held its State pageant in the auditorium of the *New Castle/Henry County Public Library.*

Community/Recreation/Visitor Centers/Boys & Girls Clubs

Community centers can convert their space to host a pageant. The *Greater Waldorf Jaycees Community Center* rents out three halls: JCI Senate Room, which seats up to 525; Giessenbier Room, which seats up to 200; and the MD Militia Room, which seats up to 130. Check with your local dance studio. Many will lease space to a pageant director when not in use, say, after the Saturday morning dance or yoga classes. Your City Hall may have generic space where you can present your pageant. *Jenks City Hall* rents its community room for various functions. Fitness centers often have facilities for rent on evenings and weekends. Be sure to check your *Parks & Recreation Department*. *Warm Beach Camp & Conference Center* in Stanwood, Washington, rents out meeting space facilities to various conference groups. The *City of Broken Arrow's Visitor's Center Gallery* can accommodate seating for 250 in its hall. Many such centers have a community/banquet/reception hall available for lease.

- *Southern Beauties and Beaus* held a pageant at the *Elliott Community Center* in Gadsden, Alabama.

- *Southern Stars Pageants* presented a pageant at the *Calera Community Center* in Calera, Alabama.

- *Pageland Watermelon Pageant* held a pageant at the *Pageland Community Center* in Pageland, South Carolina.

- Colorado's *Our Little Miss* held an event at the *Windsor Community Recreation Center* in Windsor, Colorado.

- *Miss Georgia Royalty* held a pageant at the *Tucker Recreation Center* in Tucker, Georgia.

- *Fairytale Pageant Productions* held its *Miss Alabama Belle* pageant at the *Childersburg Recreation Center* in Childersburg, Alabama.

Chamber of Commerce

Contact the Chamber of Commerce in the town where you will present your pageant to find what area halls are available for rent. Some may even have its own hall to lease, as does the *Spencer County-Taylorsville Chamber of Commerce*. As of this writing, for only $150 per day ($100 with Chamber member discount), you can rent the hall for a 125-person capacity event — which includes the kitchen and ample free parking.

Malls

Many pageant systems present its single-day events at malls, particularly those who have many children competing. Although malls can be viewed as a win-win situation, there are pros and cons for pageant producers to consider.

Most malls have a promotional court area. *Tri-State Cinderella Pageant* held a Preliminary pageant in Dover Mall's Promotional Court. If a mall doesn't have staging that can be assembled/disassembled and a crew to assemble/disassemble it, pageant officials will need to bring their own stage and crew.

The Pros: Mall staging venues are relatively inexpensive to rent. Families with young children generally like mall activities, so your chances of gaining lots of official contestants at your pageant are good. Lots of foot traffic means that your pageant will be seen. Moreover, chances are good that the Director of Mall Marketing will consider barter. Learn how to barter for a mall pageant venue by reading my book *Producing Beauty Pageants: Brokering a Pageant through Barter*, Chapter 5, "Pageant Venue Bartered" under "Malls."

The Cons: Admission cannot be charged because the mall is an open area. *Little Miss & Teen Miss North Carolina* reminds prospective contestants on its brochure, "There will be no admission for pageants held in the mall." Dressing room arrangements may be difficult, but not impossible. Larger malls may have the capability to pitch covered tents, or an employee bathroom can double as a dressing room. Some malls don't offer outfit changing rooms for pageants. When this happens, pageants need to make adjustments to the competition categories. *Arizona Cover Miss* notes, "OOC (Outfit of Choice) not offered at Malls."

Moreover, pageant vendors are not allowed to sell their products at the mall. Pageant candidates who use such services as vendor spray tanning (and makeup and hair) need to make other arrangements, or they can use the mall's services. If the mall doesn't have such a vendor, then management may allow you to bring your own service crew; however, don't assume this, and always ask.

You can also promote your pageant, for free, by having your mall event advertised on the malls' websites. To give you an example, *Simon Property Group* owns the following U.S. Malls, just to name a few: *Dover Mall*; *Greenwood Park Mall*; *White Oaks Mall*; *Coral Square Mall*; *Valle Vista Mall*; *West Town Mall*; *Panama City Mall*; *South Hills Village*; *Tyler Mall*; *Knoxville Center*; *SouthPark Mall*; *Lincolnwood Town Center*; *Upper Valley Mall*; *Northlake Mall*; *Ashtabula Mall*; *Washington Square Mall*; and *Broadway Square Mall*. If you were to have your pageant at any one of these malls, once you and the mall's Director of Mall Marketing come to an agreement, s/he can get your pageant posted on the online *Simon Malls* events calendar. Not only does a pageant event posting on a *Simon Malls* events calendar announce the pageant date, but it promotes contestant entries. Visitors to the *Simon Malls* website can read about the pageant by clicking on the "Visit Event Website" link. This will take them directly to a pageant's National headquarters. This is *free*, priceless advertising. Find a mall anywhere in the U.S. at the *Malletin* and the *Shopping Mall Directory USA*.

Theatrical Auditoriums

Theatrical auditoriums are among the best venues to stage your pageant. Many theaters have stages and dressing rooms, away from the audience and public access, which would accommodate most pageants. If your budget permits, rent the town auditorium. Otherwise, look into renting a school auditorium. School auditoriums are often less expensive and just as nice. Most school auditoriums charge a set fee, whereas most city theatrical auditoriums charge a percentage of your receipts, or a set fee — whichever is greater. Sometimes both fees are charged.

Movie Theater

Another possibility is to rent a local movie theater. Some movie theaters are rented out when shows are not in progress. Barter the use of its location in exchange for promotional advertising. It may interest the theater general managers to promote the current movies they are showing, and hence, sell more tickets. Locate movie houses in The Yellow Pages under Halls, Auditoriums, or Movie Theaters. Learn more about bartering for all sorts of potential pageant venues by reading my book *Producing Beauty Pageants: Brokering a Pageant through Barter*, Chapter 5, "Pageant Venue Bartered" under "Other Places to Request Venue Sponsorship."

Coliseum/Convention/Civic Centers

Renting the local coliseum is an expensive but glamorous way to present your pageant. Like theatrical auditoriums, coliseums charge a flat fee or a percentage of your ticket sales — whichever is greater; sometimes both. This fee does not include the cost of rental equipment and man hours. Your local coliseum's ticket office can give you additional information. Convention centers are not as expensive as coliseums. Rents are typically priced at a ten-hour per day usage. Hours in the building can sometimes be split into two time periods in the day (this could benefit two pageants that want to hold a competition the same day and split the rental cost), so ask. Some cities have a convention and civic center, both being one and the same. Civic centers are the least expensive to rent. Some civic centers have multiple rooms to rent — for example, a banquette room, a seminar room, and a classroom — all possibilities for your pageant event needs.

If you do bring in another pageant director to share the rental expense, verify that s/he has liability insurance. You don't need an uninsured director's candidate(s) pinning a lawsuit on you or the coliseum heads. Do not attempt to allow an uninsured director to ride your coattails by "sub-leasing" under your rental agreement. *Make sure that s/he is written up in the original contract and under his/her own insurance policy.*

- *Binibining Pilipinas Pageant's* Nationals take place at the *Smart Aranet Coliseum* in Quezon City, Philippines.

- The *Miss Naturally Beautiful Pageant* was held at the *Corinth Coliseum Civic Center* in Corinth, Mississippi.

- *Southern Beauties and Beaus* presented a pageant at the *Pell City Civic Center* in Pell City, Alabama, and another at *Cullman Civic Center* in Cullman, Alabama.

- *Little Miss Arkansas* presented its pageant at the *Hot Springs Convention and Civic Center* in Hot Springs, Arizona.

Cruise Ships

Can you imagine a more serene place to present a beauty pageant than aboard a cruise ship? With your production aboard a cruise ship, you must require full payment far in advance of the sailing date. The 2012 *Southern Queens of the Sea Pageants* took place aboard the *Royal Caribbean's Monarch of the Seas* from May 7th–May 11th. The official contestant package cost for the Inside Cabin Package — which included the pageant entry fee, t-shirt, photo/DVD, and cruise fare for one (per person double occupancy, taxes, and fees) — was $1,340; travel insurance was available for an additional fee. Official contestants who paid the full payment by March 15th, received a $150 discount; by April 1st, a $100 discount; and by April 15th a $50 discount. Although the cruise departed from Port Canaveral, Florida, the pageant was open to girls from Oklahoma, Arkansas, Louisiana, Mississippi,

Alabama, Florida, Georgia, South Carolina, North Carolina, Tennessee, Kentucky, Virginia, West Virginia, and Texas.

American Royalty Supreme Pageants presented its pageant on the *Celebration Cruise Ship* with Grand Bahamas Islands as its destination!

Universal Petite Pageant held its National pageant on the *Liberty of the Seas*, in 2013, on a *Royal Caribbean Cruise!*

Creative Locations

Can you imagine your pageant taking place in a castle? *Miss Tri-County Beauty Pageant* brought that imagination to life when, in 2011, pageant officials presented their pageant at the *Celebration Castle* in Long County, Georgia. The *Celebration Castle* is a unique rental venue in Southeast Georgia located in Long County near Hinesville — about thirty-five miles from Savannah. The 13,500 square foot facility — housed on ten acres of land — provides plenty of room for parking and space for outside activities. Small or large pageants are welcome here. Castles are not the only creative location to present your pageant; other locations included:

- *Kingston Spring Fling Pageant* was held in the park at Historic Kingston in Kingston, Georgia.

- *Little Miss Alabama* was presented at *The Von Braun Center Playhouse* in Huntsville, Alabama.

- *Miss Hamilton Pageant* was held at the *Bevill Business Center* on the Hamilton Campus of *Bevill State Community College* in Hamilton, Alabama.

- *Supreme Pageant System* presented the *World's Most Beautiful Baby Pageant and Model Search* 2011 at the *Super Flea & Farmer's Market* in Melbourne, Florida. Pageant officials asked candidates to arrive dressed to compete.

Backup Location

Have a crisis location plan in place. _Little Miss & Little Mister Chilli Pepper Pageant_ promoters held their pageant on the stage in front of the _U.S. Bank_. However, in the event of inclement weather, their backup plan was to present their pageant in the Community Room of the _U.S. Bank_.

Nancy Fletcher, model search manager assistant for the _Miss Hawaiian Tropic_ noted,

> We hold the pageant at an outdoor location, so we have learned to always have a backup location. We have a dressing room nearby large enough for all contestants to wait out the weather. This past year we had to rush the girls off the stage when it rained, while our staff came out with towels and mops to dry off the stage, because we didn't want them to slip in their heels on a wet floor. It added an hour and a half to the pageant time.[4]

Changing Your Pageant Venue Midpoint

There may come a time when you need to change your pageant venue during your pageant promotional effort. You may have more candidates than you anticipated, and therefore, require a larger venue. When _Star One National Pageants_ first planned its 2011 event, it was to take place at _The Clifton Center_. However, due to a terrific response, it was moved to a larger venue — _Holiday Inn Louisville_ in East Hurstbourne. Should you need to make venue changes midpoint, it's best to do so before you print and sell admission tickets. If that's not possible, make sure you have a person at the original location telling uninformed attendees that the venue has been changed to a new location.

---

[4] White, Martha C. "Lessons Learned From Planning Pageants." _BizBash_, April 29, 2008. http://www.bizbash.com/lessons_learned_from_planning_pageants/new-york/story/10595/.

Barter for Your Pageant Venue

In the dozen years I directed pageants, I bartered with nearly *every major hotel chain for 100 percent of my pageant needs*. The four title pageants that I held in San Antonio, Texas (on the Riverwalk), for example, were completely bartered with *The Westin Riverwalk*, *Hyatt Regency Riverwalk*, *Hilton Palacio Del Rio*, and *Marriott San Antonio Riverwalk*. Each provided me with a pageant ballroom, meeting rooms, dressing rooms, and a block of crew rooms — "the bottom floor" — *for each one of my respective pageants*. Then they continued participating as the Official Venue Sponsor for each respective annual event. Except for barter taxes, these trades didn't cost either of us a cent.

Rental managers of various hotels, theaters, cruise ships, etc., are often willing to barter their venue by participating as an Official Venue Sponsor. After all, an empty hotel, theater, and cruise ship during a shoulder season IS an expense to the owner — one that s/he can turn into an asset by bartering with your pageant business. Learn precisely how to barter with such venue owners by reading my book *Producing Beauty Pageants: Brokering a Pageant through Barter*, Chapter 5, "Pageant Venue Bartered" under "Plan Your Pageant during Hotel Shoulder Season."

Chapter 4

Printed Materials

Selecting a printing company to produce your pageant materials requires some thought and research. Printing companies range from the less expensive quick printers to the more expensive elaborate printing companies. Some printing companies print only quick items such as business cards, stationery, and brochures. Others print an array of items including calendars, books, and four-color items. Some printing companies send out work that needs to be typeset, while others have their own typesetting equipment on location. While most printing companies have a camera to make negatives from pictures, the quality can vary. Always ask the manager to see samples of work s/he has produced.

Most printing companies can do all the work onsite for most jobs. Nevertheless, it is best to know the company's limits. If the printing company manager subcontracts some of the work to another printing company, or to a typesetter, find out the names of the subcontractors. If you take the work directly to those subcontractors, you may get a better price. If the printing company has to send out any portion of any job, the cost of the final product can be more expensive. In addition to knowing what work the printing company can and cannot do, find out if it has a good reputation for doing quality work and if it's done on time. Check with the _Better Business Bureau_ before committing. There is nothing more frightening than waiting until the last minute for your Pageant Program Books — or not getting them at all! Find a reasonable and trustworthy source by shopping around and comparing prices. Prices vary from printing company to printing company, even within franchises.

At some point early in the pageant process, structure a list of items you will need from your printing company. Although you won't need some items until later, some will be necessary sooner. But before approaching a printing company, Courtney, from _Photo Retouching by Courtney_, who designed the cover of my _Producing Beauty Pageants_ series, can brand your pageant marketing materials so that one complements the rest. Listed below are various printed items needed to get a successful pageant business started.

Stationery

Initial stationery purchases should include business cards, letterhead stationery, and envelopes. Designing your own stationery allows you to show your creativity and your professionalism. There is no excuse for not having business cards. You can have large quantities printed at a reasonable price, so don't hesitate to give them to anyone who is interested in your business. Many pageant directors advertise *each* of their pageants on separate business cards. The late Texas pageant producer Jimmy Goodman had different business cards for every pageant he promoted. It's smart to take advantage of one of the least-expensive forms of advertising. Learn more about the late Jimmy Goodman, a.k.a. "the father of Open Call," by reading my book *Producing Beauty Pageants: Open Call*, Chapter 15, "Have Open Call, Will Travel."

Photographic Business Cards

Photographic business cards are effective because they are more striking — there isn't much more arresting than a picture of a beautiful beauty Queen! Besides, people tend to remember faces over names. Also, people tend keep pictures, so photographic business cards stand a better chance at remaining in the hands of your intended party. As a Queen's prize, publish her picture on your annual business cards, and give her several to distribute. If your royalty photos are less than perfect, you need photo retouching. After all, your pageant Queen *is* your brand ambassador! She needs to make your pageant look great. Courtney, owner of *Photo Retouching by Courtney*, is a professional photo retoucher with extensive experience in graphic design. She provides excellent services in natural, semi-glitz, glitz, and glamour photo retouching. Moreover, if you require candidates to provide top-quality comp cards, digital ports, pageant ads, photo backers, or series, Courtney can also provide those items. Be sure to note Courtney's work on the front *and* back covers of my *Producing Beauty Pageants* series.

Magnetic Business Cards

Advertising a teen pageant on magnetic business cards is smart. Any teen with a locker could be a prospective contestant (and so might be her friends). Because magnets can be used to post other reminders and whatnot, your magnetic business card will be in view of prospective contestants for possibly a long time. Seeing your card enough times might etch your phone number or company name in viewers' minds — or at least interest them to call or visit your website. A pageant director can send a prospective contestant a magnetic business card with a suggestion to use it to "post reminders in her school locker." A pageant system like _National American Miss_ can include a magnetic business card and a Finalist Ribbon in an Acceptance Package. And, it can be suggested that the recipient pin the ribbon in the inside door of her school locker — with the aid of the magnetic business card. (This beats suggesting that the ribbon be hung on the corner of a home dresser mirror — something that NAM already does!) When the prospective contestant's friends see the magnetic pageant business card after they revel in her Finalist Ribbon, they might _also_ want to earn such a ribbon and might jot down NAM's contact information.

Personal Note Cards

What better way to thank your Official Sponsors and pageant committee than with your own personal note cards? To give you an idea, my note card design included a hand holding a feathered pen writing (in my own handwriting) the words: A note from Anna. My initial order was 1,000 cards and envelopes, embossed with red ink on beige stock. The embossed design presented an appearance that the hand had just dipped the feathered pen into an inkwell and began writing a personal, flowing message. Personalized note cards are cheaper than store-bought cards and much more personable. A National pageant system can place its logo and tagline on the cards.

Envelopes/Pre-Stamped Envelopes

Imagine not having to stick another stamp onto an envelope. This can occur if you visit your postmaster in the bulk mail department of your town post office. Once registered, in lieu of stamps, you will receive a special permit that allows you to pre-print your permit number on your envelopes.

If you accept applications via the U.S. mail, have pre-addressed (business reply mail), pre-stamped, first-class envelopes printed. These envelopes have the words: "Postage will be paid by addressee." A greater response in reply mail will follow if you include these envelopes. The extra sales that you will likely make will more than compensate for the added expense when prospective contestants mail in their application, photo, and $25 application fee.

A smart thing to do for incoming mail is to print pre-addressed envelopes. Now, all that prospective contestants would need to do is place their sponsorship payment (check or filled out credit card slips that you also provide) into the pre-addressed envelope and bring it to their scheduled Pageant Workshop. If the permitted envelope is hand-delivered, you won't pay for postage.

However, you will pay bulk rate postage if it is mailed to you. The good news is that you can rest assured that it will arrive safely to you, because your address is legibly preprinted! This alleviates any problems that could have occurred with soon-to-be official contestants and/or parents addressing it, such as illegible handwriting, an incorrect mailing address, and/or leaving out the suite number or zip code.

If you have multiple use for incoming mail envelopes, at least color-code the sponsorship fee envelope (or other time-sensitive mail) for quick visibility.

For outgoing mail, consider a window envelope. A window envelope allows you to print the recipient's name and address only once — on the letter itself. When aligned properly, it will be seen through the envelope's window. No need for address labels if you purchase window envelopes. _National American Miss_ designed its window envelope with purple and blue swirling designs to bring its attention to the intended party: the prospective contestant. Trading out its brown envelope, about the same time NAM introduced Open Call into its pageant system, in 2008, was a SMART move! To view NAM's swirly envelope, visit _twicsy_ (the Twitter Pics Engine). View NAM's _new swirly envelope_ at _WordPress_, posted on January 28, 2015, by "Praying for

Eyebrowz." Learn more about the power of "the letter" by reading my book *Producing Beauty Pageants: Open Call*, Chapter 6, "The Letter."

Last, but not least, you will need Acceptance Package envelopes printed with your pageant logo — usually in an accommodating size of 11" x 13". It needs to be large enough to fit your pageant marketing materials.

Personalized Receipts for Sponsors, Advertisers, and Parents

Include the following on your personalized receipts: your company name, TIN, business phone number, business address, website address, logo, official contestant (name) line, contributor line, date line, memo line, and amount line on the receipt portion that is given to the contributor. On the stub portion (that candidates keep for their records), include lines for the date, amount, contributor, contributor's address, phone number, and boxes to check off method of payment. While most sponsors and advertisers use their cancelled check as a receipt, your pageant will appear more professional if candidates present individuals and businesses with receipts that include your TIN. The top face of the receipt is the first place you should note, in bold print, "Sponsor entry fee is not refundable." With such a bold reminder, official contestants, who begin to get jittery as the pageant draws closer, won't drop out so easily. Moreover, it reminds candidate sponsors (and advertisers) that refunds won't be granted by your pageant system, even if a candidate becomes a drop-off statistic. Learn more about drop-off by reading my book *Producing Beauty Pageants: Open Call*, Chapter 10, "Drop-Off."

You can avoid this expense altogether by typesetting a page of receipts in your Official Contestant Handbook. *Miss American Coed* includes a page of receipts for sponsors and advertisers in its National Pageant Forms Booklet on page 23. *National American Miss*' contributor receipts can be found here. If your receipt says "contributor," then it can be used for ad sales and other uses that help candidates gain pageant support (like merchants who donate products, sponsor fees, etc.). Be sure to scroll down to see the back side of the receipt — which includes NAM's logo, website address, and a description of what the pageant is about. For ideas on what to include in your Official Contestant Handbook, read my book *Producing Beauty Pageants: Contestant Handbook.*

If you're planning on hosting a pageant in Australia, you would need carbon copy receipts. At the Melbourne, Australia, *Universal Royalty Beauty Pageant*, some parents claimed they never received receipts. One parent told the *Herald Sun* they did not get a receipt after paying a pageant bill of $615. [5] Under Victorian law, receipts must be given by businesses for goods and services worth more than $75 — excluding goods and services tax GST. Failure to comply with the laws can result in fines of $15,000 for businesses and up to $3,000 for individuals. Actually, it's a good thing to provide a carbon copy receipt to *anyone* who pays by cash or any other method.

Brochures

Brochures must be visually appealing and tell your story. A brochure should include basic information about your pageant and an entry application. Sponsor logos can be included on the cover to give sponsors publicity and your pageant credibility. The cover can feature a Queen's photograph. If this is your inaugural pageant, you might include a picture of a crown and banner near roses. If you are a Preliminary director, your National director should provide you with pictures of the National titleholder. Whatever photo you use, it should be striking. The cover should entice prospective contestants to read your brochure.

Once opened, general information about the pageant should be on the left one-third page of the brochure. On the right two-thirds is the application. Though not a requirement, a brochure is usually an 8 ½" x 11" paper folded in thirds. The application should also include your Rules & Regulations, preferably numbered, and a consenting signature line. This should, of course, follow your complete, clear-to-understand pageant financial disclosures and supporting pageant marketing materials.

Brochures don't need to be two-sided. *Porcelain Dolls Nationals* produces a colorfully-striking, eight-page brochure —

---

[5] Holroyd, Jane. "Organisers Facing Fines Over Ugly Scenes at Pageant." *The Age Life & Style*, August 1, 2011, http://www.theage.com.au/lifestyle/organisers-facing-fines-over-ugly-scenes-at-pageant-20110801-1j6xc.html.

equipped with a last page, fold-over-and-staple "envelope" that follows its 23-point Rules & Regulations. View the brochure here.

When typesetting your brochure (or any other pageant forms/contracts), do not use all caps throughout your message. All-caps lettering is difficult to read and appears as if the message is being "yelled" to the reader.

Include perforation separating the application from the general information. This allows prospective contestants to keep the cover portion of the brochure — which includes the pageant highlights, address, website, and phone number. The reverse side of the brochure features the pageant's R&Rs and a consenting signature line. Remind your printing company to score (crease) and fold the brochures. You do not want a box of paper that you need to fold by hand, even if they are already scored. (At the very least make sure they are scored, because at least you *can* fold them!)

If you're a Preliminary director for a National pageant, your State or National director may provide brochures. _Miss USA_ State directors, at one time, provided Preliminary directors with four-color brochures (at a cost already factored into the franchise fee); additional brochures cost extra. They may still provide them. The use of these pre-supplied brochures could be optional. If you need help in designing a pageant brochure, Courtney, from _Photo Retouching by Courtney_, is an expert at graphic design and will provide you with a quality brochure.

Certificates

When a _National American Miss_ State promoter identifies each official contestant as a State Finalist, s/he sends her a certificate in her Acceptance Package. The certificate includes the pageant logo on the left corner along with a line that states, "This is to certify that [name]...State Finalist...National American Miss...." Visit _pledgie_ to view a NAM State Finalist certificate. This certificate might make the girl believe that she has already competed against other girls and won a Finalist position when, in fact, it only means that she is a candidate in the pageant. If you don't identify an official contestant as a "State Finalist," and you want to present such a certificate in her Acceptance Package, simply write "Delegate" or "Candidate" in the spot. _Easy Flyer Creator_ allows you to design flyers, leaflets, and certificates in just five minutes using built-in templates. It can be downloaded for free.

Flyers

A flyer is generally an 8 ½" x 11" sheet of paper with printing on one or both sides. It lists general information and a contact person. Designed properly, a flyer conveys urgency in registering. Motivate inquiries by including a picture of your reigning Queen. Attention-grabbing headlines such as: "No Height or Weight Requirement"; "Modeling or Pageant Experience Not Necessary"; "Talent Not Required"; "Swimsuit Optionals!"; "All Finalists Can Compete at the State Pageant!"; and "Girls 14–18 Eligible to Participate" capture attention. Prospective contestants procrastinate less when they are reminded by a deadline date to act quickly if they don't want to miss a great opportunity. If you still don't want to be date-specific, your attention-grabbing headline could read: "Deadline is determined by the number of entries. APPLY SOON!"

Post flyers at high schools, colleges, universities, community centers, grocery store bulletin boards, and church bulletin boards. With permission, distribute flyers during the weekends at shopping malls. There is no cost for displaying flyers on any community bulletin boards; however, request approval before posting. Include a posting deadline date on the right corner of your flyer for proper maintenance.

Application Forms

Application forms should be carefully framed to reveal significant facts about each candidate's background, training, scholastic record, physical notations, community involvement, etc. Careful thought when compiling information for your application will ensure a job well done when judges complete their judging. If prospective contestants are filling out a hard copy, remind them to continue to the back side if there is a second page. *Miss Cumberland County Fair Queen Pageant* adds additional advice:

> Please type the information and do not change the
> form. Please go over all spelling — these copies go to
> the judges. Make sure you keep a copy for yourself.

There are three things you should contemplate not asking on your application if you want lots of girls to participate. First, do not ask their weight, that is, if it's not part of your Rules & Regulations. A candidate may want to enter a beauty pageant as a goal for losing weight, so stating her weight at the beginning may embarrass and drive her away, or she may write it down incorrectly. In one pageant, a candidate who listed her weight as 115 pounds registered 140 at the weighing-in ceremonies. Some pageants do continue to have a maximum weight requirement for the candidates. When Alicia Machado of Venezuela was crowned *Miss Universe* 1996, she was warned that she might be dethroned by the organization because she exceeded the maximum weight required during her reign. Fortunately, the weight requirement was not enforced. *Miss California USA* no longer has a weight requirement, so it's likely that neither do its parent pageants *Miss USA* and *Miss Universe*.

Weight issues should be a personal thing. Before being crowned *Miss South Carolina* 2011, 22-year-old Bree Boyce lost 110 pounds — nearly half of her body weight — over three years. She didn't lose the weight for a pageant, but as a permanent change in living a healthier lifestyle. Not only did this change improve her self-esteem, but Bree learned to cope with her emotions in a positive way instead of by eating junk food. Her platform for the *Miss South Carolina* pageant was fitting: "Eating Healthy and Fighting Obesity."[6] Although Bree competed in the *Miss America* pageant and did not win, she was already a winner in life.

Second, do not ask measurements. A prospective contestant may feel self-conscious about not being fuller in the chest. She will be more confident about entering a pageant knowing she does not have to state her measurements. She may look great in a particular type of swimsuit, which may accentuate her breast size. This eventual official contestant may even *win* the swimsuit award. The year Lee Meriwether ran for *Miss America*, she was convinced that she didn't have a chance at the title being "as flat chested as I am."[7] Lee Meriwether would cringe when 34–22–35 was appended to her name. She feels that the measurement thing is silly. In case you're wondering, Lee Meriwether *also* *won* the swimsuit

---

[6] Pham, Thailan. "Miss South Carolina Bree Boyce: I Used to Weigh 234 Lbs." December 29, 2011. *People.*
http://www.people.com/people/article/0,,20556893,00.html.

[7] San Francisco Chronicle, September 11, 1986

competition. When Karen Aarons became executive secretary in charge of the _Miss America Pageant_, in 1985, she retired the tape measure stating "[measurements] are superfluous. They serve no other purpose than the public's curiosity."[8]

Third, if grade point averages are not a significant part of judging, avoid asking official contestants for their GPA. If candidates are not straight-A students, they may feel that they don't stand a chance at winning a crown in a pageant that doesn't stress academia. Many won't bother entering the non-academic pageant because it _still_ asks for their GPA.

Potential questions to use in your application include a candidate's most embarrassing moment, favorite pastime, favorite vacation location, favorite song, favorite movie, and philosophy of life. If your pageant is for younger girls, include questions such as "What is your favorite activity/movie/pet/sport, and why?" A quick Internet search can yield pageant question sites such as _Beauty Pageant Questions and Answers_, _Miss & Teen Jacksonville USA_ (includes a multitude of pageant questions on its website), and _Pageant Center_'s Pageant Questions for Children (includes an extensive list of questions for young pageant participants). _Pageant Center_ invites prospective and official contestants to submit practice pageant questions, and then it will reply answers via email. Visit _Pageant Center's_ Pageant Questions link.

Pageant Forms and Contracts

As a professional pageant producer/director, you will need to legally protect yourself (and the people you do business with) from potential lawsuits. There are several pageant forms and contracts that will help you to do just that; for example, the Statement of Intent/Deposit Form, Pre-Application Form, Rules & Regulations Form, Official Application Form, Contestant Release and Agreement Form, Alumnae Application Form, Emergency Contact Information Form, Medical Information Form, Medical Release Form, Contestant Release and Indemnity Agreement, Contestant Entry Affidavit, Sponsor Confirmation List Form, Disclaimer (a.k.a. Hedge Clause) Form, and last, but not least, Waiver of Liability and Assumption of Risk Form. Find forms

---

[8] _USA Today_, September 8, 1986

right for your pageant — and there are all sorts — by reading my book *Producing Beauty Pageants: Creating a Synergized National Pageant System*, Chapter 12, "Pageant Paperwork and Forms." It provides a description on nearly every pageant form that could benefit your pageant system. It also offers information on how to create forms in a downloadable format. To give you an idea of the types of forms a pageant system incorporated into its pageant paperwork, visit *Miss Pacific Islander of San Diego*. Be sure to scroll through all fifteen pages. Additional information on what pageant paperwork to include in your Official Contestant Handbook can be found in my book *Producing Beauty Pageants: Contestant Handbook*.

Pageant Magazine

You will need to keep your prospective and official contestants informed of your latest pageant news. Rather than typing it in a standard font, create a colorful, newsy, magazine-type publication. Your pageant magazine could also double as your Official Pageant Handbook. Be sure to include a table of contents, one that directs prospective contestants to your Refund Policy and other R&Rs (legal clauses, financial disclosures, and other pageant-supporting documents) relating to your pageant *prior* to gaining a consenting participation signature.

National American Miss features a total of four, four-color magazines comprising its State pageant Contestant Handbook. Additional information on how NAM uses its Magazines #1–#4 within its National pageant system can be found throughout my book *Producing Beauty Pageants: Creating a Synergized National Pageant System*.

Beehive Beauties produces a four-color magazine, packed full of photos and details about current candidates, great stories, suggestions, gift ideas, and coupons from local businesses. Candidates upload a high resolution photo (no cellphone photos) when they register, and it will automatically be included in the magazine. *Beehive Beauties'* magazine is its version of the Pageant Program Book. Since each magazine sells for $6 at the pageant event, they sell out quickly. Official contestants can pre-order as many magazines as they need. For more information about the magazine, visit Beehive Beauties General Information Scoring, and on the right, click on "Programs".

Pageant Newsletter

America's U.S. Miss Scholarship Program saves a tree by producing an online publication. When at the AUS homepage, click on "News & Events" (in the black box on the left). Doing so downloads its newsletter — a four-color, ten-page publication titled State Contestant Manual. *America's U.S. Miss* puts out three informative, colorful pageant newsletters: *American's U.S. Miss Pageant Newsletter (ages 3–24)*, *AUS Miss Youth Newsletter* (ages 3–8), and *AUS Miss Newsletter* (ages 3–24). The Miss division manual can be found here.

Miss American Coed provides its newsletters on a DVD.

Miss Westchester and *Miss Hudson Valley* updates its online pageant newsletter, "Smart. Beautiful. You!" on a weekly basis — the beauty of an online newsletter. The recent newsletter reported alumnae, newbie's, and prospective contestants' upcoming pageant activities, workshops, and entry deadlines. It also provided tips and answered questions about preparing for the next competition. A reminder to alumnae noted that that if they wanted to participate in the next pageant, they needed to reapply. "Smart. Beautiful. You!" follows with an "Apply Now!" link that sends prospective contestants and alumnae straight to an application. Designing winning sponsorship proposals, along with tips on how to secure sponsors, are offered to alumnae and newbies.

The *Miss American Coed* Pennsylvania State newsletter is a 16-page, four-color guide that includes a table of contents. The *Miss American Coed* California State newsletter is a 39-page black and white newsletter.

Parents' Pageant Guide

The *Miss Georgia Pageant* puts out a nine-page guide, *The Parent's Pageant Guide: A Manual of Pageant Week Guidelines for Parents*, to assist parents in understanding what will take place during the time their daughters compete for the title of Miss Georgia. Knowing that this is a stressful time for the parents, pageant staff asks them to direct their questions to the pageant office (and they include a phone number). Parents are also reminded that their Franchise and Field Directors are available to consult. The Parent's Pageant Guide topics include the following:

Contestant Arrival, Housing Information, Telephone Calls, Hostesses and Their Responsibilities to Contestants, Contestant Safety, Preliminary Competition Information, Visitation Rules, Badges Information, Gift Rules During Pageant Week, Season Ticket Information, Miss Georgia Reception Tickets, Miss Georgia Farewell Luncheon Tickets, Pageant Pictures and Videos Information, Sunday Morning After Miss Georgia is Crowned, and FAQs. Additional information about Franchise and Field Directors can be found in my book *Producing Beauty Pageants: Creating a Synergized National Pageant System*, Chapter 7, "Recruiting Directors" under "Franchise/Field/Regional/Local Director."

To give you an example of how helpful this guide is to a pageant parent, page one, Contestant Arrival, lets parents know that the pageant delegates, upon their arrival, will receive their room keys and a copy of the *Miss Georgia* Pageant Program Book. Prior to checking in, official contestants should have already taken their clothes to the theater, purchased food items, and completed errands. Once the delegates have signed into the hostess headquarters, they will not be allowed to leave the dorm area. At a specified time, delegates will meet with hostesses to discuss the week's pageant activities and will receive information regarding pageant clothing for the week. Regarding page three, Telephone Calls, official contestants are allowed to bring a cell phone to pageant week; however, cell phone usage will only be allowed when candidates are in their dorms. Candidates will be asked to leave their cell phones in the dorm at all times. The guide also notes that if an official contestant is caught outside the dorm with her cell phone, the cell phone will be confiscated and returned at the end of pageant week. Last, but not least, if the official contestant becomes ill or requires any needed items, her hostess will contact the parents or the Franchise Director. To view *The Parent's Pageant Guide: A Manual of Pageant Week Guidelines for Parents*, Google "Pageant Week Guidelines," and click on the first or second [DOC].

Final Pageant Newsletter

Send out a "Final Pageant Newsletter" to official contestants at least two weeks before the pageant. If official contestants are to turn in Emcee (Bio) Cards, for example, this newsletter serves as a reminder to fill them out and have them ready. Here is where you would remind official contestants to NOT mail in the Emcee Cards, but rather, bring them to registration. *Miss American Coed Pageants* reminds official contestants, in the Final Newsletter, to: refer to the Deadline Page to note the last day that the pageant will accept checks for the pageant; not mail any correspondence to the office after the deadline; pay any outstanding fees online using *Visa, MasterCard, American Express, Discover,* or *PayPal*; or go directly to the coed store to make those payments online up until the day noted on the Deadline Page; note cutoff dates for online payments; refer to important announcements regarding the Opening Number Outfit; view admission tickets information; view a copy of the Deadline Page for candidates' easy access; view the Pageant Contestant Checklist to ensure that they pull it all together for pageant weekend; view pageant Check-In instructions; view Pageant Workshop information; and have access to various forms — including the Roses Order Form, Optionals Contest Forms, a future candidates Recommendation Form, and a Photography Order Form. This informative, thirteen-page newsletter ONLY includes information pertaining to the pageant weekend. Official contestants won't need to consult any other pageant paperwork. Learn more about Optionals by reading my book *Producing Beauty Pageants: Optionals*.

Admission Tickets

If you charge admission, you will need to have printed Admission Tickets. For a thorough understanding of what is involved in Admission Tickets, and to not miss a lucrative financial opportunity, read the next chapter, "Admission Tickets."

Pageant Program Book

Visit various printing companies and copy centers to get bids for printing your Pageant Program Book (PPB). The more you have prepared, e.g., camera-ready material, the less expensive printing your PPB will be. Chapter 6, "Pageant Program Book," covers this topic in detail. Learn to barter for FREE printing of your PPB by reading my book *Producing Beauty Pageants: Brokering a Pageant through Barter,* Chapter 9, "In-Kind Sponsors" under "Pageant Program Book."

Stock

Your printing company representative can show you various stock options available — from stationery, custom cards, pageant forms, and admission tickets to souvenir Pageant Program Books and beyond. There are a variety of styles, textures, weights (types), and colors of stock available for your printing needs.

To keep their twelve different age divisions (six in the *National American Miss* and six in the *National All-American Miss*) at their National pageant organized, and also five age divisions in each of its nearly 40 NAM State pageants organized, *National American Miss* pageant officials use a variety of brands, colors, weights (types), and sizes of stock for their various pageant forms.

Using NAM's National pageant and its *National Forms* in this example, official contestants are initially mailed a set of pageant forms. Knowing official contestants as they do, NAM pageant officials recommend that they use the initial set of forms that they were mailed to practice writing their required information.

However, when official contestants are ready to submit the final forms, they are responsible for using the correct brand, color, type (weight), and size of stock for each of its online-available National Forms: Résumé, Emcee, Volunteer Service, Actress & Photogenic (combined card), Emcee & Academic (combined card); Talent; Spokesmodel; and Casualwear Modeling. Mandatory paper type includes: Exact Opaque, Astrobright, and Bright Hue. Specific forms are to be in colors Pink, Pulsar Pink, Ultra Fuchsia, Fireball Fuchsia, Yellow, Solar Yellow, Galaxy Gold, Gold, Terrestrial Teal, Blue, Lunar Blue, Green, Terra Green, Martian Green, Orchid, Cosmic Orange, Tan, Peach, and Ivory. (Each age group is required to use their respective [age division] colors.) Weight (type) of these papers includes twenty-four pound paper and Bristol Card Stock; size for all is 8 ½" x 11".

Official contestants who choose to use the downloadable National Forms need to take care in matching proper headings, paper weights, and colors. The reason is that official contestants typically practice on the original set of forms they receive. One form in one age division is slightly different from the "same" form from another age division. Knowing that girls don't get their printed information correct straight away, NAM pageant officials suggest that its official contestants practice on several forms until they get it down correctly. *Then* they can send in their final completed forms. Pageant officials needing seven or eight copies of a Platform Statement, Résumé, Talent, and Volunteer Service Form to include in a Judge's Contestant Portfolio, for example, find it easier that official contestants make the required copies and submit them prior to pageant weekend. Most pageants require that the copies be on white stock; however, when a pageant system has multiple age divisions, and *two* National pageants occurring *at the same event*, as does NAM (*National American Miss* and *National All-American Miss*), color-coding is the ONLY solution.

National American Miss official contestants — at its State and National pageants — are responsible for turning in said pageant forms, in the appropriate stock, whether they use the set that was originally mailed to them, or they create their own exact duplicates.

Therefore, NAM has made it easy for candidates to download its .pdf forms. While they are provided with one set of forms, pageant officials know that mistakes will be made on multiple rounds. So, it is wise that official contestants are offered the opportunity to download the very same pageant forms and, providing they match the stock and color, make their own copies. Wise candidates will take the clean, original set of pageant forms to *Staples* or *Office Depot* and have a half-dozen photocopies (or more) made of each form — in the appropriate matching stock. They can also purchase the stock and print the forms on their own personal home printers.

Candidates are also reminded that the color paper can be found at most major office supply stores. NAM also suggests that candidates not wait until the last day to purchase the paper. Those specific colors and weights may be out of stock, or the store nearest their home may not carry an unusual color/weight stock. How clever to not have around 700 National contestants calling the pageant headquarters year after year for yet another copy of the emcee card that their dogs chewed up!

Chapter 5

Admission Tickets

You can increase the likelihood of bringing in a large audience by encouraging official contestants to sell admission tickets to family and friends. This can be accomplished by offering enticing incentives for high sales, such as reserve seat passes and cash prizes. For example, official contestants selling five admission tickets can earn two reserve seats passes; ten admission tickets can earn four reserve seat passes; and twenty admission tickets can earn ten reserve seat passes (reserve seat passes still need admission tickets). After the twenty admission ticket level, an official contestant could earn a percentage of her admission tickets sold. *Miss American Coed* rewards crown pins to official contestants who sell ten admission tickets. Candidates who sell twenty-five tickets earn a crown pin plus a $25 cash award. Hand out admission tickets early in your pageant.

Structure Admission Tickets

Plan the structure of your admission tickets. Include on your admission ticket such information as your pageant date and time; venue; ticket number; raffle information (if raffling prizes from the same ticket); admission ticket prices (presale, at-the-door, reserve seating, and children prices); policy on lost admission tickets; policy on refunding admission tickets; and Official Sponsors' logos. Include a perforation to separate the stub from the ticket.

Decide what your admission ticket prices are, and then print it on your ticket. *Miss Southern Essence Pageant* charges $25 for reserved seating admission, $12 for general admission and advanced admission tickets, $15 for at-the-door tickets for adults, and $10 for advanced and at-the-door tickets for children.

Make it easier to inventory admission tickets by numbering them. If you are perforating admission tickets, be sure to include the same number on both the stub and the ticket. Then, number your admission tickets in subsequent order. Consider investing in *Number Machine Pro Windows* software. *Number Machine Pro* is an extremely versatile Windows program that will enable you to do all of your own numbering jobs in-house. You will be able to number every conceivable job — from raffle tickets to multi-part carbonless forms — right from your personal computer.

On the left side of the admission ticket, spare two inches for perforation between (what would be) the stub and the ticket. Then, include matching numbers on the stub and the ticket. If you are giving away door prizes, the stub would be the area for a purchaser to write his/her name, address, email address, and phone number. Thereby, include this information on the stub. Perforate admission tickets so that ten tickets can be stapled together at the stub. Include a second perforation slightly above where the stub would be stapled. This allows the stub to easily be detached and inserted into a raffle drum while the remaining admission tickets stay intact. Otherwise, you will need to manually detach the stubs from the staple.

A ticket purchaser could also keep both the stub and the admission ticket — hence the need for two perforations on the admission ticket. S/he will use the admission ticket to gain access into the pageant and retain the stub as proof that s/he 1) paid to attend the pageant; and 2) has (the stub with) the matching number to claim his/her prize if his/her admission ticket becomes the raffle's winning ticket. Applying this method means the raffle winner would need to be present to win.

On the other hand, people tend to misplace their ticket stubs, so consider having candidates hand out *only* the admission ticket portion and retain the stub for raffling and identifying the winner by name. Applying this method means the raffle winner would *not* need to be present to win.

Official contestants often sell more admission tickets if they are presented with a stapled book of admission tickets rather than loose ones. Additionally, loose admission tickets account for more losses. Moreover, inventory of the remaining admission tickets is easier when stapled at the stub. Give each official contestant a stapled book of ten admission tickets to sell to family and friends.

Miss Maud Pageant notes,

> The [admission] tickets you are given at the Orientation Tea will be the only tickets you receive. We will not be able to replace lost tickets!

Miss Archdale-Trinity notes that official contestants are responsible for the number of tickets they receive at the official contestant meeting. Contestants must pay for any tickets that are not returned.

Miss Brooklynn Productions reminds official contestants that there will be no refunds issued for advanced [admission] ticket purchases.

Lastly, regarding the pageant venue to include on your admission ticket, *Grand Dazzle Pageant* sometimes provides official contestants with admission tickets *before* it secures its pageant location. In this case, pageant officials note,

> If you have purchased an admission ticket, you will receive an email with location information within two weeks prior to event.

Do pageant officials mean that they will contact everyone who purchased a ticket, via email, to inform them of the pageant location? Or, will they contact every official contestant selling admission tickets to ask that they verbally inform admission ticket buyers of the pageant event location? If official contestants are selling admission tickets without a pageant venue printed on the admission ticket, they will need to contact every person they sold one to with the location. Avoid placing added stress on official contestants and their parents. Secure the pageant venue *before* printing your admission tickets. Then, print the location on the admission tickets.

Back Side of Admission Tickets

Your policy covering its loss and replacement, as well as the refunding of the admission price, could be printed on the back of your admission ticket. Or, print this information on a separate form. Then, you're free to include Official Sponsors' logos on the back side. For additional ideas on what to include on the back of your admission tickets, visit Chapter 12, "Mailshot" under "Admission Tickets."

Other Admission Tickets Information

The *Miss Magna Pageant* allows admission tickets to go on sale three weeks prior to the pageant. Admission tickets can be purchased on the website. Moreover, every official contestant is assigned twenty admission tickets to sell to family and friends.

Miss Magna's admission ticket price includes a copy of the *Miss Magna* Pageant Program Book. I often materialized admission tickets at every Pageant Workshop (that served as an entry deadline day). This allowed official contestants to immediately begin selling them during this exciting time. This is a perfect example of striking while the iron is hot. When official contestants sell out of their allotted admission tickets, they will turn in the money and stapled stubs. If they want additional admission tickets, they can obtain more at this time.

Will Everyone Need to Purchase an Admission Ticket?

Parents often wonder why they must pay admission to see their own child participate in a pageant. *Young Miss Pageants* answers this by stating,

> We prefer to rent ballrooms and banquet halls instead of competing in malls so that our contestants, the audience, and our staff feel safe. By performing in ballrooms and banquet halls we are able to control who is watching our children. This is why there is an admission fee to watch our pageants; it helps with the costly rental of the ballroom.

But seriously, why isn't *Young Miss Pageants* bartering "the bottom floor" with hotel management? Learn how to barter "the bottom floor" by reading my book *Producing Beauty Pageants: Brokering a Pageant through Barter*, Chapter 5, "Pageant Venue Bartered" under "The Bottom Floor."

At the very least, allow mothers free pageant admission, as does *Carolina Piedmont Pageant*. Will children under the age of two have free admission? *Oklahoma Princess of America* notes, "Lap children will not be required to have a ticket." However, if large families of six or more children want to attend, OPA suggests that they call in advance to secure a pre-paid, discounted price.

- *Miss Brooklynn Productions* allows children eight and under free entry, and additionally, one adult per contestant.

- *Princess of North Carolina* allows visiting royalty free admission and offers them the chance to be introduced. Royalty, of course, need to be in crown and sash.

- *American Coed Pageants*, at no charge, allows visiting Royalty and one parent admission to each of the Pageant Finals.

- *Pixie Pageants Mini Nationals* doesn't charge admission. The price of the pageant covers door badges, so official contestants can invite all of their family and friends to come cheer them on:

  We have waived door admission charges and slightly raised the contestant price to cover this fee.

- *Texas Choice Pageants of San Antonio* and *Southern Star's Miss Candyland* don't charge admission.

- The *National Southern Miss Scholarship Pageant* requires that everyone pay admission: parents, family, vendors, hairdressers, and coaches.

- *Crown Bound Pageants* reminds official contestants,

  [to] tell your fans to bring cash because admission and People's Choice votes are cash only.

- *Mystic Productions* bluntly states,

  If you are entering the building, you will be paying admission.

Admission Tickets and Pageant Program Book Combos

Encourage the sale of both your admission tickets and Pageant Program Books (PPB) by including a discount package offer for both. *Queen of Folly Beach and Edisto Pageant's* at-the-door admission for adults is $25. This price includes a PPB. *Miss U.S. Beauties National Pageant* sells admission tickets for $25, which includes a PPB; without a PPB, it is $15.

Mandatory Admission Ticket Sales

If it's *mandatory* for official contestants to sell admission tickets to the pageant, note this in your pageant Rules & Regulations. *Miss Southern Belle Beauty and Pink Ribbon Beauty Pageant* notes, in writing, the mandatory 10-ticket sale *before* prospective contestants officially register.

The entry fee for the *Miss 101 Wild West Rodeo Pageant* is $200. Official contestants are offered the option to secure a $200 sponsorship *or* sell $400 in rodeo admission tickets. Additionally,

> Contestants are not judged on [admission] tickets sales, but ticket sales will be used to determine the winner in the [event] of a tie.

While admission ticket buyers are often no-shows at pageant events, imagine having more people show up for your pageant than you have available seats. What will be your backup plan?

Admission Tickets Sales Count as Pageant Points

While it isn't mandatory for official contestants to sell admission tickets at the *Keep It Moving* pageant,

> [selling admission tickets] will give the pageant participants more points towards winning the pageant.

Keep It Moving features a Raffle/Admission Ticket. The ticket is one that serves two purposes: 1) A ticket purchased will enter a person into the raffle; and 2) it can be used as an admission ticket to the pageant. (The cost of the ticket is the same whether or not the person purchasing it attends.)

At the age of sixteen, I represented the Corpus Christi Naval Air Station squadron VT-31 in the *Miss Navy Relief* pageant (at the time, a charitable military organization). To participate in the pageant, I had to sell raffle tickets for a Cadillac. Every ticket sold counted as a pageant vote. The candidate selling the most raffle tickets was crowned *Miss Navy Relief*. As an incentive for each girl to participate, a local bank gave every candidate a $100 savings bond.

Badges/Wristbands

Will badges/wristbands that cover the entire pageant week be for sale? Admission tickets are only good for one event, so recommend to contestants' families that they purchase an all-events badge/wristband. _Admit One Products_ offers a complete selection of Event Badge Holders, Event Ticket Holders, Armbands, Laminating Pouches, Laminators, Plastic ID Cards, Slot Punchers, Straps, and Clips. Most products ship within two to six business days and are available in quantity tier pricing.

- _Kentucky Beauties_ presents a pageant in two sessions and notes,

    [you] must have [a] two-session badge to remain in audience between sessions.

- _Heavenly Angels & Dreamland Divas National Pageant_ requires all persons not competing in the pageant to have a wristband on at all times (every official contestant receives a complementary one with their all-for-one fee). Official contestants are reminded to not lose those badges because they are not replaceable.

- _America's Grand Miss National_ makes it perfectly clear,

    Door badges will not be replaced. Please do NOT ask.

- _America's True Beauties_ provides advance warning,

    Door badges must be worn at all times. Do not attempt to enter the ballroom without your badge.

FunPass Badge

Anyone attending _USA National Miss'_ fun events are required to purchase a FunPass. FunPass badges sell for $60 per person and include the cost of admission to the National Outing, The Pink Party, and the Pool Party. FunPass ticket order forms can be found in _USA National Miss'_ National Delegate Handbook (in the Forms & Reference Information section).

Admission Ticket Upgrades

National American Miss sells National pageant admission tickets for $20 per event. NAM also offers an upgrade for *an additional* $25, totaling $45. Owning a $45 upgraded ticket is like holding seven event tickets.

Miss Rhode Island USA sells Preliminary Judging admission tickets for $30, Final Competition admission tickets for $40, and Special Reserved Seating for $95. Admission tickets are not sold via mail or over the phone — *only* at the door and prior to each show.

Admission Ticket Outlets

Official contestants can serve as an outlet to sell admission tickets. Nevertheless, sale of admission tickets by an official contestant should not be a requirement to participate in a pageant. Admission tickets can be sold elsewhere. *Miss USA* admission tickets are sold on *StubHub.com*, *Ticketmaster.com*, and through the *Theatre for the Performing Arts Box Office at Planet Hollywood Resort and Casino*. *Miss America* admission tickets are available at *ACHEAPSEAT.com* and at *Ticket Luck*. Instead of the usual twenty percent, *Ticket Luck* only takes a one to two percent markup. For that reason, *Ticket Luck* doesn't spend on advertising, so customers lucky enough to find the site will save a tidy sum for themselves. Once customers purchase pageant admission tickets, the tickets are sent to them via Fed-EX. *Miss India Illinois* and *Miss India Teen Illinois* admission tickets can be purchased at *Sulekha.com*, *DESICLUB.com*, and *JAI HIND* India grocery stores. *Little Miss Texarkana* admission tickets are available at *TEXAR Federal Credit Union*, *Twisted Vine Floral Studio*, and *Bridal Castle*. *Miss Archdale-Trinity Pageant* sells pageant admission tickets at the Chamber of Commerce. *Miss Bermuda Pageant* admission tickets can be purchased at *BDATIX*.

Admission Ticket Envelopes

Admit One Products provides Ticket Envelopes (also known as Will Call Envelopes) in various sizes and styles. The online options include blank stock ticket envelopes, pre-printed ticket envelopes, and custom printed ticket envelopes. These envelopes work well for advanced admission ticket sales. These envelopes would be perfect for _Miss Southern California Cities_ and _Miss Long Beach_ pageants, as ALL advanced admission tickets sold are to be picked up at will-call (box office/window where you pick up the pre-paid tickets) on pageant day. On a similar note, _Miss Brooklynn Productions_ states that purchased advanced admission tickets are available at pageant day Check-In and filed by last name.

My favorite Ticket Envelope is the #10 String & Button Envelopes sold at _Paper Source_. Technically, it's not a Ticket Envelope; however, this open ended envelope (with a string and button closure) allows for pageant officials to place a book of ten admission tickets (or more if requested by official contestants) into the envelope and then twist tie the string to interlock the envelope. Official contestants now have a pouch in which to securely keep their admission tickets. Monies collected (and remaining ticket stubs) are placed in the pouch envelope and locked in place with a twist of the string.

Miss Archdale-Trinity takes inventory of sold and unsold pageant admission tickets. Official contestants must turn in admission ticket money and unsold tickets at dress rehearsal. Ticket Envelopes assist official contestants with admission ticket inventory. They also help candidates to not lose their money, remaining admission tickets, and stubs. On the outside of the Ticket Envelope, official contestants would fill in their name, the number of admission tickets sold, the number of remaining admission tickets, and the amount of cash in the envelope. If admission tickets are numbered, the beginning and ending sequence of numbered admission tickets can also be written on the Ticket Envelope. This type of ticket management helps official contestants and admission ticket managers with ticket inventory. It allows official contestants to be organized with their admission tickets inventory before appearing at the Check-In station, and it provides a speedier Check-In.

To stamp the front of the Ticket Envelope, I designed a self-inking stamp that had a line for the official contestant's name, number of admission tickets enclosed, amount of money enclosed (once admission tickets were sold), number of remaining admission tickets, and (two lines for the) beginning and ending sequence numbers on the issued admission tickets (this part is filled in by pageant officials before distribution). In addition, the self-inking stamp included my pageant company name and contact information — in the event the ticket pouch was lost and the founder kindly returned it. The front of each envelope needed to be hand-stamped because the String Tie Envelopes are not laser or inkjet compatible due to the closure device. Additionally, I would choose a different color pouch (Ticket Envelope) for every age division. This quick inventory gave me an estimate of how many at-the-door seats were available, for any age division, and at any given time. *Envelopper Inc.* also carries a line of String Tie Envelopes available in two sizes. These String Tie Envelopes come in many different colors, including metallic, matte, and linens. (When using a self-inking stamp, metallic envelopes are not recommended.)

Chapter 6

Pageant Program Book

Pageant Program Books (PPBs) not only provide a vehicle to earn money through advertisement sales, sponsor listings, and "spotlight" pages, they are sold to an audience. A PPB contains general information about your pageant, delegate roster photos, delegate and/or Royalty photo sessions, Official Sponsors advertisements, pageant committee listings, judges' bios and photos, and the evening's agenda. Moreover, a PPB allows a tax deduction for businesses that sponsor official contestants and/or purchase advertisements. Your PPB can be your best bartering tool when offering advertisements in exchange for products and services that benefit the pageant. Last, but not least, a PPB can promote your next pageant by including a prospective contestant recruitment advertisement. A PPB is a huge moneymaker, so select someone who has no other responsibilities in the pageant to handle it. Let this individual work on the entire book — from collecting advertisements to the printing, sales, and distribution.

Printing Cost of a PPB

The cost of printing a Pageant Program Book (PPB) varies from printing company to printing company. It also depends on the type of paper you choose, whether it's in black and white or color, the number of pages, the number of photos, how many advertising pages are included, how much typesetting the printing company needs to do, and how much of the work that you provide is camera-ready. If you provide a camera-ready copy, include your finished product on a memory stick, and take these files to a printing company. If your PPB is camera-ready, that is, *ready to go to press*, you will receive a better price, and you won't need to visit a specialty printing company. Instead, a company like *Office Depot* can produce your PPB from your memory stick. If you bring in the files by Tuesday, for example, it will be ready for you by Friday — often sooner — for your best price. Check with your printing company in advance regarding the lead time needed to get your printing done. In order to get to this level, you will need to use a software program that allows you to compose your PPB pages with pictures and text. *Microsoft Office's Publisher* can do just this, so can *Apple's Pages* (for Mac), *Apple's Pages* (for iOS), and *iWorks Apps*.

If you need help with typesetting and page layout — in addition to other printing services — you will need to visit a full service printing company. If you go this route, bring along a dummy PPB for starters. A dummy can be created by stapling pages together after you figure out the number of allotted pages for your PPB. Again, the more you can do on your own, the more you'll save on printing costs. For example, provide camera-ready ads, roster photos that are already 300 dpi (dots per inch) in the size of 5" x 7" and saved in a .jpg (compresses either full color or gray-scale images) format, and include pageant staff and judges' bios. *Gratzer Graphics* produced the *Miss Maryland USA* PPB. The specs noted that it was in black text, 92 pages, and included layout, proofreading, and placement of ads. (It already had a pre-designed and pre-printed cover.) View the *Miss Maryland USA* pageant book layout interior.

Number of Pages

Your Pageant Program Book (PPB) final page count will depend on many factors: the number of pages devoted to committee, staff, and volunteer introductions; your pageant itinerary and other front matter; the number of official contestants participating (and the number of roster photos featured on a single page); how many advertisements are sold; how many advertisements you have committed to Official Sponsors; the number of pages devoted to candidate sponsor listings; and a pageant's personal extras. Regarding candidate sponsor listings, be sure to include a limit on the number you will list under official contestants' roster photos. Some candidates will have one sponsor name to feature, while others want to list twenty-five or more! The *Tri State Baby and Prince Charming Pageant* allows a maximum of ten sponsors per candidate to be listed in the official State PPB. The rest make up "Family & Friends."

Pageant Program Book Photos

Another variable to consider before you can determine the number of pages your Pageant Program Book (PPB) will be is to know how many candidates are in each age division. Then, figure out how many will be featured on a page. Some pageants place six official contestants to a full page; others, nine. Some, like *National American Miss*, place six *and* nine official contestants on each page. NAM features six official contestants per page for its *National American Miss* National pageant and nine official contestant per page for its parallel *National All-American Miss* National pageant. Additionally, NAM features six pictures per page of both pageants' official contestants who participate in its National Optionals in a combined Optionals Contest Roster for each age division's respective PPB. (At the 2012 National pageant, the Teen and Miss divisions were combined. It was likely because the Miss division at National didn't have enough girls and/or ad sales to warrant its own PPB.) *Miss Dallas USA* features only four official contestants per page. You can view its 2009 Pageant Program Book at *issuu.com*. Learn how to yield a huge income stream by including Optionals participants' photos in your PPB by reading my book *Producing Beauty Pageants: Optionals*.

Moreover, will you feature all age divisions in one PPB, as does *Universal Royalty*? Or, will you create separate PPBs for each age division, as does *National American Miss*? If you have large numbers in each age division, it is probably best to make separate PPBs, or, at least, combine select divisions, as did NAM (with the Teen and Miss divisions), in 2012, at its National pageant.

Pageant directors generally accept black and white or color photographs for their roster photo if it will be reproduced in black and white. However, in such a situation, keep in mind that black and white photography reproduces best, whereas color photographs tend to reproduce dark and grainy. Photographs with too much background should be cropped so that the picture is a close-up of the face and hair. Candidates should not submit any over-the-shoulder or high fashion modeling looks — just a pleasant photograph showing a happy, pleasing face. They should also submit photographs that look like themselves. If candidates turn in professional photos that are too glamorous or touched up, judges may be disappointed when they finally meet them. Candidates often make the mistake of using a photo in which their hair appears to be a different color or in which the hair style is drastically different — or worse, one that's years old!

Little Miss Texarkana Pageant reminds candidates that if they want to use their photogenic competition photo for the roster photo, they are to turn in two copies of the same photo. (Do note that if the photogenic photo is to be 8 ½" x 11", and the roster photo is a 4" x 5" or 5" x 7", then appropriate sizes of the identical photo need to be submitted.)

East Coast USA Pageant requires all candidates to submit a PPB photo in a wallet size (2.5" " x 3.5"). Furthermore, they may email the photo in .jpeg (the most common image format used by digital cameras) format only.

Miss American Coed notes, "[Your program book photo] may be sent electronically for an additional $10 charge."

Miss Illinois County Fair Pageant requires candidate PPB roster photos to be a head and shoulder shot *without* a crown or sash:

> This photo MUST be 2 ¼" wide x 3 ¼" long; length between forehead and chin must be 1 ¼". [Furthermore, choose] a light gray or blue background. Photos with other background colors (including white as it blends with the page around it) will not be accepted. Make sure there is a distinction between your hair color and your clothing color. If you have dark hair, don't wear a dark color. Use medium shades of cosmetics.

Miss Perfect Pageants PPB and website photo requirements state,

> Each contestant must submit a total of six 3" x 5" photos (color and black and white) for the judges. The photo will appear in the program book. All photos must be identical. Include the contestant's name exactly as it should appear in the program book, on the back of all photos. The photos must be included with application and email a copy to ewilliamson@madetoday.net by deadline.

It was not clear how many (of the six photos) were to be in black and white and how many were to be in color. It did, however, include a Website & Photographer Release.

Miss Smiths Station Scholarship Pageant reminds candidates that, if they mail photos with their paperwork, write "Pictures Enclosed" in large bold letters on the envelope. This keeps the post office from bending the envelope and picture. Pageant officials also remind candidates to not paperclip the roster photos.

Miss Pasadena Strawberry Beauty Pageant requires that all photos be labeled with a tab stating name, category, and age division. Official contestants should label the back of their photo with their name, age, and the word "roster" on the back. Candidates are asked not to write directly on the back of the photos; a label works best.

Will candidates be expected to email the required roster photo(s) — in 300 dpi, in the size of 5" x 7", and saved in a .jpg format? If photos sent are larger than the specified size needed, pageant officials might need to charge a $10 photo reduction fee.

Miss Teen America requires that all roster photos be scanned at 300 dpi and saved as a .tif image.

Miss Conservative U.S. Pageant requires official contestants to submit one photo in high resolution and another in .jpg format.

To be certain that the photos are not returned to the sender, *Paradise Pageants* remind candidates, "Please make sure you have attached adequate postage to your envelope." If your photo doesn't quite meet the pageant's PPB requirements, send it to *Photo Retouching by Courtney*. Courtney, a pageant photo expert, offers photo resizing, retouching, background changes, and more.

Multiple Pageant Program Books

National American Miss is an expert at producing multiple Pageant Program Books (PPBs) for its State and National pageants. At the National pageant, in 2012, *nearly 700* official contestants (from both *National American Miss* and its parallel pageant *National All-American Miss*) were combined and fitted into *five* 8 ½" x 11", four-color glossy, perfect bound PPBs. Not only that, NAM needed to fit the following into the divisions' respective PPBs:

- 57 full page advertisements into the Princess division

- 166 full page advertisements into the Junior Pre-Teen division

- 118 full page advertisements into the Pre-Teen division

- 114 full page advertisements into the Junior Teen division

- 115 full page advertisements into the combined Teen and Miss divisions

Every PPB featured *only* the advertisements each respective division's official contestants sold. It's not clear if any of those advertisements were generated from drop-off official contestants. Understand drop-off and its financial repercussions benefitting pageant directors by reading my book *Producing Beauty Pageants: Open Call*, Chapter 10, "Drop-Off."

There are six age divisions in the *National American Miss* pageant and six age divisions in NAM's parallel pageant *National All-American Miss*. Official contestants from both National pageants, ages 4–6, were combined into the Princess PPB; ages 7–9 were combined into the Jr. Pre-Teen PPB; ages 10–12 were combined into the Pre-Teen PPB; ages 13–15 were combined into the Jr. Teen PPB; and ages 16–18 *and* ages 19–20 were combined into the Teen/Miss PPB. (NAM only has five age divisions at its State pageants. Moreover, there isn't a parallel pageant at the State level.)

The front of NAM's multiple PPBs features an identical cover: a group picture of the reigning *National American Miss* Queens. The back cover also features an identical cover, the parallel "All-American" pageant's reigning *National All-American Miss* Queens. Each division's front cover and spine identifies the division title.

The inside front was basically the same for the five age division PPBs — give or take a few pages that related to each respective divisions' Queens' photos, volunteer work, farewell pages, etc. Official Sponsor advertisements were identical in all division PPBs, as was the front matter that included photos and/or bios on directors, judges, and production staff.

Then comes the differences in each of the five divisions' PPBs: "I Am" Spotlights pages; *National American Miss* contestant roster photos; *National All-American Miss* contestant roster photos; Optionals roster photos of the *combined* pageants' (in the same age division) candidates who participated in Optionals contests; and last, the remaining half of the PPB featured each respective age division's participating official contestants' advertisement sales at $600[9] per page.

Had NAM included all official contestants in the National pageant *and* the advertisements participating official contestants

---

[9] It went up to $750, in 2014.

sold into one PPB, it would have been *nearly three inches thick and consisted of over 1,000 pages!* Instead, each of the five NAM PPBs *averaged* 220 pages, and each sold for $25.

At NAM's State pageants, it is my understanding that the State *National American Miss* PPB is divided by region and the number of official contestants residing within that area. With State official contestant numbers rivaling those of the National pageant, it would be necessary for NAM to feature multiple PPBs in order to fit in hundreds of roster photos and sold advertisements. Dividing candidates by region seems logical, and my guess is that the total number of regional PPBs would vary according to the number of official contestants and the number of advertisements they sold. My guess is that there are four regions: North, South, East, and West.

Universal Royalty, a fixture on *Toddlers & Tiaras*, featured one PPB at its 2012 National Pageant for all age divisions combined. And, although nearly 100 candidates participated in all divisions combined, less than half had roster photos in the PPB. (Last-minute entries were encouraged at-the-door, making roster photos impossible.) The PPB appeared to be printed on a home laser printer and then bound with a portable spiral binding, a.k.a. coil binding. Every page of UR's PPB, including the cover, was composed of a 20# stock weight. The "cover" was a 7mil Crystal Clear 8 ½" x 11" Letter Size clear plastic cover (usually sold for $17 per pack of 100). UR's PPB's page count was twenty-six sheets of paper (including the cover). UR sold each PPB for $20. To learn how to coil-bind a PPB, visit the *YouTube* video How to Spiral Bind a Book. For all of your in-home spiral binding needs, visit *MyBinding.com*.

Meeting Your Printer's Deadline

Printing companies are on a tight schedule. *Miss American Coed* sets a deadline for when Pageant Program Book (PPB) advertisements will be placed in alphabetical order. Official contestants who don't meet the deadline risk having their ads placed in available spaces in the book, and not in alphabetical order. They are also given a deadline (generally a week later) to submit their "Congratulations" and "Best Wishes" advertisements in the PPB.

Insertable Ad Pages

Advertisements that arrive *well after* the Pageant Program Book (PPB) ad deadline are at risk of being featured as loose-leaf pages and inserted into pocket pages at the end of your PPB. It is my understanding that these advertisements are printed on loose-leaf paper, trimmed to size, and then loosely inserted into the back of the PPB, inside a pocketed page. Speak to your printing company about including a pocketed page in the back of your PPB to accommodate late-to-arrive ads. These insertable ad pages allow pageant officials the opportunity to include the late-to-arrive advertisements. Candidates are warned that incoming ads that do not meet the printer's deadlines will be placed in "available spaces" or inserted into "loose pocket pages" — both located in the back of the PPB. Find out all available advertisement options from your printer.

Pageant Program Books Circulation

To arrive at your Pageant Program Book (PPB) circulation number, you need to know how many you will sell, give to official contestants, give to Official Sponsors, use as a prospective contestant recruiting tool, etc. While some candidates and their families will purchase more than one PPB, not every audience member will purchase one. Trying to figure out how many PPBs to print — your circulation number — is challenging.

Miss American Coed 2011 National contestant Jemila Whitner stated,

> [over] 3600 National program books will be printed and distributed throughout the nation.[10]

For a National pageant like MAC, where admission tickets sold can number in the 4,000–5,000 range, it's smart to print over 3,600 PPBs.

Storage can be cumbersome if you're stuck with too many PPBs after your pageant event. MAC sells the previous year's

---

[10] "Help Jemila get to the National Miss American Coed Pageant." sponsor goal.com. http://www.sponsorgoal.com/2011/11/03/help-jemila-get-to-the-national-miss-american-coed-pageant/.

remaining MAC Pageant Program Books at its coed store. *Miss Teen USA* sells *several* previous years' remaining Miss Teen USA Pageant Program Books at its online store.

Here's where deciding how many PPBs to print gets tricky. Let's say that you have six age divisions, and you print six PPBs — one for each age division. Will there be a printing (circulation) of 3,600 books per age division? Or, will the total number, 3,600, be divided by six age groups, for an average circulation number of 600 per age division? When a MAC contestant tells her prospective advertiser (or sponsor) that "[over] 3,600 National program books will be printed and [distributed]," is s/he to understand that his/her company will be advertised in each one of those *combined* 3,600 circulation PPBs? Or, is the candidate's age division circulation number, 600, the actual number of PPBs in which the advertiser's advertisement will appear? Additional information on PPBs advertisement circulation can be found in Chapter 13, "Selling Advertisements" under "Circulation Demographics" and "Circulation Information."

Encouraging PPB Sales

Miss Alabama America offers its Pageant Program Books (PPBs) at a pre-sale price of only $10, which encourages candidates (and their families and friends) to place their orders in advance. They are also sold at-the-door for $15, but there is only a limited number of PPBs for sale. Candidates are encouraged to ask anyone attending the pageant to pre-order the PPB in advance — both for savings and to avoid not having one. This presents pageant officials with a firm PPB count. Now the State pageant won't be stuck with unsold PPBs!

How Much You Can Make Printing a Pageant Program Book

The amount of money you can make from your Pageant Program Book (PPB) depends on many variables. Will you sell advertising space? If so, how much will each page sell for? (Learn more about advertisements by reading Chapter 13, "Selling Advertisements.") Will you provide camera-ready material to your printer to avoid typesetting charges that will cut into your profit? Will it be in black and white, color, or a mix? Will your printing company be an Official Sponsor, in part or in full, and sponsor your PPB? Assuming they will be sold, how many PPBs will you print? How much will you charge for each one? Some pageants charge as much as $20 or more per PPB! Learn how to barter for a free PPB by reading my book *Producing Beauty Pageants: Brokering a Pageant through Barter*, Chapter 9, "In-Kind Sponsors" under "Pageant Program Book."

Get Creative with Your PPB Cover

Imagine each State delegate in your National pageant having her sole headshot on the cover of your National Pageant Program Book (PPB). *USA National Miss* did just this, in 2012, at its National pageant. Every National delegate received a Special Edition National PPB Magazine. Each respective issue featured each official contestant's individual headshot on the cover! We're not talking about all the girls in a group photo, but rather, *each individual State delegate on her own personal magazine cover*! *USA National Miss* appears to be the only pageant that features each State delegate on the cover of her very own "Special Edition" National PPB Magazine. State delegates were also invited to include their sponsors' names on their respective covers in a caption under their respective photos.

Turn your PPB cover into an Optional contest and sell chances at winning the front and back cover spots. *Regal Majesty*, in 2016, did just this. For $40 per entry, candidates could submit a headshot for a chance at winning the coveted cover spot, or they could submit a full body photo for a chance at winning the back cover spot. To increase their chances at winning candidates could enter as many times as they wanted to and for either cover spot. Learn how to maximize your Optionals upcharge revenue by reading my book *Producing Beauty Pageants: Optionals*.

Most pageant systems feature a PPB for each age division with the identical cover, as does *National American Miss* at its National event. Why not take those five PPB's and create color differences to identify each age division's cover? *Photo Retouching by Courtney*, at minimum, can meticulously change each PPB cover's color to coordinate and complement your PPB series. Just look at what Courtney has done for my *Producing Beauty Pageants* series' covers that started with this book! The cover model began with a *Dazzles Pageant and Prom* red *Tiffany* gown. Although my PBP books' series cover ended with the identical gown, Courtney changed it to an entirely different color. That is the magic of photo manipulation!

Spare Pageant Program Books

Keep several Pageant Program Books (PPBs) as a marketing tool. Include a copy in every official contestant's Sponsorship Kit or Advertising Kit for the following year. It's a great tool to aid prospective contestants in their search for sponsors — to help them become bona fide official contestants (and not drop-offs). Last year's PPB edition can also aid official contestants in selling the current year's PPB advertisements. Learn more about drop-offs by reading my book *Producing Beauty Pageants: Open Call*, Chapter 10, "Drop-Off."

An Agent Tool

All Canadian Pageants divides its Professional Program Book (PPB) into two sections: "International Contestant Lineup" and "Sponsor Pages." Every international contestant must be in the "International Contestant Lineup" section. In addition to the sponsorship fee, every international contestant is charged $80 to have their photo printed in this section. This cost includes a complimentary copy of the PPB along with the delivery charges pageant officials incur when they send copies to various casting agents, talent managements, and scouts and personal clients who book kids through their pageant events. People who meet the age requirements, but are not in the pageant, have (in the past) sent in photos and payment so they, too, can be included in *All Canadian Pageants'* PPB. They also have a chance to be seen by agents, clients, and scouts for possible paid commercial bookings. This photo roster service could be a lucrative income stream for a pageant. Individuals not participating in the pageant would be charged a higher price to have their photos included in such a PPB.

Chapter 7

Director's Event Checklist

Successful pageant directors are not only organized, they also find a business model that works, and they continue to improve upon it. This organized system starts out with a basic Director's Event Checklist. As your pageant system progresses, this checklist is improved. It is always best to rely on a Director's Event Checklist — rather than memory — while developing your pageant.

A Director's Event Checklist should include items such as venue, hotel, pageant staff, staging, staging handbook, staging backdrops, stage lighting and audio, stage script, easels, committee checklist, flowers, trophies, crowns, sashes, sash pins, and the list goes on. While the _Miss Hospitality_ Director's Checklist features a sixty-day timeline, I prefer to have one at a ninety-day starting point. It is important that I see my entire production needs at a single glance. A director can tailor the Director's Event Checklist to fit his/her needs. This chapter features general items (in no particular order) that could be included on your Director's Event Checklist.

Pageant Staff

An organized pageant staff is essential to a successful pageant event. A detailed pageant production team checklist can be found in my book _Producing Beauty Pageants: Creating a Synergized National Pageant System_, Chapter 9, "Production Team."

Venue

One of the first items on your Director's Checklist is to choose your pageant venue. When searching for one, make sure it will accommodate your pageant needs, i.e., appropriate staging, seating availability, rehearsal time availability, judges interview room(s), hotel rooms availability (if a multi-day pageant), dressing rooms availability, etc. Additional information on selecting a venue can be found in Chapter 3, "Pageant Venues." Learn how to barter for your FREE venue by reading my book *Producing Beauty Pageants: Brokering a Pageant through Barter*, Chapter 5, "Pageant Venue Bartered."

Hotel

If your pageant requires a hotel stay, were you able to reserve discounted room rates for official contestants and their families? If so, is the discount rate only for a single night or the entire pageant week/weekend? What is the pageant room block rate and code number? How long is the offer in effect? Is there a fee for parking at the hotel? Is the parking fee the same for guests and visitors? Is valet parking available, and if so, what is the fee? Is free Wi-Fi available? Is there an Internet fee in the hotel rooms? What is the charge for outgoing phone calls? If official contestants will have more than four family members staying in a room, will you suggest they bring an air mattress? Are pets allowed? Will there be a mini refrigerator and microwave in the room? If you provide hotel accommodations for your official contestants, will official contestants be expected to room with other candidates? If so, will there be a chaperone in each room or, at least, one on the same floor?

Dressing Room

Even if candidates can change competition outfits in their hotel rooms, it is ideal to have a dressing room near your stage. Make sure that there are plenty of electrical outlets. If they are in short supply, ask candidates to come as ready as possible before arriving at the pageant, i.e., use a heating iron or steam iron before they arrive at the pageant. What about garment racks? The Macon County *Junior Miss Pageant* makes sure that there are a few garment racks, box fans, and some picnic tables in the dressing room to help keep official contestants organized and to keep them cool. Pageant officials also encourage candidates to bring their own fans, mirrors, clip-on lights, and extension cords. They don't, however, allow cell phones in the dressing room.

There are many dressing room tips offered by different pageant systems. A few are noted below:

- _Miss Greater San Diego USA_ suggests that official contestants bring a blanket into the dressing room to lay on the floor "as your 'SPACE' to put your things on" and prepare for the pageant.

- *California Cover Miss & Cover Boy* suggests keeping noise level at a minimum by not bringing radios, walkie-talkies, boom boxes, CD players, etc., into the auditorium or the dressing room areas.

- _Coastal Georgia Pageant Productions_ avoids being billed for damages caused by *Kool-Aid* (and the like) destroying dressing room carpeting. Candidates are reminded,

   We have had incidents where sauce was spilled and dresses have trailed [through] the mess. Please wait until you are finished competing to eat/drink, when you are OUTSIDE of the ballroom.

- *California Cover Miss & Cover Boy* mentions the following regarding items that are left behind:

   Any items left behind backstage or in the dressing room areas will be collected and retained for a period of ten days after the pageant. If these items are not claimed within the ten-day period we reserve the right to dispose of the property as we see fit. Any postage or handling fees are the responsibility of the parent and/or guardian who is claiming said property.

- *Southern Grace Pageants* states,

   Any items left [behind] cannot be mailed.

Foyer Entry Set-Up

When presenting your pageant at any venue (e.g., a hotel ballroom, a reception hall, or a town theater), the foyer — an anteroom or lobby adjacent to the auditorium — needs some pizzazz. One way to achieve this is by rolling out your custom pageant logo and message on banners and scrims. Made in vinyl or cloth, and in a variety of sizes, they add excitement and class to any pageant production.

Visit *Tour City*, and click on "Banners & Scrims" to view samples of custom banners and scrims. Whether you need full color or black and white (large or small) banners, digitally printed ones provide the best results. When ordering your banner(s), make sure grommets (or eyelets) and pole pockets are included on the order form for an alternative way to hang your banner(s) and for reinforcement of banner fabric. Moreover, even if there is an additional charge, ask that Velcro be sewn onto the backside of your banner's(s') edge(s), which helps keep the banner(s) in perfect position when displayed. In the event that you place your banner(s) outside, ensure that they are weather resistant and come with a certificate of fire resistance. Visit *Online Design's Fabrication Finishing Guide* to understand your banner options.

Depending on how big your foyer is, include several water station areas. To keep candidates' energy levels up, a fruit punch station is in order. Avoid sugar-laden, carbonated drinks. Consider having a snack table where you can sell pageant logoed bottled water, energy bars, dried fruit, etc. Although some pageant officials will have a pageant boutique at the pageant, a bling table set up in the foyer — a taste of what can be found inside your pageant boutique — can add some pizzazz. If you have vendors at your pageant, usually the foyer is where they will set up shop.

Staging

Appoint a stage manager to make arrangements for your stage set-up. If your pageant takes place in a hotel ballroom, make sure the hotel can provide your staging needs. Most hotel stages consist of platforms approximately two feet high and ten feet wide. If you feel that this is not high enough for the audience's view, you may have better luck renting a stage from *Fuller Street Productions*, *Frequency City Sound*, or *Stages Plus*. When you can afford to, purchase your own staging equipment. It will be worth your investment, as it has been for *National American Miss*. Or, secure a theater to better suit your staging needs.

Staging set-up also means that you will need seating arranged in a theater-style fashion. A stage manager will secure staff or volunteers to get this job done. Or, do as *Aqua Boom Scholarship Pageant* does and enlist candidates to get this job done. Just make sure that you are adequately insured. To be eligible to participate in the *ABSP*, among other things, official contestants have agreed to help with set up and clean up before and after the pageant. Of course, there is no need to make seating arrangements if your pageant is taking place in an auditorium. For a hotel ballroom or clubroom, write down specific details about seating arrangements for hotel personnel, and then discuss them at length with the stage manager. This will alleviate any seating problems that you might otherwise encounter. Learn about *Cinderella International Scholarship Pageant's* awesome Staging Handbook that it presents to its Preliminary and State directors by reading my book *Producing Beauty Pageants: Creating a Synergized National Pageant System*, Chapter 2, "Preliminary Details" under "Staging Handbook."

Staging Backdrops

When you want to add a finishing touch, accent the aesthetic, or shield the performers until curtain-time, a backdrop is the practical solution. Backdrops focus the audience's attention to the stage platform, not what is happening behind the stage. A backdrop example can be found at *American Royalty Supreme Pageants*. Click on "Photo Gallery" to view pictures of it.

A practical solution could be a *SICO* backdrop. *SICO stage backdrops* consist of drapes with many fabrics to choose from. Also featured are mobile frames that connect to the stage to suspend the drapes. Backdrop Carriers come in standard widths of 4', 6', and 8'. Backdrop drapes come in sizes between 4' x 10' and 8' x 12' — with five other size options.

Staging Canadell also provides easy to set-up adjustable backdrops that are 8' fixed height or 7' to 12' adjustable uprights with telescoping 7' to 12' drape supports. Pleated drapery comes in 8' x 8' or 4' x 8' sections or in custom lengths. Take a moment to view the drapery brochure.

If you need your logo (or your Event Sponsors' logos) featured in a backdrop setting, a step-and-repeat is what you'll need. The Women of Achievement included its logo design on its

Ms. United States step-and-repeat backdrop designed by _Faryha Graphic Design_ (see last project frame).

Scrims

Scrims are the latest tool in special effects lighting that take your stage to the next level. A scrim is a very light woven material made from cotton, flax (stronger than cotton), or a combination of both. Its light weight and translucency means it's often used for making stage backdrops. Scrims have been used extensively in theater, particularly when used for specials effects. When used for special effects, it is properly called a sharkstooth (open weave net) scrim, which means there is more open space than actual fabric. A sharkstooth scrim, when lit properly, can appear either opaque or transparent. These effects are then used to perform conceals and reveals. Sharkstooth scrim can also be used to create the illusion of distance. Scrims can be used alone or in front of black staging backdrops, as is used by _National American Miss_. In addition to using varied color lights while its logo appears through a gobo head projector (a device which produces patterns of light and shadow), NAM's use of scrims include: 1) placement in the back (fronting a black background) and 2) overhead to create a ceiling to enclose a large open space above the stage. Visit NAM's _YouTube_ channel to see some examples.

Scrims reflect and transmit light — which means that if a light from a front-of-house position is shone on a scrim, then both the scrim and everything behind it will be lit. There are several effects that can occur when using a scrim. A scrim will appear entirely opaque if everything behind it is unlit and the scrim itself is grazed by light from the sides or from above; the color is any color of light you shine on it. A scrim will appear nearly transparent if a scene behind it is lit, but there is no light on the scrim (this would typically be a spotlight). A dreamy or foggy look can be achieved by lighting a scene entirely behind a scrim. If a light with a gobo projector, or various pieces of equipment that go before a light (such as a gobo arm or gobo head projected using a halogen projector), is aimed at a scrim, the image will appear on the scrim. Any object(s) behind the scrim will also be lit and form a pattern. It appears that NAM uses a gobo projector to project "NAM," as can be seen on a NAM scrim. Google "Images for gobo projector" to view sample gobo images.

To learn about secret entrances with a scrim, shadow screens with scrims, shrinking and growing effects, silhouette screens with scrims, distance effect with scrims, and front projection and rear projection on scrims, visit *Studio Productions* and click on "What are scrim effects?" If you want to know what types of scrims are available, click on "What types of scrims are there?" You can purchase or rent scrims at *Studio Productions*, *Textum*, *Tour City*, *E C Stage Art*, and *Rose Brand*.

Stage Lighting and Audio

It is important to have professional stage lighting and audio. Hire a professional who specializes in mobile pageant production to make your pageant look spectacular in every way. Pageant audiences love to see professional lighting that includes multi-color lighting and lasers (and even fog for an after-pageant party). Professional audio is also a must for any pageant. *La Belle Fille Productions*, a Nashville, TN-based Professional Mobile Productions company offers Pro Stage Lighting and Professional Audio. In fact, even if you have three pageants in adjacent ballrooms going on simultaneously, *La Belle Fille Productions* can accommodate your lighting and audio needs. Visit a company like *B&H Photo, Video, and Professional Audio* to purchase your own lighting and audio equipment. Learn how to barter the services of a profession stage lighting and audio crew by reading my book *Producing Beauty Pageants: Brokering a Pageant through Barter*, Chapter 9, "In-Kind Sponsors" under "Stage, Lights, and Sound."

Transportation Carrier for Pageant Staging Materials and Supplies

It will be expensive to rent transportation to carry your pageant staging equipment and supplies from State pageant to State pageant, and then to National. As soon as you can afford to reinvest your pageant income, purchase your own truck and trailer. But, before you do this, contact the *Federal Motor Carrier Safety Administration (FMCSA)* to learn about trucking safety and procedure — including Carrier and Vehicle Safety; Laws and Regulations; and Registration, Licensing, and Insurance.

Kenn Maples, Associate Director of *National American Miss*, and under the business name *The Abri Company, Inc.*, in 2010, was given an active carrier company USDOT Number. Its fleet details include two total drivers operating one power unit (standard). *The Abri Company, Inc.* uses a truck and trailer that it owns. The cargo includes materials and supplies for pageants comprising of NAM's own staging equipment and a horde of trophies and the like. You can view this public information at Find the Company.

Companies that operate commercial vehicles that transport passengers or haul cargo in interstate commerce must be registered with the *Federal Motor Carrier Safety Administration* (FMCSA) and must have a USDOT Number. The USDOT Number is an identifier when collecting and monitoring a company's safety information. If you're hauling pageant cargo intrastate, many states require USDOT numbers. For instructions on completing the motor carrier identification report and applying for the USDOT Number, visit FMCSA. For registration and licensing information, visit FMCSA.

Probably the smartest thing about owning your own truck and trailer is that you can continuously store your pageant staging equipment in it. As each State pageant rolls around, and then National, you simply drive your equipment (or hire drivers) to deliver it. And, you won't need to pay for storage of your staging equipment, nor will you need to constantly load and unload from a storage unit between pageant events. Your truck and/or trailer will be already stocked and ready for your next production!

Easels

An easel is a freestanding, upright support typically used for a painter's canvas or a blackboard. It is usually made of wood and has movable clamps. You will need to purchase several for your pageant event. On your easels, you will include boards such as, "Register Here," "Contestant Dressing Room," "Photogenic Check-In," "Sign Up for Talent," "Interview Room for Pre-Teen (Teen, Miss, etc.)," "The Line Starts Here," and so on. If you have several activities going on simultaneously in different ballrooms, professional boards that describe each activity in progress should be propped on an easel next to the fitting activity. Include your pageant logo on all easel board messages. If you have Open Call, it would be beneficial to have easel boards in front of registration tables (stations); for example, girls with last names "A–E, Register Here"; "F–J, Register Here," and so on. It helps to keep a pageant organized.

Stage Script

Due to time constraints, will you require your emcee to ask the audience to hold their applause until all official contestants have appeared in a particular area of competition? Or, will s/he encourage the audience to applaud the entrance, performance, and exit of every candidate during their presentation, as does *Girls Self-Esteem Program (G-SEP) Pageants*? Regardless, make sure to also include a note for the emcee in your stage script to thank the audience for being kind to all pageant hopefuls and not just their own, as does *Miss Tennessee Charm*.

The 2006 State and 2007 Local Single Night Show Script for a Preliminary *Miss America* competition begins with an Off-Stage Announcer introducing the Opening Production Number, followed by the host introduction. Then, the host appears on stage and begins his presentation with some pageant history, followed by a Judges and Auditors introduction. The Swimsuit Production Number, Talent Competition, Evening Wear Production Number, and Evening Wear Competition soon follow. The pageant includes a Finale Production Number and ends with the announcement of the Runners-Up and Winner.

The smart thing about this Stage Script is that, while the actual Stage Script is on the right column, the left column features host instructional notes. For example, the right column makes note that official contestants are in Evening Wear and indicates to the audience that each candidate is provided with an opportunity to articulate her commitment to her platform of community service by answering a question. The notes on the left column of the Stage Script (intended for the host) remind him/her to take this action:

> It is recommended that you put a time limit on the answers to the questions of [twenty] to [thirty] seconds.

The 2006 State and 2007 Local Single Night Show Script can be found at *scribd.com*. Be sure to scroll down the entire two-column, twenty-five page script. To view the script, you would need to be a *Scribd* member. You can sign up for a free month trial.

For a *non-committed viewing*, Google these exact years and words (and also the quotes): "2006 State and 2007 Local Single Night Show Script" and disregard the "no results found" message. Click on the first [DOC] that appears for the *Miss Kentucky Scholarship Pageant*. It's the same script. (This process doesn't work on the *Bing* browser.)

A well-written pageant stage script is time-consuming. National American Miss knows this. So, to run a tight ship, NAM designed a stage script that is "[pretty] much the same from one [NAM] pageant to the [next]," said Steven Roddy of *The Pageant Planet*. An observing and calculating NAM alumnae contestant who goes by the username Macsasti noted,

> With all of that time saved [NAM] can now focus on getting more girls to come to [its] pageant, and serving [official contestants] better. NAM puts on a wonderful stage show, [it] really, really [does].[11]

Committee Checklist

Prior to organizing your pageant committee, make a Committee Checklist. This assures that all positions will be filled as you obtain help and that no detail will be overlooked. To help create a Committee Checklist, i.e., a Production Team, read my book *Producing Beauty Pageants: Creating a Synergized National Pageant System*, Chapter 9, "Production Team."

Check-In

Also known as Sign-In, Check-In happens at the pageant event registration. Bob Lee, whose daughter Violet entered the Tennessee National American Miss State pageant, recreated his daughter's NAM Check-In experience on his blogspot. Bob didn't make it clear what age division his daughter participated in. To give you an idea of the Pennsylvania State NAM pageant's Check-

---

[11] Macsasti. *"National American Miss—Scam?"* September 11, 2011. http://www.national-american-miss-scam.com/wp-admin/edit-comments.php?paged=34.

In process, a portion of information from Bob's blogspot is included below:

> Sign-In was between 4:00 p.m. [and] 5:15 p.m. During the Sign-[In] we entered all the Optionals Events Violet wanted to compete in: Talent, Actress, Casualwear, Most Recommendations, Photogenic, Top Model, Best Résumé, and Art competitions. After signing up for each event, [Violet] received a Ribbon for Participation. When she arrived to the Photogenic Events table, she also received a Trophy for entering all four Photogenic Events. After signing in we went to get her [$40] Production Outfit [pink NAM shirt, white anklet socks, and a hair ribbon], which [Violet] would use in the Actress Competition and the Final Dance Show before the Finale.

Universal Royalty director Annette Hill is her own registration director. When Annette registers candidates at her National pageant, she meets with each official contestant individually and privately behind a closed door. At the National pageant in Austin, Texas, in 2012, which took place at the _Holiday Inn Midtown_, a table was set inside the entrance of the competition ballroom, behind the forward-facing seating arrangement overlooking the stage. Candidates formed a line outside of the ballroom. A reigning Queen would bring in one candidate at a time (and/or her parent) to meet with Annette. The Queen would close the door and allow for all registration transactions to occur before releasing the official contestant and permitting the next one to enter and register. Candidates didn't need to be in order; they just needed to be at registration within their division time frame.

Registering candidates privately and individually at your Check-In yields less confusion. A registration director can focus on one candidate/family at a time. She can tend to financial matters privately, because, after all, each had different fee amounts to pay. Some won photo contests and didn't have to pay the basic entry fee; others received different discounts. It's like being on an airplane — every passenger paid a different price for a seat on the same airplane! If a mother in line (within ear range) becomes aware of a candidate who has received a great discount, and her daughter didn't, she will feel slighted since she has to pay full price.

If your pageant registration is set up in stations, place a strip of blue Painter Masking Tape on the floor a few feet away, indicating where next-in-line candidates are to stand while waiting their turn to register. Accompany this with a sign on an easel that says, "The Line Begins Here" — displaying an arrow pointing to the blue line on the ground. This helps provide some privacy for the candidate already at the registration table. Consider shielding part of an open station with a portable screen, partition, or wall divider. Your staging backdrop could double as station partitions during registration.

Early Check-In

Smartly, most pageants offer an Early Pageant Check-In on Friday (after 3:00, when candidates can check into a hotel), and a regular Pageant Check-In the following day, sometime after 8:00 a.m. Families that check into their hotel a day early presented NAM with an opportunity to thin out the larger Check-In crowd for the following day. It would, therefore, benefit the early-to-arrive candidates and pageant officials to take part in an early Check-In — to get as much registration paperwork out of the way before the rush.

Pike County's *Miss Heart of America Pageant* states,

Please DO NOT arrive early for Check-In; we have the Check-In time set so you have plenty of time to [turn in] your food collected and pick up your contestant number and stage card.

Miss American Coed includes a handy Pageant Check-In Instructions page in its twenty-seven page, 2009, Newsletter #2 (towards the bottom of the forms). It reminds official contestants of what items they need to turn in, and in what order they need to be in during pageant Check-In:

Be sure all of your papers are in the order listed below. One station will be set up for each of the areas listed. If you have your records arranged in this order, checking in will be fast and easy!

Early Online Check-In

Prior to its National pageant, in 2012, MAC official contestants could "speed through Check-In" by paying all of the fees online at the coedstore.com before they arrived at the host hotel pageant venue. When a pageant operates by cash during a pageant event, why subject yourself to hordes of cash and risk losing it if you don't need to? Could MAC have set up this online early cash payment system as a result of what MAC founding father and the late George Scarborough experienced, in the early '80s, at a National MAC pageant? George's horrifying and costly experience can be found in my book *Producing Beauty Pageants: Sponsorship Fee.*

Opening Number

If you plan on presenting an Opening Number (also known as a Production Number) at your pageant, hire a professional dance choreographer. It is frustrating for parents to watch their daughters be taught a dance number by a teenager (even if she is the reigning Queen), who is having a hard time with the routine herself! Using former Queens to teach the Production Number usually doesn't sit well with parents of current official contestants. They expect a professional to do the job, because they have invested a lot of money in the pageant. A pageant director might seek out a dance intern from a local college, or the owner of a dance studio, to put together a Production Number and teach the routine. *Miss Thoroughbred of the Bluegrass* keeps its production simple and safe by not having the weight of all official contestants on stage at one time (and risk it collapsing) by noting,

> Contestants will not be doing an opening number, but rather just a parade of contestants. Contestants will need a pink outfit of her choice.

Evening Gowns

Inevitably, official contestants will ask for guidance in securing (borrowing, renting, purchasing, or bartering) a beautiful pageant gown. *Dazzles Pageant & Prom*, since 2000, has been providing wardrobes for winners on the Local, State, and National pageant levels. A *Dazzles Pageant & Prom* gown can be seen on the cover of my *Producing Beauty Pageants* series. *Pageant Designs Tiffany Princess Cupcake* offers quality pageant dresses for the younger pageant contender. *Blush Kids* offer a lovely selection of pageant dresses for little girls.

Flowers

Present rose bouquets to your winners. Acknowledge candidates' parents, and present a rose to every mother and a boutonniere to every father — particularly if they double as escorts. Escorts can recognize official contestants with a rose as they appear on stage during the Evening Gown competition.

Consider renting vendor space to a florist so that parents or ticketholders who want to purchase flowers for their child/contender can do so, or be your own in-house florist and sell rose bouquets. It is my understanding that _National American Miss_ is its own in-house florist. At their National pageant, officials sell rose bouquets for $18 and $28, and rose boutonnieres (for escorts) for $11. A white, three rose bouquet sells for $18. Featured on "NAM Nationals, By the Numbers," in 2012, NAM sold 1,940 roses at its National pageant! If each rose averaged $5, that's an income stream of nearly $10,000! Or, if half of the nearly 700 National contestants purchased the $18 rose bouquet ($6,300), and the other half purchased the $28 rose bouquet ($9,800), that's roughly $16,000! Imagine what NAM's nearly forty State pageants with similar numbers, from all angles, generate from their in-house flower business!

If you want to keep it simple, yet elegant, consider presenting your royalty with rose bouquet scepters, such as the "Black Magic Scepter" offered at _Gillespie Florists_. Even better — have the rose bouquet scepters made with silk flowers, and you'll never need to water them. You also won't need to worry about your rose bouquet scepters falling apart as you transport them, and royalty will get to keep a lasting memento that won't wilt. You would be able to order in bulk for your best pricing. Learn how to barter for Queens' presentation bouquets and escort boutonnieres by reading my book _Producing Beauty Pageants: Brokering a Pageant through Barter_, Chapter 9, "In-Kind Sponsors" under "Florist."

Balloon Bouquets

Purchase or rent a portable, refillable helium tank, and create balloon bouquets at your pageant event. Unlike flowers, you won't have to lug a product around that may or may not sell, and they won't wilt if they aren't filled with helium. They are unsold, unfilled balloons that will keep for future use, unlike unsold, wilted flowers. _Universal Royalty Beauty Pageant_ sells Balloon Bouquets for $20.

Bubble Machine

There's nothing quite like floating bubbles to make a party out of your awards ceremony. Either rent or purchase a quality bubble machine. _Walmart_ or _Target_ is NOT the place to buy one. The American DJ Bubble Blast Machine (SKU: 1005454), at _Best Buy_, sells for $299.99. The _Bubble Blast Machine_ produces hundreds of bubbles per minute due to an advanced fan system. This product features a dual-fan lift system, drainage valve system, top-load filling container, remote with timer control, and wheels and dual handles for easy transportation. Because this bubble machine is so powerful, be sure to monitor usage. It wouldn't take long for a stage floor to become slippery! If you do use this (or any) bubble machine, run it in small durations. Be sure to ask for permission from your pageant venue management first. If allowed, plan on paying extra for janitorial services.

Tuxedos

Tuxedoed escorts will enhance your pageant. Tuxedos can also be worn by your emcee, judges, and other male assistants. Learn about bartering for tuxedos by reading my book _Producing Beauty Pageants: Brokering a Pageant through Barter_, Chapter 9, "In-Kind Sponsors" under "Tuxedos."

Music

Recorded music is the most widely used method of providing pageant music. _Golden Miss–Mr. National_ pageant officials play upbeat music for all Optionals events. They won't, however, play a candidate's music (during the beauty competition), and they won't take requests. This is done to keep the pageant fair for all candidates. Pageant officials understand that one candidate may have a routine to certain music, but they also feel that it's not fair to the majority who don't.

WI Pageant Productions keeps it simple by providing the same background music for the Beauty (Evening Gown) competition and *not* allowing official contestants to bring their own music for their moment on stage. A beauty pageant music playlist can be found on the Internet at various sites, including *Pageant Center*, *MP3 Bear*, and *Experience Project*.

While an orchestra is the nicest way to provide music, it is also the most expensive. A combo consisting of three or four musicians is a good alternative. Look into bartering with a live ensemble or DJ-provided music service by reading my book *Producing Beauty Pageants: Brokering a Pageant through Barter*, Chapter 9, "In-Kind Sponsors" under "Sound Design."

Tiaras, Adjustable Crowns, Coronets, and Bucket Crowns

It used to be easy to select a tiara or coronet to crown a pageant winner. There were not very many choices, nor many distributors. Now, not only are there more tiara and crown choices than ever before, but there are also *many* distributors.

Will Queens be able to keep their crowns after their reign? Or will they need to return them to the pageant? *Miss California International* crowns and sashes remain the property of *Peterson Productions, Inc.*, until the State pageant is concluded. This makes sense because the rhinestones can easily fall out even with the gentlest touch. *Miss Brunswick Old Fashion Days* pageant only allows the Queen to keep her tiara after her year reign; the Jr. Miss and Little Miss winners only get to keep their sashes.

For directors who have their crowns and tiaras customized, be careful how you design your crowns. You don't want to design anything remotely like an existing copyright image. Moreover, don't purchase counterfeit pageant products with (unauthorized) copyright images. The Japanese company that owns the *Hello Kitty* brand, *Sanrio*, filed a copyright transgression lawsuit in federal court, in 2012, against the Oklahoma pageant that ran beauty pageants under the name *Definitely Divas*. The suit claimed that *Definitely Divas*, now defunct, used the image without permission from *Sanrio* in its *Tickle Me Pink* pageant. Visit *Siouxsie Law*, and watch Emerald Gordon Wulf in a backstage video at a *Pink Pageant*. At the video's conclusion, you will see the counterfeit *Hello Kitty* loot Emerald wins. As it turned out, the pageant producers purchased counterfeit crowns (and trophies) that featured *Hello Kitty*. Not getting written authorization misleads people into possibly believing that *Sanrio* endorsed and/or sponsored the pageant. Moreover, unauthorized use of any copyright product, including music, is against the law.

Pageantry Magazine is a great source to find many of your pageant needs — including tiaras, crowns, coronets, and bucket crowns. Contact *Pageantry Magazine* to get on its mailing list. Also, contact *Glitzy Girl Magazine* and *Pageant Girl Magazine*. If you are pressed for time, bridal stores usually carry a line of tiaras from which to choose. Otherwise, order your crowns and tiaras early. Delivery can range from two to six weeks from most U.S. suppliers — longer for special orders, custom creations, or when ordering from out of the country.

Tiaras

The tiara, which has rhinestones along the front and is open in the back, should only be used for Local or Preliminary pageants. This type of crown is worn right on top of a candidate's head with the front section even with the front of her ears. While most have side combs that hold them in place, some tiaras just have a metal bar that grips the wearer, allowing her to pull her hair over the bar; gravity holds the tiara in place.

Let's take a price journey of one tiara: the #11914 Large Butterfly Cluster Tiara, made in China. This tiara is used by many pageants in Canada, *Miss Gambia USA*, and in the U.S. by *Distinguished Young Women Scholarship Pageant* and *National American Miss*, just to name a few. As of this writing, it sells for $44 at *Rhinestone Jewelry Corporation*. The very same tiara can be purchased "on sale" for $199.95 at *GlamForLess.com*, $176 at *Ejools.com*, and £ 61 at *Secret Sparkles*.

If you want to purchase the #11914 Large Butterfly Cluster Tiara directly from China, you can get each unit (tiara) for about $10 *when you order ten dozen pieces*. (Smaller orders could be negotiable.) Delivery time is about fifteen to twenty-five days, but there's no guarantee on this shipping timeframe. Visit *Yiwu Yiso Jewelry E-Business Firm*. The #11914 Large Butterfly Cluster Tiara can also be found at *Alibaba*. At one time, it was identified as model number BC0181; it may have changed. Be sure to scroll to near the bottom of the page to notice that, as of this writing, there are 104 pages of crowns and tiaras in their inventory. If you want a custom crown, *Yiso Jewelry* can design one for your pageant theme.

Crowns

The *Miss USA* crown is *almost* a full circle and adjusts to the wearer's head. Adjustable crowns have a gap in the back, which is connected at the bottom by a sliding bar. The wearer must pull a section of her hair up through the center of the crown, draping it over the bar. Some titleholders make the mistake of wearing this crown flat on their heads. It should be placed on a girl's head like a tiara, with gravity holding the crown in place. The *Miss USA* crown is most liked by beauty Queens. *Dina, Inc.* creates crowns for *Miss USA* and its State winners. Additional information about *Dina, Inc.* can be found in the section below titled, "U.S. Crown Manufacturers."

Coronets

A third type of crown is known as the coronet. It is the most difficult crown to wear, and it is worn by *Miss Americas* and by its State winners. Coronets cannot be adjusted to fit varying head sizes. A metal bar runs across the diameter of the wearer's head, or four hoops are provided at the base for bobby pins and rubber bands to secure the crown in place.

The Best Crowns is the official crown manufacturer for the *Miss America Organization*. All work, excluding metal finishing, is done in-house using *Swarovski* Austrian crystal stones.

Holly Hardwick Crowns is another option, if you want a *Miss America*-inspired crown design. The styles offered at *Holly Hardwick Crowns* are not reproductions or replicas of the *Miss America* crowns. They are totally different designs and include tiaras as well as full crowns. For an extra income stream, pageant officials can purchase dolls crowns and tiaras for resale in its pageant gift shop. Contact *Holly Hardwick Crowns* to find out if there is a bulk price discount.

Other crown sources include *The Glitzy Crown*, *Tiara Connection*, *Wholesale Crowns*, and *Rhinestones and Tiaras*.

Bucket Crowns

Bucket Crowns are the latest crowning trend. A bucket crown stands over 6" tall, and the band is a full circle and approximately 6" wide (with four small rings in the center for securing to the hair). Bucket crowns are typically plated in Sterling Silver. They are intended for ages fifteen and up. The nice thing about a bucket crown is that the winners can place a small light in the center of the crown (on a nightstand) and the crown doubles as a night light. *Porcelain Dolls Nationals*, in 2015, awarded a 70" crown.

If you do take photos of Queens wearing bucket crowns, and the crowns *are* too big to stay in position, they *will* crash and destruct if a hand isn't holding the crown in place. One option is to use Photoshop to erase any hand or arm that is propping the bucket crown in place. Learn how to use Photoshop by listening to free photoshop tutorials. Better yet, hire a professional to do this for you. Courtney, from *Photo Retouching by Courtney*, is skilled at correcting even the most complicated photos and will provide you with flawless results.

Visit *Rhinestone Jewelry Corporation* to view its inventory of bucket crowns. If you need large quantities at the best prices, purchase bucket crowns directly from China. View bucket crowns created by *Yiwu Yiso Jewelry*.

Light Up Crowns

New to the pageant scene, at least to *Porcelain Dolls Nationals*, in 2013, was the girls' 14" light-up crown. This beautiful custom-designed crown included a battery pack (located on the inside back) that took two AA batteries; it also had an on/off switch. The custom-made *Porcelain Dolls Nationals* girls' crown included AB and crystal stones in the design of a doll in a royalty chair. Kathy Raese, *Porcelain Dolls Nationals* director, along with *Alabama Wholesale Crowns* crown designer Kelly Kirkland, became a trailblazing team. Not only did the duo design the light up crown with beauty in mind, but also with practicality. The light-up crown doubled as a night light. The Dudes' light-up crown was a 4" Blue AB stone crown with surrounding lights. To yield an even more stunning effect, the AB rhinestones were replaced with blue sapphire rhinestones. *Alabama Wholesale Crowns* brought *Porcelain Dolls Nationals'* design "to light," first from its Alabama shop via a prototype, and then from its outside manufacturer.

Alabama Wholesale Crown designer Kelly can team up with any pageant director to design a custom, light-up crown, or any crown of his/her choice. Kelly can be emailed at awccustom@gmail.com.

AB Rhinestones

Not to be confused with battery-operated light crowns, when rhinestones have the term "light" in front of the color, notes *Rhinestone Jewelry Corporation*, it means that it is a paler rendition of the actual color itself and referred to as semiprecious gem colors. AB rhinestones are created by applying an Aurora Borealis (AB) coating to the stone. In light refraction, this coating makes a prism effect, which usually reflects all of the colors in the rainbow. Generally, the base color will be seen through this coating. At times, the coating will completely alter the stone's color. *Rhinestone Jewelry Corporation* notes,

- Jet AB is not black, but rather it shines green.
- Crystal AB is the result of an AB coating on a crystal rhinestone. It will disperse mild colors in all ranges:
  - Swarovski AB coatings replicate blues, greens, reds, and gold tones. Swarovski are absolutely the finest stones available.
  - Czech stones mirror other gold and yellow tones. Czech (and some Asian) cut-crystal stones are very close in quality to *Swarovski* Austrian cut-crystal stones. However, the quality is less than *Swarovski*.
  - Korean stones do not have AB coatings.
  - Chinese stone makers are now matching AB coatings of better makers quite well.

AB rhinestones are made by polarizing the glass. The stones come in special colors and usually reflect two or more colors, depending on the direction of the light source. Aurora borealis crowns and tiaras can be found here.

Crown Wholesalers

Pageant tiaras, crowns, coronets, and bucket crowns can be purchased at wholesale prices at *Rhinestone Jewelry Corporation*. Located in Brooklyn, NY, *Rhinestone Jewelry*

Corporation designed and copyrighted the crystal tiara featured on the cover of the *Producing Beauty Pageants* series. The Small Mediterranean Spray Adjustable Crown, item #15895, stands approximately 5" tall, is sterling plated, and wholesales for $43.50 each. Although minimum quantities are part of a formula that allows *Rhinestone Jewelry Corporation* to offer low prices, the featured tiara on the *Producing Beauty Pageant* series' cover can be purchased individually. Excellent customer service means that your tiara(s) is/are often shipped the same day — to any country in the world. Other wholesale crown manufacturers include *PeacockStar*, *Alabama Wholesale Crowns*, *Wholesale Crowns*, *The Glitzy Crown*, *The Best Crowns*, and *Tiara Connection*.

Crown Manufacturers

When I asked *America's Gorgeous Girls* director Ms. Lauren who her crown manufacturer is for her custom crowns, she wisely replied:

> That is one thing that I cannot tell. I'm under contract with a few other [pageant] systems not to share our crown source — it's a small company in China and if they are too busy it will take forever to receive our product. I already have to order at least three months in advance. One thing you [should know] about China is customs. Terrible! Even if your crowns are supposed to arrive they can be stuck at customs for days, especially if it is a big order. I have had it happen once and it was very stressful![12]

If you need many tiaras/crowns/coronets/bucket crowns to honor winners and/or to sell in your pageant boutique, and they aren't custom made, you can buy them directly from China. One place to start your wholesale crowns and tiaras search is at Ali Express. You will like the prices at this wholesale site, not to mention the free shipping and even greater discounts for multiple orders. Holding a "Flower Power" pageant? Purchase the Pageant Peace Symbol Tiara DST HG-971 for only $19. If your budget only permits $5 per tiara, you will find many other options. Need a beautiful 4" full crown for $25? Order the Rhinestone Crystal Diamond Tiara Crown (minimum order six pieces). Need a 6" red,

---

[12] Personal email, May 1, 2014.

white, and blue star crown for $15? Order HG804. Another star crown option, the 6" Pageant (HG802) Crown, sells for $17.50 each (minimum order six pieces). Need a 5" Rainbow Pageant Crown? A dozen crowns will set you back $249.80. All suppliers are verified by Alibaba.com, the global trade company.

Visit Alibaba's country search to find other Chinese manufacturers for your tiara and crown needs. Here you will find better prices, but expect to purchase in larger quantities, such as 300 pieces, three dozen, ten dozen, 120 pieces, etc. You can purchase a bucket crown for $5, for example, but you would need to order a minimum of 120 bucket crowns in order to yield that price. If you have a huge pageant system with many Preliminary and State directors, this is certainly the way to go. On the other hand, if you can't afford the stress that accompanies dealing with China customs, have a U.S. crown manufacturer like Dina, Inc. be your crown source.

U.S. Crown Manufacturers

A pageant system would be hard-pressed to find crowns and tiaras made of *Swarovski* crystals from crowns manufactured in China. Two crown manufacturers, Dina, Inc. (manufacturer of the Miss USA crown) and The Best Crowns (manufacturer of the Miss America crown), proudly produce *Made in the USA* products made with *Swarovski* Austrian crystal stones. My experience is that Czech and Asian "crystal" stones will probably work fine in a small venue, i.e., sparkle in the 20th row or so, but if you want your crown's sparkling effect to be seen by the audience sitting in the last row of a large theater, your crowns need to be made with *Swarovski* rhinestones.

Dina, Inc., makers of the *Miss USA* crown, hail from Cranston, Rhode Island. The company has four employees and occupies a non-descript building on Dyer Avenue. Even so, owner John Bordieri said that he has no trouble finding customers, and despite not having a company sign on its building, customers certainly have no trouble finding *Dina, Inc.*

Not only is *Dina, Inc.* the official crown and tiara designer for *Miss USA* and its State winners, *Dina, Inc.* provides crowns and tiaras made with *Swarovski* crystals for many of the *Miss America* State winners and its princess program titleholders. For the *Miss Universe* pageant, *Dina, Inc.* also makes crown pins.

The making of tiaras and crowns is labor-intensive. While the brass frames are molded by machine, the rest of the process is hand-made. *Dina, Inc.* uses *Swarovski* rhinestones — which come in 500 foot roles — that need to be cut to length. Then, each rhinestone is individually soldered into place. Finally, the crowns and tiaras are washed in *Tide* detergent for about 15 minutes.

Because the work is so labor-intensive, *Dina, Inc.* contracts out some of the production work. While you will find about 200 crown and tiara styles on a wall within its shop, *Dina, Inc.* also accepts custom orders. *Dina, Inc.* prides itself on its impeccable customer service. It can turn crowns and tiaras over quickly *and* make them the way customers want. If needed, *Dina, Inc.* employees will work on Christmas, Easter, or any other holiday to complete an order. Besides crowns and tiaras, *Dina, Inc.* makes doll tiaras, crown rings, crown pins, and scepters.

The Best Crowns is another quality crown company that manufacturers its products in the U.S. — as far back as 1949! With over sixty years of manufacturing experience, *The Best Crowns* is able to meet your needs for high quality, competitively priced crowns, tiaras, and scepters, including custom design work. *The Best Crowns* started manufacturing fashion jewelry and crowns in 1949. All work, excluding metal finishing, is done in-house using *Swarovski* Austrian crystal stones. Moreover, *The Best Crowns* stands behind its work. In the event that you damage a crown, it can be repaired, in most cases, at no charge. *The Best Crowns* offer an extensive line of crowns and tiaras. Compare its pricing and selection, and you'll see why it has been around for over sixty years.

As with any crown manufacturer, there are legalities. In respect to *The Best Crowns*, its terms of sale is that all sales are considered "final." In the event you receive a shipment damaged in transit, you must contact *The Best Crowns* within *24 hours* in order to file a claim with the carrier. OPEN YOUR ORDER UPON RECEIPT AND INSPECT THE MERCHANDISE TO ASSURE NO DAMAGE HAS OCCURRED IN TRANSIT AND THAT ALL MERCHANDISE IS IN THE SHIPMENT. In the event that *The Best Crowns* chooses to accept a return of merchandise, there will be a 25% restocking charge. You will be responsible for all shipping fees, including the fees for return of the merchandise.

H&R Pageant Supply is also a pageant supply company proudly featuring Made in the USA crowns and tiaras. Other products include boy's and men's crowns, contestant numbers, crown and sash pins, pageant trophies, scepters, stock sashes, and custom sashes. If you need a rush order, call 1-800-787-8777. If it is after business hours, leave a message and a daytime phone number. View H&R's trophies here.

Czech Manufacturer

In 2014, Donald Trump, who co-produced the *Miss Universe* pageant along with *NBC Universal* between 2002 and 2014, succeeded in bartering with *Diamonds International Corporation* for what happened to be the loveliest *Miss Universe* crown ever designed. Paulina Vega, who hailed from Columbia and became the winner of the 63rd installment of the *Miss Universe* pageant, for the very first time was crowned with Czech-produced crown. According to the manufacturer, the whole production process of the diamond crown, from earliest sketches to final production, took nearly four months. The 2014 *Miss Universe* crown design is reminiscent of the Manhattan skyline and required the work of ten people. Valued at $300,000, the crown contained 311 pieces of diamonds (total 11 CT), five pieces of Blue Topaz (100 CT), 198 pieces of Blue Sapphire (30 CT), and Crystal (33 pieces). It was set in 14k gold – Au 585 – that had a net weight of 220 g of gold. The total weight of the spectacular crown is 411 g. As part of a projected ten-year cooperation with the Miss Universe Organization, starting in 2014, DIC is also on the hook to produce stunning crowns for *Miss USA* and *Miss Teen USA*. Moreover, as part of the cooperation, the 2014 *Miss Universe* pageant promoted DIC globally — to 180 countries. The advertising benefits that DIC gained from the cooperation agreement — $150 million dollars per year — will amount to approximately 1.5 billion dollars in 10 years. There is no question that *Miss Universe* and DIC mutually benefited by barter. Learn how to barter for your crowns by reading my book *Producing Beauty Pageants: Brokering a Pageant through Barter*, Chapter 9, "In-Kind Sponsors" under "Crown Company."

Miss Curacao, in 2015, was crowned with a stunning crown designed by DIC. It was set with three blue aquamarines and one yellow lemon quartz — representative of the national colors of Curacao. The base of the crown was made of 14 ct white gold, with a total weight of nearly 170 g. The crown's design symbolized the open sky, sea, and sun: representing Curacao on one side and the national colors on the other. The crown was designed to give the impression of a boat docking on one side, and the logo of *Diamonds International Corporation* — DIC — on the other. The crown is not only of beautiful design, but it is also a perfect hand-made product of Czech jewelers, goldsmiths, and fitters, who spent almost 2,000 hours designing and manufacturing it. View both the *Miss Universe* crown and the *Miss Curacao* crown at DIC's website.

Sashes

Some people call it a banner; others, a sash. But, by any name, it is an accessory most closely identified with beauty Queens. A sash adds to the regal appearance of your Queen and pageant. A sash is a "sign" the public can see a titleholder bearing and identify with the pageant she represents. *Miss America* paved the way with its titleholders wearing sashes.

Essence Pageants treats sashes as credentials. State representatives must wear the sash provided by the pageant at all times:

> Please wear your State sash when exiting the plane. Never leave your hotel room without it. You will not be admitted in [any] facilities without it.

Miss USA official State contestants are issued three sashes that drape from the right shoulder to the left hip: one to wear at all times until the candidate departs from the host city, one to wear during Preliminary judging, and one to wear only on the telecast. Shorter versions are provided for the swimsuit competition. In a recent campaign, "Discover the Power of the Sash," *Miss USA* officials stated:

> The power of the sash allows our contestants to build a local, regional, and sometimes even a national presence that can enhance their brand and change lives.

In-House Sash Company

Some pageant systems produce their sashes. It makes sense for a pageant system that has tens of thousands (or more) of prospective contestants participating in its pageant system *each year* to produce in-house sashes. It is my understanding that *National American Miss* produces its sashes in-house — at least the black (stamp) print on white satin ribbon featuring each State title at its National pageant. *Cinderella International Scholarship Pageant* also has an in-house sash production company in which it produces printed satin banners. *Cinderella* Executive Staff Member Donna Breen stated,

> Our State directors let us know what they need [at their expense] and we print titles for them, along with our custom slipper design, onto satin banners.

However, for its embroidered banners, both employ outside embroidery companies to do the honors. *Cinderella International Scholarship Pageant*, for example, employs Cyndi Neely, owner and embroiderer extraordinaire of *From Wishes to Stitches Embroidery* (cinderellagrammy@swbell.net). Cyndi creates sashes for its Local, State, National, and International Queens. (Although it appears as an extension of CISP, Cyndi Neely's email noted above is her own personal business address and is not a part of *Cinderella*.) Cyndi's handiwork can be seen on the cover of my *Producing Beauty Pageants* series.

Custom Sashes

There are a number of companies from which to order custom-made sashes. You are aware that *From Wishes to Stitches Embroidery* (cinderellagrammy@swbell.net) will create reasonably-priced custom satin sashes. Cyndi even uses filler for a slightly plush effect. It's no wonder *Cinderella International Scholarship Pageant* has employed Cyndi's services for many years, having the need for adult, youth, and toddler sashes.

The *Miss America* sash maker, *The Sash Company*, also crafts each pageant sash by hand, and like Cyndi's sashes, they have Velcro closures and are tailored at the shoulder for an excellent fit.

If you're on a tight budget and want a lovely sash at a reasonable price ($15), visit *Majestic Sashes*. When ordering custom sashes from *Majestic Sashes*, allow two to four weeks. A local company may need only a week's notice, while an out-of-town company may need several weeks. Other sash companies include *Rainbow's End*, *Holly Hardwick Crowns*, *Royalty Sash Co.*, *KD Creations*, *Banners Plus, LLC*, *Ladybug Designs*, and *SasheDesigns.com*. Visit *KD Creations* to view a selection of crowns for embroidery that can be embroidered onto sashes.

Strip Sashes

Coastal Pageant Productions awards Strip Sashes, a.k.a. Strip Banners, to official contestants for its Superlative Awards. Strip Banners are (typically) blank satin sashes. It is up to the winners to have their titles embroidered on their sashes — at their expense. Most Superlative Award winners generally receive a trophy and tiara. A Strip Sash makes it that much nicer for those winners; most will gladly pay the embroidery expense. Moreover, Strip Sashes make it possible for directors to create spur-of-the-moment awards to present. At *Rainbow's End*, in addition to embroidered sashes, you'll find Strip Sashes. Learn more about Superlative Awards by reading my book *Producing Beauty Pageants: Optionals.*

Half Sashes

County fair, festival, and 4-H candidate awards often require a Half Sash. *Hodges Badge Company* sells a variety of Half Sashes, such as the Contestant Half Fair, Festival & 4-H Award Sash. It is a custom, hot-stamped satin sash with a gold rim or satin center. Half Sashes are available in your choice of stock or custom center design. A 3" rosette matching the ribbon's color is included at the hip. Pricing is based on the number of characters, including spaces. Standard size is 3" x 36". Pins are included but unattached.

Two Layer Sashes

Hodges Badge Company sells a variety of two layer sashes, such as the 2 Layer Contestant Award Sash. It comes in a standard adult size of 3" x 52" with a loop size of 60". The child's size is 3" x 40" with a loop size of 40".

Pre-Titled Sashes

Avoid the higher embroidery costs by ordering your sashes with titles already printed in a gold foil on a high-quality, double-faced satin ribbon. *Alabama Crowns Sashes* has an extensive line of such sashes, both in 40" ($2 each — designed to pin at one shoulder and at the opposite hip) and 70" ($3 each — wraparound sash) lengths — all with preprinted titles. For example, in-stock titles include Queen, King, Photogenic, Overall Winner, Hi Point

Winner, Supreme Winner, Talent Winner, Prettiest Hair, Prettiest Smile, Best Dressed, Countess, Count, Duchess, Duke, Finalist, Contestant, Prince, Princess, Academic Winner, Miss Congeniality, Most Beautiful, Most Handsome, First (Second, Third, and Fourth) Alternate, Interview, Costume, Swimsuit, Sportswear, Portfolio, Sweetheart, Personality, and Model. Either length will work for a child or an adult. Custom titles are also available for only $8 each. (Do not try to use the 40" sashes as a wraparound for a child because the title is printed in the center of the sash, and it will not work.)

On-Site Embroiderer

If you provide an embroiderer at your National pageant, as did *Miss American Coed*, in 2012, winners can customize their banners minutes later! Not only did the embroiderer monogram/embroider banners, she was available to alter production number outfits and tend to minor pageant attire repairs. *Cinderella International Scholarship Pageant* employs Cyndi Neely, owner of *From Wishes to Stitches Embroidery* (cinderellagrammy@swbell.net), for on-site services at its International pageant. As noted earlier, one of Cyndi's sash designs can be found on the cover of my *Producing Beauty Pageants* series. *The Glitzy Crown* not only provides crowns for sale, they also offer sash embroidery service at *TGC Sashes*.

Sash Pins

Most sash companies sell crown sash pins. Pinned at the bottom, sash pins keep ends together; pinned at the top, they keep the sash from falling off of the shoulder. Visit pageant product sites such as *Tiara Connection*, *Allens Crowns & Trophies*, and *Crown Chic Boutique* to view sash pins.

London Strawberry Festival Queen states,

> Buttons, badges, and pins may be worn on the BACK of the sash. These must be limited to those associated with festivals/events attended or crown pins. Do not wear pins on your sash that are not related to your reign. Pins may not be placed on baby sashes due to safety. A few crown and strawberry pins may be worn on the front at the top or bottom of the sash but

cannot cover or interfere with the title or run down the sides of the sash.

Magnetic Sash Pins

The idea for a magnetic crown pin came to Sydney Swanson, a former *Miss Nebraska National Teenager*, quite by accident. Sydney's sister, Kirsten, who shows horses, wore a magnetic number holder — a magnet with a crystal on it — on her leather clothing. With such clothing worn when showing horses, pins cannot be used to pierce and hold numbers. Soon, the idea to create a magnetic crown pin to hold a queen's sash together (and not destroy the sash fabric with piercing pins) was born. Being a true millennial, Sydney found a manufacturer in China who would build a prototype for the proposed magnetic crown pin. After many emails, and a couple of prototypes, the design was completed, and the first order of magnetic crown pins arrived. The magnetic crown pins retail for $20 and wholesale for $10 at *The Crown Box*. There are several ideas to take into consideration when ordering magnetic crown pins at wholesale prices. One is that magnetic crown pins can be sold as a sponsorship fee fundraiser. Official contestants can raise their sponsorship fee by purchasing the pins for $10, and then selling them for $20. For every sale, they earn $10 towards their sponsorship fee. Another idea is that pageant officials can award a magnetic crown pin to every official contestant who turns in a full page of Contestant Referrals. View this lovely magnetic crown pin (made with 53 cubic zirconia diamonds) at *The Crown Box*. *America's National Teenager Scholarship Organization (ANTSO)* recently purchased 1,000 units.

Trophies

A trophy is a symbol of victory. Often made of metal or plastic, it doesn't have much monetary value. Still, it celebrates success. Whether you assemble trophies in-house, or purchase them assembled, these tangible symbols of distinction are proof of a pageant winner's success. Learn how to barter for trophies by reading my book *Producing Beauty Pageants: Brokering a Pageant through Barter*, Chapter 9, "In-Kind Sponsors" under "Trophies."

In-House Trophy Production

Many National pageant systems have an in-house trophy shop to produce trophies. Create and register your own trophy company name, and then contact a trophy manufacturer to purchase trophy parts direct. Reduce your trophy costs by screwing the nuts and bolts yourself.

Engraving Machine

It wasn't long ago that manual engraving machines (also known as pantograph machines) were the only type of engraving equipment available on the market. These were replaced with rotary engraving machines, so we no longer had to insert individual pieces of brass type into a slot and manually trace the characters to engrave an item. Now, we can type in a message or import graphics directly into the computer as the rotary engraving machine etches the plaque.

Next came laser engraving machines, which simplified the engraving process even further. Instead of using engraving cutters, the laser used a beam of light to mark materials.

If you are considering purchasing engraving equipment, it's good to know how these two marking methods compare. "Rotary vs. Laser: Which is Best?" explains both machines and the latest developments in each.

The *RayJet Laser Trophy and Awards Engraving* machine makes it so that you can engrave plaques from your office. Easy-to-use software allows you to engrave text, logos, and images. If you prefer a rotary engraving machine, *Gravograph* is one place to visit.

Creative Trophy Ideas

Tired of presenting standard trophies? *The Glass Slipper Natural Beauty Pageant* enlisted Jack Vrtar of *Custom Glass Etching* to custom etch all of the beautiful crystal Glass Slippers that are awarded at every TGS pageant. Enlist *Custom Glass Etching* to create a custom trophy for your pageant.

Little Miss & Teen Miss North Carolina presents 6' custom lighted trophies. For standard lighted trophies, they can be purchased from a number of locations. *TrophyKits.com* features lighted column trophies in 8", 9 ½", and 11". These trophies are available in quantity tier pricing. They include seven flashing patterns ("AA" batteries are included). Simply purchase the "Beauty Pageant" parts, and then assemble. Other light-up trophy companies include *Alabama Wholesale Crowns*, *Wholesale Crowns*, and *Award Creations*. Any of these trophy companies will accept orders for custom trophies.

At one time, *Krystal Pageants* presented its winners with seven-foot musical trophies. In my research, I was not able to locate a trophy company that made musical trophies. It's likely that they can be custom made.

Online Trophy Companies

There are several online companies from which to order pageant trophies. *Crowns Awards* offers several beauty pageant trophies to choose from, including its Beauty Chaplet Trophy, Floating Medal trophy, Beauty Solstice Insert Trophy, and StarBell Beauty Trophy. Other trophy companies include *The Trophy Depot*, *Riherds*, and *QuickTrophy*. All offer a 24-hour turnaround. *Crown Awards*, *QuickTrophy*, and *The Trophy Depot* provide free ground shipping for orders over $100 within the continental U.S.; *Riherds* provides this for orders over $500.

Trophy Checklist

Always have a prepared Trophy Checklist for the title awards you need. A Trophy Checklist prevents forgetting to order trophies for any division.

Medals

Beauty medals are sometimes used at pageants and presented to Runners-Up, Semifinalists, Finalists, and/or Lineup and Optionals award winners. Each of the five *Little Miss and Mister Italianfest* finalists receives medals for their accomplishment(s).

Pre-Manufactured Medals

Visit *Crowns Awards* to view its line of beauty medals. The 2 ½" Galaxy Star Insert Medal (item number CM40BKCUSRG) features a multi-level design. This medal is available in gold, silver, and bronze. It includes your pageant logo, for FREE, on 50+ piece orders. There is a $35 one-time logo fee for orders of less than 50 pieces. Pre-manufactured medals feature a neck ribbon of your choice. Quantity-tiered pricing is available. For example, at 100 units the price per unit is $2.79; at 1,000 units, it's $1.59.

Also available is the Spin Wreath Beauty Medal (item number CM01SPRG). It features a rotating center design and is available in Gold, Silver, and bronze. It includes an activity insert and neck ribbon of your choice. Each unit sells for $3.29. If you purchase six units, your cost would be $2.79; 100 units costs $2.29. There are even greater discounts if you purchase in quantities of 500, 750, or 1,000. Imagine presenting a spinning beauty medal — each featuring your pageant logo on the front and website address on the back — to every official contestant in your pageant. An official contestant can hang it in his/her locker. This could present an opportunity for priceless advertising when his/her friends stop by and "give it a spin." Visualize every anointed "State Finalist" (official contestant) in your State pageant receiving such a memento indicating that s/he is a "State Finalist" — even if about 50% of them inevitably become drop-offs. Or, present such a medal to every fully-registered "State Finalist" — i.e., official contestant — the moment she pays her complete sponsorship fee. (Fewer drop-offs occur after the latter.) Now you'll likely have competitors working "on the double" to complete their payment because they want this brag medal *soon* to show their friends. Both medals come with same day shipping. Learn more about drop-offs by reading my book *Producing Beauty Pageants: Open Call*, Chapter 10, "Drop-Off."

Custom Made Medals

Imagine awarding custom designed medals with your logo etched or cast in *real* copper, bronze, or brass material. Columbia Trophy and Metal Products, makers of the NFL Championship Trophy, Golden Globes, and Country Music Awards, among others, will create a stamp or cast of your pageant logo and/or pageant design onto your pageant medal. *Columbia Trophy and Metal Products* provides quantity-tiered pricing — perfect for a National pageant system. Such a quality pageant medal at the end of a lovely ribbon likely means that it will remain on a winner's vanity mirror for years to come. Additionally, *Columbia Trophy and Metal Products* also provides top quality, American Made trophies.

Robes

Not only will you find pageant sashes at _SasheDesigns.com_, but you will also find a selection of pageant robes. With pageant robes, it is not necessary to purchase them often since you may loan them to your titleholders. _Regal Majesty Pageants_ does just this. Winners are presented with either robes or a caplet, and it is their responsibility to return these items at the end of their reign.

In the event that titleholders are not able to attend most of the major events, the robe must be returned immediately upon request. If a robe is damaged, titleholders will be required to pay [a] $100 replacement fee; if the caplet is damaged there is a $50 charge.

Princess of North Carolina offers additional advice:

> These capes will be dry cleaned before returning (DO NOT WASH). Return capes on hangers with name and $20 [for dry cleaning] attached in an envelope. If cape is lost or stolen it must be replaced and/or repaired at the expense of the parent or guardian(s).

Scepter

Held in a Queen's hand, a scepter is a symbolic ornamental staff showing a sense of divinity. A pageant event is the perfect ceremonial occasion for your Queen(s) to carry a scepter, such as the 20" long by 3" in diameter _Red and Silver Round Velvet Scepter_ featured on the cover of the _Producing Beauty Pageant_ series. It retails for $29.99 at _Shindigz_, and is available in blue, black, and red. The other colors you see on the various _Producing Beauty Pageant_ series are modifications done by Courtney of _Photo Retouching by Courtney_. Be sure to visit _Shindigz_ here to view their reasonably-priced selection of scepters that are ready to be shipped out in time for your pageant event. If you prefer to purchase the _Red and Silver Round Velvet Scepter_ on _Amazon_, click here. Although the scepter was "expected" to arrive the day after the cover photo shoot, it arrived two days _before_. Either way, expect excellent customer service and a timely-shipped product. _Anderson's_ also has a reasonably-priced selection of scepters.

First Aid Kit and Other Emergency Tips

The _Cinderella Scholarship Pageant_ reminds its Local and State directors to:

- keep a well-supplied First Aid Kit.

- keep a list of emergency telephone numbers (fire department, police department, ambulance, nearest hospital, etc.) posted in several accessible locations throughout the staging facility.

- know the location(s) of the firefighting equipment and the fire alarm box in the pageant facility (and how to use the equipment).

CSP also notes that a registered nurse can usually be acquired to be on duty (in uniform) throughout the pageant in the event his/her services are needed.

Panic Table

Porcelain Dolls Nationals provides a _free_ Panic Table in the ballroom for candidates' last-minute needs. The Panic Table was created by director Kathy Raese's then-teen daughter, Isabel, in an attempt to help alleviate candidates' (and their mothers) panic attacks prior to competition. Items on the Panic Table are free to official contestants and mothers and include such products as _Band-Aids_, double sticky tape, hair spray, hair brushes and combs, sewing kits, instant tanners, body lotions, fake nails, nail polish (clear and French), glue for nails, stones, fabric, teeth whiteners, fake eyelashes and glue, assortment of different kinds of makeup (such as mascaras, blushes, lip glosses, eye shadows, liners), mirrors, toothpicks, wispy tooth brushes, makeup wipes, curling irons, flat irons, bobby pins (all colors), safety pins, ponytail holders, baby diapers, water spray bottles, emery boards, _Visine_, scissors, rubber bands, cotton balls, _Q-tips_, lint remover, nail clippers, and last, but not least, hand sanitizers. Of course, the list continues to grow as Isabel sees what other items are needed. Kathy Raese noted,

If someone mans the Panic Table, we will have a steamer for those last minute wrinkles!

Even if you cannot budget such items for free on your panic table, offering these items for sale affords convenience to official contestants and their families.

Contestant Numbers

You will need to number official contestants for their order of placement. While I find it easiest when candidates appear in alphabetical order by last names, as does _Miss Alabama Palm State Scholarship Pageant_, other pageant systems have them draw for numbers. Still, others assign numbers based on deposits received, using the postmarked dates on the envelopes as a reminder. National pageants often line up candidates alphabetically by state, and the same applies for official contestants representing their cities at a State pageant. For a change, reverse alphabetical lineups.

Rosette Numbers

A professional touch can be achieved by using rosette numbers — a number centered on a rose-shaped arrangement of ribbon. Companies that sell pageant rosette numbers include _Shop for Awards_ and _Banners Plus, LLC_. When ordering your numbers, remember to order several blank rosettes. In the pageant rush, official contestants may misplace their number and need a replacement. Just have heavy duty markers ready. At the _Macon County Fair Pageant_, candidates (except Princesses) are each given a rosette identifying their pageant number. Pageant officials state, in writing, that the rosettes are NOT a keepsake. They are to be returned after the pageant, or there will be a $7 replacement fee.

Button Numbers

Candidate button numbers come in a variety of styles. _Shop for Awards_ sells ribbon numbers. _Six Cents Press_ sells customized, made-to-order pin-back buttons from your artwork. Choose from a dozen popular round and shaped button sizes with a metal pin-back, or you can purchase a DIY Button Making Kit. _Miss West Deptford Township_ keeps cost down by asking that custom button numbers be returned after the pageant. Candidates that do not return them are charged a $2 replacement fee.

Badge Numbers

National American Miss provides official contestants with numbers on card stock and inserts them into a plastic sleeve holder that is attached with a safety pin-like backing. These vertical nametag holders can double as number holders, as they do for NAM. They can be purchased at any office supply store. *Office Depot* sells the Pin Style Name Badge Kits, Business Card Size 12 ¼" x 3 ½", Box of 100 (Item #303529), for $19.99 (includes white inserts). *Staples* sells the Avery Top Loading Pin Style Name Badges, 1 ¼" x 3 ½", item number 538165, for the same price. The kit includes clear plastic badge holders and badge inserts. (It didn't specify how many were in the box.). *C-Line Products, Inc.* sells the Pin Style Name Badges Kit with inserts, 3" x 2", 100/Box, for $29.15. Inserts are Laser/Ink Jet friendly.

Laminated Numbers

If it is not in your budget to purchase rosettes, design your own set of numbers (using stencils and a black permanent magic marker). Once you create a set of numbers, make copies and keep the master for future use. Former Texas pageant director Karen Kemple made contestant numbers for pageant candidates by cutting thin, white cardboard in the shape of the Texas state. Then, she tacked on adhesive numbers, followed by lamination. Safety-like pins were glued to the back (purchased from a craft store). Lamination machines can be found in office supply stores and educational product stores. *KD Creations* features a variety of reusable laminated contestant numbers that come with a closeable safety pin attached to the back. Laminated contestant numbers can be customized to match the theme of your pageant.

Number Placement

Specify, in writing, where official contestant numbers are to be worn (left or right hip). Judges are accustomed to being instructed as to where the number is placed, so if a candidate is wearing her number on her left hip while others are wearing it on the right, judges might not see the "leftie" during lineup.

Miss England official contestants wear their numbers on their left wrists — a red circle with white numbers — in a bracelet-like fashion. The red circles, about an inch bigger than candidates' wrists, are placed there so as to not take away from the beauty of their competition outfits. These "rosette-like circles" are attached to an elastic band and worn as a stretch bracelet.

Face of Europe official contestants wear rosettes on their left arm — a black number on a white button, trimmed in ribbon and secured with Velcro. The ribbon color that encircles the rosette depends on the age division within the pageant; for example, the Junior division wears red rosettes; the Teen division wears white rosettes; and the Senior division wears blue rosettes. To be more precise, Teen and Senior division candidates wear their rosette numbers on their left wrist, and Junior division candidates wear them above the left elbow.

Iris Festival Beauty Pageant requires that parents who accompany their younger children on stage wear the numbers themselves (and _not_ the official contestants).

Titles as Numbers

Promoters of the inaugural _Kentucky Fried Chicken_ (KFC) pageant numbered the _2012 Miss KFC Pageant_ candidates in a clever way. Instead of receiving numbers, candidates were "numbered" _Miss Zinger_, _Miss Hot and Spicy_, _Miss Hot Wings_, _Miss Biscuit_, etc. They were judged in five areas: Interview, Introductory Speech, Best Sports Wear, Best Talent, and Best Evening Wear. The candidate who scored the highest in three of the five areas — who appeared as _Miss Original_ — was crowned _Miss KFC 2012_.

Numbered Lineup Chairs

To avoid congestion and confusion in the backstage area, _Cinderella Scholarship Pageant_ provides lineup chairs for official contestants, each numbered (on the back) with the candidate's corresponding number. Numbered chairs make it easy for pageant staff to spot a missing participant and know exactly who is missing! It also provides candidates with an opportunity to rest.

Score Sheets

Arrange your score sheets approximately two weeks before your pageant. On the score sheets, include candidates' names, lineup numbers, a space for every competition score, an area for judges' critiques, and a line for each judges' signature. You will also need a set of Semifinals, Finals, and Placement Ballots. For additional information, see Chapter 16, "Scoring Procedure" under "Score Sheets."

Bio/Emcee Cards

There isn't anything much more frightening than for a candidate to walk on stage and have nothing be said about her because her bio card could not be found. It is the stage manager's responsibility to review all of the bio cards, with the emcee, in order to see that every official contestant's card is included.

Supply your emcee with bio/emcee cards for every candidate, Official Sponsor, judges' introductions, etc. Printed on index cards, various announcements and candidate introductions can be communicated to the audience. Keep the cards from getting out of order by hole-punching the corners and inserting a ring. Combine bio/emcee cards from each age division onto one ring. If the emcee drops the cards, s/he can quickly find the next candidate because the cards continue to remain in numbered order. Moreover, color-code cards for every age division. You will need a set of bio/emcee cards for every area of stage competition.

Beehive Beauties has a unique way of describing official contestants on stage. When prospective contestants sign up for the pageant, they receive a questionnaire, and when they become official contestants, some of their answers are displayed on a Jumbo Screen for the audience to view as each contestant appears on stage. The emcee only needs to look up and read key points, and there's no chance that s/he will drop any bio cards! Still, have some hole-punched bio cards (that are secured by a ring) as a backup.

Miss Black Texas USA reminds candidates to, "[write] all answers in third person." The _Junior Miss Pageant_ reminds candidates that their bio information will be read to the crowd. Therefore, if they don't want something read to the crowd, candidates shouldn't include it on their entry form:

For example, if you want the emcee to introduce "Melissa Muirheid," [don't] write down that her name is "Melissa Renee Muirheid" because that is what [the emcee] will read!

Master/Mistress of Ceremonies (Emcee) Information Guide

A script must be developed for your emcee to follow. Make this information available at least two weeks before the pageant so the emcee can review it. Also, provide a list of your official contestants so that the emcee can practice pronouncing difficult names. Have candidates provide phonetic spelling of their names (for example, Mel · uh · knee for Melanie). Scripts play a role in helping pageants to run smoothly, and a pageant that runs smoothly is likely to attract additional and returning competitors. Make sure that your script is well written and uses proper spelling and grammar. Hire a professional editor, such as Courtney, from *Photo Retouching by Courtney*, a graphic designer who also holds an English degree. She is the editor of my *Producing Beauty Pageants* series and offers editing for your Emcee Information guide. Additional information regarding Master or Mistress of Ceremonies scripts can be found in my book *Producing Beauty Pageants: Creating a Synergized National Pageant System*, Chapter 12, "Pageant Paperwork and Forms" under "Master/Mistress of Ceremony Script." A Local pageant script can be found at the *Miss Kentucky Scholarship Pageant* website under the "Miss Division." The Local Single Night Show Script for a Preliminary *Miss America* competition is also worth looking at.

Pageant Itinerary/Schedule

You will need a Pageant Itinerary (schedule) for your pageant event. If you have more than one age division, you will need a separate schedule for each division. It would be best to print each division's Pageant Itinerary in a different color. The *Miss Rodeo Wyoming Pageant 2013 Itinerary* can provide helpful guidance.

National American Miss' National Schedule of Activities for the *National American Miss* competitors and *National All-American Miss* competitors includes a color key code.

Additionally, at the National pageant, in 2012, not only did NAM have a table with every division's schedule placed in a page protector and taped to an 8' table, but the table was also manned by a NAM staffer telling official contestants the following:

> [new] this year is the ability for contestants to download all schedules (in PDF [Portable Document Format]) onto their *Smartphone* and to [go] onto the Internet or Safari.

All that a NAM official contestant needed to do was to key into her Smartphone this link: http://www.namiss.com/PR/, for example, to pull up the Princess schedule; /JP/, to pull up the Junior Preteen schedule; /JT/, to pull up the Junior Teen schedule; /TN/, to pull up the Teen schedule; and /MISS/, to pull up the Miss schedule. This information is, of course, for *National American Miss* official contestants. If girls were in the simultaneous parallel *National All-American Miss* pageant, they would need to add "AA" to the following PR, JP, JT, TN, or MISS. To view the All-American Princess schedule, for example, official contestants would need to key into their smartphones: http://www.namiss.com/PRAA/. This convenience will have NAM saving a tree by not needing to print 700 (and likely more) copies of the National Pageant Itinerary for both its 2012 National pageants (*National American Miss* and *National All-American Miss*), and at least as many official contestants at *each* of its approximately forty State pageants! Have a backup plan in place if your system goes down.

Why must official contestants fumble with keying a set of http address letters into their smartphone when they can use a QR code scanner that's available for free on the app store? It can be downloaded, at any time, to snap a picture of a QR code, and the QR code's image will then link them to NAM's various itinerary schedules. Learn how QR codes can benefit a pageant system by reading Chapter 8, "The Internet," under "QR Codes." Courtney, from *Photo Retouching by Courtney*, is a graphic designer and editor, and can integrate QR codes into any of your pageant marketing materials.

Judges Information

Approximately two weeks before your pageant date, send your judges an informative newsletter packet. This should include the mechanics of judging, a time schedule, judges' dress code for the interviews and pageant evening, and a judges' scoring guide. If you use a Judges' Affidavit, include one here. A sample Judges' Affidavit can be found at the *Miss Kentucky Scholarship* pageant website under "Judges Forms." A comprehensive explanation of a judging panelist's responsibilities can be found in this book, Chapter 14, "Judging." Pageant forms, including a Judge's Affidavit, can be found in my book *Producing Beauty Pageants: Creating a Synergized National Pageant System*, Chapter 12, "Pageant Paperwork and Forms." It is important to have judges sign a Judges' Affidavit. It will make him/her think twice about abandoning judging responsibilities at any point during a pageant competition.

Pageant Party

Schedule an official contestants' pageant party. Pageant parties provide a perfect opportunity for candidates to make friends with other candidates. Colorado's *Our Little Miss* hosts a Cupcake Party immediately following the pageant. *America's Theme Pageants* features multiple parties, for all ages, after competition. They include Family Jackpot Bingo, Fun Time Dance Party with *The Party Maniac*, and a Slumber Party Movie Time — all with free babysitting available.

What's a pageant party without games? Official contestants love a prize wheel. Prize wheels can be purchased at a number of places, including *Prize Wheel Advantage*, *The Store Gameops*, and *Displays2Go*. Pageant candidates love fun, so having a *Plinko Board* (sold at *Displays2Go*) adds excitement to a pageant party. *Lil Miss Lux Pageant* featured huge blowup dice. Every official contestant was able to roll the dice at the after pageant party. Candidates could roll one to six, and there were six different prize selections to choose from.

During the *Miss Teenage America* pageant, in 1972, pageant officials showed a movie about *Dr. Pepper* during pageant week. After the film ended, candidates were asked how many bottles of *Dr. Pepper* had appeared in the film. The candidate citing the correct answer (989 bottles) won a TV!

To keep younger divisions occupied, place jelly beans in a jar and ask candidates to guess the number of beans. The candidate closest to the actual count wins. Then, all the contenders can eat the jelly beans at the pageant party.

Official Queens' Photos

At the conclusion of your pageant, have your pageant photographer take multiple pictures of your Queens and Runners-Up in their crowns and sashes. Take these pictures *before* you release the winners to family and friends and before they receive flowers and gifts.

If you need to book a photographer, visit _togally_. At *togally* you can search ratings, reviews, and portfolios before hiring a photographer — nationwide.

If you're looking for a photographer that has experience on both sides of the camera, Robert Goold, of _Robert Goold Photography_ has *also* been a professional model for over twenty years. Some of his own modeling photos can be found _here_. _Men's Health_ magazine couldn't have picked a more fit and attractive model to put on its June 2000 cover than Robert! You can find Robert's photography work on the cover of my *Producing Beauty Pageants* series.

Backup Queens' Photos

Miss American Coed temporarily takes the crown (and sash) off of each newly-minted Queen (in their respective age divisions), and places it on the heads of the First Runners Up in each respective age division. This allows First Runners Up a "prepared backup opportunity" to have their "Official Queen Photo" taken. In the event any reigning Queen(s) are unable to fulfill their royalty duties, MAC is prepared with backup photos of the First Runners Up as replacements for its pageant marketing materials. Now, all division MAC Queens *know* that if they don't complete their reign as promised, the First Runner Ups are positioned as immediate replacements.

Look After Official Contestants

Never lose sight of what your pageant is about: the official contestants. _Pageants UK_ editor Lucie Hide notes,

> Think of how you would like to be treated, and then focus your efforts on looking after your contestants,

guests, and sponsors — ahead of looking after yourself if you want to survive in this business. Keep everyone well informed of times, dates, rules, and any changes whatsoever. Good communication is essential.

Angels of Light Beauty Pageants crowns every angel in the pageant. The question pageant officials ask is, "Which title will your angel win?" Examples of the titles include: Angel of Speech, Angel of Summertime Dress, Angel of Dressy Dress, Angel of Casual Dress, Angel of Scholarship, Angel of Talent, Angel of Volunteering, Angel of Accessories, etc. The pageant even includes a Special Needs division; however, it is referred to as "Rare Angels." Pageant rules state,

> All contestants are given ground rules prior to the pageant. They are instructed to have respect for EVERY contestant. Staring, pointing, laughing, teasing, etc., will result in disqualification or in forfeit of titles.

British Columbia director Liz McKinnon makes sure that every official contestant leaves the pageant with amazing prizes and wearing a crown.

America's Natural Supreme Beauties pageant officials present every candidate with a rhinestone crown pin (and other gifts) at Check-In.

Chapter 8

The Internet

The Internet is a tool that can help leverage your pageant business. If you are a newbie on the Internet, take a basic computer class at your community college. You can also visit *Internet Basics*. This lineup of *free* tutorials includes *Internet 101, Chrome, Internet Safety, Facebook 101, Mozilla Firefox, Blog Basics,* and *Social Media.* You can also hire a high school or college "computer geek" to help you as needed.

Your Own Website

There are many tutorials on how to create your own website. Your first tutorial could begin with learning how to set up and register your domain and name. Next, choose a Web Host, and sign up for an account. You can then begin designing your website pages. When those three points come together, you'll be ready to test your website.

First, make sure you are set up to collect credit card information so that you can begin accepting payments. Once your website works, get it noticed by using Google's *Link Submission Page.* Christopher Heng of *thesitewizard.com* has a free tutorial on how you can create your own website. His tutorial is intended for the beginner, and it takes you step-by-step through the entire process. As the steps become more involved, his guide will provide links to relevant articles that will help you to gain a better understanding of how a website works.

Free Website

Many pageant directors start their pageant business with a temporary website, often designing it themselves. Later, when their business grows, they often hire a professional website designer to design a new, more efficient website.

You can create a free website at a number of sites. *Little Miss Georgia-World* and *South Texas Pageants* created their free websites at _Webs_. *Mississippi Sweet Pea Pageants* created its free website on _Yola._ Arizona's _Our Little Miss_ built its free website on _Wix.com_. _America's Talented Beauties & Cuties_ created its free website at _Angelfire_. _Forever Beautiful Pageants_ and _Texas Rhinestone Beauties Glitz Pageants_ created their free websites at _Weebly_. *Yellow Rose Pageantry* used the free website templates available at _intuit_ to create its website.

Learn how to barter for a FREE website by reading my book *Producing Beauty Pageants: Brokering a Pageant through Barter*, Chapter 9, "In-Kind Sponsors" under "Website Sponsor" subheadings: "The Pageant Barter," "The Traditional Barter," and "The Independent Barter."

Hire a Professional to Create Your Website

If creating your own website isn't for you, enlisting a professional to get a website up and running is the best way to start a pageant business. If you do hire a developer to create your website, make sure that *you* own your domain name. Often, website designers purchase the domain names *in their own names*. This means that they can restrict your access to your own website.

Begin your professional website designer search by visiting other pageants' websites. On the websites you like, scroll down to the very bottom to see if the website designers are posted. _Miss Texas USA_ pageant's website was designed by BarronSmiaath90@gmail.com. _Miss California USA_ enlisted _Digital 7 Media_ to *redesign* its website. _Miss Arkansas USA's_ website was designed by _Vanbros and Associates_. _Miss USA's_ website was designed by _ILS_. Although *Miss Texas USA, Miss California USA*, and *Miss Arkansas USA* pageants are preliminaries to _Miss USA_, each enlisted different Web designers. _International Junior Miss'_ website was designed by _123Triad_, and _Silver Scope Web Design_ designed _Royal International Miss'_ website.

Silver Scope Web Design's skilled team of developers recommends that both State and Regional beauty pageants have a well-designed website — one they can help pageant directors to create. A quality website can draw attention to your pageant, and quite possibly, attract prospective contestants and turn them into official contestants. An impressive website will likely also attract Official Sponsors. When you visit *Silver Scope's* website, you will see that it incorporates several strategies to help target groups to your pageant website, including 1) displaying Official Sponsors along with special offers they provide and 2) optimizing your website to rank well under selected key phrases in popular search engines. Included in your pageant website development by *Silver Scope Web Design* is the ability to accept online registration for new candidates. Visit *Royal International Miss* to see one of several pageant that websites *Silver Scope Web Design* developed.

Search Engine Optimization

Establishing a good online reputation is a start towards achieving a number one ranking position for your pageant system. Big brands generally have good reputations and rank at or near the top of any search results list that is returned by a search engine. Since Google is the dominant search engine, Search Engine Optimization (SEO) techniques usually focus on increasing rankings in Google.

You can manipulate your rankings to get your business rank near the top by using various methods that are legal and not get penalized by Google. A top ranking in a Google search result attracts the lion share of visitor clicks. For example, the number 1 position gets a lot more clicks than the number 2 position which gets vastly more clicks than the other 8 listings in the Search Engine Result Page (SERP).[13]

The obvious ways to get to the number one position include things like the following:

- building a search engine friendly website

- including organic/free/natural listings such as news, video, maps, places, blogs, images, social updates, and last, but not least, shopping on your website

---

[13] Anderson, Shaur. "How to Get to Number 1 On Google Without Breaking the Rules." Hobo Internet Marketing, 7 Apr. 2016. http://www.hobo-web.co.uk/how-to-get-to-number-1-on-google/.

- including keywords and key phrases within your site, but be CERTAIN to match your list of selected keywords and key phrases to the content within your website!

If you need an SEO expert in the field of pageantry, look no further than *PageantReady's* website developer and SEO expert Charlie Hoff. Learn more by visiting *PageantReady's Facebook page*, or call 877-2-PAGEANT (877-272-4326). You can also hire *hobo Internet Marketing* to help drive more business to your website. The awesome team at *hobo Internet Marketing* will check your website against best practices recommended by Google, identify reasons for a traffic loss, and deliver the insight needed to repair previous rankings damage and get you more free traffic from Google searches in the future. To get started, you can begin by using the Best SEO Tools for 2016.

Website Cost

Silver Scope Web Design hears this question all of the time. Websites are much like houses in the way that different houses have different prices. Depending on what you want in or on your website, and how fancy you want it, the prices will vary. The *Silver Scope Web Design* team will work with you to design a website that fits your needs and your budget. Quotes are always free, and there is no obligation. Visit *Silver Scope Web Design's* bid page.

Own Your Material

If you hire a consultant or contractor to do work for you, as a general rule, anything s/he invents or creates will belong to him/her, unless you have made a contractual agreement in advance. If you get someone to write a piece of software, for example, even though it was for your company, the contractor may own the software and be able to do with it what s/he wants — even give it to your competitor! The same goes for design. You may have to pay more to get the rights assigned to you, but depending on what you're having done, it may well be worth it.

Having a work-for-hire provision in your agreement may not be enough to cover this. Your agreement should include a fallback clause that states that, in the event any copyrightable material does not qualify as a "work made for hire," the material is assigned to you. The agreement should further explicitly assign other types of intellectual property to you, such as trade secrets.

Updating Your Website

Universal Royalty Beauty Pageant director Annette Hill, in 2012, completely revamped her website. Annette went from an ample, informative website, to a bare, uninformative one. In 2015, Annette revamped her website yet again, this time to a more appealing one.

Miss American Coed went from a bare and uninformative website to an organized and informative one. A prospective contestant can find out what it would cost to participate in a MAC State _and_ National pageant _before_ she even fills out and signs a legally-binding Official Application. It's no wonder that, since 1984, the year after its inaugural pageant, MAC continues to display an A+ with the _Better Business Bureau._

Miss Teenage Canada — formerly _Miss Teen Canada-World_ — recreated its pageant website to include a long-running, informative blog. Key information on how to apply for _Miss Teenage Canada_ is linked at the top of the website, and when business is done — or even before it starts — people who want to stay and visit the blog are welcome to do so...and stay for as long as they want. The only thing missing at the _Miss Teenage Canada_ website, as of this writing, is an online store!

Pageant producers often feature a bare website, thinking that there will be less upkeep required for the website. There is no need to have price changes, for example, because there isn't a financial disclosure page to update. Have a new rule to include? No need to change it here because Rules & Regulations aren't posted on a bare website! Those directors think that they will save money by going bare, when, in fact, they _lose_ sales. Most prospective contestants "will NOT buy a dress" without a price tag on it AND without understanding the store's Refund Policy!

Moreover, pageant producers who feature an uninformative website are counting on prospective contestants to contact them with any and all questions. On the other hand, if their website is ample, they likely think that prospective contestants won't contact them. (Usually, the opposite holds true for both.)

This generation is getting smart about such tactics. Many would-be prospective contestants likely won't contact the pageant, but, instead, query their questions at various social media places.

Those replies are not controlled by pageant officials and often dampen any future enthusiasm there may have been to participate in the pageant.

So, how many total entries did Annette have in her National *Universal Beauty Royalty* (combined divisions) pageant, in 2012, after she revamped her website? *Less than 100 in all age divisions combined!* Annette was even pushing last minute entries "at the door!"

Whether you are revamping your website, or using your existing one, there are several tips that can help you to keep it razor-sharp:

- Periodically check your website to see that all sections work as you had intended. Just because it worked last month doesn't mean it still works the same. Glitches happen.

- If you put links on your website, check to make sure linked sites still exist.

- If you include your home address on your website and you live in an apartment or condominium, rather than state your address as 1234 Grove Street, Apt. # B, state it as 1234 Grove Street, Suite B. It will give the appearance that you work out of an office building rather than an apartment.

- When you have blank pages on your site — if your Official Application or newsletter includes a blank page between sections — make sure you include on those blank pages "Page Intentionally Left Blank." Otherwise, people who are in a hurry will think that the previous page was the last one, and they will not bother to scroll down to see if additional information follows.

- Periods are not necessary when bulleting incomplete sentences. When you do have periods at the end of bullets, make sure that each bulleted point is a complete sentence and that *each one* ends with a period (and not just some). Consistency is important.

- Include plenty of space between information. Words are highlighted by space — vital to your message being seen. Therefore, overcrowding a page with information tends to overwhelm readers.

Princess of North Carolina includes a Countdown Clock at the bottom of its home page. When I wrote this, the 2012 clock read "82 days, 1 hours, 39 minutes, and 11 seconds left until State." When I performed a second editing on this book, the clock read "69 days, 15 hours, 26 minutes, and 11 seconds left until State." Moreover, when you click on any of the homepage buttons, e.g., "About Us," "Information," or "FAQs," the clock continues to appear on the bottom of each page. On a third editing, the clock read "295 days, 23 hours, 1 minute, 55 seconds." This, of course, was for the 2013 pageant, because, as of this writing, the 2012 pageant took place 296 days ago!

Parents and official contestants find it helpful when pageant officials include a "Map and Directions" page on their website, as does *Diamonds & Dolphins Pageant*. Moreover, DDP included the Room Block ID number of the host hotel. If you do this, be careful that only official contestants and their families have access to this privy information. Otherwise, anyone viewing your website can become "we're with the pageant" people and use up all the limited blocked, discounted rooms.

If you include a FAQ on your website, ask the question and then state the answer. Don't begin your answer with "Answer." Reading "Answer" after every question is redundant and annoying. Likewise, don't type the word "Question" before every question and then state the answer. At the top of your FAQ, include the sub-heading "Questions & Answers," having the word "Questions" in red and "Answers" in blue as your key. Then, type all the FAQ questions in the color red and responding answers in the color blue.

Last, but not least, make sure your content is designed so that your page can fit on various smaller screens, e.g., tablets, iPads, small laptops, and cell phones.

Licensing a Website Platform

When the *Miss Rhode Island* pageant needed to redesign their outdated website, they turned to *Digimix* for help. Not only did the *Digimix* website team design the best *Miss Rhode Island* website, they also built a website platform especially for beauty pageants. The *Miss Rhode Island* website features a titleholder's roster where a visitor can view all previous titleholders, by year, or explore each winners' profile. Official contestants can easily log in to the site to build their own profile, just like they would with *Facebook*. Candidates can also connect their profile to their *Twitter* account, and their latest tweets will automatically appear on their *Miss Rhode Island* profile pages. The *Miss Rhode Island* website also has an events calendar and management system, a press release system, and a customizable homepage. Any pageant system can contact *Digimix* to learn more about licensing the *Digimix Beauty Pageant* website platform. After all, *Digimix* owns the rights.

A Website in Motion

Imagine a pageant website having an introductory "cover page." This is how I would describe National scholarship pageant newcomer *Miss All-Star United States'* beckoning website. At one time, three pictorial frames bled to the edge of a computer screen — each initially three seconds long — which made up the introductory part of its website: two still images and one cinematic clip. In the first motionless frame, you saw two girls on bikes; in the last, a profile of a girl looking at her laptop as though she was applying at colleges — at the suggestion of its motto, "We Believe in Education." But it's the motioning frame (nestled between the two still frames) that seemed to encourage a prospective contestant to step right in and join the girl already "participating" in its scholarship program. That video clip was aptly branded: "Dream it, Believe it, & Achieve it — Our Queens are Innovative Community Leaders." It was a pioneering introduction to *Miss All-Star United States'* website and program.

News Rotator

While visiting *Miss All-Star United States'* website, scroll down each frame to view the information below. Once you scroll down, the frame locks in place. (If you want to visit the next frame, simply click on the center right side arrow.) Notice the rotating "news" panel towards the bottom of the page. A rotating scene like that is powered by a News Rotator like *Planavsky.com*. A News Rotator is a Javascript module that you can easily implement on your website. You can add any amount of news story "panels" to the module by using some simple Javascript declarations. It is also possible to change the look and feel of the model (such as height, width, and color) by editing the CSS that comes packaged in the small script noted below *Planavsky.com's* site. All instructions concerning what to edit, in order for the script to fit your website, can be found at *Planavasky.com*. Simply copy and paste the code into your site HTML. Then, follow the instructions in the code to configure the module to your liking and include your news panels. *National American Miss* also includes *Planavsky.com* on its website's homepage — both at its beckoning header and at its "In [the] News" sections.

Be creative with your slideshows, videos, and collages. You can do just that by using *kizoa*, a free video maker, slideshow creator, and collage builder. *All World Beauties Pageants* employs *kizoa* to present its slideshow presentation.

Sister Pageant Website

If you have more than one pageant in your system, include a separate "Sister Pageant" link on *each* pageant website, as does *America's Grand Miss*. When you arrive at *America's Grand Miss'* website, scroll down to the bottom, and click on "Visit our Sister Pageant." When you arrive at its sister pageant, *Tropical Dream Stars USA*, you will see a "Sister Pageant" link on the top left side of the site. When you click on it, you will be taken to *America's Grand Miss*. Including a "Sister Pageant" link on each individual pageant website can prevent all of your pageants' information from being crowded onto one website.

In yet another example of a different pageant system, when you visit *USA's Pageants*, scroll to the bottom of the home page, and click on its sister pageant, *MGN Scholarship Pageant*. As expected, when you arrive at the *MGN Scholarship Pageant*, a link on the bottom right corner will take you *USA's Pageants*.

Contestant Area

Create a Contestant Area on your website, as did *Miss Teen America*. Once official contestants are completely registered for the pageant, they will be given a user name and password. Only then will they be able to access the Contestant Area. It will be up to the pageant director to determine when the prospective contestant becomes an official contestant. (Will it be when she makes an initial deposit, pays the first sponsorship installment, or pays the entire sponsorship fee?) Then, the official contestant can access the Contestant Area.

Your pageant registration can run more efficiently by including a Shopping Cart in the Contestant Area of your website, as does *Emerald Pageant Productions.* At the "Shop," official contestants can pay, in advance, for various mandatory entry fees, Optionals fees, a modeling clinic, an "I'm Proud of You" Pageant Page (defined in my book *Producing Beauty Pageants: Contestant Handbook*), Pizza Party tickets, and pageant event tickets, just to name a few.

The Contestant Area can house pageant literature far beyond the initial pageant forms and pageant marketing materials official contestants initially receive. This literature should NOT include *additional* financial disclosures and pageant information that should have been received when competitors were prospective contestants. *That* would be unethical. All of this information should be provided to competitors upfront — prior to signing the Official Application that becomes a legally-binding contract when they pay the first sponsorship fee installment and become official contestants.

An ideal place to include pre-made Pageant Workshop tutorial video clips would be at the Contestant Section of your website. A pageant director might feature a video on proper pageant makeup application, how to negotiate steps on a pageant stage, how to perform pivot turns, how to grip and use a standing or hand-held microphone, how to answer on-stage questions, how to prepare for judges' interview, how to enter a room, how to make eye contact how to sit, what not to do with your hands while sitting, how to get up from a chair, etc. Imagine having snippet video clips that do all of the work for you. The candidate wouldn't need to leave her home to attend a Pageant Workshop, well, except for the *free* one that you promote as an entry deadline, as does _National American Miss_ right after its Open Call. Moreover, many candidates will still choose to attend the (pageant weekend) $25 Pageant Workshop and put the tutorial video clips knowledge "into full action." Learn more about pageant workshops by reading my book *Producing Beauty Pageants: Creating a Synergized National Pageant System*, Chapter 10, "Pageant Workshops."

Pre-Application

When a prospective contestant finds a pre-application on your website, her immediate excitement could motivate her to instantly complete and submit it. A pre-application includes basic information, such as the prospective contestant's first and last name, date of birth, home address, home phone, cell number, email address, and if your pageant is for girls seventeen and under, her parents' or guardian names, and a signature line. If your non-scholarship pageant has an academic slant, as does *Miss American Coed*, you would ask what school grade or year of college and GPA (grade point average). What is smart about MAC's pre-application is that prospective contestants are able to type in the requested information as soon as the application appears on the screen. Although less committing, a MAC Pageant mailing list offer is also ideal because prospective contestants are likely to submit it due to their excitement and interest. No application fee is charged for the pre-application or mailing list offer, so the applicant will likely submit both. From these sieves, MAC builds the *best* type of pageant mailing list.

Establish a Quality Pageant System with Your Website

Using *Miss American Coed*'s business model as an example of a quality pageant system, if a prospective contestant doesn't want to fill out an online pre-application or the Official Application (contract), she isn't rushed to do so. Instead, if she wants to further investigate the pageant system, she can do so; and, she will learn it ALL at MAC's website. She doesn't even need to be an official contestant to do this.

Any prospective contestant can be privy to complete financial disclosures at MAC's website. A prospective contestant can first read about MAC's Official Application and Rules & Regulations for its State pageant; Official Application and Rules & Regulations for its National pageant; State pageant Newsletter #1 and Newsletter #2; National Pageant Application; National Appointed Application; National Newsletter #1; National Victory Newsletter #1 (from MAC's Victory parallel pageant); National Advertising Information; National Sponsorship Information; and its National Hotel Reservation Form that lets her know that she will not only be responsible for making her hotel reservation at the _Hilton at Walt Disney World Resort_, but she will _also_ be responsible for that expense...*before* committing to a MAC State or National pageant. All that a MAC prospective contestant needs to do is click on the "Newsletters & Downloads" link, on the left side of MAC's homepage, to start the information process.

Moreover, the prospective contestant can visit MAC's store by clicking on the "Pay Fees" link. A *fully-detailed* alphabetical list of pageant costs that could be associated with her pageant age division can be viewed when she clicks on "Index." Now the prospective contestant is NOT financially clueless when she fills out the Official Application (contract) to participate in a MAC State (or National) pageant and commits to it when she (or her parent/legal guardian) sign the contract, and thereby, set into place the Refund Policy and other legally-binding clauses. (That contract won't be activated until she pays her first sponsorship installment.) The prospective contestant can question any fee to see how it could relate to her *before* she (or her parent/legal guardian) signs the legally-binding Official Application (contract). This prospective contestant is completely aware of MAC's full financial disclosures *from the State pageant to the National pageant* — BEFORE she participates in a MAC State pageant. Parents WANT to know what the pageant will cost them in its entirety — BEFORE their daughters financially commit. MAC has been on solid foundation, since 1983, when its first National pageant was introduced.

Posting Event Results

Will you post results for the outcome of your pageant? Doing so would help parents determine if they want their daughters to participate in your pageant. Mrs. Sanchez, a concerned pageant parent, logged onto _National American Miss_' website under "Event Results." She found that, between 2007 and 2011,

> [a] number of names winning most of the competitions [were] (Taylor Longbrake, Bayli Ray, and Terra Gonzales Hammonds). Next we will go to 2008 and 2009 Jr. Pre-Teen and we see the same names. Now we will go to the 2010 and move up to

Pre-Teen and again the same girls winning. 2011 we graduate to Jr. Teen and the same here. [14]

NAM posting its "Event Results" helps parents like Ms. Sanchez in their research...if they know where to look. If they don't like what they see, as didn't Mrs. Sanchez (and her daughter), they can choose not to participate in the pageant. While I wouldn't recommend placing Event Results due to the first and last names typically being posted, NAM's Event Results page IS its most visited webpage. It would be difficult for NAM to let go of its #1 most popular webpage.

If your candidates are underage, it is best to not include their last name in your results posts. *Southern Grace Glitz* only posts first names and last initials in the Events Results. Protecting the privacy of your official and alumnae contestants is your number one priority.

Know Your Website Statistics

According to *SiteSentral.com,* and as of this writing (June, 2012), *National American Miss'* website ranked #406,038 *in the world* among over thirty million websites, based on the *Alexa Traffic Ranking*. Its estimated pageviews were 1,249 per day (37,461 pageviews per month). *Miss England's* website ranked #1,372,612; its estimated pageviews were 179 per day (5,381 pageviews per month). *American USA Beauty Pageant's* website ranked #1,460,279; its estimated pageviews were 169 per day (5,058 pages per month). *East Coast USA Pageant's* website ranked #4,619,806; its estimated pageviews were 53 per day (1,599 pageviews per month). *Miss All Canadian Pageants'* website ranked #6,985,675; its estimated pageviews were 35 per day (1,057 pageviews per month). *Miss American Coed's* website ranked #2,243,475; its estimated pageviews were 110 per day (3,292 pageviews per month). *Universal Royalty's* website ranked #3,589,968; its estimated pageviews were 69 per day (2,057 pageviews per month). *America's Grand Miss National's* website ranked #6,986,314; its estimated pageviews were 35 per day

---

[14] National American Miss—Scam? "Why Are Our Girls Expected to Compete with Professionals?" September 21, 2011, http://www.national-american-miss-scam.com/2011/09/by-sanchez-why-than-are-our-girls-expected-to-compete-with-professionals/.

(1,057 pageviews per month). _Miss Heart of the USA_'s website ranked #1,875,968; its estimated pageviews were 131 per day (3,937 pageviews per month). _Tropical Dream Stars'_ website ranked #9,309,674; its estimated pageviews were 26 per day (793 pageviews per month). _Royal International Miss'_ website ranked #3,802,547; its estimated pageviews were 65 per day (1,942 pageviews per month). Last, but not least, _Porcelain Dolls Nationals'_ website ranked #10,744,646. Its estimated pageviews were 23 per day (687 pageviews per month). None of these take into consideration the pageant system's _Facebook_ or other online accounts, which often outnumbers website visits.

As noted, these results are based on the _Alexa Traffic Ranking_. As _alexa.com_ noted,

> The traffic data are based on the set of toolbars that use _Alexa_ data, which may not be a representative sample of the global Internet population.

The importance of _Alexa Traffic Rank_ is relative, so it's probably best to not put too much reliance on this index. Still, many Internet users find that _Alexa_ is a very fair score. _Alexa_ not only uses traffic as an input for its traffic scores, but the bounce rate, pages visited, and the time each visitor spent at the pageant's website are also part of the calculation. Websites with more or less the same traffic, but lower bounce rates and higher visitor duration times and higher "pages visited" figures, scored much higher.

So, if you're wondering how it is that _National American Miss_ has over a thousand MORE pageviews _per day_ than any of the pageant systems featured here, wonder no longer. The answer to the SECRET of NAM's success can be found in my book _Producing Beauty Pageants: Open Call._

Increase Pageviews

To get lots of pageviews per day, get professional help from the start. Have your blog designed by a professional, and get someone to add in the proper SEO plugins since the old blogging tricks _still_ work best. Build a passionate community around your blog. Last, but not least, getting a RSS subscriber is getting somebody who is totally committed to receiving your content every single day. You will come to cherish RSS readers in a way that you would never think about _Twitter_ followers or _Facebook_ Likes. The social subscribers are doing it as an impulse, but a RSS reader is somebody who wants to instantly get your content *every single time you publish it*. Read 10 Simple Tips to Get 250,000 Page Views Per Month for additional excellent ideas (and to learn blogging tricks).

Note Precise Statistics

If you do offer businesses the opportunity to be featured on your website, as does *Little Miss Precious Pageant*, when you note that your site has "more than 30,000 viewers," is that per week, month, year, or since the website has been up? Remember to include the time period, such as 90,000 visitors *per year*, and give accurate sales information.

How to Extract Marketing Intelligence from Your Website

The most successful pageant producers gather competitive intelligence from their websites using very precise measurement tools that reveal such information as: who is accessing the website (IP address and the cookie ID, if used); where the website is being accessed from (IP address); how often the same user has accessed the website (if cookies are used); how long the user stayed on the website and what content they accessed while they were there; which other websites have linked to this website; what search queries are used to find this website; and where the website ranks within search engines. Many tools, such as *Google Analytics*, are free and can provide a wealth of information with minimal intrusion on how users interact with website content. Other techniques, such as requiring cookies or having users fill out forms on the site, can yield additional details. By gaining this intelligence, a pageant producer can determine: if his efforts are cost effective, if and which advertising venues are resulting in sales, and last, but not least, whether the website content is presented in a manner that effectively maximizes user experience and the promotion of the pageant.

WhoLinks2Me, a free Domain Analyzer, is an online service that allows you to find inbound links and keywords information about a website. You can learn how to install code to see who is linking to your website by following the four easy steps at the site.

If you've ever wondered who visits your pageant blog, *StatCounter* is a site you can use to see what your readers are interested in and what visitors most like about your blog. By placing *StatCounter's* invisible code on your blog, you'll get answers to questions like: How many people visited my blog today? Who links to my blog? Does my blog show up in search engines? What are my most popular blog posts? Do my readers click on the links that I recommend?

Tracerlock.com is an automated online service which scans thousands of articles published on news sites, online trade journals, and e-zines looking for new matches for your information requests. On the downside, by using this website, your competitors can monitor you, and you can monitor them.

PDF Forms Search Engine

PDFfiller.com search engine is a Web service built to help anyone find and fill out any form. If a pageant's forms are in a PDF (Portable Document Format), all forms that prospective contestants find are automatically made fillable through the magic of *PDF filler*. A prospective contestant who wants to fill in the forms on her computer screen can do so. She would simply upload your form at *PDFfiller*, click anywhere on it, and start typing. She can sign your form, and then, she can print, email, fax, or export the form right from her computer. Pageant directors can save a tree by requiring prospective and official contestants to find any of their pageant forms on the *PDFfiller* search engine. The *Miss & Teen Jacksonville USA* pageant master paperwork link at *PDFfiller* is an example. While at *PDFfiller*, type in *Star Bright Pageant*, and a few of its pageant forms appear. You can even find pageant forms for *Miss Black Deaf America*, *Cinderella International Scholarship Pageant*, *Our Little Miss*, and *Miss Bright Star of America*, to name a few. The *Universal Royalty Little Miss America High Glitz* form can even be found...*in Spanish!*

Survey/Suggestion Box

If you don't feature a Survey/Suggestion Box at (or following) your pageant, include an Online comments field on your website, as does *Georgia Benefit Pageant Systems*. As a new non-profit pageant organization, GBPS pageant officials strive to be the best. They also know that they will make mistakes, and things will not go as planned. They offer official contestants and parents an opportunity to make comments, opinions, suggestions, or requests, and to submit them in the website Comments/Suggestion Box. GBPS will not hold this against any candidates or parents. GBPS pageant officials have already made a lot of changes at one of their pageants and will continue to do so until most candidates are pleased. Being busy, pageant officials don't see or hear everything that goes on at their pageants. They ask candidates to be their eyes and ears, and they promise to do their very best to improve on every suggestion. Learn how to create a non-profit pageant system and maximize financial support by reading my book *Producing Beauty Pageants: Directing a Fundraiser Pageant*.

National American Miss invites official contestants to fill out the "National American Miss Pageant Survey" after every State and National pageant. Official contestants are to identify their age division by clicking on the appropriate circle. Next, they are asked to rate and comment on a variety of topics on a scale of 1–10, including: 1) how well NAM informed her on preparing for the pageant; 2) if the check-in process was smooth and organized; 3) if the NAM staff was friendly and helpful; 4) to rank the host hotel; 5) if the competition/rehearsals started and finished on time; 6) to rank their overall pageant experience with NAM; 7) to write a comment or testimonial (maximum 500 characters); 9) to note one thing that they will remember most about the pageant (maximum 500 characters); and 10) to write the official contestant's name and email address (optional). Imagine having many candidates and/or their parents writing glowing testimonials, and then including the best ones in your pageant magazine or Official Contestant Handbook! View NAM's pageant survey, or build your own survey form at *Wufoo*. Learn how to create a thorough Official Contestant Handbook by reading my book *Producing Beauty Pageants: Contestant Handbook*.

FlipSnack

Place your Official Contestant Handbook (or pageant magazine) on your website using _FlipSnack_. _FlipSnack_ is all that you need to publish an online Official Contestant Handbook (or pageant magazine). _FlipSnack_ will transform your PDFs into online flipbooks. It works and looks great across all digital platforms, making it easy to sell directly from the pages of your digital publication. Simply select one or more PDF or JPG files to start, and turn your PDFs into a beautiful flipping book.

Starting today, you can create every page of your flipbook right within _FlipSnack's_ content editor (starting from scratch), or you can edit your existing PDF by adding elements to it. You will be able to find options to create and delete pages, as well as add many elements, such as text, images, videos, links, audio, shopping buttons, social media buttons, and more. Live chat is available 24/7. The beauty of _FlipSnack_ is that the Basic editor is free for 15 pages per PDF; up to 3 flipbooks per collection; 10,000 daily opens; up to 7 days of statistics; and it is embedded with a watermark. Additionally, you won't need to register. Beyond the free Basic Editor package, various paid _FlipSnack_ packages can be found on its go premium page. Visit _Royal International Miss_ to view its National Contestant Handbook, created by using _FlipSnack_. RIM's Texas State Handbook and Eastern State Handbook are also _FlipSnack_ flipbooks, while Oklahoma State Handbook is not a flipbook at all. Notice the ease of using a flipbook as compared to scrolling down a document. Create an outstanding Official Contestant Handbook by reading my book _Producing Beauty Pageants: Contestant Handbook_.

Social Media Image

Social media are forms of electronic communication through which users create online communities to share information, ideas, personal messages, and even videos. It also serves as a platform to network, talk, and bookmark online. Social media has become the leading conduit because it's fun, and can be a platform for advertising, publicity, and/or promotion. Businesses of all types and sizes are experimenting with social media marketing. Examples of social media include _Twitter_, _Facebook_, and _Pinterest_.

Probably the most successful pageant system to carefully craft its social media image is _National American Miss_. It has become an expert at creating and sustaining a carefully crafted image on its favorite social media sites: _Facebook_ (a social site that connects people with friends), _Instagram_ (a site that allows you to share photos with family and friends), _Pinterest_ (an online pinboard), _Twitter_ (a place to connect with friends and share _your_ breaking news), and _YouTube_ (a video-sharing site).

At its National pageant, in 2012, NAM provided a free workshop, "Social Media & You," in which official contestants were given advice on how to create their own personal brand. A NAM staffer presented a slide show onto a screen from a laptop, in front of NAM National candidates, _while_ a video cameraman recorded the presentation. Former and alumnae NAM pageant girls were featured in the slide show, with the NAM logo next to (or on) them. They appeared on the screen (at various times) while the NAM staffer talked about the best types of pictures to use as a profile on candidates' social media sites.

The NAM staffer also explained how official contestants could create usernames that don't sound inappropriate. Candidates were informed that they have the power to create their own positive image. The NAM staffer also showed them how to produce and distribute that power because, as NAM State Finalists (official contestants), they are NOW in a role model position! These "NAM girls" are taught how to create their own personal brand — whether it is posting photos of them helping a cause, or their day-to-day activity photos — in which it is suggested that they wear their NAM sashes for such photo ops.

National American Miss knows that the youth are living life online. NAM has positioned itself to teach official contestants how to best use this tool to present a clean image for themselves, and ultimately, spotlight the NAM brand in a positive way when they post their pictures. NAM girls are even encouraged to change inappropriate usernames _and_, if necessary, to unfriend. This is great power of suggestion! The _free_ NAM Social Media Workshop teaches official contestants how to properly post their NAM pageant experience. Cultivating such clever marketing techniques makes NAM look GREAT on any social media site that NAM girls use to post.

National American Miss knows that social media gets its pageant message out in an extreme way. What better way to do this than by teaching official contestants the how-to's in a _free_ Social Media Workshop? And, if your Social Media Workshop is videotaped at your National pageant, the video can be edited and presented, in uniformity, at all State pageant workshops. Additionally, your "Social Media & You" video can be posted in a "Contestants Only" area.

The NAM staffer closed the free "Social Media & You" session by talking about the effect that _Toddlers & Tiaras_ — and particularly _Honey Boo Boo_ — has had on NAM's efforts to recruit official contestants. With (nearly) 700 girls competing at the 2012 National pageant alone (and not including about the same number of girls competing in _each_ of NAM's nearly 40 State pageants), it didn't seem like _Toddlers & Tiaras_ and _Honey Boo Boo_ combined had any negative effect on NAM's candidate recruiting efforts!

Social Media Class or Online Course

If you are new to social media, take an online Social Media class. Such courses are usually offered in a series. It often begins with the basics of launching and managing a social media platform, and it eventually covers more advanced skills like developing a long-term content strategy and using software to monitor multiple social platforms. Karen Clark, social media expert and author of _Social Media for Direct Selling Representatives: Ethical and Effective Online Marketing_, can teach you how to incorporate all forms of social media into your pageant system. Learn more about how Karen's social media business, _My Business Presence_, can help you to weave social media connections into the fabric of your pageant business. An example of Karen integrating social media with a pageant system, albeit via a _National American Miss_ candidate, can be found in my book _Producing Beauty Pageants: Creating a Synergized National Pageant System_, Chapter 1, "Becoming an Innovative Pageant Producer" under "Synergize via Official Contestants."

YouTube

The most popular social media gem is _YouTube_, and _National American Miss_ knows it. NAM utilizes _YouTube_ more successfully than any other pageant system. NAM links girls from all over the United States with videos of current (and past) Queens, as well as current (and past) official contestants. NAM encourages official contestants to upload their NAM experiences on _YouTube_. Guidance to do just that is also provided. Such promotional efforts are priceless. NAM Queens and official contestants create videos for free, and in a sense, they are "NAM employees" who don't get paid.

To show you an example, visit Zoey Francis' _National American Miss_ Mini Montage, a 47-second _YouTube_ medley of pictures. Zoey, not even double-digit in age as of this writing, garnered nearly 1,500 views since her June 2, 2012, posting. Now, look at a NAM State teen official contestant who posted her NAM three minute video during a State pageant. She begins filming herself in her hotel bathroom after having attended a NAM "Get Acquainted" party at her State pageant. The video was posted on July 3, 2007, and, as of this writing, nearly 75,000 viewers have viewed her goofy NAM message! Talk about free, continuous social media promotion for NAM!

Using a free hosting service like _YouTube_ to post any pageant promotional video is smart. Young girls flock to _YouTube_ to get "the scoop" on any pageant they are considering entering. After all, NAM officials know that _YouTube_ is the number four search engine as of this writing![15] If you Google "National American Miss YouTube," you will net quite a few NAM _YouTube_ videos. Granted, not all NAM _YouTube_ videos are posted by Queens. Current and former official contestants are also encouraged to speak/post about the pageant. After years of _YouTube_ videos being uploaded by prospective contestants, official contestants, and pageant officials, NAM corralled them into its own NAM _YouTube_ Channel and placed a link on its website. Learn how to make your own _YouTube_ channel by visiting "How to Make A YouTube Channel 2014." Ignore previous years' tutorials; this one includes _Google Plus'_ new features.

"Like" and "Fan" on Facebook

The _Facebook_ brand carries with it a sense of safety, authority, and trust. Having _Facebook's_ logo connected to your pageant website will make your website look and feel more legitimate and trustworthy (at least in the eyes of _Facebook_ users). It's a free

---

[15] "The top 500 sites on the web." _Alexa._ April 22, 2014. http://www.alexa.com/topsites.

advertising tool that relies on referrals and recommendations — just as a pageant system does.

An important way to promote your pageant system, pageant event, and pageant website is to get social media sites' tools working for you, especially the *Facebook* "Like" and "Fan." The beauty of *Facebook's* "Like" and "Fan" tools is that, when prospective and official contestants employ either one on a pageant's *Facebook* page, a tsunami effect benefiting the pageant system occurs. Pageant promoters have the opportunity to have their brand followed by "fans," keeping them up-to-date with pageant information currently posted on their *Facebook* pages. That is, as long as those "fans" don't click on the "Remove me from Fans" at the bottom of the menu.

The "Like" button, by contrast, is a link placed by pictures, wall posts, and status updates on *Facebook*. Depending on their email settings, if users click on "Like," they are sometimes notified when other users "Like" the same post or picture. A buildup of "Likes" amongst prospective and/or official contestants aid in generating even more girls to sign up for the pageant. After all, if other people like the pageant, then it *must* be a good pageant. So, they sign up. *National American Miss* knows this all too well. Imagine the number of girls that NAM pageant officials link its pageant information to when, as of this writing, nearly 60,000 girls have "Liked" them on their *Facebook* page. When prospective (and official) contestants "Like" a pageant system's page, they will start to see stories from that page in their News Feed. The page will also appear on the prospective contestant's profile, and she will also appear on the page as a person who likes that page.

Imagine having nearly 60,000 "Likes" on your pageant system's page. This gives your pageant page a chance to go "viral" as friends recommend your pageant to their friends, who then recommend it to their friends, and so on. A tsunami of amazing results occurs from "Likes." Learn more about how to encourage prospective and official contestants to "Become a "fan"" of your *Facebook* page. To understand "What 'Like' Means" on a Facebook post — in comparison to just being a "Fan" — visit the PC World page. To learn how to incorporate the Facebook "Like" button on your page, visit internetmarketingsolution. To learn how you can design your Facebook page so that more people will "Like" you, visit Kevan Lee's "How to Create and Manage the Perfect Facebook Page for Your Business: The Complete A to Z Guide." If you prefer to speak to a social media expert, contact **Karen Clark** at *My Business Presence*. Karen has extensive experience in integrating pageant information with social media and vice-versa. If you prefer to accelerate your pageant business immediately by using social media marketing, Social Media For Direct Selling Representatives: Ehical and Effictive Online Marketing (Volume 1), authored by Karen Clark, will help you learn the best ways to use *Facebook, Instagram, Pinterest, LinkedIn,* and *Twitter,* and it will also help you to learn how to avoid the common pitfalls of using social media for your direct selling business. The generic information in Karen's book will help even a pageant system.

Build Your "Likes"

National American Miss introduced its "NAM Connection Game," in 2012, to National candidates and rewarded them for liking NAM on *Facebook.* This motion added nearly 60,000 *additional* Likes (as of this writing) to its Facebook "Likes" tally. (Learn about the "NAM Connection Game" by reading the next section below, "Up Your Online Game.")

To a *Facebook* visitor, seeing a large "Like" number says these people care about this particular pageant and what it's about. For a pageant system, "Like" lets them know what the passive fans (prospective contestants) and active fans (official contestants) are about. These "Likes" reveal a lot about the people who are fans of the page by providing a class of digital records similar to Web search queries, Web browsing histories, and credit card purchases. These "Likes" also drive the *Facebook* algorithm that decides what content to display in *Facebook* users' news feeds. Pageant producers can take advantage of this, not only to promote its site, but also to discover things that are no longer ephemeral — no longer fleeting — because they can "think ahead" of those girls and create meaningful content on its website (and in the pageant) in order to keep the active fans within its pageant system until they age out.

This is important for pageant systems like NAM, whose goal is to register, say, a seven-year old prospective contestant (they start at age four) into her first State (and then National) pageant, and then retain her until she ages out at twenty. Along the way, this official contestant's *Facebook* "Likes" allow the pageant director to keep up with her ever-changing likes and predict what her future tastes lean towards — even *before she figures it out for herself!* This presents an opportunity for pageant producers to make changes in the pageant business model along the way for the greatest chances of retaining the girl in its labyrinth until she ages out. Most importantly, not only does it cage the "bird" (official contestant), it draws in her "flock" (friends) as well. As the saying goes...birds of a feather flock together. Imagine having a bird like this one in your flock of candidates:

> Even though I didn't win anything, I walked away a different person. I got participation awards though, I got the Portfolio Award for doing Photogenic 4 times, I got the Outstanding Participation award for selling ads, and the Spirit of America award for doing 5 or more Optionals. I plan on continuing Pageantry and hope to get far with it. I hope it continues to help me with my career. I am participating in NAM again this summer and cannot wait to see what this time brings me.[16]

Learn what Optionals can do for your pageant system's bottom line — and how not to miss financial opportunity when designing your Optionals — by reading my book *Producing Beauty Pageants: Optionals.*

This was written by a NAM official contestant who didn't receive a callback, but rather, a mailback letter informing her she was accepted as a State Finalist (official contestant):

> "You have been selected as a state finalist for the National American Miss Jr. Teen New Jersey Pageant," that was the first sentence I saw when I receive [sic] my acceptance letter from the NAM pageant. It's what made me start to purse [sic] my dreams. [17]

Miss Speckled Perch offers a Spirit Award to the candidate with the most *Facebook* "Likes" for their picture on the *Miss Speckled Perch Facebook* page during the pageant. One winner is awarded for the younger divisions (Tiny, Little, and Princess), and one winner is awarded for the older divisions (Jr. and Miss).

---

[16] "My National American Miss Journey!!" April 18, 2012. http://www.namissblog.com/2012/04/my-national-american-miss-journey.html.

[17] Ervin, Alison. "My National American Miss Journey." This, Is my life blogspot. April 9, 2012. http://ali13singer.blogspot.com/2012/04/my-national-american-miss-journey.html.

Candidates are asked to email their pictures to the pageant so that they can be uploaded to the pageant's *Facebook* page. Then, the official contestants would need to go on *Facebook* and invite all of their friends and family to "Like" their photo and share the picture with friends. *Facebook* keeps track of the "Likes," and the pageant has no control over the results. The sooner official contestants submit their photos, the sooner they are uploaded, and the longer they have to garner "Likes."

Miss American Coed rewards *Facebook* "Friends" with a $50 *Facebook* discount on their entry fee. (To receive the discount, official contestants are requested to note "*Facebook* Friend — $50 Discount" in the comments field of the online shopping cart before they check out.)

Up Your Online Game

If you want to be a competitive pageant system, not only will you need an online presence, but you will also need to ramp up your online game. No other pageant system is more of an expert at doing this than *National American Miss*. All you need to do is Google NAM, and you'll find it *all over the Internet*.

One example of NAM's aggressive online presence could be witnessed at the 2012 National pageant when *National American Miss* State Queens and *All-American Miss* State Queens — all nearly 700 official contestants — were introduced to the new "NAM Connection Game." These official contestants could play the game by simply "liking us" on *Instagram*, *Twitter*, and *Facebook*, for example, and by taking various NAM pageant event pictures (of themselves and/or other NAM State Queens) and posting them on the various social media sites. The National official contestants could earn a total of sixty points for their efforts. (The points didn't count for any area of competition, only a trinket prize.) Official contestants simply filled out a form stating where they posted their social media photos and noted what they "Liked." When their efforts added up to the required 60 points, the official contestants took the form into the NAM Gift Shop and received a rhinestone crown pin. (Most official contestants also ended up making a NAM gift shop purchase, for example, a logo pageant sweatshirt or t-shirt to put that *"free"* crown pin on!)

When NAM's goal for each site (*Instagram*, *Twitter*, and *Facebook*, for example) had been reached, NAM would donate $1,000 to the Hurricane Sandy relief. (And, it was a tax write-off for NAM.) Imagine having to pay out $1,000 for the work of nearly 700 girls. That's approximately $1.45 per candidate for maybe an hour's worth of work *per candidate — less than minimum wage*!

Understanding that their participation in the "NAM Connection Game" benefited Hurricane Sandy victims, official contestants — all (nearly) 700 National candidates — took part in promoting NAM to their friends! They were encouraged to do it during Nationals week, from their iPhones or laptops. Talk about the best publicity and it would cost NAM only $1,000 plus the cost of (nearly) 700 rhinestone pins (at wholesale prices if purchased in bulk from a China manufacturer)...*if* all *National American Miss* and *National All-American Miss* official contestants participated and *if* NAM's goal was reached! What's more, NAM is striking while the iron is hot, i.e., getting a huge number of official contestants to work and "Like" the pageant during National pageant week while they are still excited — *before* pageant winners are announced. Getting NAM's publicity train chugging before the 2012 holidays, and before its 2013 rounds of NAM State Open Call sessions and State pageants began, is sheer marketing genius!

Leave State or National official contestants no time to be bored at your pageant. Guide them in your social media pageant marketing game *before* your current pageant year ends. Employing official contestants by way of a "Pageant Connection Game" likely means that your *Facebook* "Likes" *alone* will grow by however many candidates are in your pageant! (And, if those girls ask members in their network to also "Like" NAM, the wildfire spreads.) Imagine NAM featuring the "NAM Connection Game" for all of its approximately forty State pageants that feature similar numbers — and usually more! Although NAM started its pageant system, in 2003, it wouldn't be until January, 2009 — about a year after it introduced Open Call into its pageant model — when NAM joined *Facebook*.

If NAM had offered the "NAM Connection Game" after crowning, well, the "iron" would have cooled down, and very few official contestants would have participated. It's all in the clever timing on NAM's part along with hiring an MBA as National Director of Marketing — LaKishia Barber-Edwards — to come up with such social media promotional ideas!

Encourage Online and Other Promotions Participation

Kentucky Beauties offers official contestants a chance at winning a gorgeous custom satin sash, round crown, $50 pageant cash for State or Nationals (towards registration fees), and the *Kentucky Beauties Overall Community Queen* title. To participate, candidates would need to spread the *Kentucky Beauties* pageant word at various locations — including on social networking sites — to receive points for each. *Kentucky Beauties* also provides participating candidates with an Appearance Validation Form that they are required to fill out. The form includes: Name; Date of Appearance; Type of Event; Appearance Type (a note to attach a copy of a newspaper article, radio announcement, or television copy); Contestant Signature line; Parent Signature line (if under 18); and Representative Signature line. They award points as follows:

- *Facebook/Twitter* posting: twenty-five points

- Tag the pageant's page to the candidate's post: 100 points

- *Facebook* subscription: 50 points (for each system)

- Participate in a local parade: 150 points

- Community events: 200 points (make appearances at festivals, fairs, concerts, ribbon cuttings, grand openings, etc., in crown and sash, and email photo to pageant OR post to their personal *Facebook* page)

- Crowning appearances: 150 points (email photo to pageant OR post to their personal *Facebook* page)

- Helping at other Preliminary pageants: 150 points

- Refer three quality prospective contestants: 300 points, and

- Media appearances: 500 points each

Each participant in the Community Program receives a trophy. Different size trophies are awarded based on official contestant involvement: 100–200 points, 6" trophy/crown; 250–500 points, 12" trophy/crown; 550–750 points, 18" trophy/crown; 800–1000 points, 24" trophy/crown; 1100+ points, 3' trophy/crown; overall points, 6' trophy/round crown/rhinestone sash. The candidate with the most appearances and/or community points at the end of the pageant would be the recipient of the *Kentucky Beauties Overall Community Queen* title and awards. (*Kentucky Beauties* also offers a civic Queen title, which is based on military donations; the prizes are the same as the above breakdown.)

If you want to understand more about mastering your online marketing, visit Marie Forleo's free video series about online marketing. She will show you how to market more and sell better — whether you are just starting out or have been in business for some time. There are some major changes in the next five to ten years on the Internet, so it's important that you up your online game now before these changes happen.

QR Code

A QR code — a type of "quick response" barcode in two- and three-dimensional matrixes (not to be confused with Quadratic Response Code) — lends exclusivity to a pageant system's promotion. It's a bridge that digitally connects people to traditional advertising and marketing. Users with a camera phone equipped with the correct barcode scanner application can scan the image of the QR code to display text, contact information, connect to a wireless network, or open a web page in the cell phone's browser. Employment recruiters have started placing QR codes in job advertisements, and it won't be long before Contestant Recruiters use QR codes in their search for prospective candidates. Read 11 Reasons You SHOULD Be Using QR Codes at Your Place of Business to gain some insightful information. Pageant systems that turned to technology and that are employing QR codes in its pageant marketing materials include *Dream Girls USA* and its sister pageants *Young American Miss*, *Miss AmeriQueen*, and *Real Girls USA*. Even county fair pageants like *Marion County Fairest of the Fair Pageant* are getting into the QR code action.

Not only are pageant systems using the interactive QR code, *Prestigious Beauty Pageants* — a haven of world beauty pageant news — also employs its own QR code. It provides teaser headlines and other interactive tools that eventually route traffic to its website, one that receives nearly 600 pageviews per day (at the time of this writing), according to *CuteStat.com*. *Pageantry Magazine* employs QR codes in various manners, including one for subscriptions to its outstanding source of pageantry information.

"Tween-Time" Ideas for QR Code Inclusion

Anytime you can capitalize on "tween-time" — when people are in between point A and point B — is the best time to bring your QR code "store" to the people. Take, for example, an official contestant's friend who purchased an admission ticket. Prior to attending the pageant, s/he can scan the QR code provided on the front of the admission ticket to discover the pageant's website where she can learn about the next "State Finalist" search or Open Call dates — or whatever it is that you are promoting to this select group in possession of this one particular QR code. Maybe you are encouraging every ticketholder to write a future prospective contestant's name on the back of the ticket. That QR code might have also invited the admission ticket holder to earn a chance for a prize in the subsequent drawing. Now, you have a *motivating* built-in leads builder. Not only is the friend happy about a chance at winning the prize in the secret drawing, but the friend's sister might be interested in receiving "the letter" inviting her to your next Open Call!

Another "tween time" to include a QR code is at an Open Call. The cover of a presentation folder, typically presented at a pageant Open Call, would be an ideal place for a QR code. Let's use, as an example, a California State *National American Miss* Open Call. At one Chula Vista Open Call session, in 2015, prospective contestants were given a glossy, white NAM-logoed pocket folder and two pieces of pageant marketing materials: 1) an Official Application — a one-sided, non-carbon copy photocopy, to be returned right after it was signed, which was right before the session started; and 2) "What Happens Next" — a one-sided flyer (that is ordinarily a two-sided flyer at other NAM State pageants). After prospective contestants filled out and signed the legally-binding Official Application, they had about 30 minutes to sit and wait for the Open Call session to begin. They sat in silence without having any pageant financial disclosures or other pageant supporting materials in hand to read. Moreover, this particular Open Call didn't include a free photoshoot to keep prospective contestants preoccupied, and a spiral-bound photocopy of

Magazine #1 was presented at the conclusion of the Open Call session.

What would have been ideal for these "tween-time" people is if NAM would have included a QR code on the front of its Official Application (contract) with a directive leading to NAM's financial disclosures, such as their Refund Policy (exactly what money isn't refunded once it is turned into NAM), who pays for the "optional" weekend hotel expense, what prizes "the bottom line" line up with, how official contestants can EARN the premium prize, etc. This knowledge should be accessible to applicants *before* requiring a consenting signature on the legally-binding contract (Official Application) that they are required to sign before the Open Call session begins.

Still, a QR Code is no substitute for full financial disclosures and complete pageant marketing materials, in writing, presented with a verbal explanation — BEFORE requiring a contractually-binding signature on an Official Application.

QR Codes that Rock

Whatever QR code you design, it should not be boring, and it need not be in black and white. Create Customized (Colored) QR Codes shares ideas on how you can generate beautiful, useful, colorful ones, and with the help of *QR Hacker*, this tutorial will show you exactly how to get your first multi-colored QR code.

Ideal Places for a Pageant QR Code

There are many things to do with — and many worthwhile ways to employ — a QR code in your pageant marketing materials. What can I do with a QR Code? can help you figure them out and explain how to employ them in a variety of ways, including bridging your URL destination, *vCard*, *YouTube* videos, *Facebook*, *Twitter* Follow, Tweet, *Google Maps*, *LinkedIn* Profile, *LinkedIn* Share, plain text, contact information, *Skype* username, and Application URL. Why not use a QR code to direct people from your pageant blog to your *YouTube* video; from your *YouTube* video to your pageant website; and/or from your website to your blog? To learn how to do this, visit *MMiScan*.

Returning to the example of the Chula Vista *National American Miss* California Open Call session, in 2015, NAM's scheduled presenters — and its presentation equipment — were stuck in another state due to inclement weather. Although NAM had a team of seven Open Call presenters, none could be present on this day. Instead, a fill-in presenter conducted the Open Call and presented sparse financial disclosures and other supporting pageant materials, and the information she presented via NAM videos could not be heard due to a missing sound system! QR codes on the cover of the glossy folder could have bridged prospective contestants to NAM's digital pageant marketing materials, say, to the exact pages of their complete pageant marketing materials and full financial disclosures provided at its pageant website, that is, if NAM posts them.

A QR code can also be placed on the front cover of your pageant magazine, flyer, brochure, pageant receipts, business cards, blogsite, social media sites — any pageant marketing materials and paperwork that floats around on land and on the Internet — to promote or bridge whatever it is you want promoted or bridged. After all, each different QR code can lead to a different pageant marketing material or promotion.

If you have a blog, include a QR code on your website that bridges to it. This can lead prospective contestants to your blog, which they then can read at a later, more convenient time, and not just while they are at your website "store" window shopping. It's likely that your blog will convince these "window-shopping, prospective contestants" to revisit your website and shop, pay the application fee, hit the submit button, and *become* an official contestant or "State Finalist" — whatever you label a pageant candidate.

If first-time visitors use their phone's barcode app to retain your blogsite information for a later "tween-time" to read, your blog might just be the convincing tool that those prospective contestants need as a motivation to revisit your website and become official contestants. And just think — this all started with a QR code!

As noted in the previous chapter, in 2012, NAM had nearly 700 official contestants at its National pageant; in 2013, they had nearly 800. This is a huge number of girls to keep informed. Official contestants with a smartphone would be able to key in an http address leading them to their respective age division's weeklong pageant itinerary. Why not use a QR code here? It would be the perfect time for a QR code, and you would save a tree! Moreover, a pageant producer won't need to pay for man-hour power to make itinerary hardcopies, lug them to the National pageant, risk that the wrong color paper was used for the wrong age division, lose them in transit, etc. It's much cheaper and easier to incorporate a QR code and attach it to your "Welcome" board in the lobby check-in, inside the Pageant Program Book pages, etc. (And have a single hardcopy itinerary taped to a table as your backup.)

Change Your QR Code to Reflect Recent Updates

Change the QR code on your website or *Facebook* page to reflect current surprises for girls who register by a certain day. Suggest that visitors share the QR code via any share button via *Gmail*, *Facebook*, *Pinterest*, email, etc. *Instagram* is a great spot to upload a QR code if you want prospective contestants to download whatever app that you want downloaded. *Pinterest* is also an ideal spot because, with a QR code, you can link prospective contestants to your FB page, specific boards, or to pictures you've already pinned to your board. You will give visitors the opportunity to link to your pageant website and the ability to share it with friends.

But do more than the basic black and white "block-o-blocks." Demonstrate what your app does, and tie it to your brand. Make the ad your app. Show them — don't tell them — how to download your app. But before you upload your QR code app, test it repeatedly to make sure it is able to be scanned. Test it again. Continue to test it multiple times, testing it from various distances, and then have three other people test it. You'll be viewed as an innovator in the pageant industry, not as incompetent. Last, but not least, personalize your QR code, and drive it to retail.

Personalize Your QR Code

You can make your QR code a personal, scan-to-find-out message. For example, the viewer can discover that her application fee will be waived if she uses the encrypted message that was revealed as a result of scanning the pageant's QR code. This coupon might also encourage her to apply to be an official contestant. If she has already paid the application fee, it's too late; she would have needed to scan the QR code sooner. Learn how to Use QR Codes Creatively and incorporate secret prizes (attend the "free" Open Call or attend the one "free" Pageant Prep Training Session). The young generation loves QR codes and the surprises that they can hold!

Print a page of QR code stickers with your contact information and stick them on anything that you would want returned if it were lost or stolen, e.g., laptops, business equipment, your camera, phone, etc. Your "contact me" information is included on the QR code. Such a QR code would be ideal for a large pageant system with lots of staging equipment.

Pageant promoters who use _MailChimp_, a popular email marketing platform, can use its latest feature Pyow to send a unique QR code to each email recipient. These emails are then printed out and redeemed at retail. Many pageant systems use email to promote their pageants, so why not include QR codes in those messages?

QR codes can also work well for pageant systems employing mailshot, as does _National American Miss_. NAM already waives the $20 NAM Official Application (its official contract) fee for any prospective contestant attending Open Call who fills it out (and signs it) _before_ Open Call begins. A QR code can take it one step further. NAM could make a big deal out of the freebie via a QR code on "the letter" that is mailshot to thousands upon thousands of prospective contestants before they attend Open Call. This would work well because NAM doesn't note the avoided cost directly on "the letter." It simply says that it's FREE to attend Open Call. This could make the prospective contestant believe that ordinarily it might cost to 1) attend Open Call; 2) submit an application/photo; 3) attend a Pageant Prep Training Session; and/or 4) participate in a professional photoshoot. These are all FREE for prospective contestants attending a NAM Open Call. Why not include four strategically-placed QR codes, in various pageant marketing materials, making a big deal out of these freebies?

If you are a pageant system which already doesn't charge an application fee — also known as a tollbooth fee — make a "big deal" of your "application fee" by promoting your "free application fee" in a QR code. It's natural that everyone — prospective contestants included — love a bargain. Learn more about "the letter" by reading my book _Producing Beauty Pageants: Open Call_, Chapter 6, "The Letter." Learn more about NAM's free photoshoot by reading the same book, Chapter 3, "Free Photoshoot." Learn more about how NAM employs its contract — Official Application — by reading the same book, Chapter 9, "Official Application."

QR Codes on Your Website

If you want to increase traffic to your website, learn how to correctly use QR codes. Learn how to do this by reading Websites with QR codes and How to Use QR Codes to Improve Your WordPress Website's User Experience.

Create Your Own QR Codes

Visit *The New York Times Blog gadgetwise* to learn how to make your own QR codes. Reading How to Make a QR Code in 4 Quick Steps can help you to create your own QR codes. Online generator QRStuff.com creates codes for free. The Google URL Shortener will also create a QR code file from a shortened link — just click Details to see the image file. Other QR code-generating sites include Kaywa, Qurify, and Delivr.

Hire a Professional Graphic Designer

If you're not up to doing it yourself, hire a professional graphic designer to incorporate your QR Code(s) into your pageant marketing materials. Courtney, from *Photo Retouching by Courtney*, is an expert at integrating QR Codes into pageant graphic products. Such products can include flyers, posters, brochures, admission tickets, raffle tickets, pageant magazines, Pageant Program Books, pageant marketing advertisements, business card magnets, refrigerator magnets, car magnets, and more. These QR codes could link to exclusive discounts, information, special deals, raffle prizes, etc. Titleholders could include them on their autograph cards and photo business cards, linking the viewer directly to their platform, website, or an exclusive promotion.

Social Media in Action

On the evening that one National American Miss prospective contestant's mom found out that her daughter, Sofia, was accepted to compete in the New York State NAM pageant, she took to social media. The Sofia C. NAM Sponsorship Collection account was created on *EventBrite* to solicit sponsors to contribute towards her daughter's sponsorship fee. She also announced the same on Sofia's newly-created pageant *Facebook* page. Each account linked viewers to the other — the start of her synergy — and eventually to the *Eventbrite* checkout for easy payment.

Sofia's *Facebook* page also gave readers additional details as to how her mother was going to raise the sponsorship fee:

> I am going out to buy some more water bottles and cupcake making supplies to sell at the park today to try to raise money for the pageant. There is also [Sofia's Eventbrite link] where you can "buy tickets" to the event as a donation to help me along in my fundraising efforts. Please post on your wall also to get the word out for me. Thanks. I get the free photo shoot pics tomorrow night on disc, expect to see them very soon. :) She is really very excited & I am happy to be able to do something to make her feel good about herself again.

See how clever this social media thing is? Sofia's *Facebook* page presold the viewers, who eventually visited the linked *Eventbrite* page. The *Eventbrite* contribution page not only solicited the sponsorship fee, but it made it easy for people to pay any portion of the sponsorship fee via an "Order Now" button. It also provided even more convenient payment options such as *PayPal, AMEX, Discover, MasterCard,* and *Visa.* Moreover, the account could be set up with "Monthly Deposits" and "Coupon Codes."

The *Eventbrite* page also directed viewers to Sofia's *Facebook* page for additional information. While on her *Facebook* page, we learn that Sofia's mom noted that she would soon be posting the free photoshoot photos that were taken at the Open Call. When that synergy happens, NAM pageant officials will likely gain even more people visiting its website, resulting in additional Open Call attendees and official contestants.

Sofia's mom also invited readers to post Sofia's pageant information "on their wall," meaning, on *the readers' Facebook* pages to synergize NAM to greater heights. To NAM's benefit, Sofia's mom placed NAM's pageant link on Sofia's *Eventbrite* and *Facebook* pages — which *attached to the friends' walls that permitted the synergized connection.*

Why did Sofia's mom stop synergizing at just two social media sites? Why didn't she know to include even more popular sharing links? As a pageant producer, do as NAM pageant officials do at its National pageant, and teach a "Social Media & You" pageant workshop; however, begin at your Preliminary or State pageants levels. Learn how pageant directors and candidates can synergize simultaneously by reading my book *Producing Beauty Pageants: Creating a Synergized National Pageant System*, Chapter 1, "Synergize Your Pageant" under "Teach Prospective Contestants to How to Synergize" and "Encourage Official Contestants to Synergize Your Pageant with Social Media."

Networking Social Media

When Bethany Jones posted her daughter's participation on her newly-created NAM *gofundme* page in an effort to raise money for the *National American Miss* Iowa State pageant, she noted:

> I have 1259 people in my networks, all it takes is a $1 and we are good to go, including all of the entry fees, travel costs, an interview outfit, and a formal dress for her to wear! On average, Sponsors donate anywhere from $10.00–$50.00.

Now, imagine nearly 700 (or 800) official contestants in your National pageant (or similar numbers at your State pageant) reaching out to *their* respective networks! Encouraging official contestants (and their families) to network social media into their sponsorship efforts will strengthen your pageant promotional efforts.

Social Media Spreads Like Butter

When *National American Miss* official contestant Esther N. was presented with the opportunity to win $50 by recommending (the most) girls to NAM, she took her *prospective contestant search* to *Yahoo! Answers* to spread the word:

> I was recently given an amazing opportunity to recommend girls for this pageant because I am a contestant. Any state, it doesn't matter. SO if ther [sic] are any parents or young ladis [sic] who would like to take me up on my offer please e-mail me.

> It is an amazing experience and one can trully [sic] grow as a person! I LOVE NAMiss

for more info go to the official website @namiss.com

And then there is NAM contestant Vanessa and her posting on *Yahoo! Answers:*

> Hi, my name is Vanessa and I'm here to ask for referrals for next year's pageant in a state (U.S.A. only) near you. namiss or national American miss is not a beauty pageant it is based off of poise Communication skills and your unique and individual personality. This competition is for girls only from ages 4–20. By compete [sic] ing [sic] in namiss you will learn valuable skills like introducing your self [sic] to a live AUDIENCE, walking on stage for a personal appearance, and gain skills in an interview with the pageant judges. There is something for every girl at National American Miss. And this opportunity of a life time can be yours. All you have to be willing to do is give out your address to me, I would consider through e-mail because you never can be sure about some people on the Internet. If you are under 14 years of age ask for a parents [sic] permission to give out your address.
>
> *Disclaimer
>
> I am not in anyway [sic], shape, or form, getting paid for promoting National American Miss. All thoughts and opinions are my own.
>
> Thank you and have a wonderful day :)

Yet, the most rancid posting on *Yahoo! Answers* comes from NAM contestant Mona Joyce:

> OMG! I'm in the national american miss [sic] pageant too! And it's not very expensive. You have to raise like $450 by asking for money from friends/family or doing fundraising things... It may seem like a lot of money. But its [sic] actually really easy to raise it. I did things like: Had my dad go to a bar and put a donation jar up with my face on it. People put alot [sic] of money in there (because they were drunk lol).

Controlling Social Media Content

Some pageant systems attempt to control social media content that pertains to its pageant name. Whether it works, or not, remains to be seen. Nevertheless, it's probably a good thing to have something in writing to help guide official contestants' busy social media fingers.

Ms. America Pageant explicitly states in its Rules & Regulations,

> Contestants are not allowed to use their title name in any electronic address or Social Media without the written approval of the *Ms. America Pageant*.

Ms. Latina International includes a clause that official contestants must consent to:

> I acknowledge and agree to provide the *Ms. Latina International* Pageant Organization my permission to view at random, my personal social media websites I am a member of, subscribe to, included but not limited to [and it lists the ten popular sites].

Advertise on Social Media Sites

In addition to ramping up their social media game, many pageant directors add to their online persona by purchasing advertising on _Facebook_, for example, to advertise and promote their pageants. For about 19 cents per click, prospective contestants can see information on their pageant. There are a number of ways in which pageant directors can reach the demographic they are specifically targeting. Such advertisements can reach the profiles of single girls between the ages of eighteen and twenty-five, for example, who like to model. Pageant directors can even choose the state they are targeting. Think of the "click fee" as postage for mailing information to prospective contestants during the "snail mail" days.

Official Contestant Website and Social Media

Pageant systems are encouraging candidates to create their own website and Public Figure page featuring the pageant system's information *and* a link to pageant headquarters. *Essence Pageants* invites official contestants to build a website that features its pageant information — one that includes a link to pageant headquarters — for people interested in learning about the pageant. Pageant officials even present an award to the candidate with the best overall website. Judging includes professionalism, ease of use, and functionality.

USA National Miss allows State Queens to create a website to promote each State Queens' title and to include photos of appearances. The National office must be aware of any website that candidates intend to create to promote the *USA National Miss* State title. The guidelines include:

> You may NOT include your phone number, home address, or any other identifying information on your website. Remember that the Internet is public domain, and anyone (even people with wrong intentions) may view your site. Free websites abound on the Internet. We suggest *Webs.com* for a quick and simple website creation that will not cost you any money.

> You may create a "Public Figure" page on *Facebook* to promote your title and generate support for your journey to nationals. An example of how to set up your *Facebook* page name: *USA National Miss Georgia Teen* — Your Name.

> You can create a blog to write about your year as the State Queen. There are many free blog sites on the Internet.

National American Miss official contestant Hadassah Ayanna created her personal NAM pageant website at *weebly.com*. Headings at her website include: Home, About NAM, State Cover Girl Title, Optionals Contests, Become a Sponsor, Tips & Advice, Q&A's, and Blog. *National American Miss* official contestant Cassie Graham created a detailed NAM sponsorship and campaign at *raiseBIG.com*. *National American Miss* official contestant Kristen Clark created a NAM Ad Program website. Be sure to click on the left links to view the complete ad information.

Candidate Profile Page

Miss Gateway St. Louis Pageant requires its Outstanding Teen candidates to set up a profile page on *Miss America's Outstanding Teen/Children's Miracle Network* website. While it is the hope that each official contestant at the Local level will raise funds for CMN, it is NOT a requirement to enter a Local Preliminary, and there is NO minimum amount of fundraising required.

Miss Arab USA directs applicants who register (and pay the non-refundable, $50 registration/application fee) to a private area on the pageant website to create their personal online profile. The Judge's Committee reviews all participants' profiles, and then selects the Top 100 applicants for phone interviews. The Judges' Committee then selects twenty (from the Top 100 applicants) to become Semifinalists. The 2012 Semifinals was held July 10th–14th at the *Talking Stick Resort* in Phoenix, Arizona. The twenty selected Semifinalists were then required to submit a final pageant registration fee of $250.

The Semifinalists were responsible for their own travel expenses to and from the pageant location. The *Miss Arab* Organization was responsible for the official contestants' local transportation, hotel accommodations, and meals. Once Semifinalists arrived at the *Talking Stick Resort*, they entered into a one week program where they were trained for the Final pageant.

The Judging Panel then selected five girls (from the twenty Semifinalists): one as *Miss Arab USA* 2012; one as *Miss Arab USA First Runner-Up*; one as *Miss Arab USA Second Runner-Up*; one as *Miss Arab USA Third Runner-Up*; and one as *Miss Arab USA Talent*.

National American Miss official contestant Alaina Walker's online profile, "It's My Time to Shine," is a thorough official contestant website. Click on the "Sponsorship" link at the top of the homepage, and you will find NAM's Sponsorship Information Packet. Click on the "Advertising" link, and you will find NAM's "Advertising Information Packet." Additionally, if you scroll to the bottom of the homepage, you will find links to "Alaina's Bio/Résumé"; "Alaina's Blog"; "Please Sponsor Alaina!"; "Purchase Pageant Tickets"; "Purchase Banquet Tickets!"; "Please

Support Alaina by Purchasing an Ad!"; and so on. Any link selling a product (admission tickets, advertising, etc.) offers payment options that include *Mastercard*, *Visa*, *Discover*, *American Express*, and *PayPal*. Alaina's free website profile was created on *weebly*. The website is pretty impressive for an eight-year-old on her second year at bat with NAM!

Language Translators for Pageants

Skilled translators take care of every single detail of the translation process, no matter how big or small. Professional language translation services make sure that every word reads and sounds locally correct. *TranslatorsCafé.com* is a directory of translators, interpreters, and translation agencies that provide language specialists to translate your material. *American Translators Association* can help you find the skilled translator that you need.

When you visit the *Miss Brazil* website, a pop-out field box appears to the right of its homepage and asks if you want to translate the page. To the right of that box is an "Options" field, and under that are two additional options — one that says "Translate," and the other, "Nope." When I click on "Translate," I am offered several languages to choose from. Even better, when you Google *"Miss Brasil"* on Google's search engine, you will note "Translate this page" next to its URL address. Click on it, and *Miss Brasil's* entire website is translated into English. While at *Miss Brasil's* website, the "Translate" bar at the top lets you choose a translation in *any* language — Chinese, Dutch, and even Ukrainian! Even *Miss America* and *Miss Universe's* Google links don't offer a "Translate this page" link. It's no wonder the *Miss Brazil* website — *Miss Brasil* untranslated — is nearing one million page views as of this writing! It's your website traffic stats that corporate Official Sponsors want to see.

The World's Most Beautiful Woman provides translations in twelve languages — including French, Spanish, and Portuguese — on its website. Think you need to be a worldwide pageant to benefit from translation? *Miss West Africa UK* includes English, French, and Portuguese translations. Many U.S. pageant systems, at a minimum, should include a Spanish translation on the website, as does *National American Miss* (for its FAQs). Even better, *Sophisticated Beauties & Beaus* includes a Spanish link at the top of its website. When you click on it, you will be taken to an impressive Spanish version/translation of the site.

Don't stop at website translations. Need downloadable forms in Spanish? Visit _Little Miss/Mr. L.A._, and scroll to the end to notice that it has downloadable forms in both English and Spanish. _Miss Africa Belgium Beauty Pageant_ includes three hotline numbers for voice information — in three languages! For English, dial 0499-920-400; for French, dial 0499-920-392; and for the Netherlands, dial 0499-920-623.

Trade Links with Other Pageants

Pageant directors can build strength in their pageant systems by teaming up with other pageant directors and exchanging links. Pageant directors banding together can mutually benefit, particularly if they coordinate their pageant dates and not fragment the market in an identical area. _Miss Heart of the USA_ invites other pageant directors to exchange links. Other pageants that trade links include _America's Gorgeous Girls_, _All Star Kids_, and _The Regal Princess Pageant_.

Email

Turn your emails into a pageant-advertising campaign. _MailChimp_ makes it easy to design exceptional email campaigns, perfect for any pageant system. _MailChimp_ team members will help you design email newsletters, share them on social networks, integrate them with services you already use, manage subscribers, and track your results. _America's Gorgeous Girls_ has a strong pageant email campaign. To subscribe to its email promotions, email aggcalifornia@yahoo.com. When you do send an email to this address, you will receive an automated response. Today's auto response (February 14th) was:

> Hello Gorgeous Girl!
>
> Thank you so much for your interest in West Coast America's Gorgeous Girl and Simply Gorgeous Girl. Your email is very important to us. Our next pageant is Sassy Safari and is scheduled for March 30th, 2013, in Las Vegas, Nevada; April 13th, 2013, in Riverside County, CA; and May 5th, 2013, in Oxnard, CA! Paperwork for Sassy Safari is available on our website! We hope you can join us for all the FUN!!!

We will respond to your email very soon. In the meantime, please feel free to visit us at http://www.aggcalifornia.com/ to download your pageant paperwork or visit us on *Facebook* via WestCoastGorgeousGirls! I hope to meet you soon!

Kentucky Beauties, who, as of this writing, was back from its successful inaugural year, included the following in its auto response email: a link to obtain Preliminary entry forms, a link to register online, a description of the pageant highlights, and contact information.

Emma — an email content hub — describes a quality email marketing campaign, ironically, comparing email marketers with the *Miss America* pageant. The *Emma* blog, "3 lessons email marketers can learn from the Miss America pageant," makes excellent comparisons between how the *Miss America* pageant operates and how email marketers (in general) *should* operate. Make time to read these short lessons.

Weblog

A weblog is a website that consists of a series of entries arranged in reverse chronological order, usually updated frequently. The information can be written by the site owner or by contributing users. The *Miss Connecticut Pageant* launched an *Activity Weblog* in an effort to further communications between the pageant and pageant family. Included in the weblog are photos, links, and comments about the "happenings and what's going on" within its pageant.

Forum

Faces of Europe added a Forum to its website for official contestants. Click on "Contact," and then on "Forum," to access it. Here is where official contestants can share their experiences, ask advice from other candidates and pageant officials, and learn about their experiences. *Miss American Coed* provides a useful pageant forum that is open to prospective and official contestants. Here they can find information on MAC's National Stage Layout, gown rules, information on its National application for candidates who attended a State pageant, what kinds of gifts Princesses exchange with each other, and last, but not least, additional information on attending the National pageant. Posted on March 24, 2010, "New Gown Rules!" had, as of this writing, over 4,500 views! A Forum can be a great support system for prospective and/or official contestants. Stats for MAC's forum visitor log includes the day's viewer count; today (January 22, 2015) that number is 19. It also states that the most viewer usage on a particular day stood at 268 (for January 25, 2014). There were more people visiting the forum at the end of January in 2014 than compared to January of 2015. It may have been that MAC began promoting its State pageants earlier in 2014 than in 2015.

Blog

If you're not already blogging, then create one. You can blog about anything that markets your pageant. For a better understanding, read How to Start a Blog, by Amy Lynn Andrews. Another tutorial is How to Make a Blog—2012—Step by Step for Beginners! by Tyler Moore. When it comes time to start a blog, you will need to decide whether you want to host the blog yourself, or if you want to use a free blogging service that hosts for you. A tutorial on how to make this start is How to Start a Blog: From Topic Choice to Implementation.

Podcast

A podcast is a type of digital media file formatted to be played on the iPod and other MP3 players, hence "podcast." A podcast is downloaded directly from a streaming Internet source. A podcast is distributed on the Internet using syndication feeds, or free-use websites, and is hosted or authored by a podcaster. The media files are downloaded onto a computer, either a home PC or a Mac, and then directly downloaded onto a digital media device like an iPod or other MP3 player. Many people simplify the podcast definition simply by calling it an online, prerecorded radio program over the Internet. *Pageantry Magazine PodCasts* can be viewed by clicking the image or header, at which point, you will be redirected to its corresponding page. *FireFox* and *Safari* internet browsers work best. If you don't see or hear the podcast, you will need to download the latest version of your preferred media player: *Quicktime*, *Windows Media Player*, or *Real Player*. You can also download *Pageantry's PodCasts* for free on *iTunes*. If you're looking for a particular pageant system, type it in the search box, and chances are you'll hear its success story. Your pageant system might be the next featured story!

PageantCast podcaster and host Tim Kretschmann offers some advice if you want to be a featured story:

> If you want to get on *PageantCast*, you can begin by sending or emailing a headshot, an email address for communication, a short bio, your Skype Address (Webcam is now required for remote interviews), and let me know your time zone.

PageantCast is in Central Standard Daylight Savings Time. Be sure to advise Tim if you have times that work best for you. Since there is often a serious backlog, don't be surprised if *PageantCast* has to set the interview out quite a ways into the future. So, how does Mr. Kretschmann determine who appears on *PageantCast*? He tries not to cover a single pageant system and only covers teens and above in female pageants. Often directors contact him, and this generally helps in putting together the final interview.

Message Boards

Porcelain Dolls Nationals director Kathy Raese finds Message Boards to be one of the best places to post her upcoming pageants.

> I purchase top spots at all major boards. My favorite four include *Texas Pageant Board*, *The Hot Spot*, *Bravo*, and *Hip Hip Hooray*.

Kathy isn't kidding. Visit the sites to see her pageant ads — posted right at the top!

Create your own Message Board ads. To learn how, visit *MyBannerMaker.com*. You can create the best banners and buttons, for free, using the banner template creator to build out your website or *Facebook* profile with the latest graphic design layouts.

You can also enlist a message board advertising banner designer like *GlamKIDS.net*. *GlamKIDS*.net is a one stop shop for pageant comp cards, digital portfolios, advertising banners, custom web design, and much more. Work is usually completed within 2–3 days. Banner price includes banner and banner code. GK also offers posting for 30 days, for an additional charge. To view a sampling of pageant systems who enlisted its services, click here. Other quality banner designers and their email addresses include *Glitter Banners* (GlitterBanners@aol.com); *Banners Gone Wild* (bannersgonewild@yahoo.com); *Bee Seen Posting* (lexilou@cox.net); and *Maw's Posting Service* (lu-lu2@cox.net).

Pageant Emporium, an Online Guide to the pageant world, features an alphabetical list of Pageant Message Boards. Other beauty pageant message boards include, but are not limited to: *charmingbelles.com*, *ARK-LA-TEX-OK Natural Pageant Board*, *L.A.T.O. Pageant Tell All Board*, *ourcutebabies*, *Simplicity Pageants Pageant Vendor Classified Message Board*, *Arkansas Pageant Resource*, *Congrats, Ads, and Positive Posts Message Board*, *Do-It-Yourselves Moms' Message Board*, *The Florida Bravo Board*, *Glitter Banners Message Board*, *Michigan Bravo Board*, *Mississippi Pageant Sisters Message Board*, *New York Bravo Message Board*, *Shining Starz*, *Dreamstar USA*, *Louisiana Pageant Opinion Board*, and *Virginia Board*.

Chat Boards

Chat Boards, a.k.a. pageant message boards, are generally for informational purposes only. There are rules to follow when posting, so get your point across without breaking them. For example, no large fonts or large spacing; keep posts short; no repeated (re)postings of messages still on the main page; if you post your pageant, do not let it roll off of the board before posting again — just to name a few. Boards are generally updated within approximately one to two weeks after the current featured pageant has ended. *Porcelain Dolls Nationals* director Kathy Raese noted,

> Chat Boards can be very unnerving and ugly, so don't put too much stock into them.

Some of the Chat Boards Kathy has used included the *Yellow Board*, *Purple Board*, *Green Board*, and *Florida Board*. To give you an example of the number of visitors that viewed the Yellow Board, as of January 2015, it had 2,229,033! Other Chat Boards include Pageant Guru Message Board, Georgia Pageant Discussion Board, Child Beauty Pageants—Just Mommies Message Boards, Arkansas & Missouri Pageant Information Board; Circle of Moms, Charming Belles, Texas Pageant Boards, The Doll Palace Forum, and last, but not least, a Message Board List providing hundreds of other pageant message boards links!

Online News Sources

Online news sources have become a major media player in the world of advertising. We should no longer solely depend on print, radio, and TV media in our pageant marketing efforts since we now have online news sources to help pageant directors get their message out — and usually for *free*. Information regarding Online News Sources can be found in Chapter 9, "Breaking into Media" under "Online News Sources."

Virtual Pageant Program Book

Hearts and Crowns, in 2009, featured a virtual Pageant Program Book (PPB) at its National pageant. The virtual PPB included pictures of every official contestant and was projected during the pageant. After, the Virtual PPB was edited into its pageant DVD. For information about selling virtual ads in your Virtual PPB — including Benefits of Virtual Ads, Packaging of Virtual Ads, and Virtual Ads Company Information Form — visit Chapter 13, "Selling Advertisements" under "Virtual Ads."

Online Pageant Program Book

Supreme Pageant System keeps pageant costs down by "printing" an online Pageant Program Book (PPB). Scroll down the site to view candidates from both their Glitz and Natural pageants. When you arrive at the bottom of the online PPB, click on the "Front Cover Winner," "Centerfold Winner," and "Back Cover Winner" to see who graces these coveted spots.

In my research, I found that many pageant systems posted their official PPB and/or pageant magazines/newsletters on *issuu*, a printable publication site. View the 2012 *Miss Teen World Puerto Rico* online magazine, 2011 *Miss Hispanidad* online PPB, 2012 *Miss Hispanidad USA* PPB, *Miss Asia USA* PPB, *Miss India Holland* pageant magazine, *Miss Brazil Canada* pageant magazine, *Miss Chipao Malaysia 2013* PPB, *Miss Deaf America* pageant newsletter, *Pacific Pageants* pageant magazine, and *Miss Asian America* PPB.

Free Software

Before buying computer software, visit _CNET.com_ and search for the word "free." You'll get a list of free software that you can download. These are just a few of the free software legally available for you to download:

- *GIMP* is a powerful Photoshop replacement.

- *Open Office* is a word processor, spreadsheet, presentation maker, and more. You do not necessarily need to spend money on *Microsoft Office. VLC Media Player* can play almost any piece of video, and it comes with a bevy of video kodacs.

- *VLC* can transcode video and share it over a network.

- *Ad-Aware Free Antivirus* + protects your personal home computer from malware attacks.

- *Avast Free Antivirus* protects your PC against the latest viruses and spyware.

- *AVG Antivirus Free* protects your computer from viruses and malicious programs.

- *Avira Free Antivirus* detects and eliminates viruses.

- *True Image by Acronis* is a backup and recovery program that synchronizes your files in a simple and reliable way.

- *inFlow Inventory Free Edition* keeps track of inventory, from purchasing to sales, with reports and business document creation.

- *Quick Logo Designer* can help you design attractive logos with 2,200 logo templates that you can customize with 5,000 graphics and effects.

- *Sothink Logo Maker Professional* allows you to create awesome logos and vector artworks.

- *doPDF Free PDF Converter* allows you to transform any printable document into PDF format.

- *Primo PDF* enables you to print to PDF from *Windows* applications and optimize the PDF output.

- *Free PDF to Word Converter* allows you to convert PDF files to Word file format.

- *CutePDF Writer* allows you to create *Adobe* PDF files with the push of a button.

- *Google SketchUp* allows you to create 3D models and upload them to *Google Earth*.

- *PDFill PDF Editor* allows you to open, view, edit, and save PDF files without *Adobe Acrobat*.

- *PDFill Free PDF Tools* allows you to combine, split, encrypt, rotate, crop, apply a header to, watermark, and convert PDF files.

- *Easy Flyer Creator* allows you to design flyers, leaflets, and certificates in just five minutes by using built-in templates.

- *PDF4Free* allows you to create and write PDF files, as well as convert other files to PDF format.

- *Project Dogwaffle Free* allows you to express your artistic skills by drawing, sketching, animating, and painting.

- *Adobe FrameMaker Templates: Borders and Tables* allows you to create certificates and documents using specific *FrameMaker* templates.

Chapter 9

Breaking into Media

You can generate thousands of dollars of free advertising if you know what advertising paths to pursue. You are aware of free online publicity options and Internet vehicles, such as blogging, podcasting, and social media, but let's talk hardcopy here. In the years that I have directed pageants, I have bartered for *one hundred percent of my media advertising*. The key is tying various types of media as Official Sponsors. A basic principle of my pageant system has always been to not purchase what can be donated or traded. Do your pageant's bottom line a favor by increasing publicity at little or no cost to you. Learn how to barter for traditional advertising by reading my book *Producing Beauty Pageants: Brokering a Pageant through Barter*, Chapter 6, "Media Partners."

Public Service Announcement

A public service announcement (PSA) — also known as a public service ad — is a message in the public interest disseminated by the media without charge. A good PSA can generate excellent results, at no cost, if accepted by the public affairs department. You cannot use public service announcements to solicit funds; however, you can solicit official contestant participation.

Send your PSA to radio (and TV) stations in the area from which you are recruiting contestants. Remember to send your PSA to colleges and universities. Many have its own radio (and TV) stations. Insider tip: There is a special meaning to a radio newsroom's "Blue Monday." Because staffing is short on weekends, and not much happens on Sunday night, filling up the Monday morning newscast can be a challenge. Your PSA might be most welcome on a Monday morning broadcast.

For the best PSA results, find out the name of the station's PSA director. Learn how much lead time s/he requires in order to be able to include your PSA on the air. Also, know the length that the PSA needs to be and the submittal deadline. Although stations receive frequent requests for public service announcements from national organizations, most are more receptive to local information. Take the time to make the information interesting to the public. It is also wise to include a cover letter that gives some background on your pageant organization.

Radio Stations as Official Sponsors

Radio stations can be retained as Official Sponsors. I approached my first radio station by writing to the General Manager. He invited me to the station to discuss details, after I presented my offer in a brief letter. My request was that the general manager give me 150 thirty-second (:30) recorded commercials to promote my pageant, in exchange for promoting the radio station. I also asked that they provide a station personality to host the pageant. How I bartered thousands of dollars of free radio publicity can be found in my book *Producing Beauty Pageants: Brokering a Pageant through Barter*, Chapter 6, "Media Partners" under "Radio Official Sponsor."

Internet Radio/Podcasts

Some Internet radio stations broadcast 24/7, while others are more accessible like podcasts (via *iTunes*, etc.). Getting sets on such stations or shows is reasonably easy, by comparison, to some of the other formats: Just listen in, spot a gap, and ask. It is perfectly possible to set up your own pageant podcast or to be featured (or sponsored) by an Internet radio station.

College/Non-Profit Radio

Non-profit radio stations are (generally) independent, small concerns where DJs entirely pick their own playlists. Non-profit radio stations (generally) welcome such promotions as a well-run pageant production. Include one in your pageant promotional efforts, especially if you are a non-profit pageant system. Learn more about non-profit pageants by reading my book *Producing Beauty Pageants: Directing a Fundraiser Pageant*.

Community Radio

Apart from music, community radio tends to be intensely local in flavor and have a wide mix of programming. If you have a list of other Official Sponsors that you plan to get onboard with your pageant promotions, and there is a community radio station that you intend to approach for barter, it will help gain their support if they are aware of your current media partners. Learn more about bartering with radio stations (and other media partners) by reading my book *Producing Beauty Pageants: Brokering a Pageant through Barter*, Chapter 6, "Media Partners" under "Radio Official Sponsor."

Internet Talk Radio

Talkzone.com, an Internet talk radio, has a "Pageant Talk Radio" segment. When arriving at the site, you will find hundreds of Queens and pageant directors' stories featured as guests on the roster, along with each appearance date. Other guests include modeling agency owners, success strategists, pageant judges, image consultants, personal trainers, pageant website designers, clothing and swimsuit designers, plastic surgeons, and even a visit by Jamie Kern Lima, creator and CEO of award-winning *It Cosmetics*. Jamie teaches countless pageant winners how to contour their abs with makeup and to use certain lip colors for a whiter smile. Who needs plastic surgery when you can contour your abs with makeup? Fitness experts also appear on various segments to help official contestants whittle their waists with exercise. The beauty of *Talkzone.com* is that every guest featured — and there are hundreds — has a "Click here to visit her/his website." Pageant producers/directors and royalty should make an effort to appear on *Talkzone.com*.

Television and Radio Talk Shows

The marketing impact television and radio talk shows offer proves to be advantageous for all pageant systems. It provides pageant officials with a "live" tool in which to advertise and promote their pageant before, during, and/or after the event. Many pageant systems attribute their success to television and radio talk shows.

Syndicated Newsmagazines

If you DO have a unique angle to your pageant, approach syndicated newsmagazines like *Inside Edition*, *Access Hollywood*, *The Insider*, *Entertainment Tonight*, and *The List* to promote your pageant. Pageants that have a unique angle to its system stand a better chance at being featured in a syndicated newsmagazine. *Miss Plus America* was featured on *The Insider* and *Entertainment Tonight*. Visit *The Insider's* clip *and Entertainment Tonight's* clip to view the segments. MPA was also featured on *Dr. Phil*, *Taboo*, and *The Mike Huckabee Show*. You can often see pageant stories featured on any one of these newsmagazines, including *Inside Edition*. While *Inside Edition* managing editors look for scams, cover-ups, and crime feature stories, a unique pageant story could interest their viewers. Submit your *Inside Edition* story ideas.

Syndicated Appearance

It just so happens that *Inside Edition* correspondent Megan Alexander, a.k.a. Megan Cournoyer, is heavily involved in the pageant industry. Megan and her husband, Brian Cournoyer, have owned State directorship of *National American Miss* Northern and Southern California, Indiana, and Washington, since 2003, under National directors Steve and Kathleen Mayes and Associate Directors Kenn and Lani Maples. In fact, Megan (and her husband) helped the Mayeses and Mapleses form NAM, in 2003, after both sets of National directors abruptly left their respective State directorships at *Miss American Coed*. Additionally, as a child, Megan participated in *Miss American Coed*, under then-MAC State directors Steve and Kathleen Mayes. Megan was even crowned *Miss Washington American Pre-Teen*.

At the conclusion of many NAM pageants — and in her *Inside Edition*-mode — Megan often interviews key NAM pageant officials and titleholders. You can view these videos on *YouTube*. In the October 11, 2012, video "NAM: Interview with Kenn Maples Associate," Megan introduces herself as "Megan Alexander," her *Inside Edition* moniker, and not Megan Cournoyer, her *National American Miss* state director name. Then Megan begins her "interview":

So, Ken, people are watching here right now and they hear the word "Pageant." And they wonder, "What is a pageant?" There is a lot of stereotypes out there in the media. How is NAM different?

Kenn Maples, co-director of NAM, replies:

NAM is very different. We are not a beauty pageant. In fact, less than five minutes ago I had a young lady that's a part of the hotel say to me, "I'm against pageants. But I've been here watching you guys and I'm so impressed. You have completely changed my mind about what the word 'pageants' really means." She says, "You have the most outstanding bunch of ladies that [I've] ever seen." And so we're really excited about the things we're doing with National American Miss with our young ladies. We're dealing with life skills. We're not here for makeup for our little girls.

Megan interjects,

Not allowed to wear it!

During the interview Kenn is wearing a NAM "staff" badge; he is a NAM multi-state director. Megan Alexander, who is also Megan Cournoyer and a NAM multi-state director, isn't. So when the average future prospective contestants view this video, they likely see an "*Inside Edition*" interview featuring *Inside Edition's* Megan Alexander! It might appear to them that they are seeing two sides: a reporter's side and the pageant's side. After all, they probably only know Megan as Megan Alexander of *Inside Edition*, and they likely don't know that she is also Megan Cournoyer, co-director (along with her husband, Bryan Cournoyer) and owner of several NAM State pageants!

Now they are hearing about how positive NAM is from Associate Director Kenn Maples, because Megan Alexander/Cournoyer — the *Inside Edition* reporter — guided the interview into positive pageant territory! This certainly helps to cultivate a positive pageant image, something NAM officials are an expert at.

If you're going to craft an image for your pageant system, learn from the nation's biggest pageant system and expert publicity crafters — NAM — and design a positive one for your pageant! If you don't have Megan Alexander/Cournoyer interviewing your pageant officials or official contestants at your pageant, find a local television host to do the honors. Videotape the segment, and upload it on *YouTube*. Even a local TV personality can help you craft a great image.

Create Your Own Syndicated Newsmagazine Appearance

Megan Alexander was also the correspondent for *Inside Edition's* "Toddler's & Tiaras" episode. Megan is in a position to guide that interview in the direction of her choosing, even angle it to benefit NAM. Another pageant story Megan reported was one about *Miss USA*: "Miss USA Pageant Official Photos Too Sexy?" Another was about *Miss America*: "Miss America Responds to Criticism." Pageant producers who keep their pageant systems in good standing likely won't be featured on *Inside Edition*!

Public Access Television

Public access television is another good medium for promoting your pageant. If your community has cable TV, it probably has public access channels that provide free air time. Cable stations use public access channels to fill up otherwise empty channels and to allow groups and individuals to air their messages. You may be permitted to develop your own program — in this case, produce your pageant — using one or more video cameras at the public access studios. Since the resources aren't large, and your production expertise is probably limited, you'll want to keep anything you produce for public access as simple as possible.

To arrange utilizing public access television, speak to the cable television's program director. You will need to work closely with the program director to develop your project and schedule your air time. It will be worth the effort if your pageant program fits within its guidelines. I can attest that getting a pageant on air through a cable channel works. My first pageant aired bi-weekly, for two months, on our local *Time Warner Cable* station, and the cable company wasn't even an Official Sponsor! Learn how to gain free cable TV airtime by reading my book *Producing Beauty Pageants: Brokering a Pageant through Barter*, Chapter 1, "A Bartered Pageant Production" under "Cable TV Official Sponsor."

If your pageant is aired on television — even a public access television channel — remember to include promotional advertising for your *next* pageant. This can be done by announcing and/or scrolling your website address and phone number on the screen intermittently throughout the show. Interested prospective contestants watching the show can note your contact information.

Public Broadcasting Television

Viewer-supported *Public Broadcasting Television*, *PBS*, is a non-profit public television service. Generally, beauty pageants do not fit into a *PBS* schedule; however, PBS may consider airing a pageant tailored similarly to that of *America's Junior Miss* (now known as *Distinguished Young Women*) where judging standards include scholastic achievement, community service, and concern and involvement in human relations. After all, PBS looks for programs that not only inform, but also inspire and educate, and it helps that DYW is a non-profit pageant system. Find help in creating a non-profit pageant system by reading my book *Producing Beauty Pageants: Directing a Fundraiser Pageant.*

Television Affiliates

Incorporate a network affiliate (or affiliated station) into your promotional efforts. Send your request to the station's general manager/program director, and follow up with a call or visit. Be sure to ask him/her for an appointment to discuss details. If s/he appears reluctant, make him/her aware that, given the opportunity to hear you out, this may be the offer that s/he cannot refuse. *41 WMGT* sponsored the 2010 *Little Mr. & Miss Cherry Blossom Pageant.*

Cable Television

Check with your local cable television station about the possibility of sponsorship. An important advantage of cable television companies is that your pageant can be promoted on more than one network. Since the prices are more comparable to radio than to a network affiliate, trades are easier to arrange.

You can barter for cable advertisements. In Corpus Christi, Texas, *Athena Cablevision* sponsored my Texas pageants with thousands of free commercials, on many local cable stations, including on the local *MTV* affiliate! Learn more about bartering for free cable advertising by reading my book *Producing Beauty Pageants: Brokering a Pageant through Barter*, Chapter 1, "A Bartered Pageant Production" under "Cable TV Official Sponsor."

If your cable advertisements barter agreement doesn't include production, contact a television commercial producer like *Stapp Production* who specializes in Television/Radio Production. SP staff can create television and radio commercials, which includes writing and audio preparation.

Newspapers

Producing beauty pageants is news, perhaps not front-page headline news, but news nonetheless. Beauty pageants have made news since the early 1900s. The thousands of newspaper articles that I found when researching information for this book indicate that pageants are no fading star.

Newspapers as Official Sponsors

A newspaper is an effective medium to secure as an Official Sponsor. Offer the newspaper general manager a similar promotional trade as your radio and TV Official Sponsor. *The Telegraph* became an Official Sponsor for the 2010 *Little Mr. & Miss Cherry Blossom Pageant*. Learn how to secure a newspaper Official Sponsor by reading my book *Producing Beauty Pageants: Brokering a Pageant through Barter*, Chapter 1, "A Bartered Pageant Production" under "Newspaper Official Sponsor" and in Chapter 6, "Media Partners" under "Newspaper Official Sponsor."

High School Newspapers

Remember to send your pageant press release to high school journalism departments. Once you register official contestants from a particular school, take a group picture, and send it to the school newspaper department, along with a press release. Be sure to attention your request to: Journalism Dept.

Calendar of Events

Advertise your pageant in the "Calendar of Events" section of your local paper. Calendars of events are listings of future events specific to your area. Sometimes called "Datebook" or "Community Bulletin Board," it may be helpful in promoting your pageant event. All calendars of events have deadlines — anywhere from a week to three months in advance, depending on the publication. Although it is generally free to the public for inclusion, there is no guarantee that your information will be published. With the ever-growing number of pageants in San Antonio, Texas, a local newspaper created a special section in the Sunday edition called "Pageant News." If your newspaper doesn't have such a section, ask that one be created for you.

Pageant tabloids, newsletters, magazines, and pageant websites often include a calendar in which you can advertise your upcoming pageant. *Pageantry Magazine* has a calendar of pageants at the end of its magazine. The *Pageant Center* includes a pageant calendar where you can promote your pageant. *The Pageant Planet* has a pageant directory that includes a "Pageant Calendar" in the first section of its site, located in the blue box on the right. *Turn for the Judges* includes an "Announcements" section. Scroll down to the "TFTJ Café" and click on "Find Your Perfect Pageant System and Start Winning." On the left side (under "TFTJ News Links"), click on "Pageant Calendar." *Glitzy Girl Magazine* has a "Right Now" section featuring what's going on in the contestants' lives when they are not competing, and if newcomer *Pageant Girl Magazine* doesn't feature a Calendar of Events, just ask.

Press Release

In 1983, I discovered the press release. Up until then I didn't realize that the pictures and blurbs appearing in the paper about local events and people were submitted by the public. I believed that there was a reporter seeking out those stories. The average person doesn't realize that the media needs him/her. Newspapers are constantly looking for stories that it can run. Send press releases to local newspaper editors regardless of whether or not you have them as an Official Sponsor. Remember to also send press releases to high school and college/university newspaper editors. Many publish their own newspapers; some on a weekly, or even a daily basis, and most have online versions.

A press release should be short and to the point: it should include the five W's and one H: Who, What, Where, When, Why, and How. The press release should never exceed two pages, and should always be limited to a single event. Write the press release as if it were going to be published word-for-word in the newspaper. Always read it over, because spell check is not infallible. If you have two pageant events scheduled on different days, write separate releases. Remember that assignment editors file correspondence by date, so always include one.

A press release should contain a release line with the basic information. If the information can be used at once, enter "For Immediate Release" in capital letters near the contact's name. If the information cannot be released immediately, include when you would like the article to be printed. Also, note the date when the PSA may no longer be used. Next, write your attention-grabbing tagline. For tagline ideas, refer back to Chapter 3, "Start Your Own Pageant Business" under "Create Your Pageant Tagline."

One rule that should never be broken is: Type and double space all press releases. The material should contain the name, address, email address, and phone number of your pageant organization, plus a contact person. Include a clear, contrasting picture to help promote your story. Keep the copy simple and clean. Always indicate where the press release ends. Otherwise, a busy editor might wonder whether there was a second page to the release. That is why reporters and writers always indicate the ending of the story with END or # # #. A cover letter should be included with all press releases.

Include photos with your press release, but take care to send high-quality prints. *Miss Hispanidad USA Pageant* permits official contestants' family and friends, at various promotional functions, to take photos to promote the pageant. While pageant officials allow such candidate photos, they permit ABSOLUTELY NO HORNS or photobombs. The last thing a pageant director wants to see in a press release is a horned candidate photo, or worse!

Want-Ad Newspapers

Want-Ad newspapers, such as the *Penny Saver*, *Ad Sack*, and *The Thrifty Nickel*, only print want ads. In my experience, Want-Ad newspapers have been a GREAT pageant marketing vehicle to advertise my pageants. Not only are these newspapers free to the public, but a wide variety of people scan them for bargains. Approach the owner or manager about Official Sponsorship. Imagine the coverage your pageant will realize when a free *Pennysaver* is inserted into the mailbox of every home in your targeted areas! If you place a display advertisement, ask that your ad be positioned on the first or front page of the paper, preferably on the right hand corner. Believe me, it pays to know this, and if there is a "model" category, this might be the place for your classified pageant advertisement. Otherwise, choose the "miscellaneous" category — particularly if it's next to the employment section.

Magazines

A National pageant system placed a non-sponsored, half-page advertisement in *Seventeen* magazine. Prospective contestants, who wanted to learn more about the pageant, were invited to fill out and submit an application. Part of the initial entry requirement for every registrant was to send a $20 photo evaluation/application fee that was refundable if girls didn't "make it" into the pageant. With thousands of girls sending their $20, the advertisement more than paid for itself. But do your homework. Not all magazines will produce successful results. Better yet, offer to trade leads with such magazines. Learn how to barter for magazine leads (and advertisements) by reading my book *Producing Beauty Pageants: Brokering a Pageant through Barter*, Chapter 1, "A Bartered Pageant Production" under "Magazine Official Sponsor" and Chapter 6, "Media Partners" under "Magazine Official or In-Kind Sponsor."

Press Kit

State and National pageant promoters encourage candidates to publicize their participation in the pageant through their community newspapers and online news sites. Pageant officials also provide official contestants with a Press Kit, which usually includes a standard press release, candidate bio, an introductory letter on an official letterhead, and other supporting pageant materials. To gain perspective on how to produce a pageant Press Kit, visit Rhonda Shappert's *Winning Through Pageantry*. Rhonda, the author of *Pageant Secrets* and *10 Insider Secrets to Winning*, provides excellent material on creating your own pageant Press Kit. *Miss Newark Pageant* ten-page *Press Kit* can be found at *issuu*. A quality Press Kit will guide a pageant contender to a successful news release submission.

Miss American Coed reminds official contestants in its newsletter to:

> Get Media Coverage! A Press Release will be sent to you soon. Make several copies of it. Call to make appointments with News Editors of daily and weekly newspapers, radio, and TV stations in your hometown. Wear a nice outfit and take last year's National Program Book and a picture with you.

If you encourage candidates to seek out press promotion in newspapers, radio stations, and TV, include information from this chapter in your press kit.

Via its blog, *National American Miss* reminds official contestants of what they received in their Acceptance Package:

> You all received a press release in your packet #1...I encourage all of you to send it to your news stations, radio stations, and newspapers....and just like Jenny Jones, you could be featured in the news for YOUR ACCOMPLISHMENTS of being selected as an OFFICIAL NATIONAL AMERICAN MISS STATE FINALIST!![18]

In another blog, NAM congratulated the girls "[who] are receiving their acceptance calls!" and then reminded them,

> Don't forget the power of sending out your press release — this is a great tool to help raise sponsors.

---

[18] Maples, Breanne. "Gearing up for summer pageants." NAMISS ROCKS BLOG! http://namissrocks.blogspot.com/2010/05/gearing-up-for-summer-pageantsfirst.html.

National American Miss also posted a clipping of a NAM State Finalist that made the "FRONT page of her local paper!"[19] *National American Miss* certainly knows how to motivate official contestants into nailing free media coverage — all while promoting its pageant system.

Media Kit

A Media Kit is crucial to the success of a National pageant system. While a Press Kit is designed to help individual candidates seek the release of their own personal press, and press for their personal sponsors, a Media Kit is designed to get the media to pick up the pageant's story *and* as an aid in securing and promoting Official Sponsors. A Media Kit can include such pages as: introduction, company profile, mission, history and relevance, press release, judging criteria, the pageant's market demographic, and a pageant brochure. *Miss Plus America* includes a Media Kit on its "About MPA" link. When the drop box appears, click on "Sponsors." To the right, under "Sponsor and Media Kit," is a download link. Although in Spanish, *Miss Latina Dallas'* fourteen-page Media Kit can be found at *issuu*.

High School Yearbook

Remember to advertise late-summer or early-fall pageants in high school yearbooks. Advertising your California State scholarship pageant in several California public high school yearbooks is smart planning. Repeat for every respective State Open Call schedule and State pageant within your system.

Student Directory

A student directory, supported by paid advertisements, lists the names, addresses, email addresses, and phone numbers of participating students. Find out deadline dates and general

[19] "Cournoyer, Megan and Brian. "National American Miss Press Release." Namiss blog. April 13, 2011. http://www.namissblog.com/2011/04/national-american-miss-press-release.html.

information — including potential barter — by contacting the school's journalism department. In addition to high schools, student directories can also be found in most middle schools. A pageant advertisement would be highly visible, for years to come, in such directories.

Specialty Advertising

A smart and inexpensive place to advertise beauty pageants is on emery boards (nail files). A specialty advertising company can print your pageant logo, website address, and phone number on the back. Locate a company by Googling "Specialty Advertising Companies." Other specialty advertising products include pens, hats, Frisbees, t-shirts, key chains, mirrors, cups, etc. For more specialty advertising ideas, visit Chapter 18, "Pageant Boutique."

Network with Other Pageants

Hearts and Crowns Pageant Productions allows other pageants' paperwork to be included in its registration packets for a cost of $50. Payment can also be sent through *PayPal* to HeartsandCrowns@yahoo.com, with a reminder of adding four percent. *Hearts and Crowns* allows pageants to list its pageant information on its Hearts and Crowns Pageant Message Board. They also provide tables for pageant forms and flyers at its pageant event. *American Royalty Pageants* once allowed pageant directors to solicit pageant material at its pageant; however, pageant officials received complaints from official contestants that competing pageant directors were bothering them as they were preparing for competition. Instead, for a fee of $50, ARP will place pageant paperwork (that it is provided) into contestant gift bags. ARP pageant officials also offer competing pageant systems the opportunity to purchase an advertisement in its Pageant Program Book. *American USA Beauty Pageant* warns official contestants and their families that:

> Soliciting of any other pageant system (unless prior approval from American USA director is received) is not allowed. If you [choose] to do so, you will be disqualified without refund.

Pageant Program Books

Generate another pageant income stream by selling Pageant Program Book (PPB) advertisements to other pageant systems. *America's Gorgeous Girls* sells PPB advertisements directly at its "Advertise with Us!" website page. Where possible, purchase an advertisement in various PPBs to promote your pageant. Remember to include your own pageant advertisement that promotes your next pageant event *in your own* PPB! Offer to barter with other pageant directors for PPB ad space. Learn to barter for PPB advertising by reading my book *Producing Beauty Pageants: Brokering a Pageant through Barter*, Chapter 9, "In-Kind Sponsors" under "Pageant Program Book."

Online News Sources

You can begin greasing your pageant publicity wheels by sending your pageant press releases to a variety of free online press release news sources and business directories. *International East Coast Pageants* uploaded its pageant press release on *Classified Ads.com*. On the left side of the post, a viewer could read that the press release was posted on November 15, 2011, updated on December 31, 2011, and expired on September 13, 2012. One year of free advertising is what this pageant system gained from this free posting. Furthermore, a contact person and telephone number was included on the left side. By the time the post expired, there were over 500 views on this one free site alone! Smartly, pageant officials included a listing of the entire year's pageant events and its website address — a free one created by using *Wix.com*. It would have been better if a link to its website was included, instead of just a website address.

There are many free online sites to submit your pageant promotional material. To get your pageant post out, advertise your pageant on free online classified sites such as the *Chandler & Brownsboro Statesman*, as did *Sunburst Beauty Pageants*. UK's *Miss England* sent a press release promoting its 2012 event to this edition of *starnow*. By the summer of 2012, there were nearly 9,000 views at the free post! (To view most of the pageants' press releases, click on the online newspaper link provided next to its names.) *Miss Nigeria* promoted pageant entries at *Beauty Pageant News*; a press release that promoted a *National*

American Miss pageant was uploaded at *thepress.net*; NAM had another pageant story featured in this edition of *Edmond Life & Leisure*; *Miss American Coed* promoted its pageant in *AllEvents.in*. Notice, under the site heading (*AllEvents.in*), the dozen cities you can reach, so be sure to send a separate release to each listing if you want to reach those cities. NAM also posted at *Free Press Release*; *Cutie Pie Glitz Pageant* promoted its pageant at *auditionsfree.com*; *International Pageant Productions* submitted its pageant press release to *Free Press Release*; *Altamaha Southern Miss Pageant* posted its press release on *brycancountynews.net*; *Miss India UK* posted its pageant press release at *The Free Library*; *Little Miss African American Scholarship Pageant* sent its pageant registration press release to *Kickmag*; *Indian Princess Pageant* posted its press release at *Free Press Release*; *Miss Priss Pageant* posted its press release at *Family & Kids Community Digest*; UK Pageant directors can look into posting its pageant information on *uk.starsinmyeyes.tv*; *Little Miss and Mr. Las Vegas Beauty Pageant* promoted its event at *Free Press Release*; *Miss Beautiful Princess UK* promoted its pageant at *starnow*; and *Miss Black Africa UK* and *Face of Europe* sent pageant press releases to *Auditions and Casting Calls*.

Free Online Classifieds

Advertise your pageant on these FREE online classified sites, as did *Candy Kiss USA Pageant System, LTD*: *My AdMonster.com Free Classified Ads*; *FreeAdvertising4.com*; *USA BizBook.com*; *iLeeg.com Free Local Classifieds*; *BloomingtonSuperAds.com*; *BoiseSuperAds.com*; *Socializr*; *ClassifiedAds.com*; *Pittsburgh City Paper*; *Event Monsters*; *CommunityHotline.com*; *Classifieds Earth*; *Advanya Free Classifieds*; *50 States Classifieds.com*; *Quick Ads Now* ; *Reminder News*; and *Close By Me*.

The list goes on. In fact, other online sites *Candy Kiss USA Pageant System* advertised on included: *USNetAds.com*; *Hoobly.com*; *Univision.com* (a free Spanish classifieds site); *adsglobe.com*; *Free Advertising Online of Connecticut*; *Classifieds Ad Board*; *ebay classifieds*; *bigclassified.com*; *Best Way Classifieds.com*; *Pennysaver USA.com*; *Myadsclassified.com*; *sell.com*; *CommunityHotline.com*; *USMarketAds.com*; *USMarketDB.com* (*Twitter* version); *freeadlists.com*; *Locanto.com*; *backpage.com*; *FreeAdsCity.com*;

ZeroCostClassifieds.com; *NY ClassifiedAds.com*; *NYC Pennysavers.com*; *BigClassifieds.com*; and last, but not least, *USFreeads.com*.

If you are looking for even more free places to advertise your pageant, look no further. *The Grandfather of All Links* has been gathering free advertising sites since 1994. It updates its site several times a month, removing bad links and adding new ones. Better yet, don't waste time submitting sites by hand. Use its Cyberfetch Submitter software, or use its Advertising Services. Drive prospective contestants to your pageant website by making it findable. Professional search engine submission can be your solution if you want a fast presence across the web for your pageant website.

Social Media Site Value

If you think posting on free classifieds might be a waste of time, consider, for example, that a site like *USMarketAds* is very popular on *Twitter* and *StumbleUpon*, with nearly 9,000 *Twitter* shares as of this writing. According to *CoolSocial.net*, a website social media analyzer, *UsMarketAds* scored a 59 on Social Media Impact. A Social Media Impact Score is a measure of how much a site is popular on social networks, and it gave this site a 3 out of 5 stars. *USFreeads* scored an 82% on Social Media Impact across the following: *Facebook*, *StumbleUpon*, *Twitter*, *Delicious*, and *Google Plus*. It is liked by 487 people on *Facebook*; it has 126 *Twitter* shares; and it has 11 *Google Plus* shares. The Social Team scored it a 4 ½ out of 5 stars. You can check any social media site at CoolSocial.com.

Free Online Business Directory

Promote your pageant system in online business directories. It's an opportunity for you to tell the world who you are and what you do differently. The Ultimate List: 50 Local Business Directories is a great resource to use in order to compile a list of directories in which to list your business.

Hotfrog, a global company based in Sydney, Australia, is a tool for you to create demand for your pageant business from within business directories. *Hotfrog* can help you to convey exactly what's different about your pageant system and help you to put its unique approach in front of prospective contestants searching online. People search online for all kinds of products and services every day — beauty pageants included. The keywords you choose for your profile are matched to the words prospective contestants enter into search engines. Your business stands to rank higher because *Hotfrog's* aim is to help get your pageant website listed in Google's search results. Registration takes less than five minutes, and it's free, so add as much detail to your profile as you want. You can even create coupons to incent prospective contestants into visiting your pageant website or attending your Open Call. Learn more about promoting Open Call by reading my book *Producing Beauty Pageants: Open Call*, Chapter 7, "Promote Open Call."

You can find other top places to list your pageant system at the *Vertical Response* blogsite's article, *The Top 20 Places Your Business Needs to Be Listed Online*. The ones most ideal for a pageant system include:

Google

Listing your pageant system on *Google Places for Business* should be at the top of your priority. *Google* outperforms every other search engine. Registering for a business listing on *Google* is easy and free. Business listings appear in *Google Maps*, and happy customers can leave reviews on your *Google Plus* page. Create you *Google Places for Business* listing by clicking here.

Bing

Bing is the second most visited search engine on the Internet. If people aren't searching on *Google*, chances are they're searching for your pageant business on *Bing*. Create an account on *Bing Places for Business*, and then create your *Bing Places for Business* listing.

Yahoo!

Yahoo is the Internet's third most popular search engine, bringing in millions of searches per day. A *Yahoo Local Basic* listing is free. Create your *Yahoo Local* listing by clicking here.

Yelp

Yelp is probably the best place on the Internet for prospective contestants to find a quality review. If you're looking to tap into the word-of-mouth advertising world, then *Yelp* is the place to start. Create your *Yelp* listing by clicking here.

MerchantCircle

MerchantCircle is an online directory that helps small businesses connect with local customers and other local small businesses. It offers free marketing tools to help build your pageant system.

Yellow Pages

Yellow Pages is the online version of a modern day phone book and allows you to list your business in an organized directory. Create your *Yellow Pages* listing by clicking here.

White Pages

White Pages is the online equivalent of the white pages in a phone book, and it's a great way to make your business contact information available to over 200 million people. Create your *White Pages* listing by clicking here.

Superpages.com

Superpages.com is another online directory. It includes unique features like cars for sale, lottery results, and helpful tips for finding business services. It also places the local weather listings right on the home page along with a *Facebook* sign-in option. Create your *Superpages* listing by clicking here.

Foursquare

Not only is *Foursquare* a popular business directory, it's a popular social networking site. It can be connected to your *Twitter* so prospective and official contestants can Tweet you. Prospective contestants can also check in and comment on your pageant system — ultimately leading them to become official contestants by participating in your pageant. *Miss American Coed* is a *Foursquare* fan. Create your *Foursquare* listing by clicking here.

DexKnows

DexKnows is a popular online directory that not only allows a business listing; it also provides a way for you to track how your customers engage with your profile, thus allowing you to track your online reputation. This detailed information is available through reporting tools, which allows a pageant system to monitor its ratings and reviews. Create your *DexKnows* listing by clicking here.

Becoming Your Own Public Relations Agent

Now is the best time to become your own public relations (PR) agent and generate significant, positive exposure. Begin by gathering names and addresses of Local and National editors and reporters. Then, use Social Media to your advantage. To better assist you with your free PR campaign, read *Free Publicity 101* by Cathy Stucker and the *Kindle* Edition of *Power Publicity: How to Get Rich and Famous With Free Press Coverage* by Sheil Danzig.

Chapter 10

Prizes and Awards

Having an impressive list of awards and prizes for everyone attracts a more diverse and larger group of candidates. In a Local or Preliminary pageant, the major objective for most candidates is to win the title and continue competing in the ensuing State or National pageant. Nevertheless, it is important that you arrange an array of gifts for the Runners-Up and for each official contestant. All candidates — not just the winner — should be compensated for their hard work. Awarding special titles and corresponding trophies or medals, at the very least, makes more (if not all) candidates feel special. You can attract a better group of contestants if you have an impressive list of prizes for everyone. Prospective contestants are more likely to enter the pageant if they know that they will receive something even if they don't win the crown. Be sure to spread these gifts out so that several contestants receive some type of award. Gift packs for each official contestant are easy to assemble. It can include items such as suntan lotion, panty hose, lipstick, movie passes, shampoo, costume jewelry, and other items local stores or cosmetic companies donate. Because awards are important to candidates, begin arranging your list early. Learn how to barter for prizes by reading my book *Producing Beauty Pageants: Brokering a Pageant through Barter*, Chapter 7, "Barter Your Prize Package" and Chapter 9, "In-Kind Sponsors." But, before reading this book, strongly cement your prize foundation by reading my other book *Producing Beauty Pageants: Creating a Synergized National Pageant System*, Chapter 3, "Prize Structure."

Most Popular and Least Popular Prizes

R.D. "Bob" Marshall of the *International Pageant Group and Production Committee* (and former editor and publisher of out-of-print *Pageant Review*), in the early '90s, did research through his TQ Club Questionnaires. It was discovered that the most-wanted prizes included cash (number one by all results), followed by scholarships, portfolios, screening tests, trips, large trophies, tiaras, clothing, and jewelry. The least-wanted prizes included scepters, photos, banners, flowers, luggage, and small appliances. Of the appliances, TVs and VCRs were more desired than others, such as radios. Now, computers and iPads would top that prize list!

As a rule of thumb, Mr. Marshall recommended that parents find pageants that offer prizes that equal the amount of money it costs to enter. At the same time, he doesn't fault pageants that offer less of a prize package. After all, pageants exist for vanity, ego, and/or fun.[20]

Mr. Marshall suggested that pageant directors combine the more-desirable awards with the lesser ones. Arrange the awarding so that more candidates obtain an award (even if it's a small trophy). Include an Overall Winner (of all ages) who will receive the major award — the most sought after one. Mr. Marshall also made one additional suggestion: Where automobiles or large awards are involved, use them as a door prize rather than as an award. This way, all official contestants will have a chance at winning. This makes for a much better pageant because all candidates are entered into the free drawing and will feel closely related to the event taking place.

National American Miss agrees. Rather than present a *Ford Mustang* to a single pageant winner, NAM includes every National-qualifying candidate (who are present) into the drawing. Additionally, NAM noted their odds of winning:

> [NAM] expects anywhere from 400–800 National Participants at the 2011 National American Miss pageant finals, but the actual number may exceed those estimates.

View NAM's "National American Miss' Ford Mustang Convertible Drawing Rules." A car giveaway promotional piece can be found in NAM's 2014 Experience National American Miss Open Call take-home DVD. Understand how the "Silent

---

[20] Reinhard, Katherine. "Pageant Price Tags Are Not Pin-sized Parents Pay Top Dollar So Kids Can Compete." *The Morning Call*, March 18, 1991, http://articles.mcall.com/1991-03-18/features/2780423_1_international-pageant-group-miss-daughter.

Salesman" works in this DVD by reading my book *Producing Beauty Pageants: Open Call*, Chapter 5, "The Silent Salesman... and Other Subliminal Messengers."

As a group project at your Pageant Workshop, ask official contestants what prizes would entice them to compete again if they did not win the title the first time. This is an excellent way of finding out what awards will influence alumnae to recompete. *Universal Royalty* surveyed prospective and official contestants (on its *Facebook* post) to find out — in the event they should win the Ultimate Grand Supreme title — if they would prefer to win $10,000 cash or a car. Forty-two official contestants and/or parents responded to the survey. From those respondents, 95% percent chose the cash! One responder replied,

> Cash — Taxes will have to be paid on both, but at least the winner will have an option on what [she] would like to spend the leftover cash on.

Another replied,

> Cash, unless money is provided for the taxes on [the car].

However, if you've received a *Ford Mustang* via barter, as does NAM, since 2003, you don't look a gift horse in the mouth. Keep your cash reserves, and barter for a car to raffle or to present as a Queen's prize. Learn more about bartering for a car by reading my book *Producing Beauty Pageants: Brokering a Pageant through Barter*, Chapter 8, "Vavoom and Varoom."

Cash — Popular While it Lasts

National American Miss State Queens win a $1,000 cash award. It looks GREAT on pageant paperwork — NAM State Queens winning a $1,000 cash award. Many prospective contestants even think it's a college scholarship! NAM even provides [all cash awards] to the recipient with an admonishment to use the funds for their education![21]

---

[21] Kessler, Glenn. "National American Miss pageant: Fact checking its award claim." *The Washington Post*, May 25, 2015. https://www.washingtonpost.com/news/fact-checker/wp/2015/05/25/national-american-miss-pageant-fact-checking-its-award-claims/.

But, let's look at NAM's pageant model structure. NAM State Queens win their $795 entry fee waived for the National pageant, $350 for transportation expenses to (but not likely from) the National pageant in Anaheim, California, a *John Robert Powers School Systems* scholarship, two VIP tickets to *Disneyland*, and $1,000 cash.

This cleverly-designed prize package is calculated to get the winning State Queens to the National pageant — *before they pay taxes on this prize package*. But, more on that later.

NAM State Queens are on their own to pay their approximately $1,000 hotel tab at the National pageant. But wait — they just won $1,000! Now, every NAM State Queen can make it to the National pageant in November with their free airfare *and* prize money to pay their $1,000 hotel bill! Remember — this is before the taxman reaches in to grab his share of the winner's prize package (come the 15th)! NAM certainly was clever in designing its State Queens prize package.

So, when NAM State Finalist (official contestant) Aisha Williams noted on her *sponsor goal* fundraising page,

> If I win the NAMISS pageant I will receive $1,000 that I will put toward my college funds.

NAM State Queen mother Beth Anne countered,

> When you win, NAM hands you a check for $1,000 and $300 for your child's airfare to the National pageant. But, the kicker is NAM structures its event so that you are in a hotel for seven nights and the $1,000 is gone right there.[22]

Many prospective and official contestants think that the hotel expenses for the NAM *State* Queens — going into the National pageant — is paid for by pageant officials. NAM official contestant Dava C. was one such believer:

> [NAM will] pay for your airfare and your hotel-ing [sic][23]

Here is an example from another:

---

[22] email. December 6, 2012.

[23] LeRoy, Bridget. "Dava on the Runway." *The East Hampton Star*, August 11, 2011. http://www.easthamptonstar.com/?q=Education/2011811/Dava-Runway.

[the] winner in each category receives a six-night stay at the host hotel...[24]

...if you become a State Queen and advance to the National pageant.

NAM State Queens *don't* win their hotel expenses paid at National — unless they earn a hotel stay for one night or more, depending on the number of $600[25] ad pages they sold in the State Pageant Program Book (PPB), and *if* they chose the hotel as their prize.

An official contestant need not be a State Queen to shoot for that goal. But, she would need to sell two $600[26] page ads — $1,200[27] — in the State PPB for a guaranteed qualification to participate in the National pageant. She would still need to secure a $795 National sponsorship fee and pay the required $80 for an Opening Number outfit. And, then there's the hotel expense — never mind Optionals!

The question a pageant producer should ask himself/herself is: Will the cash prize benefit the winner? If not, consider giving Queens a bigger payout.

Winners' Taxes

National American Miss State Queens better save all of the cash part of their prize package because, come April 15th of the following year, they will need to pay taxes on ALL of their winnings.

NAM State Queen winnings, as you are aware, consist of the $795 paid entry to the National pageant; $350 airfare; a *John Robert Powers School Systems* scholarship likely valued at $1,000; two *Disneyland* tickets (around $200 in value); and $1,000 cash. The cash "value" will dwindle to about $500 after the

---

[24] Halm, Julie. "Student to compete in National American Miss pageant." *Lancaster/Depew Bee*, June 6, 2013. http://m.lancasterbee.com/news/2013-06-06/Local_News/Student_to_compete_in_National_American_Miss_pagea.htm l.

[25] It went up to $750, in 2014.

[26] In 2014, *National American Miss* increased full ad pages to $750.

[27] In 2014, it totaled $1,500.

winner pays taxes — less if she doesn't decline the pricey *John Robert Powers School System* scholarship! It's not clear if she will be responsible for the taxes on the "hotel expenses paid to attend the following year's pageant to crown [her] successor."[28] Assume that she will be responsible for those taxes because the "[hotel] expenses paid to attend the following year's pageant to crown your successor" is listed as a major prize in the Queen's prize package; it's in writing for the IRS to see. Since it's in writing, NAM pageant officials are likely not required to pay barter taxes on that hotel expense if they did, indeed, barter for that "prize;" however, if NAM pageant officials did pay for them, then they would still write it off. Either way, all State Queens will need to declare it as part of their winnings... and pay taxes.

How much winners will pay in taxes depends on what state they live in; however, it's likely that they'll pay nearly half of the total package value. And, if a NAM Queen participated in ad sales and won any prizes from the *non-bulleted prize list* noted in NAM's Magazine #1, page 4, she would need to carve out an even bigger chunk from that already-dwindled $1,000 cash prize to pay taxes. She might end up having to *raise* money to pay those taxes just to keep those prizes! There goes the $1,000 cash prize to pay for the week's hotel stay at National — never mind NAM's "admonishment to use the funds for [the winning recipients'] education."[29]

If you're rushing the herd through Open Call, then don't count on candidates reading the fine print and complete financial disclosures in your pageant marketing materials before they sign a legally-binding contract: the Official Application. It would behoove pageant officials to verbally inform official contestants, at Open Call, and before parents and prospective contestants sign the contract (Official Application), to be prepared to put aside cash to pay taxes should they win *any* prize package valued at $600 or more. (And yes, even the waived $750 entry fee to the National pageant will be taxed).

If you're a non-Open Call pageant system, highlight (in yellow) this financial disclosure, and, in your Official Contestant

---

[28] National American Miss Magazine #1, 2014.

[29] Kesslar, Glenn. "National American Miss pageant: Fact checking its award claims." The Fact Checker, *The Washington Post*, May 25, 2015. https://www.washingtonpost.com/news/fact-checker/wp/2015/05/25/national-american-miss-pageant-fact-checking-its-award-claims/.

Handbook (or magazine), include a table of contents directing readers to that precise tax information page.

When presenting any prize package to winners, inform them (verbally and in writing) of their impending tax bill — *before* they accept the prize package and spend the cash on *part* of her hotel room expense at your National pageant. Allow winners the opportunity to decline any part of their prize package to avoid a large tax bill. At the very least, allow winners the option of putting aside their respective $1,000 cash prize (or whatever cash prize you offer) to pay income taxes — at the expense of their participation in the National pageant and paying for their week-long, $1,000 hotel bill! Fill in her spot with an Appointed Representative Program (ARP) girl! Learn more about developing your own Appointed Title Program by reading my book *Producing Beauty Pageants: Creating a Synergized National Pageant System*, Chapter 6, "Appointed Titles Program and National Qualifying Avenues."

Pageant producers who give away paid entry fees (waived) into their National pageant to *each* of their State winners, on the other hand, receive a HUGE tax write off that enables them to preserve more of the cash that they *do* earn. Entrepreneurship certainly has its benefits.

Declaring Prizes

Official contestants need to know that they will need to declare any prize(s) they win. It's not just cash that will be taxed. Winners will pay taxes on the fair market value of any property they win, even if it is less than $600. So, official contestants will need to be prepared to come up with the cash needed to pay taxes due on cash and non-cash prizes, for the year which it was presented. If a State winner's prize package is valued at more than $5,000, the sponsor must withhold 25 percent of the prize value for federal taxes and may have to withhold state taxes as well. A huge chunk of a $1,000 cash prize will already disappear from the start.

If a candidate wins a car, or other expensive merchandise, she may be required to give the sponsor (car dealership if it is the donor) cash to pay the federal tax withholding before the sponsor will release the non-cash prize to her. For example, if a candidate won a $25,000 car, she may have to give the sponsor $6,250 for the federal tax withholding before the sponsor will give her the car. She may also have to pay the state withholding up front. It would behoove all pageant producers to have an accountant doing their taxes in order to keep pageant winners current on the ever-changing tax laws.

Prizes and awards will increase a candidate's tax bill, but the question of how much tax she will ultimately need to pay depends on the value of her winnings and the amount of her other income. Prizes are taxed as ordinary income. (Sometimes a pageant director will include a cash award to help cover taxes on the prize, but the cash is *also* taxable income to the winner.) Winners residing in the thirty-nine states that impose a state tax will also be required to pay a state income tax. If an official contestant wins in a state where the prize is taxable, a tax return must be filed with that state. Winners can avoid all taxes on a prize if they refuse to accept the prize(s). The title, however, is tax-free!

Coastal Pageant Productions states on its 97.3 KISSFM *Little Miss & Teen Miss St. Patrick's Day* entry form,

> Any valuation of the prize(s) is based on available information provided to the Company, and the value of the prize awarded to a winner may be reported for tax purposes as required by law. Each winner is solely responsible for reporting and paying any and all applicable taxes. Each winner must provide the Company with valid identification and a valid taxpayer identification number or Social Security number before any prize will be awarded. Prizes are not transferable, redeemable for cash, or exchangeable for any other prize. Any person winning over $600 in prizes from a station will receive an IRS form 1099[B] at the end of the calendar year and a copy of such form will be filed with the IRS.

Kudos to CPP for including this important legal tax information, in writing, with the first form (contract) that a prospective contestant receives: the Official Application. And, more kudos to CPP for providing copies of the Official Application to the prospective contestants *before* they pay any part of the entry fee.

Winners Planning for their Tax Bill

In the event that they do win cash and prizes, help official contestants plan for their tax bill in order to optimize their winnings. Remind candidates to save all expense receipts, such as their preparation costs such as competition outfits, accessories, makeup and hair expenses, and pageant costs such as coaching, entry fees (if they paid for it themselves), Optionals fees, mandatory fees, registration fees, Check-In fees (if different), hotel room expenses, traveling expenses, photo and video package fees, etc., for the calendar year. It is my understanding that they can deduct these costs from their winnings and reduce their tax bill.

Say a pageant winner agrees to accept a prize of a four-year college scholarship to a not-so-popular university, valued at $80,000. She signs for the prize, and then chooses not to attend the university. She may still be required to pay income tax on the non-cash $80,000 scholarship prize, whether or not she used the prize that she accepted. She could face serious penalties if she accepted the prize and couldn't pay the taxes. It would behoove pageant directors to provide prospective contestants with a clear definition of their prize package's tax ramifications. They should also advise official contestants, in writing, to put aside cash to pay taxes on those prizes. Additionally, remind candidates that if they win, they can *decline* a prize they don't deem worthy of paying taxes on. Often, the prize cannot be sold, even on *eBay*, for the amount needed to pay the tax bill!

The "Miscellaneous" or "Asterisked" Part

The "miscellaneous" part of the *97.3 KISSFM/Little Miss & Teen Miss St. Patrick's Day* Entry Form states, "No purchase necessary to participate or win." If the entry fee for the pageant is $75 [plus Optionals], the "No purchase necessary to participate or win" statement should *not* be included in the "Description of Contest/Participation." A pageant producer wouldn't want to provide a refund to every candidate, due to what appears as a contractual gaffe, since a purchase *is* necessary to participate and win, because a sponsorship/entry fee is just that.

The "asterisked" part of *National American Miss'* "It's YOUR time to Shine!" undated brochure leads prospective contestants to www.namiss.com/car for its *Ford Mustang* drawing details. When you arrive to the site and click on the National American Miss' Ford Mustang Convertible Drawing Rules box on the upper left corner, rule #3 states, "NO PURCHASE NECESSARY TO WIN," but rule #4, the ELIGIBILITY rule, states:

> Drawing is open only to persons who, according to
> the pageant rules for the National American Miss,

are qualified for and participate[30] in the 2015 National Finals of the National American Miss pageant (the "Finals").

However, on the 2016 "This year's grand prize is a New Ford Mustang Convertible, to be given out live via webstream in a random drawing among all girls who are in attendance. How awesome is that?!" flyer, it states:

All you have to do is qualify for Nationals at your [State] level competition, and then attend the drawing at Nationals!"

There isn't any mention of needing to participate in "the Finals." To participate in the National pageant, in 2016, a girl would need to raise a $795 sponsorship/entry fee and pay an $80 Opening Number outfit fee. Maybe NAM meant that girls could, at minimum, only participate via the paid Optionals, or by selling ads in their Pageant Program Book, in their quest to earn guaranteed National Cover Titles, and *then* be qualified to partake in the *Ford Mustang* drawing. It's quite possible that girls could "qualify for and participate in the [year] National Finals of the National American Miss pageant" by participating in any one of the free National Optionals: Academic Achievement, Art Contest, Best Thank You Note, Volunteer Service, National Scrapbook Contest, Best Résumé, and Most Promising Model. Regarding the Most Promising Model free Optional, in order to qualify, candidates need to pay for Photogenic **and** Casual Wear Modeling Optionals — each at $175! If so, once those girls qualify for the National pageant, at their State pageant, all they would need to do is show up on the *Ford Mustang* drawing day, fill out a Participation Order Form at Check-In, turn in their Volunteer sheet, and be present for the drawing. They won't even need to book an overnight hotel room; however, they would need to arrange for their own transportation — from wherever state they hail from.

Social Security Number

A Social Security Number (SSN) is a form of identification (like an account name), not an authentication (like a password). A pageant

---

[30] Emboldened and italicized by author.

director will require that candidates provide a Social Security number, in the event they win a prize in the amount of $600 or more.

Don't ask for candidates' SSN number until after they check-in at the pageant event, or, if possible, only ask the winner after she is chosen — as does Kathy Raese, producer of *Heavenly Angels* and *Porcelain Dolls Nationals*. And, certainly don't ask that candidates write it down on an Official Application that needs to be submitted online, handed in-person to a pageant official or volunteer, or via the mail! Asking that every prospective or official contestant write down her Social Security Number (or the last four digits), in our identity-theft world, is ludicrous. In the case of asking for the last four digits, it's NOT a password to validate the identity of the contestant.

Depending on when the Social Security Number was issued, it may follow a pattern which could make it easy for an identity thief to make an educated guess (to fill in the blanks), if the last four digits are given. In the AAA-BB-CCCC Social Security number format, the AAA is a number that represents the state in which a person applied for the SSN. If your SSN starts with 530, that is a number specific to Nevada. If you applied in New Mexico, the number is 525. So, if a candidate stated her last four digits, and she was born in Nevada, an identify thief will only require ninety-nine guesses to *guarantee* that s/he will predict her SSN. The second group of digits (BB) is handed out in a semi-sequential, chronological order. A good explanation of how these numbers are issued is provided in the "GROUP NUMBER" section at *Structure of Social Security Numbers*.

Both *National American Miss* and *Porcelain Dolls Nationals* give away cars at their National pageants. *National American Miss* and *National All-American Miss* National candidates were asked to write their complete SSN on the 2012 National Official Application; it wasn't asked on its State Official Application.

While official contestants are forewarned to be prepared to show their Social Security number at the *Porcelain Dolls Nationals* pageant, PDN doesn't ask for it on its National application. Candidates are forewarned, however, to bring their Social Security numbers to the National pageant to present during check-in. At the pageant's conclusion, paperwork featuring candidates' SSN's is shredded.

Miss Growing In Grace asks (at the top of its Application Packet) that official contestants write only their "LAST 4 DIGITS SSN#."

Universal Glitz N Glamour Pageant doesn't require Social Security numbers on an Official Application, but reminds the parents of the candidates to,

> Please bring your child's Social Security Number to crowning. *If* your child wins an award of $600 or more, you must fill out a W-9 to receive the award. Contestants agree as a condition of entering the pageant that the prize winner is responsible for any and all taxes associated with their receipt of the prize.

Learn more about barter taxes (and other legal aspects of barter) by reading my book *Producing Beauty Pageants: Brokering a Pageant through Barter*, Chapter 11, "Legal Aspects of Barter."

Structure, Secure, and Award Your Prize Package

There are pageant directors who offer huge prize packages — often in the range of thousands of dollars — but who never award them. Any promise to official contestants, written or verbal, should stand. It's often the director's intention to give out big prizes only to find out, at the last moment, that s/he cannot afford them or get them sponsored, or worse, the Official Sponsor who promised prizes never had intentions of awarding them.

America's National Teenager Scholarship Organization, whose tuition scholarships are awarded by named institutions which provide the terms and provisions for its use by recipients, states,

> ANTSO (its State and National directors) [have] no control over such scholarships and its terms.

If pageant officials secure the tuition prize for their winner(s), and upholds their end of the barter bargain with the named institution, and *still* the institution does not honor the tuition prize for the winner, in my opinion, a pageant promoter who arranged and stated the prize in writing is responsible for the prize value. But, most pageant directors don't choose this default plan, and it is spelled out in the Rules & Regulations, as in *Miss Angelic Queen*'s R&Rs:

> Sponsors are responsible for their donations. WE CANNOT ACCEPT RESPONSIBILILTY FOR THE REDEMPTION OF SPONSOR PRIZES. IF YOU HAVE PROBLEMS CLAIMING A PRIZE, PLEASE REPORT IT TO OUR OFFICES SO THAT WE CAN CONTACT THE SPONSOR AND/OR REMOVE THE PRIZE FROM OUR SPONSOR LIST. Sponsor prizes must be viewed strictly as bonuses. They are not a part of the official Miss Angelic Queen prize package.

If the sponsored prizes are "viewed strictly as bonuses" and are "not a part of the official prize package," then *don't* list them on the Queen's prize package. Then, you won't need to "remove the prize from [the] sponsor list." Don't set yourself up for a bait and switch tactic from the start.

Miss Bright Star of America states,

> All prizes and awards are subject to fulfillment by the sponsors. *Miss Bright Star of America* pageant and its producers assume no responsibility for the failure of the sponsors to fulfill their commitment.

USA's Pageant will (at least) substitute another prize of equal value, should a sponsor not come through with a promised prize or award:

> *USA's Pageants, Inc.* is not responsible for the failure of sponsors to provide promised awards and prizes. *USA's Pageants* reserves the right to substitute another prize of equal value, if a specified prize becomes unavailable.

These "prize loopholes" aren't what official contestants expected when they signed up. It is NOT the responsibility of the pageant winner to chase down the prize; it's the pageant director's. Then, if necessary, the pageant director can take legal action against the Official Sponsor. Candidates deserve the prizes they were promised when they entered the pageant. Cencio Cahilig, director of _Miss Philippines USA_, in 1977, stated,

> Often, it's not knowing what [sic] we're going to come through with prizes.

Know what you actually have by structuring (in writing) and securing (in possession) your Queen's prize package *before* you begin promoting your pageant. Otherwise, have a legal backup plan in place.

Porcelain Dolls Nationals, *Dream Girls USA*, and *America's Grand Miss National*, on the other hand, state,

All prizes are guaranteed.

Learn the pros and cons of *National American Miss'* prize structure by reading my book *Producing Beauty Pageants: Creating a Synergized National Pageant System*, Chapter 3, "Prize Structure."

Prize Contribution Link on Your Pageant Website

When you begin securing your prize package, include a prize contribution link on your pageant website. One never knows when a company or individual might desire or want to donate products to the winners and/or all official contestants. *Miss Black Georgia USA* includes a contact email link for any person, business, or organization wanting to contribute prizes to the pageant system.

But, just don't start with your website. Begin promoting your prize contribution needs at the Google search site browser. When you Google "Contact/Miss California USA," the keywords that a searcher first sees, even before clicking on their site, are:

HELLO! LET'S TALK. If you would like to talk to us about a sponsorship opportunity or you have a question about the upcoming state pageant, please get in touch.

Wow — such gripping, bold keywords. This message, in itself, has a great chance of linking intrigued web surfers right to *Miss California USA*'s page. While the message is vague (is it referring to sponsors for an official contestant or to sponsor gifts for the Queen's prize package?), a *Send USA Message* page asks for your name, email address, subject, and includes lines to write a message. Any business wanting to associate its product or service with the *Miss California USA* pageant can present its offer right here and hit the submit button. Like *Miss California USA*, include a prize contribution link for people to sponsor products or services.

State Your Prize Package

Prospective contestants want to know what the Queen's prize package will be *before* they commit to a pageant. Knowing that there is a valuable prize package for the winner can greatly increase the number of participants — especially if they, according to a popular pageant-critiquing website, have a "lottery mentality." It's no wonder Miss Texas USA has hundreds of participants every year — the winner's prize package is valued at over $90,000!

Pacific Miss Asian American Beauty Pageant, for its 2011 event, spread the prize package between the winner and two Runners-Up. The winner received $10,000 cash, a CHOUETTE watch valued at $1,850, an *Image Consultant* scholarship valued at $9,450, and a Beauty Cosmetic package; First Runner-Up received $5,000 PLUS all of the above; and Second Runner-Up received $3,000 in cash PLUS all of the above. In addition, the Top 15 official contestants received an *Image Consultant Training Program* (valued at $2,000 each), provided by *C&D Success Image*. Moreover, all candidates were featured in the documentary TV show: *Miss Asian American Journey*. Nowhere on the prize list did it mention the winner's prize package as including "an official crown, banner/sash, and trophy." Those are awards, not prizes. It should go unsaid that winners receive them — it's a pageant! Take the awards off of your prize package list, and make room for real prizes.

Be careful what you value your prizes. There are tax consequences for the winners. No Queen will want to lose even more of what's left of her $10,000 cash winnings to the tax man after already paying taxes on the cash and watch. Winning a $9,450 image consultant prize that may or may not be worth that amount can eat up what's left of the winner's $10,000 cash prize! Educate your winners on prize-accepting repercussions. Then, let them accept or decline any prize. It might even be to the winner's advantage to decline both the CHOUETTE watch and image consultant, just so she can keep more of the $10,000 cash.

Are you giving a college scholarship to the winner? If so, what if the winner is already in college (or has already graduated)? Can she receive a cash replacement value? Can the scholarship be applied towards her student loan or Graduate school? What if the winner is undecided as to which college or university she will attend? Will she have access to the college funds when she is ready to attend college?

Miss Teen Canada International Scholarship Pageant allows the winner to attend any college of her choice, stating,

> You must attend an accredited university or college to receive the scholarship. It is not a cash award. If you have a student loan, it may be applied directly towards the loan. The scholarship is not awarded to the titleholder; it is a scholarship to be used for education and is paid directly to the educational institute.

P.E.A.R.L. Girls states,

> All scholarship monies will be sent directly to the pageant winners' university of choice. Pageant contestants have up to two years post pageant date to submit all documents necessary for their scholarship to be processed for the university of their choice.

In its prize package listing, in 2013, *Miss Texas USA* included a $45,600 scholarship for the winner to attend *Lindenwood University* — a campus *and* online university in St. Charles, Missouri. The Top 5 Finalists each won a $40,000 college scholarship, and Semifinalists won a $29,600 college scholarship. With the high costs of higher education, such a gift would be most welcome to the majority of pageant candidates! Still, winners should be educated, in advance, about tax consequences. Although taxes might not need to be paid until the scholarship is activated, it is my understanding that, once official contestants sign in acceptance, they are responsible for the tax bill — whether or not they cash in the scholarship. Suggest to prospective contestants during Open Call — or in your pageant paperwork if you're a non-Open Call pageant — to speak to a tax accountant about potential tax ramifications. Learn more about how Open Call works by reading my book *Producing Beauty Pageants: Open Call*, Chapter 4, "How Open Call Works."

Step Prize Package

American Beauty Pageant offers a Step Prize Package. If a division has at least ten delegates in it, the winner of the pageant receives $1,000. After this goal is met, the pageant's step prize package steps in. For every five additional delegates entered in a division, the prize increases by $500. For example, if there are fifteen delegates in the Jr. Miss division, the prize package for the winner will be $1,500. In addition, the pageant prize package includes autograph cards, Christmas cards, return airfare, luggage fees (maximum two bags), hotel, and meals. It wasn't clear if airfare was included. Of course, it goes without saying that pageant officials award a crown and sash to Queens.

Universal Glitz N Glamour Pageant notes that, if there are over sixty candidates in one division, it will add one Mini Novice Supreme (0–12) and one Grand Novice Supreme (13 & up) title, which will be awarded the same prize package as the Overall Supremes. If there are over 750 official contestants in the entire pageant, additional prizes will be added to the prize packages. Rather than say "additional prizes," spell out exactly what those prizes (and their amounts) are before a prospective contestant fills out and signs an Official Application (contract) and pays a deposit. For a better understanding of Grand Novice Supreme, Mini Novice Supreme, and Overall Supreme, read my FREE e-book *Producing Beauty Pageants: A Guide to Pageant Terminology.*

Prorating

Prorating means to divide and distribute proportionately. A pageant director will often prorate a cash prize if, for example, there are less than the minimum number of candidates expected who entered the pageant. Therefore, the cash prize is based on the number of entries and proportionately distributed. If you prorate, present details in writing before a prospective contestant fills out an Official Application and pays a non-refundable deposit and entry fee.

Little Miss Colorado prorates its cash prizes if there are less than fifty contestants, as follows:

50+ contestants = Full payout
45–49 contestants = 90 percent payout
40–44 contestants = 80 percent payout
35–39 contestants = 70 percent payout
30–34 contestants = 60 percent payout
25–29 contestants = 50 percent payout
20–24 contestants = 40 percent payout
15–19 contestants = 30 percent payout
10–14 contestants = 20 percent payout

1–9 contestants = 10 percent payout

Cash for _Miss Elite Colorado_ is prorated if there are fewer than five contestants:

3–4 contestants = 75 percent payout

2 contestants = 50 percent payout

1 contestant = 25 percent payout

Miss Latina Pageant prorates the bond amount if there are less than sixty-five entries.

Novice of the Year Nationals will prorate [regular] bonds with less than fifty official contestants, that is, all except for the Mega Supreme $5,000 bond. The Mega Supreme bond is guaranteed no matter how many candidates participate; however, if the [regular] bond is $1,000, and there are twenty-five official contestants, the bond will be prorated to $500. Not surprisingly, the pageant has never needed to prorate.

Glitz and Glam Pageant's prorate system includes,

> All cash prizes will ONLY be awarded if there are fifty or more female contestants in each Glitz and Glam division and twenty or more male contestants in the Glam! (Boys and girls do not compete against each other.) Example: If there are fifty female contestants in Glam and only forty-nine in Glitz, we will only award cash prizes to the Glam division. There must be at least twenty-five male contestants total in the pageant for cash prizes to be awarded to our male supreme winners.

Porcelain Dolls Nationals director Kathy Raese, who doesn't prorate cash prizes regardless of the number of entries, scoffs at pageant directors that do this, but that don't put it in writing:

> Many pageant directors state that a certain dollar amount will be awarded. But then they don't award the prize money because they didn't meet the pageant entry goal numbers, and nowhere in the pageant paperwork does it state anything about prorating!

What's worse than complete financial disclosures being presented after a contract is signed? Non-existing (not in writing) but enforced financial disclosures...such as prorating. In such an event, pageant officials are unfairly making up the rules as the game is played.

Pageant Dollars

Pageant Dollars are "monies" earned and/or won during a pageant. Pageant Dollars must be used at the pageant where they were obtained. *Showtime Beauty Pageants, Inc.* presents Pageant Dollars for candidates to use at SHOWTIME BEAUTY PAGEANT, INC. events *only* and states this in its Good Faith Agreement. Otherwise, these Pageant Dollars have absolutely no monetary value. *Simply Gorgeous Girls* features Gorgeous Girl Cash. SGG notes that Gorgeous Girl Cash has no cash value, but it is intended to be used as a gift card towards the State pageant in the form of "credit" that can be used to pay for entry fees. Think long and hard before giving away such income streams. Learn more about Good Faith Agreement by reading my book *Producing Beauty Pageants: Creating a Synergized National Pageant System*, Chapter 12, "Pageant Paperwork and Forms."

Savings Bonds

If your pageant provides savings bonds to the winners, will they need to provide you with their Social Security number upon crowning (or within two weeks)? If they don't, will you forfeit the savings bond? Will you have a minimum official contestant rule in order to present savings bonds? Can winners take a fifty percent cash equivalent on the bonds? Whatever your rules, state them in writing.

Crowning Beauty states in its Rules & Regulations that a minimum of *thirty-five* contestants are required to award full amounts of bonds. Yet, on the last line of the "Please Read and Sign Release," it states that bond amounts are based on *thirty* contestants. Legally, CB is required to make the payout on thirty contestants even if it meant thirty-five.

Miss Bright Star of America awards all monetary scholarships "[during] the *next* year pageant crowning ceremony." So, when do the "monetary scholarships" begin earning interest for the titleholders? Is it when they won this money? Or is it a year later when they are given their prize? This arrangement appears to be an interest-free loan to the pageant director!

Southern Glamour notes that bonds are guaranteed and will not be prorated.

East Coast USA Pageant states that all savings bonds will be awarded in cash equivalency at the conclusion of the pageant evening.

Fun Prizes

My Royal Crown allows official contestants, after each State pageant, a visit to the *Royal Treasure Chest* to select a gift of their choice. Moreover, cute welcome gifts are provided to every official contestant at registration. Pageant directors can obtain such prizes for *free* by bartering In-Kind, if they make the effort. Learn how to barter In-Kind for free prizes by reading my book *Producing Beauty Pageants: Brokering a Pageant through Barter*, Chapter 9, "In-Kind Sponsors."

Storybook Pageants doesn't present beauty awards (other than Beauty Supreme). Rather than awarding every candidate Runner-Up titles for beauty, each candidate is awarded a title, a 5" crown, and a trip to the prize table.

Door Prizes/Raffles

Start early to round up your door and raffle prizes. The pageants listed below offer some good door prize tips:

- *Heavenly Angels Pageants* not only offers quality door prizes, but there is always a raffle table set up to sell raffle tickets — up until the door prizes drawing. As a bonus, twenty-five raffle tickets are sold for $10.

- *Little Miss Morgan County* raffles sporting goods gift cards.

- *Pretty in Pink Pageants* candidates can sell 50/50 raffle tickets. Ticket profits from sales are divided: fifty percent to the official contestant, and fifty percent to the pageant system.

- *Miss Marshall-Putnam Fair Pageant* requires all official contestants to sell (or purchase) five books of raffle tickets at $5 per book.

To encourage pageant entries from each candidate, *Crystal Doll Pageants* held a drawing to give away two tickets to see Justin Bieber live in concert. All a girl needed to do to earn raffle tickets was to participate in any CDP pageant. The contest started on July 1, 2012, at *Fresh Faces* and ended on October 14, 2012, at *Southern Gem*. For every CDP a candidate entered, including pageants that were held in between these two events, she earned an entry into the drawing. The more pageants the candidate entered during the raffle period, the greater her chances of winning. A candidate could also earn one extra entry into the drawing if she entered Photogenic and the Overalls, or she could earn two extra entries into the drawing if she entered Photogenic, Overalls, *and* Ultimate Supreme. The concert tickets winner was drawn at *Southern Gem* on October 14th, 2012, in Long Beach.

A raffle ticket drum is in order if you provide a raffle at your pageant. One can be purchased at _Raffle Drums_, _Displays2Go_, and _Tripp Plastics_.

Souvenir Gift Trade

Many children's pageants require official contestants to bring a small gift to give to each participating candidate. Candidates at the Washington _Cinderella International Scholarship Pageant_ see the gift exchange as a memorable part of competition. CISP requires every contender to bring a minimum of 100 gifts for the other participants, staff, judges, and reigning Queens. The souvenir gifts are tokens of friendship from the candidates' area and may be donated to them by their city, state, Chamber of Commerce, or merchants in their area. They don't need to be expensive or identical in kind; however, they cannot be brochures or literature. Some ideas include lollypop pens, locker mirrors, combs, pencils, candy, hair clips, or mood rings — novelty items offered at the _Oriental Trading Company_ or from the $1 *Target* bin. CISP officials encourage candidates to use their imagination in preparing their souvenir gifts, including hand-made gifts by the candidates or a family member. At the end of the Souvenir Exchange Party, awards are given (in every age division) for the "Most Original Souvenir" and "Best Overall Souvenir."

When to Collect Souvenir Gifts

Pageant officials typically collect souvenir gifts at registration. Then, they will provide tote bags and place one of each novelty gifts into every tote bag. However, not all pageant officials want to be responsible for the gifts prior to gifting. Instead, they require that official contestants take their novelty gifts to their hotel room after hotel check-in. Then, when they go to pageant check-in, candidates are only to bring *one* sample novelty gift to registration. This system keeps pageant officials from being responsible for the gifts, lugging them around, and finding a place to store them until they are needed. If you have 100 candidates, and each brings 100 novelty gifts, this is a lot of merchandise for which to be accountable.

A great marketing idea is to provide totes that feature your pageant name on the front in order to hold all those goodies. *Lil Miss Lux Pageant*, in 2012, gave every contender a "We Got This in the Bag" tote that featured an image of a purple diamond ring between *Lil Miss Lux* and "We Got This in the Bag." It was filled with all kinds of amazing goodies. All tote bags had a ring inside — one of which was a *real $600 antique diamond ring!*

Offer Souvenir Gifts with Parents' Permission

Make it clear (in writing) to official contestants and parents, as does _Glamour Girls Pageants_, that items *of any kind* cannot be handed to candidates during competition. This includes gifts, toys, food, candy, or any other item that may either be a distraction to a contender or cause soil to her face, hands, and/or clothing. Furthermore, candy or other edible gifts may *only* be offered with parental approval.

Making Souvenir Gift Exchanges Non-Mandatory

Participating in pageants is costly enough. It is best not to make your souvenir gift exchange mandatory. If you do include a gift exchange in your pageant festivities, consider candidates who cannot afford to participate. They will be sad to not be a part of the festivities.

Today's Girl Youth Organization has a non-mandatory gift exchange. A few weeks prior to competition, pageant officials will give every participating official contestant ALL candidates' names from their age group. While not every candidate will participate in the gift exchange, ALL will go home with a tote bag filled with novelty gifts because every official contestant who *does* participate will bring one for every candidate in their age division.

Royalty Gifts

Some pageant systems require every candidate to bring a gift for the outgoing and incoming Queen. If so, state in writing if the outgoing and incoming Queen gift(s) need(s) to be wrapped or unwrapped. If you expect the gift to be wrapped, and you don't state this, be prepared to wrap them at registration; official contestants won't be carrying wrapping paper. Even if you do state it in writing, *still* be prepared with gift wrap for candidates who "bought their gift on the way to the pageant." For candidates who didn't have time to purchase their two $5–$10 outgoing Queen gifts for their respective age division, for their purchasing convenience, *Miss Georgia Girl* features a gift table with items in the $5–$10 range.

Glamour Girls Pageants asks that each candidate bring, for her age division only, a $5 cash gift to present to incoming beauty royalty. If there are fifty candidates in any given division, the beauty winner from that division will receive forty-nine $5 bills! Although not required, it is suggested that official contestants bring a similar gift to outgoing royalty.

Honoring returning royalty is very important to *Southern Beauties and Beaus*. Therefore, pageant officials ask each candidate to bring six $5 bills. This money will go to the Queens/Kings in their respective age division and for the overalls in their breakdown. If the returning candidate is a Queen, she will get $5 from everyone in her breakdown. If a returning Overall Winner, she will also get $5 from everyone in her age division. Every official contestant is asked to place each $5 bill in an envelope (labeled with each candidate's name and age division) and hand them over at registration. Pageant officials, in turn, will make each returning royalty their own special money tree. Official contestants are reminded that they could be on the receiving end of their own special money tree next year.

America's Model Miss, on the other hand, does not ask candidates to bring gifts for returning royalty. AMM provides those gifts.

Keep Your Promise

Numerous pageants have started up across the country as profit-making ventures, playing on the ambitions and vanities of parents to extort large entry fees, and offering token or worthless prizes. Doug Conn, a Louisiana modeling school owner, says,

> A particularly heartless gimmick is to promise a college scholarship to the parents of a six-year-old girl, who will then have to track the contest organizer down twelve years later.

If you offer valuable prizes to your winners, pay up promptly. If you are concerned about children's educational welfare, present long-term savings bonds.

Thousands of winning candidates have never received the prize money, trip, or car they were promised. When Jayne Kennedy was crowned *Miss Ohio USA*, in 1970, she was the first African American to win the title. The prizes and jobs promised to the winner disappeared the next day. Promoters of this sort leave winning candidates disappointed, frustrated, and feeling jilted or humiliated.

Distribute prizes when you say you will — whether it is the day of the pageant, or at the end of a Queen's reign. Most pageants are set up to award prize packages right after the candidate wins the title. Minimize the hoops that a titleholder must go through in order to claim her prizes.

Miss/Mr. Edwardsburg Pageant presents most of its awards at the *end* of the reign. All scholarships are awarded upon the successful completion of the Queen's reign. This was decided upon by the pageant committee. In order for the titleholder to claim the scholarship, she must notify the college or university (admission office) where she is enrolled. She is to ask Admissions to send a letter to the pageant organization stating that she, the titleholder, has been admitted and is enrolled as a student for the current term. Included in the letter should also be the name and address of to whom the check will be sent. Awards are granted after the successful completion of the titleholder's reign. The titleholder has two years after the completion of her reign to collect the scholarship prize. If the titleholder doesn't complete her reign, she won't receive the college scholarship.

Crawford County Fair Queen receives a monetary cash award of $750. She receives $250 when she is crowned and the remaining $500 when she completes her reign. This likely means that the winner won't receive the IRS form 1099[B] at the end of both calendar years (and a copy of the form filed with the IRS) because the prize was split into two years — neither exceeding $600. Still, check with your tax advisor.

Miss Teen America scholarships are divided into four equal installments. The winner can only claim one installment *per year*. Furthermore, all scholarship requests must be accompanied by a tuition bill. Scholarships must be claimed within five years of the award and must be used in consecutive years. Second through fourth year scholarship requests must accompany a current transcript showing a minimum GPA of 3.2.

Promoters have been known to rescind on prizes for their Queen, along with her title, because she did not live up to her contract. According to an article published in *The New York Times*, Virginia J. Reichardt lost her *Miss Connecticut* title and prizes, including her official car with her name and *Miss Connecticut* emblazoned on its flanks. Thomas Curtiss, the executive director of the pageant, characterized her as an irresponsible young woman who did not attend Local pageants and who did not appear at Official Sponsors' events. Eventually, *Miss Connecticut* and the pageant board members ended the legal battle with an out-of-court settlement.[31]

What Not to Promise

Never promise fame and fortune to titleholders. Rarely does their coronation translate into a fortune or a life as a celebrity. Even though many pageant directors feel that one of the quickest ways to stardom is through the exposure of winning a pageant, never promise stardom.

---

[31] Freedman, Samuel G. *The New York Times*, Section B, Page 2, Column 5. June 18, 1982. http://www.nytimes.com/1982/06/18/nyregion/beauty-queen-battling-to-regain-her-crown.html

When to Post Awards

Official contestants like the element of surprise when it comes to awards presentation, whether it is announcing the Runners-Up and Queen or an Optionals award. Noted one *National American Miss* official contestant,

> [what] I didn't like is [that NAM] listed the top five in every Optionals except for photogenic, so crowning wasn't very interesting since I already knew I hadn't placed in four of my five Optionals.[32]

Keep your awards ceremony a surprise until the very end. The element of surprise is a HUGE part of a fun pageant!

---

[32]"National American Miss?" YAHOO! Answers.
http://answers.yahoo.com/question/index?qid=20110917164212AAfY7LO.

Chapter 11

Recruiting Prospective Contestants

There are a number of ways to recruit prospective contestants for your pageant. In Chapter 8, "The Internet," we learned the importance of recruiting prospective contestants via social media and other electronic vehicles, including message boards, web advertising, and podcasts. In Chapter 9, "Breaking into Media," we explored other methods of communicating pageant messages to prospective contestants. Next, in Chapter 12, "Mailshot," you will learn how to employ a successful direct mail campaign. This chapter, "Recruiting Prospective Contestants," focuses on old school recruitment approaches — reaching out to prospective contestants to sell your pageant — to establish personal connections.

Old School Official Contestant Recruitment

When I began producing pageants, in 1983, there wasn't much choice but to recruit prospective contestants via "old school" techniques. The Internet and social media weren't around yet. Looking back, old school methods were (and still are) among the best ways to recruit pageant candidates. Approaching a girl and inviting her to learn about your pageant was (and still is) a huge compliment. This chapter focuses on how and where to recruit prospective contestants and the recruitment tools needed.

Recruitment Tools

There will be times when you are presented with planned and unplanned opportunities to recruit girls into your pageant. Be prepared for such occasions with an arsenal of recruitment tools. Recruitment tools can include, but not be limited to, Recruitment Forms, clipboards, carabiner pens, *Bic* pens, brochures, and business cards. A carabiner is a metal loop with a sprung gate used to connect components — usually to fasten a 24" corded pen — and can be attached to a clipboard. Carabiners can be purchased at *Staples* or *Office Depot*. To view what they look like, visit *Quality Logo Products* or *Amazon.com*. (Regarding *Bic* pens, take the caps off of each one and roll the pen on paper until ink flows. Then, with the ballpoint down, return the primed pens to the box to keep them ink-primed.)

If you are recruiting from locations that have a large group of girls standing in line, in addition to the ink-primed *Bic* pens, you will need to distribute Recruitment Forms (on clipboards) to garner their contact information. The type of information featured on your Recruitment Forms can include: prospective contestants' name, age, date of birth, mailing address, zip code, home/cell phone number, and email address. Frame each contact template in a "box." Now, include several "boxes" on each page (one side only), so that maybe ten or twelve fit onto one side. Make sure there is enough writing space since young girls have large handwriting. Above these contact template boxes, include a line that states something to the effect of:

> Please fill this out if you want FREE information about the Miss XYZ Pageant.

If you're an Open Call pageant:

> Please fill this out if you want FREE information about the Miss XYZ Pageant and Open Call [Photoshoot, if you provide one within your Open Call].

To drive your Open Call statement, add a FREE photoshoot to the sessions. You will have more interest from "looky-loos" prospective contestants and a better chance at converting them into official contestants when they show up to "only" collect free photos. This is one of *National American Miss'* best tactics.

In my pageant promoting days, I filmed pageant commercials for every single pageant that I produced. Instead of a Photoshoot, I included commercial filmings. Learn how I obtained FREE commercial filmings from TV Official Sponsors by reading my book *Producing Beauty Pageants: Brokering a Pageant through*

Barter, Chapter 6, "Media Partners" under "Television Official Sponsor."

Learn how and when to put together those FREE commercials by reading my book *Producing Beauty Pageants: Creating a Synergized National Pageant System*, Chapter 14, "Airing Your Pageant on Television" under "Create a Pageant Commercial."

Don't just promote a pageant, have a hook, such as an Open Call, and to work the Open Call hook, have a catch to it, such as a group Photoshoot promoting an Official Sponsor's product that was donated in barter. Now, you'll likely have an even greater percentage of girls pre-sold on your pageant — even before they realize it — because they're not exactly sure what it is that they're going to learn at the FREE Open Call they were "selectively" invited to attend. Understand the mesmerizing power of Open Call, and how to *properly* integrate it into your pageant system (for optimum success), by reading my book *Producing Beauty Pageants: Open Call.*

Always have a dozen carabiners that are attached to clipboards, readily available — each with a stack of Recruitment Forms — in a tote bag. And remember to ink-prime those carabiner pens. In a large group gathering, simultaneously hand the prepped clipboards to interested girls. After the last contact box is filled out by the now-prospective contestant, take the completely filled out Recruitment Form off of the top and place it on the bottom of your clipboard stack to expose a new page. Continue this process with all of the clipboards while you rotate fresh Recruitment Forms to the top of each stack.

For an even larger-scale recruiting effort, have a couple of boxes of ink-primed *Bic* pens and a large stack of loose Recruitment Forms available in your tote bag. Interested girls who are standing in line have time to fill out their contact information. Don't require a consenting signature at this recruiting time. Conclude by presenting prospective contestants with a pageant brochure and a business card. Tell them that you will send pageant information (or an Open Call/photoshoot/commercial invitation) so that they can look forward to learning about your outstanding program. This is not the time to present your pageant marketing materials. At this early time, prospective contestants will likely lose it (or toss it). Their number one concern is the event that they are at, not your "cold call" visit. A business card and a brochure would be the exception. Those items can be easily tucked away.

Approaching Prospective Contestants

Equipped with a dozen clipboards and ink-primed carabiners, you are prepared approach a large gathering of prospective contestants. Introduce yourself and your pageant program. Invite the first dozen interested girls to simultaneously write down their contact information. Let them know that you will mail them your program information. Then, invite the next interested dozen prospective contestants to do the same. Present your business card and exciting pageant brochure, but preserve your hook (Open Call and/or photoshoot/pageant commercial) to regenerate future interest. Let the "Silent Salesman" introduce that information, beginning with "the letter." Learn more about the "Silent Salesman" by reading my book *Producing Beauty Pageants: Open Call*, Chapter 5, "The Silent Salesman...and Other Subliminal Messengers." Understand the power of "the letter" by reading the same book, Chapter 6, "The Letter."

Where to Recruit Prospective Contestants

There doesn't seem to be a shortage of places to recruit prospective contestants. A list of recruiting places can be found below:

High Schools

High schools are an ideal place to recruit prospective contestants — particularly if your pageant is a scholarship one set up similarly to *Miss America* or *Distinguished Young Women*. Ask school officials for permission to distribute pageant marketing materials. Arrange to make broadcasted announcements at their campuses via the school's closed-circuit television or PA (public address) system. Announce your recruitment booth location, time, and day. Ask to make an appearance at a student pep rally to promote your scholarship program. Get permission to set up a booth at the next scheduled school dance by contacting the school's ASB (associated student body) office. Show up at a homecoming game and recruit homecoming candidates. Ask to leave your pageant brochures in the scholarship forms display.

Cheer/Drill Team/Pep Squad

High schools have an all-girls drill team, cheerleading, and pep squad. Contact each team's manager to request an opportunity to speak to team members. In return, offer to provide a pageant official to judge their officer and team end-of-season tryouts.

Yearbooks and Student Directories

Pageant promoters sometimes go from high school to high school successfully recruiting prospective contestants from yearbooks (shelved at most high school libraries). They even purchase a student directory to cross reference names and contact information to yearbook pictures. Recruitment is easy because most school directories include students' addresses and phone numbers. When you come across a student (from a yearbook photo) that you believe would make an ideal candidate for your pageant, make note, such as "Suzie is ...S.A.F.E." You might gain access to her cell number, home number, mailing address, and/or email address if she elected to include it in the directory. If you are an Open Call pageant, this would be the perfect time to invite Suzie to a session to learn about your program. If you don't Open Call, and you do have her telephone number, call Suzie and ask for her permission (or her parents') to send her pageant marketing materials. This professionalism makes it "First Class" mail, not a "Second Class" mailshot!

Recruiting via yearbooks and student directories would be an ideal job for official contestant recruiters. Gain insight on how Official Contestant Recruiters operate (like those working for *Miss Texas USA*) by reading my book *Producing Beauty Pageants: Creating a Synergized National Pageant System*, Chapter 8, "Official Contestant Recruiters."

Malls

Show up at the next department store model search or fashion show to recruit. These model searches and fashion shows are sometimes advertised in newspapers, usually in a Sunday edition. Look on the mall's website calendar under "Calendar of Events" to find announcements on mall promotions. Girls auditioning for department store model searches often make ideal pageant candidates and are generally receptive to pageant information — especially if you have modeling (school) scholarships and portfolios as prizes. Consider tying in a mall's chain store as an Official Sponsor into your pageant. Then you could include those Official Sponsors in various pageant literatures stating, "Applications available at participating ... stores." When *Dillard's* department store had model search events, I showed up with a folder of Recruitment Forms, a box of ink-primed *Bic* pens, business cards, and brochures. I handed these items to girls to fill out while they stood in line.

Modeling Agencies/Schools

Many pageant Queens are known to have been recruited into a pageant system through a modeling agency. Joe Rinelli, a stockbroker at the time, also doubled as a *Miss Texas USA* contestant recruiter. He discovered *Miss Texas USA 1986* Christi Fitchner — who ultimately won *Miss USA* 1986 — at the *Kim Dawson Agency* in Dallas.

Approach modeling agencies and modeling schools. Many will post information of this nature on its electronic bulletin boards and newsletters, and therefore, might welcome your pageant information. Keep the agency in mind when bartering an In-Kind modeling scholarship prize, when recruiting for judges, when bartering active leads, and as an Official Sponsor. Modeling and talent agencies do like pageantry. After all, in 2015, *WME-IMG Talent Agency* bought the *Miss Universe* pageant system from Donald Trump after NBC sold its share to Donald that same year. Learn how to barter for your *entire* pageant system by reading my book *Producing Beauty Pageants: Brokering a Pageant through Barter*.

Acting/Cheer/Dancing/Baton Twirling Schools

Acting, cheer, dancing, and baton twirling schools are ideal places to recruit and trade active leads. And, remember to barter for school scholarships. Learn more about bartering for such prizes by reading my book *Producing Beauty Pageants: Brokering a Pageant through Barter*, Chapter 7, "Barter Your Prize Package" and Chapter 9, "In-Kind Sponsors."

Photography Studios

You can find quality photography studios in your *Yellow Pages*. You can also find some in the classified section of photography magazines. Many advertise model shoots for young girls, women, and men, so this can be another good source for prospective contestant leads. Offer to trade leads with a reputable photographer. Always research *anyone* you do business with, at the very least, through the *Better Business Bureau*. One quality photography studio is *The Right Light Photography* — the setting for the cover photo of the *Producing Beauty Pageant* series.

Movie Auditions/Filmings

Movie filming events present a good opportunity to recruit prospective contestants. The movie, *Bring it On*, starring Kirsten Dunst (2000), was filmed in San Diego, California. Other movies filmed in my neck of the woods included *Anchorman* (2004), *Top Gun* (1986), and *Almost Famous* (2000). And, yes, there were hordes of girls at every filming site — even if Tom Cruise, Will Ferrel, Kate Hudson, or Kirsten Dunst weren't around! The late Aaron Spelling, casting director for the series *Charlie's Angels*, held an "Angels 88" search in San Diego, California. Thousands of girls auditioned, providing me with an ideal opportunity to also recruit for my California pageants.

No town is too small for a movie filming event. I had the opportunity to recruit hundreds of girls into one of my Texas pageants, in 1985, during auditions for the movie, *The Legend of Billie Jean* (starring Helen Slater). It was predominately filmed in Corpus Christi, Texas, so I showed up at the audition location equipped with pageant recruitment tools. But, don't just stop at one location. A movie filming schedule is often extended into nearby towns and cities. For instance, *The Legend of Billie Jean* also filmed scenes in Flour Bluff, Kingsville, and Aransas Pass — perfect Texas towns for pageant recruitment! Additionally, two of the movie scenes were filmed in Colorado.

MTV hosted (and filmed) a Spring break event on Padre Island beach in Corpus Christi, Texas. It provided me with a great opportunity to interact with thousands of prospective contestants. Be sure to wear plenty of sunscreen and a hat in order to prevent sunburn during the hours that you spend garnering prospective contestant leads — other items to leave in your tote bag.

245

Your Own Pageant

Featuring a Referral Program or a Recommendations Program in your pageant is a popular way to build leads. If you are an Open Call pageant, mail an Open Call invitation. If not, cold call those prospective contestants. It's imperative that you "go to the girls" to "get them to come to you." Understand the importance of "going to the girls" to "get them to come to you" by reading my book *Producing Beauty Pageants: Open Call*, Chapter 1, "Open Call," under "Not Understanding the Covert Variable: A True Case Study."

In the Meantime, More Recruiting

As an Open Call pageant, and during the weeks prior to each Open Call, I am my own Official Contestant Recruiter at a modeling school/agency, the mall, the town fair, cheer/dance/twirling functions, and/or thumbing through town newspapers, high school yearbooks/student directories, etc., recruiting prospective contestants for the second, third, fourth, etc., pageant Open Call.

After speaking to each group who attended their scheduled Open Call, the no-shows were invited to attend yet the next Open Call. I repeated this scenario up until two weeks before my pageant event — when all official contestant roster photos and sponsorship names were submitted to the printing company to be included in the Pageant Program Book. Candidates who applied after the final deadline were registered into the very next pageant — which I began recruiting immediately after the current pageant, and often *before*.

Greater Numbers with Personal Contact

National directors who promote State pageants without State directors (or State directors without Preliminary directors) need to make every effort to personally connect with prospective contestants. If a pageant promoter cannot physically meet prospective contestants, arrange to connect via a Skype meeting.

If a pageant promoter can meet prospective contestants in person, setting up a Skype Open Call meeting is the best solution.

Skype Meetings

Pageant directors can establish personal connections by arranging Skype meetings (or telephone conferencing) with prospective contestants. Skype (and telephone) conference meetings work well, particularly with an Appointed Titles Program (ATP). Directors will be able to hear and/or see prospective delegates' enthusiasm for the pageant — which means selling the pageant will be easier, and a personal connection has been formed, which is better than solely mailshot.

Pageant officials who have an ATP integrated into their "non-Open Call" pageant system might not realize that they ARE an Open Call pageant. Their Open Call "locations" are their computers and the U.S. mail! Establish an effective ATP into your pageant system by reading my book *Producing Beauty Pageants: Creating a Synergized National Pageant System*, Chapter 6, "Appointed Titles Program and National Qualifying Avenues."

So, why not hone your Open Call skills and learn everything about a pageant system's BEST KEPT SECRET? For added relations with prospective contestants, consider having one or two Queens present, along with your presenter, during a Skype Open Call meeting. Learn how to integrate a Skype Open Call into your pageant by reading my book *Producing Beauty Pageants: Open Call*, Chapter 14, "Open Call Styles."

Part-Time Open Call Meetings

Wise (and predominately) non-Open Call pageant directors will arrange part-time Open Call dates, *even if only in select states*. It's the BEST way to sell a pageant to prospective contestants — particularly in the pageant-favoring states of Texas, Florida, New York, Ohio, Nebraska, Arizona, Georgia, California, Tennessee, Kentucky, Washington, Mississippi, Alabama, Oklahoma, and last, but not least, the Carolinas. Even if a pageant system wants to remain a predominantly non-Open Call pageant, the pageant system might choose only pageant-favoring states for Open Call. For the rest of the states, the pageant system can apply an Appointed Titles Program or Delegate-At-Large program via mailshot and/or employ other Open Call styles: Phone Open Call,

Open Call Forum, and Teleconference Open Call. Learn about all Open Call styles by reading my book *Producing Beauty Pageants: Open Call*, Chapter 14, "Open Call Styles."

Contestant Recruiters

Pageants that have Contestant Recruiters generally fare better with candidate entries. Contestant Recruiters are "Open-Calling" every time they personally speak to prospective contestants. It was the muscle that Richard Guy and the late Rex Holt — Guyrex — flexed throughout the '80s with their *Miss Texas USA* and *Miss California USA* franchises. Learn about Contestant Recruiters and the secrets of their trade by reading my book *Producing Beauty Pageants: Creating a Synergized National Pageant System*, Chapter 8, "Official Contestant Recruiters."

Cold Calling

When Dee Dee Hintz received a phone call from a *National American Miss* pageant official saying that her then seven-year-old granddaughter had been recommended by an anonymous source for the NAM pageant, she was leery. After finding out that the pageant wasn't like a *Toddlers & Tiaras* event, she accepted the cold call. Then, she took her granddaughter to the Open Call, from which she received a callback, and ultimately registered her into the pageant! [33] Learn how NAM successfully integrates callbacks by reading my book *Producing Beauty Pageants: Open Call*, Chapter 16, "Callback."

The late South Texas pageant producer, James Matthew Goodman, Jr. — Jimmy — was an expert at getting prospective contestants to register into his pageant via cold calling. In the '80s, Jimmy had (quietly) become one of the most successful Open Call pageant producers in U.S. history, having produced hundreds of beauty pageants — some accounts say thousands — in the South Texas region. He was most successful at bringing in newbies,

---

[33] "Byron-Bergen Second-Grader is a Finalist for 'American Miss.'" *The Batavian*, May 29, 2012. http://thebatavian.com/tags/national-american-miss-pageant.

simply by cold-calling *while alumnae returned through the back door*! Jimmy didn't have a website or cell phone, and he didn't spend a dime on advertising. A one-man operation, Jimmy had an incredibly successful method of recruiting around 200 fully-paid, official contestants into every pageant division — for multiple pageants per year — during a time when the Internet or cell phone wasn't around. Jimmy simply picked up a landline phone (he had rolls of quarters in his car and found the nearest phone booth if he wasn't at his home office), and called names he picked up from high school yearbooks/student directories, town newspapers, and referrals. Jimmy's story and business model can be found in my book *Producing Beauty Pageants: Open Call*, Chapter 15, "Have Open Call, Will Travel."

Building Referral Mailing Lists

In addition to a template including a name, address, zip code (if you require the Zip +4 digits, spell that out too), and email address, include a line on your prospective contestant referral page for a complete phone number — including brackets for the area code. Otherwise, a prospective contestant might only place the last seven digits of the ten-digit number: the prefix and line number. She might leave out the first three digits: the area code. Better yet, in a small font, write "area code" digits near the brackets. Some young girls might not know what the brackets are for and *still* leave out their area code number. Leave plenty of room for the referring candidate to write the three blocks of numbers. Additional information on securing quality referrals can be found in my book *Producing Beauty Pageants: Contestant Handbook*.

Your Own Website

If you don't think a National pageant can draw in traffic, think again. I don't need to remind you that, in 2012, *National American Miss* received over 1,200 pageviews per day! Learn how to garner more pageviews by reading 10 Simple Tips to Get 250,000 Page Views Per Month.

Chapter 12

Mailshot

The most popular method of promoting a pageant is via a mailshot campaign. It allows pageant promoters — particularly those who don't employ Open Call — the opportunity to blanket a greater area for prospective contestants. For non-Open Call pageants, mailshot — a borrowed UK term describing a bulk distribution of unsolicited marketing material — is part of a one-step process to get girls to register directly into the pageant. For Open Call pageants, mailshot is part of a two-step process to get girls to attend Open Call and then register into the pageant via a pageant workshop (or some other motivating registration function). Whether you are an Open Call or non-Open Call pageant, mailshot is a big, expensive part of your pageant business model.

How Mailshot Works

You will need to start with quality prospective contestant leads for your various age divisions. Such leads can be obtained from a number of sources. For some outstanding leads sources, read the "Mailing Lists" section towards the end of this chapter. Armed with strong leads, you will aim your mailshot target with bullseye accuracy.

Mailshot Target in Action

Assuming you don't Open Call, you will mailshot pageant marketing materials to several thousand girls to get about 2% of them to act. Interested prospective contestants — those 2% — will typically end up registering for your pageant. They would receive an Acceptance Packet that includes pageant paperwork, detailed sponsorship information, sponsorship fee envelopes, Contestant Handbook, and last, but not least, a Press Kit to help them secure their sponsorship fee and promote the pageant.

Girls who didn't reply to the first offer would receive a second mailshot offer, and maybe even a third. Meanwhile, new leads from a different source are prepared for their first mailshot. This will go on until the desired result occurs, time permitting.

If you are an Open Call pageant, mailshot plays an even *bigger* role. If you're yielding National American Miss-like entries, you likely have a mailshot target of 10,000, which will yield approximately 4% of your overall target — 400 fully-registered official contestants — after a series of drop-offs occur between the first mailshot Open Call invitation and when the second sponsorship installment is paid. This 4% gain is impressive because most non-Open Call pageant systems only yield about 2%. (I am not factoring in NAM's online applicants or straight-to-register mailshot, which ordinarily would be simultaneously going on, and probably contributes to the 4% return presented in this example.)

In order to get about 2,000 girls to attend Open Call, NAM needs to mailshot about 10,000 Open Call invitations — "the letter" — to its target. From the 10,000 mailshot, about 2,000 will attend Open Call. From that number, about 800 will accept entry and pay the first sponsorship installment.

The 1,200 girls who attended Open Call, but who didn't register for the pageant, are usually mailshot a second pageant invitation. It's now a straight-to-register offer because they already attended Open Call and were already invited to the free Pageant Prep Training Session (to pay the first sponsorship installment) but didn't attend. If they decide to participate after all, they will pay the sponsorship fee online. If they want to attend a Pageant Prep Training Session, it will cost $25. They won't be required to pay the $20 application fee because it was waived at Open Call.

From the 800 girls who did pay the first sponsorship installment, about half of them will step up to pay the second (and last) sponsorship installment. The remaining 400 girls, who only paid the first sponsorship installment, become drop-offs and leave NAM a HUGE silent income.

Meanwhile, all no-shows at various levels of the drop-off ladder are mailshot extended entry deadlines to participate in the current pageant. (It carries over to the following year's pageant, provided that the girls don't age out.) Understand how NAM drop-off numbers works by reading my book *Producing Beauty Pageants: Open Call*, Chapter 10, "Drop Off" under "Drop-Off Ladder" and "Silent Income from all State Pageants Combined."

Scatter Your Mailshot Aim

Mailshot only to a few girls from one specific source per pageant event. Let's use a cheerleading squad as an example. Invite only three or four girls from the same cheer squad to your pageant or Open Call. It will appear as though you *are* singling out prospective contestants — particularly when they received an invitation, but the majority of the squad didn't. You stand a better chance that those three or four girls — 100% of them — will participate. If you want the remaining squad girls to participate, let the three or four cheerleaders that you do have refer them. Then, they will also become "carefully-selected" prospective contestants because *they* were referred. Repeat this across all U.S. high school cheer squads, and you have a group of quality candidates.

If you're wondering how to reach only a few select girls on a cheer squad, one way is to obtain mailing lists from various cheerleading magazines. Not every girl on a cheer squad subscribes to a cheerleading magazine, but for those who do, this is your opportunity to mailshot your pageant invitation to those leads. If three or four girls from the squad are subscribers, then those are the girls who will receive your pageant marketing materials. But, you don't need to tell them that you obtained their names from a generic list. Instead, those recipients might believe that they had been "carefully selected" from the squad or other source. Cheerleading magazines to invite as an Official Sponsor include: *American Cheerleader Magazine, Inside Cheerleading*, and *Texas Cheerleader Magazine*. (You can do the same with gymnastics and dance magazines.) Learn how to barter with magazine editors by reading my book *Producing Beauty Pageants: Brokering a Pageant through Barter*, Chapter 6, "Media Partners" under "Magazine Official or In-Kind Sponsor."

Don't Address Mailshot to Minors

Don't address a pageant invitation to a minor. Also, don't include the full name of the referring minor on your "you-have-been-referred-to-me-as-a-potential-candidate letter." Both are a violation of the Federal Trade Commission rules. Even if it were legal, take into consideration the parents of the minor recipients. The last thing a pageant director needs is to hear a parent saying, "I am disgusted that this organization can reach out to minors without their parents' permission!" It also renders ineffective to include on a Referral Form: "By signing this, I hereby allow [pageant name] to use my daughter's name in our marketing campaign material." A parent's signature would render useless in this case, because using a minor's name in marketing material is *still* illegal.

A Fine Line between Selected and Blanketed

National American Miss is an expert at making prospective contestants believe that they have been "chosen" or "selected" to receive Open Call information. It is my belief that these girls are not singled out. A UK Model Scout also agrees. In her *Yahoo! Answers* response to a prospective NAM contestant who believed that she was carefully selected, she described how unsolicited Open Call invitations work:

> You won't have been singled out; it will be a blanket mailshot to girls your age. It's an advertising ploy, not necessarily a scam. Many companies use it, not only in modeling. If you mailshot a set number of households, or a demographic, 2% of them will react. Companies need to send out several [thousands] of mailshots to get anywhere near enough interest in whatever it is [it offers].[34]

First and Second Mailshot

When you're in the mail-order business, it is often necessary to mailshot at least twice to see results. The first mailshot serves to entice the recipient, and the second to motivate the recipient to act. Pageant officials will mailshot two attempts to prospective contestants, per pageant season, and a third, if time permits.

One pageant organization let me in on a comical story. In sharing this behind-the-scenes account, pageant officials asked not to be identified. At one time they employed a humorous and

---

[34] "Is it worth the money to join National American Miss?" *Yahoo! Answers.* http://answers.yahoo.com/question/index;_ylt=ArmfKR_YrxT7zGoQrvLTqcHB _Nw4;_ylv=3?qid=20120220131808AApkNZj.

clever technique to recruit prospective contestants from their *second* mailshot, but first, let me tell you about their *first* mailshot.

The first mailshot included only a postcard inviting girls to participate in their pageant. These girls could do so by visiting the pageant website (and completing an online application), or by calling the pageant headquarters.

All invitations were identified by a code on the postcard mailer. The code was ultimately a list-cleaning tool.

From the first mailshot, about two percent of its target paid a deposit and registered. Those names were taken off of the first mailing list. The remaining prospective contestants — those who received the postcard yet chose not to register — became the "inactive list" leads.

The cleaned "inactive list" was positioned for a second mailshot. Pageant officials used an identical postcard, only this time they manually crumbled each postcard and then flattened each one out. Then, they stuffed each one into an envelope with a note that read,

> Please do not throw this out again. We're confident that if you understood what our pageant is about, you would participate in our program!

Would you believe they had *nearly* a five percent return on the second mailing? Some prospective contestants even wondered how pageant officials knew that they'd tossed it — no kidding!

When Miss Texas USA needed a striking postcard — one that pulled in record-breaking prospective contestants (and eventual) official contestants — pageant officials employed *PostcardMania's* services. The *PostcardMania* marketing consultant had a discussion with pageant officials to fully understand the dynamics of their business and situation. Then, to achieve their marketing goals, *PostcardMania* team members suggested a DirectMail2.0 campaign to *Miss Texas USA* pageant officials. To learn more about the DirectMail2.0 campaign and the amazing results *PostcardMania* achieved for *Miss Texas USA* — which culminated into over a quarter-million online ad impressions — visit "Houston Beauty Pageant Company Case Study." Contact *PostcardMania* at its website portal or visit its *Facebook* page: PostcardMania — Postcard Marketing Experts.

Information to Include in Your First Mailshot

If you are a non-Open Call pageant, your first mailshot should be a simple invitation for the prospective contestant to visit your informative pageant website. It's not the time to mailshot complete financial disclosures and supporting pageant materials. Your informative pageant website, such as, for example, _Miss American Coed_'s website, lets prospective contestants decide how much information they want to read BEFORE filling out an Official Application.

If you're an Open Call pageant (and mailshot prospective contestants Open Call invitations), include your URL (Uniform Resource Identifier) to lead prospective contestants to _your_ informative website.

Meanwhile, "the letter" (Open Call invitation) can entice prospective contestants to attend your Open Call, as does the one _National American Miss_ sends out. View NAM's 2015 Open Call invitation to see how it reads. (This particular Florida State Open Call didn't provide a free photoshoot — proof that Open Call, in itself, is enough enticement to get prospective contestants to attend.) View NAM's accompanying envelope here.

After prospective contestants (and their parents/guardians) attend Open Call, a spokesperson should begin the session by telling them about its pageant program. At this time, s/he _should_ also present, verbally and in writing, _complete_ financial disclosures and supporting pageant marketing materials. _Then_ the Open Call spokesperson can invite prospective contestants to fill out an Official Application (contract) and gain a legally-binding signature. I would NEVER allow my daughter, Mia, who appears on the cover of my _Producing Beauty Pageant_ series, to participate in a pageant system that requires a legally-binding signature _before_ dispensing complete financial disclosures and other pageant supporting materials — verbally and in writing.

A pageant system won't need to mailshot a heavy Acceptance Package with complete pageant marketing materials, supporting materials, and complete financial disclosures IF it was thoroughly presented at Open Call. Learn how to draw HUGE crowds at your Open Call by understanding the psychology of an Open Call. This information can be found in my book _Producing Beauty Pageants: Open Call_, Chapter 2, "Psychology of an Open Call." To understand the power of "the letter," read the same book, Chapter 6, "The Letter."

Information to Include in Your Second Mailshot

Besides serving as a motivator, second mailshots serve as an extension for prospective contestants to do what the first mailshot requested. A second mailshot is a leads nurturer. It affords pageant officials an opportunity to mine for official contestants from the same leads — albeit angling from a renewed and heightened state, and thus, presenting to the prospective contestants a more enticing "new" offer.

If you're a non-Open Call pageant, your second mailing should include the same information as the first mailing, only with a new "extended" deadline and a new hook. An opportunity to participate in a group photoshoot to promote an Official Sponsor's product is one hook. Offering an opportunity to be photographed at the pageant by the famed photographer "X," for example, is another. Just keep hooks slightly different from the first mailshot invitation to the second.

If you're an Open Call pageant, the Open Call itself *is* the hook *even if prospective contestants didn't act on the first mailshot offer*. Maybe it was because those girls didn't have a photo that they were asked to bring, they got cold feet, or they forgot to mark their calendars. Maybe they just needed more time to research the pageant. Now, having just been offered another chance to look into the pageant by being invited to attend a different Open Call, their enthusiasm is often renewed, and you'll garner a few more interested prospective contestants who will submit the necessary materials by your second deadline date. If you don't have additional Open Call sessions, invite those prospective contestants to register online by offering a new entry deadline along with the photographer "X" information.

Again, a second mailshot is not the time to include full pageant marketing materials. Do you think that the *Miss California USA* and *Miss California Teen USA* pageants, in 2012, would have had *over* 400 combined entries if it stated, in any of its Open Call invitations, that its entry fee was $1,700 (slightly less for the teen division) before they had the opportunity to meet with these girls in person and *then* present complete financial disclosures and supporting pageant materials (before requiring a contractual signature on an Official Application)? *Miss California USA* officials might have scared away a good number of prospective contestants! The entry fee, in 2013, was $1,875 (slightly less for the teen division)! The financial disclosures for *Miss California USA* and *Miss California Teen USA*, and other pageant marketing materials, are shared with prospective contestants at Open Call or after a pageant representative contacts prospective contestants from their online pre-application submission.

Mailshot Campaign

Direct-mail techniques, or tips, will greatly increase the response to your mailshot efforts. Not only is getting prospective contestants to open their mail vital to a successful mailshot campaign, but so is getting them to *read* it.

Folding

Gain a competitive edge by knowing smart folding (and stuffing) tips. Fold your literature in an accordion fashion to expose an attention-grabbing headline. First, place attention-grabbing information, such as an Open Call, photo shoot, Pageant Workshop, or pageant commercial filming information, in this forefront view, followed by other pageant marketing materials. It will be the first thing a prospective contestant's thumb touches as she pulls the literature out of the envelope. It could be the difference between reading the information and ditching it. If your attention-grabbing headline is buried in the folds of your pageant marketing materials, it might continue to be buried — right into the trash!

Inserting

Place your attention-grabbing banner first into the envelope, *backwards*, and in an accordion fashion with the promotion facing front. This helps your target to immediately see the banner when opening the envelope. People tend to open their mail from the back side and pull out the information from the same angle.

If your envelope features a window that displays the contact's mailing address, still place the attention-grabbing banner backwards if you want it to be the first piece of pageant marketing material (in a slew of others) you angling them to read.

If your envelope features a window, and you only include one piece of pageant marketing material like an Open Call invitation, then a contact's name and mailing address (on the invitation) needs to be aligned to the window.

Outer Envelope

The outer envelope is known as the headline of direct mail. Half of the battle is to get that envelope opened. Fortunately, people do open most of their mail. The problem then is to pique interest or curiosity in the reader to examine the contents. You want your mailshot to be the one that's "saved for last." The obvious approach to accomplishing this goal is to pre-sell. This consists of putting the offer — headline — right on the front of the envelope. Some headline ideas include: "You Could Be the Next *Miss Golden State* Winner!"; "Girls Needed for the Miss XYZ Pageant Commercial Filming!"; or "There Will Only Be One *Miss South Texas* and it Could be You!"

Or, just print an enticing design on your envelope, as does *National American Miss*. View NAM's swirly envelope at *twicsy* (the Twitter Pics Engine). View NAM's *new swirly envelope* at *WordPress*. Be sure to scroll down under the new swirly envelope to view NAM's 2015 Open Call invitation.

You won't need to peel another address label if you use window envelopes. If you do bleed your envelope design on a corner of your pageant envelope, continue the bleed onto the back. This way, your striking envelope can be spotted whichever side it lands in your targets' mailbox/slot. Accompany the continued bleed on the back side with an inviting message, such as your tagline.

Reply Envelope

It pays to have a reply envelope. Even with the restrictive postal design requirements for business reply mail, there is room to make the envelope interesting. Typefaces, reverses, colors, borders, and bleeds are all tools that can provide a sense of design and value even with strict adherence to postal requirements. Your company name and the way the envelope is addressed can also help with the sale. For envelopes other than business reply mail, the only additional requirement is that you must fit the reply envelope into the outer envelope, so it must be large enough to accommodate pageant marketing materials. Successful pageant promoters will provide a self-addressed reply envelope. Smart ones will include a "Postage Paid" reply envelope. For information on prepaid postage envelopes, visit your post office or go online.

Miss Plus America doesn't supply reply envelopes. Instead, it requires that _all_ snail mail MUST be sent Priority Mail because it accompanies a tracking number. Good advice. _Miss Illinois USA_ also offers some good advice,

> Unless you are specifically requested to do so, there is no need to spend additional money on Priority or Overnight mail; regular first class will suffice and will not cost you extra money. If you do decide to send something to us using a faster method of delivery, please make sure you waive the need for our signature. We are unable to sign for our packages on a daily basis and it will only further delay our receipt of your package if we have to wait to sign for them. This applies to all mailings you send in to Pageant Headquarters.

Business Cards

Include _two_ business cards in your mailshot. They are small, so it is easy for prospective contestants to file one away and give the other to a friend. Heighten your promotion by sending business cards with a printed hook on the back. For example, if all of your Runners-Up and winner advance to another pageant, print on the back: "Top 5 Contestants Advance to the Miss ... Pageant!" or "You Could be the Next Miss Golden State!"

Postcards

When you want to get your message out to lots of prospective contestants, postcards are fast and cost-effective. While they often serve as a follow up (or reminder) tool, postcards can be used for initial contact, Open Call invitation, online applicants' second connection, birthday cheers, and last, but not least, to decline prospective contestants entry. If you don't want to employ a designer, create your own postcard using _PsPrint_ postcard templates. If you need graphics for a magnetic postcard, one that will stay put on your target's refrigerator for all of her visiting friends to see, *Photo Retouching by Courtney* will create graphics for your postcard magnet.

Initial Contact

In addition to swirly envelopes, *National American Miss* also uses postcards in its mailshot campaign — mostly when Open Call is not included. One NAM official contestant recalls,

> One day [I] got a postcard in the mail that said, "[Would] you like to join the pageant?" It was a $20 entrance fee and if you didn't get in you would get $20 back. [I] figured [I] might as well see what happens. So [I] sent it in and [I] got a letter back saying, "Congratulations, you are a state finalist."[35]

Notice the hook in the first mailshot postcard? NAM's hook is that you would "get $20 back" if you didn't qualify to enter the pageant. The recipient is made to think that she had nothing to lose by sending in $20 — cheap validation. In the second mailshot, the prospective contestant received a letter (not "the letter") inside NAM's swirly envelope stating that she became a "State Finalist." You don't need me to tell you that the hook words here only mean "official contestant." The first mailshot served to entice; the second served as a motivator.

Open Call Invitation

Reach prospective contestants via an Open Call postcard campaign. Visit *Miss Central Massachusetts'* "Open Call Every Sunday" postcard. Designed and printed by *RMG Printing* (RomanMarketingGroup@gmail.com), MCM's Open Call postcard was the perfect solution to its mailshot campaign to recruit girls for its Princess (5–7), Little Miss (8–12), Teen (13–17), and Miss (18–27) pageant divisions. To view MCM's general pageant invitation postcard, also mailshot-designed by *RMG Printing*, visit "Become the Next Miss Central Massachusetts." Both postcards were designed E.D.D.M. (Every Door Direct Mail)-ready for mass mailing. Before you decide to integrate E.D.D.M.-

---

[35] Salisbury, Andrea. "Dedham Teen Prepares for National American Miss." *Dedham Transcript*, March 4, 2010.
http://www.dailynewstranscript.com/news/x1759786430/Dedham-teen-prepares-for-National-American-Miss#axzz28m4MPq50.

ready postcards, read some outstanding advice from *PostcardMania's* Maniac Marketing blog.

Online Applicants' Second Connection

National American Miss' second mailshot to online inquiries are slightly different. In this case, the first mailing isn't considered a mailshot, because prospective contestants made the first move: they applied online at NAM's website. Those specific girls will receive the initial pageant marketing materials that Open Call attendees receive; however, the applicants from the group that didn't come up with their first sponsorship installment are now targeted for a motivating mailshot.

That mailshot — a 12" x 7" postcard — features, on the left 1/3 side, a reminder that the recipient is *still* a "State Finalist" and that NAM hadn't heard from her in quite some time. There was still time to be a part of its awesome event. Then, it glosses over the prizes up for grabs: thousands of dollars in cash awards, scholarships, trophies, modeling scholarships, trips to *Disneyland*, etc. The post card recipient is reminded that she will be presented with a trophy on stage for already having been selected as a "State Finalist."

On the right 1/3 side of the postcard NAM notes that the "State Finalist" could call (or mail) in her sponsor payment to secure her spot in the pageant:

We accept all major credit cards.

Below that, tiny iconic images of *Visa, MasterCard, Discover,* and *American Express* cards authenticate the implied action. Above those images, and in red ink, is suggested:

If you are into doing things yourself, and you have some free weekends, have a bake sale, a garage sale or a car wash! Make bracelets and sell them, or set up a lemonade stand. All these things are a perfectly fine way to raise money!!

On the center 1/3 of the postcard, NAM includes five paragraphs on how the "State Finalist" can obtain her [$480] sponsorship fee — in a combined 18 sentences.

Birthday Cheers

Another clever strategy *National American Miss* employs is to mailshot normal-sized postcards with a birthday greeting. The birthday postcard becomes either the second or third mailshot, depending on when the applicant's birthday is, and when NAM fires off its second mailshot. The birthday postcard shows the recipient that NAM really cares about her and that she is still welcome to take part in its pageant. Young, impressionable girls *like* to feel wanted.

The front of the 2014 NAM birthday postcard included a group photo of 2013's *National All-American Miss Queens* (in gown, sash, and crown) holding balloons and party horns. NAM's logo and website address are strategically placed on the bottom right corner. Receiving this hyper-colorful postcard is as if the postman sprinkles confetti all the way into the recipient's hands. You *feel* confetti coming down like you just *won* the pageant! On the back of the birthday postcard is nothing but a simple birthday greeting:

> Your birthday is a special day! I wish you lots of love and happiness. Make this your best year ever!

NAM is betting that "your best year" will be to win the pageant THIS year. NAM's "Silent Salesman" starts early in its promotional process, even before Open Call sessions begin. Learn more about NAM's "Silent Salesman" by reading my book *Producing Beauty Pageants: Open Call*, Chapter 5, "The Silent Salesman...and Other Subliminal Messengers."

Decline Entry

According to NAM mom Jennifer, *National American Miss* also sends postcards to decline entry:

> Well, in a few days we should either get a phone call saying she's an Arizona State Finalist or a post card saying she's not.[36]

Jennifer's daughter didn't receive a declining postcard, but a callback inviting her to become a NAM Arizona State Finalist. In

---

[36] "What is National American Miss? Another Beauty Pageant?" *Coupons and Friends.* January 21, 2013.
http://browse.feedreader.com/c/Coupons_and_Friends/289511381.

my extensive research for my *Producing Beauty Pageant* series, I have yet to find a NAM prospective contestant who received a declining postcard — or the postcard itself — so I can't write about it or a "declinee's"[37] experience.

PostcardMania: A Case Study

A Houston-based Preliminary to the *Miss Texas USA* pageant enlisted *PostcardMania* marketing experts to create a pageant-winning postcard to attract prospective contestants into its pageant. The postcard design used a bright blue color scheme to engage prospective contestants. It also featured a picture of two gorgeous pageant Queens to get postcard recipients interested in participating. The prospects could visualize themselves (or their child) wearing the crown, and it compelled them to call to find out more information. The headline read: "You could be the next!" and then invited the reader to think about what it would be like to be a pageant winner, while the picture of the Queens reinforced the glamour that comes with winning.

The Preliminary pageant wanted a way to promote its pageants that was both easy and effective. The *PostcardMania* marketing consultant had a discussion with the producers to fully understand the dynamics of their business and then suggested its DirectMail2.0 campaign to achieve their pageant's marketing goals.

A DirectMail2.0 campaign consists of many distinct marketing strategies integrating together to result in a complete and complimenting marketing program. This means that it creates leads, nurtures leads, and even tracks the results of the postcard campaign so that pageant producers can continually build off success. And all of this happens automatically. The main drivers of the campaign are the direct mail postcards and the automatic online follow-up. For the lead generation portion of the pageant website, the automated follow-up portion of the campaign kicks in. Prospective contestants that visit the website are automatically tracked and followed via banner ads after they leave the site. The ads *Postcardmania* created match the design style of the postcard, even using the same images. This helps immediately orient prospective contestants when they see it, so

---

[37] Maybe *Webster Dictionary* will add "declinee" to its next printing.

they know who the ad is from, and they can focus on the content of the message.

In the first five days, the Preliminary pageant received 259 online follow-up ad clicks and 245,718 total online ad impressions (number of times the ad was seen). Over the next 15 days, the Preliminary pageant received another 49 banner ad clicks and 73,330 more online ad impressions. As of this writing, the Preliminary pageant was able to add 1,900 people to its online follow-up list. To put these results in perspective, this means that, over a period of twenty days, 308 people a) went to the pageant website (most likely due to the postcards), and b) returned to the site via the online follow-up banner ads. It is unlikely that prospective contestants would have returned to the site without the banner ads to remind them. That is the power of automatic online follow-up that _PostcardMania_ can accomplish for you.

Mailing Lists

Ever wonder how you (or your daughter) received pageant information when you (or your daughter) were in high/middle/elementary school? How did pageant promoters find you (or your daughter) in order to send pageant literature?

Pageant producers purchase mailing lists from list brokers. _Alloy Media & Marketing_'s high school market will allow you to select from this group by choosing ethnicity, class year, age, zip code or county area, gender, etc. You can even be more selective, for example, by purchasing the names of all teen subscribers to a particular teen magazine. Lists are normally purchased on a one-time use, i.e., "seeding names" are inserted in your order. If you mailshot more than once, the company you purchased the one-time list from will spot it and possibly take legal action. However, when a prospective contestant contacts you from your mailshot, you now own the right to mail that girl future pageant marketing materials. If you intend to mailshot to the same list for a second time (minus those who made personal contact with you), you will need to repurchase it. Be sure to comparatively shop for mailing lists. While _Alloy Media & Marketing_ has magazine subscribers' lists, you might be able to rent the same list directly from the publisher for a lower price. Or, barter for mailing lists, as does _National American Miss_ with _American Cheerleader Magazine_ and _Dance Spirit Magazine_. Learn how to barter for leads with direct mail companies and with magazine publishers by reading my book *Producing Beauty Pageants: Brokering a Pageant through Barter*, Chapter 6, "Media Partners" under "Direct Mail Official Sponsor." *International Pageant Productions* pageant officials invite prospective contestants to "Join Our Mailing List" at their blog!

Magazines

I wrote my last teen article, "Secrets of Teen Millionaires," in 2008, for the now-defunct teen magazine *Cosmo Girl!*[38] (Its sister magazine, *Cosmopolitan*, continues to thrive.) That year the economy took a particularly sharp downward turn leading into The Great Recession. Loads of teen magazines — *Cosmo Girl!* included — folded. (And so did hordes of pageant systems that didn't include Open Call in its business model, but that's another book.) For those still around, and even for some of the new ones, contact publishers to purchase their subscribers list. Or, offer to barter same-demographics mailing lists. A magazine editor might also be interested in becoming an Official Sponsor of your fantastic program. After all, subscription rates are down these days! Learn how to barter with magazine editors by reading my book *Producing Beauty Pageants: Brokering a Pageant through Barter*, Chapter 6, "Media Partners" under "Magazine Official or In-Kind Sponsor."

Contestants

One of the best lead generators is official contestants. Their enthusiasm for your program helps them to garner prospective contestant referrals for current or future pageants. There are many ways official contestants can go about collecting referrals, i.e., building leads. They include 1) typing friends' names into the pageant website's referral page link portal; 2) writing their friends' names (and contact information) on a pre-printed Contestant Referral form; 3) retrieving their school directories and carefully selecting names (and contact information) to include on the Contestant Referral form; 4) gathering referrals from dance, gymnastics, or other schools (twirling, modeling, acting, cheer,

---

[38] Stanley, Anna. "Secrets of Teen Millionaires." *Cosmo Girl!* April, 2008, Vol, 10, Issue 3, page 88.
http://connection.ebscohost.com/c/articles/31813936/secrets-teen-millionaires

theater, etc.) they attend; and last, but not least, 5) incorporating synergy.

Referral Link

Don't wait to build a mailing list through official contestants. Invite *prospective* contestants to insert referrals onto your website referral portal, as early as their first visit. Include a "Refer a Friend" link on your website *and* in your email campaign.

The beauty of having a referral link portal on your website and email campaign is that the leads will have already been entered into your database. No need to employ a data processor. All you need to do is print labels, and you're ready to mailshot to your target market.

Even before a girl becomes a *National American Miss* official contestant, and even before she pays a $20 application fee (when applying online) — yet after she "Accepts" NAM's "specific conditions of use" — a prospective contestant is brought to NAM's "MyNAMiss Registration" page. Here she can click on "My Referrals" and is immediately offered an opportunity to "add your first referral" on a referral template at the portal. When she completes all asterisked boxes, her referral page is submitted. At the top of the "Successfully-Submitted" page, she will find another "Add New Referral" button available to her. She clicks on that and a "New Referral" template appears, giving her yet another opportunity to add an additional referral. It will go on for as long as her referral list warrants.

If the next referral is a sister at the same household, it won't process. This prevents mailing multiple pageant marketing materials to the same household. If the referral stems from a different address, then it takes, and NAM's "My Referrals" list continues to grow. Official contestants can return to the page and continue adding referrals.

Prospective contestants can also add referrals if they paid the $20 application fee. Then, their referrals stick, even if the prospective contestant's pageant career is cut short and she doesn't pay the first sponsorship installment. NAM builds referrals with prospective and official contestants.

But the downside to having a referral portal on your website is that a *prospective* contestant *can* delete her referrals before final submission, i.e., simply by abandoning her shopping cart and not paying the $20 application fee. Or, an official contestant who becomes disillusioned with the pageant can delete the referrals before the pageant ends. (At least with the prospective contestant, while she opted out of the pageant before paying the $20 application fee, her referrals might not have.) Talk to your website designer to come up with a way for referrals to stick once they are keyed into your referral portal.

American Nation Pageants includes a "Refer A Friend!" page on its website. It asks for the prospective contestant's name, state of residence, email address, telephone number, age, and the referring person's name. Following the prompts, I filled in the required asterisked fields and then hit the submit button. The transaction didn't take. I tried again, and it didn't work. So, for the one non-required, non-asterisked field (telephone number) I had left blank, I filled it in. As it turned out, every field needed to be filled out, not just the asterisked fields. This time it did take, but that was the end. Although I wasn't through referring, there weren't any more open field portals to refer prospective contestants.

Official Contestant Handbook

Dedicate four pages in your pageant newsletter/magazine to "referral lists," i.e., two back-to-back referral pages. *National American Miss* includes four referral pages in its Magazine #3. Even if you feature blank pages in your handbook, include loose referral forms with your pageant marketing materials. Candidates often don't want to write in their Contestant Handbook (Magazines #1 to #4) and tear out the pages, or they don't make copies. Loose forms can be folded and tucked into candidates' tote bags and brought to school or to dance classes to be filled out.

Referral Awards

A Contestant Referral Award is an award that prospective or official contestants can work toward with minimal effort. Entice official contestants to respond to this contest by crowning the candidate who turns in the most names and addresses — leads — the Miss Hospitality title. Consider awarding official contestants who, for example, turn in a certain number of pages, and not just to the overall winner who submits the most leads. Remember to include the count from your website referral portal. Consider rewarding a free Optionals entry to prospective contestants who refer a certain number of active leads. Consider "active leads" as prospective contestants who are invited to, and who attend, your Open Call. Learn how to be selective about giving away lucrative Optionals by reading my book *Producing Beauty Pageants: Optionals*.

American Royal Beauties breaks down its Referral Program awards opportunities into *registered* groups that include 3–5 official contestants, 5–9 official contestants, and 10+ official contestants. Each respective groups' awards affords free Optionals competitions and other perks. In the 10+ group, free entry into the National pageant is awarded if ten or more girls that the official contestant referred *register* into the current pageant. Granted, official contestants can refer pages and pages of leads, but unless their leads translate into official contestants, it won't count towards *ARB's Referral Program* awards. What would make their referral page even better is if ARB included an unlimited portal field to build its mailing list, as does *National American Miss*. Detailed information on NAM's Referral Program can be found in my book *Producing Beauty Pageants: Contestant Handbook*.

School Directories

One of the least expensive ways to build leads is to purchase middle and high school directories. They often include the students' first names (and their respective grades), their parents' complete names, mailing address, telephone number, and/or email address. Be smart by not blanketing the entire directory in one mailshot. Contact the school's ASB (Associated Student Body) to purchase a school directory. For a nation-wide canvassing of school directories, use a *Patterson American Education* directory to lead you to the school. Official contestants often use their school directories to build leads onto their referral forms.

Modeling Agencies/Schools

Modeling agencies/schools might have lists to sell. Better yet, offer to barter your list of active leads. Learn how to barter for leads with modeling agencies and schools by reading my book *Producing Beauty Pageants: Brokering a Pageant through Barter*, Chapter 7, "Barter Your Prize Package" under "Modeling Agency/School." Additional information can be found in the same book Chapter 9, "In-Kind Sponsors" under "Acting/Modeling/Cheerleading/Baton Twirling Schools."

Referral Program

You likely already have ideas on how to build your own Referral Program within your pageant system. Additional ideas to add to your success can be found in my book *Producing Beauty Pageants: Creating a Synergized National Pageant System*.

Admission Tickets

Print a referral template on the back of admission tickets, thereby inviting ticketholders an opportunity to refer a prospective candidate for future pageant information. The template should include the name, age, home address, email address, and phone number of a referral. Also, reserve the back of your admission ticket for a Silver Official Sponsor (anyone who pays to advertise a coupon or advertisement on the back of every admission ticket), as does *Boar's Head Pageant*. You can use money from this ad sale to purchase a demographic mailing list.

Pre-Application/Pageant Website

Display a pre-application with a referral portal on your website. The referral portal can include fields asking for the prospective contestant's name, age, date of birth, home address, zip code, email address, and phone number. Also, remember to include a link at the bottom of this page: "Send this page to a friend." Now, the prospective contestant becomes a Contestant Recruiter even before she becomes an official contestant.

Synergy

If your pageant system isn't synergized, it won't play ball in the big leagues. The synergy needs to come from two angles: pageant officials and official contestants. In fact, it wouldn't hurt to start synergizing prospective contestants, as does *National American Miss* at its Open Call. My book *Producing Beauty Pageants: Creating a Synergized National Pageant System*, can help you realize synergy paths you might not know exist. In today's pageant field, it can make the financial difference.

Emailshot

Bring together old school and new school by incorporating a pageant emailshot campaign parallel to your mailshot campaign. *Kennedy Pageant Productions* includes a Subscribe to our Email

List portal. Be sure to scroll down the home page to view the portal field box. Anyone can subscribe because an age field is not included. But, if you plan to email pageant information, how will you know if the recipient fits the pageant's age demographic? Include age and date-of-birth fields.

Emailing to Minors

If you plan to email pageant information to minors, read *Children's Online Privacy Protection Act* (COPPA), 15 U.S.C. §§ 6501–6508, which contains a requirement that the Federal Trade Commission (FTC) issue and enforce a rule concerning children's online privacy. The Children's Online Privacy Protection Rule, 16 C.F.R. Part 312, on April 21, 2000, became effective. On August 1, 2012, the Federal Trade Commission announced that it issued a Supplemental Notice of Proposed Rulemaking to modify certain rules under the COPPA. You might also want to read "FTC Complaint Filed Against Sites That Market To Kids."

Email Campaign Takes Flight

As I write this, I received a colorful pageant email invitation from *East Coast Starz*' "Now Boarding, No Delays, Book Today" emailshot campaign. The subject line of the email stated:

> Calling All Models to Board this Amazing Flight!
> FREE PHOTO SHOOTS!

At the beginning of the email content is a flyer featuring photos from three amazing photography studios: *Candy Kid Photography*, *LeRed Photography*, and *Gallery Row Studio*. It accompanied an announcement stating that its photographers will be at the *East Coast Starz* pageant: a hybrid between a pageant and a fashion show. Then came the enticing bait:

> Just Added: Amazing Editorial Designer Showcase Bonus Shoots! Every registered contestant will get the opportunity to shoot with Olesja Mueller [Gallery Row Studio].

The "just added" information would be PERFECT for a second emailshot. Even if you know from the start — your first emailshot — that this opportunity will happen, keep it for your second emailshot, unless you have something even more exciting to offer. It could be the hook you need to convince on-the-fence prospective contestants to become official contestants after all.

East Coast Starz' emailshot campaign not only calls for all pageant girls, but fashionistas can also board this flight! As I scroll down the email, it features young fashionistas in the prettiest of clothes, shot by some of the best photographers. There are links at the top of the email for prospective contestants to connect to ECS' pageant paperwork, online registration, and hotel room information. Featured at the bottom is a "Forward this email" link. Girls are encouraged to:

> Get your Boarding Pass...before the flight is OVERBOOKED! Only 15 contestants accepted per group. All groups close to full!

East Coast Starz' emailshot is the golden bullet of a successful pageant email campaign. Contact ECS to get on this flight or to be placed on its standby list.

Mailshot, EMailshot Again

When then prospective contestant Hadassah thought about entering a *National American Miss* pageant for the first time, it wasn't because she received just one invitation to its Open Call:

> I've been receiving letters from them for at least seven years to compete in NAM.[39]

On the seventh invite, shy of her 18th birthday, Hadassah participated in her NAM State pageant. It may take two — or seven — mailshots to hit that target!

---

[39] "Hadassah (February 2011): NAM." *National American Miss – Scam?* April 24, 2011. http://www.national-american-miss-scam.com/2011/04/hadassah-february-2011-nam/.

Chapter 13

Advertisement Sales

Selling advertisements offsets the costs of producing your Pageant Program Book, and it can also be one of your largest income streams.

Advertisement Sales: A Prerequisite or Not

Official contestants who want to sell advertisements in your Pageant Program Book (PPB) can do so. Nevertheless, selling advertisements should not be a prerequisite for participating in the pageant, but if it is mandatory, as in _Miss Teen America_, be sure to stipulate this financial disclosure before prospective contestants sign a contract (Official Application) and activate the legally-binding clauses. It would be unethical to divulge this financial disclosure _after_ prospective contestants turn in their first, non-refundable sponsorship installment and become official contestants, and if it is "[mandatory] that every contestant sell at least one ad," as notes _The Glass Slipper Natural Beauty Pageant_, do they mean a business card-size, a quarter page, a half page, or a full page ad? _Kentucky Beauties_ requires official contestants to sell at least a one-half page advertisement in its PPB. Candidates who do not meet this requirement are charged an additional $50 along with their entry fee. _Miss American Coed_ PPB ad sales are not required at the State pageant; it is only required at National. The _Mr. and Miss Greek God & Goddess_ pageant officials warn prospective contestants, before they legally commit to the pageant by signing their Official Application, of the following:

> Final contestants are to sell a minimum of $100 worth of ads for the Pageant Program Book; this will be explained further in Informational Meetings once the Final contestants are selected.

World's Perfect Teen notes,

If you won a State Pageant (and you have won your $895 entry fee), you are required to purchase a second advertisement page for $225. Please submit your second page and payment at the same time as your complimentary advertisement page.

One thing to make clear, as does *Miss Lake Charles USA Pageant* is that,

Selling ads [do] not increase your chances of winning...

...unless it does.

Built-In Advertisements

If you do make advertising sales for your Pageant Program Book (PPB) a criterion, consider building the advertisement copy cost into the sponsorship fee. *World's Perfect Teen* charges an $895 entry fee. Not only does this fee cover the cost of a candidate's National opening number outfit, but it also includes a full page advertisement that every official contestant receives for "free" in its PPB. Pageant officials who want a guaranteed advertisement from every official contestant should build the PPB advertising cost into the sponsorship fee.

Salute Advertisements

Miss Oklahoma pageant identifies Pageant Program Book (PPB) advertisement sales as "Salute Ads" in its Congratulatory Ad Pages & Salute Ad Pages Contestant Information guide. The Salute Ad is an advertisement page in the PPB dedicated to the official contestant. The Salute Ad is an opportunity for official contestants' hometown businesses, chamber representatives, employers, community leaders, sororities, teachers, friends, and family to show their support. *Miss Oklahoma* pageant officials arrange it so that such advertisement sales are a win-win opportunity: participating candidates receive a rebate from the advertisements sold *and* exposure in the PPB. Pageant officials hint that every official contestant "should be able to sell a minimum of four ads," but remind them that the rebates only kick in after five pages are sold. As of this writing, a full page color advertisement costs $750; a full page black and white ad costs $300. They also hint that some official contestants sold over thirty pages!

Signature Page

Official contestants who find it hard to sell advertising pages in the _National American Miss_ Pageant Program Book can choose to sell a Signature Page. Alexandra Curtis, _National American Miss All-American Teen_ 2011, says:

> A Signature Page is where a contestant has her family and friends throw in some money, they all sign the page, and you can design it and put a picture of yourself [in the advertisement] — but the money has to equal $600[40]!

Spotlight Page

When official contestants want to purchase advertising pages in your Pageant Program Book (PPB), consider offering a rate that is less than what businesses would pay. _Miss Connecticut USA_ makes up to ten PPB pages available per official contestant. Candidates can choose as many as ten full-page ads or twenty half-page ads — or a combination of the two. State pageant officials believe that this is a great way for candidates to gain added recognition and exposure by "spotlighting" their photo more than once in the PPB. Spotlight Pages are $300 for a full-page ad and $200 for a half-page. _Miss Connecticut USA's_ Special Spotlight Pages guide can provide helpful tips.

National American Miss' "I am" Spotlights sell for $195. The advertisement measures approximately 3" x 7 ½" — which means three spotlight ads fit on a single (PPB) page. This translates to NAM charging $585 for a full page of spotlight "ads." (While a full page PPB ad went from $600, in 2013, to $750, in 2014, it appears that the cost of the Spotlight page has remained the same.) For every "I am" Spotlight entry each NAM official contestant makes

---

[40] It's likely that the signature page, in 2014, went up to $750 — it line with the full page ad price increase of the same amount.

in the National PPB, the candidate receives one credit towards the Spirit of America Award. An official contestant who earns five credits earns a Stars and Stripes trophy. Candidates who want to purchase an "I am" Spotlight will find a Photo Card in a section of NAM's black & white portion of its National Pageant Guidebook . On page "w" of the forms section of the National Pageant Guidebook, it asks candidates to "Tape Your Color Picture Here" in the box to the right of the form:

> Please use double stick tape or tape only the very edges of the picture. Please write your name gently on the back of your picture. School photos are fine!

Pressing a hand-written name too hard will indent the name of the candidate on the picture and reproduce with the indented name! "I am" candidates are gifted an "I AM" t-shirt when they arrive at the National pageant. To view the "I am" Spotlight, visit page "w" in The Official National Pageant Guidebook (a black and white forms section following the color pages, where the order form is the first mention of cost). If these links don't work, Google "National American Miss Guidebook," without the quotes, and you'll likely find the most recent NAM guidebook. Then, click on "Guidebook." When you arrive on that page, you will have three options: 1) Download Official National Application; 2) Download NAM Guidebook — Color Informational Section; and 3) Download NAM Guidebook — Black & White Forms Section. The Spotlight ad information, except for the cost, appears in the color portion of the Guidebook. The $195 cost does, however, appear in the Black & White Forms Section. This is an illustration of springing the price on competitors the last minute, and it is something that I do not recommend.

Miss California United States makes it easy for official contestants to purchase a spotlight ad by including a Spotlight Ad and Headshot Upload page on its pageant website. Candidates can register for a spotlight ad by filling in their name and contact information, uploading their spotlight photo, and listing up to five sponsors for that particular purchase.

Circulation Demographics

I researched different pageant systems with the most advertisement sales in their Pageant Program Books (PPBs), and I compared Advertising Program informational packets. It wasn't what was included in the demographics that was vital to each system's success. Rather, it's what most left out: *circulation*.

Let's say that you have a National pageant system and feature multiple age divisions in your various State and National pageants. You produce multiple PPBs — one for each age division. Every official contestant who sold an advertisement has her advertiser's ad displayed *only* in her respective division's PPB, but often, official contestants — newbies in particular — are not aware of this practice and can't relay this information to prospective advertisers. A candidate simply takes direction from her State or National pageant's Advertising Program packet — which usually doesn't include circulation — and presents prospective advertisers with the opportunity to purchase an advertisement in "the PPB." The prospective advertiser often presumes that his ad will be included in one comprehensive PPB and be seen by 100% of the *overall* pageant audience.

The prospective advertiser might investigate the pageant and discover that approximately 500 official contestants sold approximately 4,000 admission tickets (averaging eight per candidate). S/he might assume that 4,000 people will comprise of the audience. The candidate, who is trying to sell an ad, might have told the prospective advertiser that the PPBs will be "distributed" to the audience. The prospective advertiser might assume that "distributed" means "PPBs complimentarily handed out to the audience with every ticket purchase" and will likely believe that his/her ad WILL be seen by 4,000 people.

The prospective advertiser is probably not aware of several factors. For one, not everyone who purchased an admission ticket will attend the pageant event. Another is that a PPB is usually *sold* to the audience, and last, but not least, and typical of a multi-age division pageant system, is that each age division generally has its own PPB. This means that the prospective advertiser's ad would *only* appear in the respective candidate's division PPB. For a pageant system featuring five age divisions, for example, his/her ad would be seen by approximately one-fifth of the audience. In this scenario, the prospective advertiser would not be aware that the *true circulation is about one-fifth of what s/he might have been led to believe.*

Even if the pageant system produced one PPB for its entire State or National pageant(s), and it sells x number of admission tickets, often it's still not one-for-one. Generally, just a *percentage* of the tickets sold translate into the circulation number of a PPB. If a PPB is priced relatively inexpensively, i.e., $10, maybe five or six out of 10 people would purchase one; at $25, maybe two. If the entire (combined age divisions) 4,000 audience members wanted to see all of the advertisements in every age division's PPBs, at $25 per PPB, they would need to pay $125 for all five age division PPBs. It's not going to happen, and for people who purchase admission tickets, yet don't attend the pageant, it is likely that zero PPBs are sold to them. (Having online access to a free PPB would be ideal for no-shows — at least to add them into a circulation count.)

This scenario doesn't factor the PPBs that are gifted to non-attending family and friends into the circulation. It also doesn't include the people who view it, for free, as a virtual PPB at a digital publisher like _issuu.com_ — as you would see if you viewed _Miss Asian Global & Miss Asian America's_ PPB. (A viewer doesn't even need to look at every single page of its 120-page PPB in order to include his/her visit into a PPB's circulation number!) Nor does it consist of virtual PPBs that are typically displayed (and rotated) on several TV's located in the pageant ballroom, as does _My Chance Novice Nationals_. It also does not include advertisements that are inserted on the pageant DVD, as also does _My Chance Novice,_ and last, but not least, it doesn't take into account the advance purchases of PPBs sold at a pageant website to people (who may or may not attend the pageant event). View _Diverse Dreams' Beauties of America's_ advance PPB purchase _Tickets & Program Magazines_ link.

Your circulation number will improve with success from marketing PPBs via various sales avenues and from visits to the free online version. Now, instead of _Miss American Coed_ National contestant Jemila Whitner, in 2011, citing "[over] 3600 National program books will be printed and distributed throughout the nation,"[41] she can reference the previous year's true circulation number — which usually is larger when including online PPB versions. You now have proof that x number of people downloaded your PPB at _issuu_, visited your PPB website link, and purchased x number of them. How do you think _USA Today_ has the greatest circulation number of all major newspapers? Not only does _USA Today_ include paid subscribers in its circulation figure, but the free online version is _also_ factored into its circulation count!

---

41 "Help Jemila get to the National Miss American Coed Pageant." sponsor goal.com. http://www.sponsorgoal.com/2011/11/03/help-jemila-get-to-the-national-miss-american-coed-pageant/.

The bigger the pageant system, the more complicated its PPB advertising program becomes. It's no wonder most pageants keep the PPB circulation number out of its advertising material; however, if a pageant system has a no Refund Policy for PPB ad sales, accurate circulation numbers should accompany it.

Advertising Sales Kit

Give official contestants advertising sales tools to help them reach their Pageant Program Book (PPB) advertising sales goals. A typical pageant Advertising Sales Kit can include, but isn't limited to, an Advertising Information Booklet (a.k.a. Advertising Magazine), Advertising Sales Information Form, an actual PPB, Advertising Order Form/Contract, Advertising Order Form Cover Page, Advertising Rate Sheet, Receipt Book, Lanyard, Crown/Sash, Advertising Sales Letter, and Circulation Information. If you require that advertisements be camera-ready, direct delegates to *Photo Retouching by Courtney* for affordable, high-quality, camera-ready ads. Don't let the name fool you. *Photo Retouching by Courtney* not only produces book covers like my *Producing Beauty Pageant* series, she also offers advertising and graphic designs at probably the best prices around.

NAM's Advertising Information Booklet

No other pageant system has as many Pageant Program Book (PPB) advertising ad page sales as *National American Miss*. For this reason, NAM's *Advertising Program* magazine information — presented to newly-minted official contestants at its Pageant Prep Training Session — is featured in this example. It is a colorful, fourteen-page, slick publication that breaks down its PPB advertising program in the following ways:

- Page one indicates premium prizes that State Finalists (official contestants) can win if they sell one and two pages of advertising.

- Page two includes information for winning a free hotel night at the host hotel as a premium prize. Learn how to barter for thousands of dollars in FREE hotel rooms to dispense as premium prizes by reading my book *Producing Beauty Pageants: Brokering a Pageant through Barter*, Chapter 7, "Barter Your Prize Package" under "Hotel Rooms as Premium Prizes."

- Page three notes Finalist Level (one small ad), Silver Level (half-page ad), Bronze Level (three small ads), and Gold Level (one complete ad page or ten small ad spaces) Awards (prizes). It continues with State Ambassador Awards (two complete ad pages or twenty small ad spaces); Platinum Level Awards (three complete ad pages or thirty small ad spaces); Platinum-Plus Level Awards (four complete ad pages or forty small ad spaces); Diamond Level Awards (seven complete ad pages or seventy small ad spaces); and Diamond-Plus Level Awards (eight complete ad pages or eighty small ad spaces). *Each of these levels can earn between one and eight premium prizes.* The Diamond Level Awards winner(s) can substitute a paid trip to the National Pageant (in place of the group of premium prizes) OR $1,000 cash — whichever a participant chooses. The Diamond-Plus Level Awards winner(s) can substitute a $1,500 college scholarship, a $1,100 cash award, OR a laptop computer in place of the group of premium prizes OR the substituted National Pageant paid trip.

- Pages four, five, and six provide the basic "Advertising 411!" It leads official contestants directly to what they need to know *and* do when they first decide to sell ads. These hand-holding tips include: 1) sitting down with parents to discuss a goal plan; 2) making a list of all the people they can approach to sell ads to; 3) *not* using the phone or writing letters to prospective advertisers; 4) writing down what to say to prospective advertisers when visiting them *in person*; 5) reading a sample script of what to say in an advertising sales pitch; 6) suggesting that candidates practice what to say to prospective advertisers in front of a mirror; 7) reminding candidates to approach relatives and friends in their PPB ad sales search — including those who live out of state or even out of the country; and last, but not least, 8) reminding candidates that Fridays, Saturdays, and Mondays may *not* be good days to visit busy store owners and managers to sell PPB advertisements.

- Page seven reminds official contestants they can include their photo on each complete PPB ad page — words that encourage many ad sales! It also includes an ad size and price rate card.

- Page eight is a contact list page that has lines for candidates to write down who they contacted and on what date/time.

- Page nine features ten photos of NAM's previous years' *National* advertising title winners.

- Page ten has additional advertising information, such as Ad Copy, Ad Layout, ad photos, Ad Record Sheet, and ad deadlines. Moreover, it is noted that additional Ad Layout and Ad Record Sheets can be found in the MyNAMiss Section of the pageant website. This section is a Sign in/Register area only for official contestants.

- Page eleven of the Advertising Program magazine features a rough sketch Ad Layout.

- Page twelve provides a completed Ad Layout.

- Page thirteen includes an Ad Layout Sheet. All that official contestants would need to do is circle their age division, i.e., Princess, Jr. Pre-Teen, etc., and write in the candidate's name, city, and state. While the Ad Layout Sheet is blocked into eight business card-size ad spaces, an official contestant can use half of the page to arrange her half-page ad, a quarter page to arrange her quarter-page ad, etc. Therefore, it would behoove a pageant system to include a sample page displaying various size advertisements templates — as is posted on page fourteen featuring a mosaic of various ad sizes: 1/10 page ad; a 2/10 page ad; and a 3/10 page ad and highlighting the official contestant's photo.

- Page fourteen — the back cover of NAM's Advertising Program magazine — consists of an Ad Record Sheet whereby candidates can list the advertiser, ad size, and ad cost as they make each sale. Participating candidates can check off lines for the prizes they want if they have sold $600 (or more) in ads — one being the only ($1,500) college scholarship a candidate can earn at *any National*

American Miss pageant...IF she sells eight full pages for a grand total of $4,800[42] and IF she chooses that *earned* prize.

Nowhere in the NAM State *Advertising Program* magazine does it indicate that any *National* official contestant has the opportunity to sell twenty full page PPB advertisements, for a grand total of $12,000[43], at the *National* pageant to have the option to substitute a (not to exceed) $2,300 cruise in place of the premium prizes! But it *should* be since NAM permits PPB advertising pages sold at the State pageant to count ONLY towards the National titles of National Cover Girl, National Cover Model, and the National Cover Miss titles. (NAM won't re-award prizes at the National pageant that were earned at the State pageant.) That information should be synergized.

If a National candidate wants the National Cover Girl title, it requires selling seven full PPB ad pages. If the candidate already sold three pages at State, she would only need to sell four additional pages at National in order to "earn" the impressive National Cover Girl title! It's easier for the participating candidate to sell $2,400 in ads at the National pageant, rather than $4,200. And NAM won't miss a lucrative financial opportunity from what might otherwise be a missed income opportunity. Moreover, the State ads count won't take up space in the already-crowded National PPB, because those ads were already advertised in the State PPB.

This is ratcheting up strength in NAM's already-strong State and National PPB advertising program. It doesn't get smarter than this. But it shouldn't surprise you. NAM National Director Steve Mayes holds a BA in Finance and an MBA. NAM Associate National Director Kenn Maples holds BS degrees in Economics and Business.

NAM official contestant Alaina Lakera Walker took a few pages from NAM's National Advertising Program magazine and synergized it into her personal pageant website page. To view NAM's rate sheet, Order Form, Ad Layout Sheet, and Credit Card Form (which wasn't included in NAM's State Advertising Program magazine noted above but, instead, loosely accompanied the

---

[42] In 2014, Pageant Program Book ad pages went up to $750. But, it's my understanding that the prize values remained the same.

[43] In 2014, $15,000.

Advertising Magazine), scroll a quarter of the way down Alaina's
weebly page.

MAC's Advertising Information Booklet

Miss American Coed Colorado pageant officials created an
outstanding Advertising Information Booklet that is helpful to
official contestants participating in its Pageant Program Book
(PPB) advertising sales program. It begins by introducing the
various levels of advertising awards participants can choose to
win. It explains how candidates get started, what to do when they
are ready to go out and find advertisers for the PPB, and provides
an example of what they could say when presenting their pitch. It
also lists good advertising prospects, what to do when a
prospective advertiser says "No", and provides information on
how official contestants can win the National Hostess Title. In
fact, every official contestant who sells ten pages of advertising is
named National Hostess _if_ she attends the National pageant. She
will receive an official National Hostess crown, banner, trophy,
and any award for which she qualifies. To receive a National
Hostess title and earned awards, an official contestant must take
the National trip (and not the cash award), and she must attend
the National pageant. In 1983, MAC developed the National
Hostess Program. Additional advertising information can be
found in MAC's Advertising Information Booklet, such as
advertising sizes and prices, what to obtain in the way of
advertising copy, information on advertising layouts, about
photos in advertising, an advertising record sheet, advertising
deadlines, and a note stating: "Advertising payments are non-
refundable." Note: MAC has different ad page requirements for
different states. If you hail from Colorado, for example, you are
expected to sell four pages of ads for Hostess; if you are from
Arizona, you are expected to sell two pages. Moreover, the
advertising page prices might also differ from state to state.

Miss American Coed official contestant Brittney added
synergy to the MAC Advertising Packet by attaching a self-created
advertising FAQ. The questions she fashioned included: Is it tax
deductible?; Can I have a receipt?; What do I get out of
sponsorship?; What are my funds going to pay for?; Is the
advertising Local, State, [or National?]; If I can't buy an
advertisement but I want to help, what can I do?; What is the
pageant all about?; Is this just another beauty pageant?; and What
made you want to join this pageant? Brittney then customized her

answers to fit her pageant's goals. Candidates should keep their answers brief for ease of "scanning" the page. Moreover, they should consider the most important questions, and then list them first since some people may only read the first few questions. Personally, I would list "Is this just another beauty pageant?" right at the top. This is usually the main issue prospective contestants have to overcome. Then, on to "What do I get out of sponsorship?" followed by "Is it tax deductible?"

Advertising Sales Information Form

The Advertising Sales Information Form typically includes the various sizes of Pageant Program Book (PPB) advertisements for sale and their costs. It also indicates if advertisements need to be camera-ready. Selling advertisements can be easier if it isn't mandatory that advertisements be camera-ready. Some businesses do not have access to camera-ready advertisements, and official contestants might not think (or cannot personally afford) to enlist a graphic designer to create the advertisements. Moreover, the cost for the advertiser to produce a camera-ready advertisement may argue against placing one in the PPB.

The Advertising Sales Information Form reminds official contestants that they can publish their picture in every full page advertisement sold, if the purchaser doesn't object. It also reminds them that the candidate pulling in the most advertisement dollars wins the Cover Girl award and notes the details of that award. (If you have more than one Cover Girl winner, note those details here.)

While selling advertisements for the National PPB is not mandatory, *Pure American Pageants* will only accept advertisements from candidates that make up a full page.

Visit *All Star Kids* to view its Sponsorship and Fund Raising Suggestions: Endorsement Form/Ad Sales Form.

A variety of advertising forms that American Coed Pageants use can be found in the MAC National Pageant Forms Book. Scroll down several pages to find samples that include Ad Record, Various Ways to Arrange Your Ad Pages, and Ad Layout forms.

Pageant Program Book

Your Pageant Program Book (PPB) can be used as a promotional aid when included in the Advertising Sales Kit. If you are new at producing pageants, you won't yet have a previous years' PPB. Simply create an advertising template — which would include the various sizes of the advertisements offered for sale, or visit other PPBs posted online, and use its ad pages as a guide, particularly if your ads will be the same size(s).

Advertising Order Form/Contract

Another tool to aid official contestants in selling Pageant Program Book (PPB) advertisements is the Advertising Order Form (a.k.a. Advertising Contract). It lists the advertiser, sizes, and costs of each PPB advertisement; features a representative signature line; and includes other details specific to each pageant that would seal the contractual deal.

Ultimate Panche Pageant includes the following in its Pageant Program Book Advertisement Contract: circulation number, full advertisement page size, submission deadline for camera-ready advertisements, materials accepted (digital and hard copy required), digital format specs (JPEG—PC formatted), where digital files can be sent (and the deadline), where hard copies can be sent, who to make checks payable to, where to mail in checks, pageant contact information, advertiser contact information, and a representative signature line and date. (Advertisers are also given the option to turn in hard copy advertisements to official contestants.)

Miss California United States includes two payment options on its Advertisement Order Form: 1) if paying by check, the form asks for the official contestant's name, business name, telephone number, amount received, check number, advertiser's address, ad size, payment made online, and to check boxes for: ad attached, ad sent via email, or ad coming later; 2) if paying by credit card, the form asks for name on credit card account number, expiration date, company name, authorized amount, CVC (the three numbers on back of a credit card), cardholder's name, and cardholder's signature.

Advertising Order Form Cover Page

Queen of Folly Beach and _Edisto Pageant_ ask official contestants to fill out a Program Book Advertisement Information order form for every advertisement they sell. The order form is required to be attached as a cover page over every advertisement that is sold and submitted.

Advertising Rate Card

Businesses can learn more about advertising in your Pageant Program Book (PPB) by visiting your website. Customers want to be able to connect with your business, so provide your website address in your advertising sales information. *Miss Teen America*, at one time, dedicated a page on its website to providing advertising sales information — which included page size, dimensions, and rates. All that an advertiser needed to do when purchasing advertisements was to scroll down the page to find payment options, as well as options on submitting copy-ready advertisements.

What are your PPB advertising rates? Most pageants include a set price on advertising space, i.e., one for a full page, one for a half page, one for a quarter page, and one for a business-card size. *Miss Archdale-Trinity Pageant*, on the other hand, has one size and two prices: one for Commercial and another for Family/Non-Commercial. A full page advertisement for Commercial use is $299; for Family/Non-Commercial, it is $100. *Miss Black Louisiana USA* charges an extra $25 for color advertisements.

If you do sell your PPB backside cover, inside back cover, inside front cover, and even the front cover, what will each sell for? *Miss Nevada United States* sells the PPB inside back cover for $750, inside front cover for $750, and back cover for $1,000. Additionally, their eighth page ad sells for $75, quarter page for $100, half page for $175, full page for $300, and a two-page spread for $550.

Probably the most important set of numbers a pageant system can include on the Advertising Rate Card is the Taxpayer Identification Number (TIN) — a nine-digit tax ID number — as does *Regal Majesty Pageant*. The TIN makes it easier for advertisers to deduct the costs of advertising on their tax forms. At the very least, it builds an immediate trust in the eyes of businesses that advertise. Additional information on TINs can be found in Chapter 2, "Start Your Own Pageant Business," under "Tax Identification Numbers."

Receipt Book

Provide a receipt book for every participant selling advertisements. If you do not have receipt books with your company name, purchase receipt books from any office supply store, or include a master page of receipts in your Official Pageant Handbook. Then, remind candidates to make copies of it. Require that every official contestant present a receipt to every person or business purchasing an advertisement. Ideas on developing a strong Official Contestant Handbook can be found in my book *Producing Beauty Pageants: Contestant Handbook.*

Lanyard

If you already include lanyards in your Sponsorship Kit, official contestants can wear them when they sell advertisements for the Pageant Program Book (PPB). *National American Miss* gives out membership cards (name tag) and ID tags for its weekend (State) pageants, so I presume those cards can slip right into the lanyard pouch. It makes your pageant system look good when official contestants appear "official" as they seek sponsorship support or PPB ad sales.

Crown/Sash

Some pageant systems include a crown and/or sash as an aid tool in official contestants' Sponsorship and/or Advertising Sales Kit. This makes it possible for candidates to wear their anointed State or National titles while seeking prospective sponsors/advertisers to whom they sell sponsorship/Pageant Program Book (PPB) ads. If you cannot afford to give them to your candidates, incorporate the expense into the sponsorship fee or deposit. For participating PPB ad sales candidates, the crown and sash would be a helpful tool in the PPB Advertising Sales Kit. At the very least, provide title-identifying satin ribbon sashes.

If pageant officials at *National American Miss* wanted to increase its already-astronomical PPB ad sales, and if they don't already have one, they might invest in a ribbon printing machine similar to the one featured in the above *YouTube* link. The ribbon printing machine is for hot foil printing on satin ribbon sashes.

Any pageant system wanting to increase PPB ad sales might consider making satin ribbon sashes from its own in-house, heat transfer equipment. In NAM's example, each "State Finalist" could be presented with a satin ribbon sash in her Acceptance Package. The foil lettering might read: *National American Miss State Finalist*. It wouldn't even need to feature the year or even the state name, so leftover satin ribbon sashes could be used for any of its State pageants, for any year. Official contestants can choose to wear their sashes when seeking sponsorship support *and* PPB advertising sales. With NAM official contestants already numbering between 500 and 1,000 in many NAM State pageants, that's a whole lot of satin ribbon sashes to letter-foil press. But, then again, that's a whole lot of sashes hanging on the corners of official contestants' dresser mirrors advertising NAM to their visiting friends. Moreover, those satin ribbon sashes have a way of appearing in social media photo ops. Who needs a "State Finalist" ribbon on a string when a satin ribbon sash does a better job at promoting?

Advertising Sales Letter

An Advertising Sales Letter helps official contestants to focus on one targeted group of advertisers at a time. *Miss Plus America* pageant officials suggest that candidates target advertisers, i.e., approach only retail stores, attorneys, health organizations, or manufacturers. Target dentists, for example, and direct your Advertising Sales Letter to that group. In my *Miss South Texas Teen* pageant, in 1986, official contestant Kellie Kolaya targeted her efforts to selling Pageant Program Book (PPB) advertisements to oil companies. When one oil company purchased an advertisement, she would tell another oil company that so-and-so just bought one. When that oil company found out that so-and-so bought an advertisement, *it* also purchased one. That year the PPB was filled with South Texas oil company advertisements!

Advertising Packet

One year a *Miss American Coed* official contestant, Rachel, had a great experience finding advertisers. One day, and on a *Thursday*, Rachael went out to sell her mandatory two pages of ads for her National Pageant Program Book (PPB). She made an Advertising Packet with information about herself, the pageant, advertising information, the benefits of becoming a sponsor (in addition to the PPB ad sales), and her contact information — complete with her photos. Then, Rachael went to *Kinko's* and made color copies.

Next, she decided to go to one of the bigger cities. It was a good idea. She was well-received when distributing Sponsorship Packets at large car dealerships, wearing her crown and banner. One dealer even considered buying two PPB ad pages himself! In all, Rachael went to about fifteen dealerships — *BMW, Cadillac, Ford, Mitsubishi, Subaru, Dodge, Nissan*, etc. Those managers all told her they would get back with her on Monday regarding the number of pages that they would buy! Granted, two or three of the dealership general managers were not as welcoming to Rachel, but others, would comment "Hey, it's *Miss Indiana*! Good job!" and "Look everyone, *Miss Indiana* is walking in our door!" *She* was wearing a sash.

Rachel suggests that official contestants be prepared when they walk into a dealership. Bring any paperwork you need so that you are well prepared. Go up to a salesperson, introduce yourself, shake his/her hand and ask him/her, "Who can I speak to about sponsorship?" Then s/he will take you to that person — where you'll introduce yourself again and then hand over your paperwork. Then, Rachel would explain to him/her,

> I am looking for sponsors for my pageant for whom I can run ads for throughout my year, in the program book, in any appearances that I do, and for whom I can represent for any necessary promotions!

Along with her contact information, Rachel included a cost breakdown on her handout. She answered all questions and did as much explaining as she could, in a short period of time. After all, these people are very busy, so expect to be there less than ten minutes — sometimes not even five! Just as MAC pageant officials help candidates hone their interview skills, they help them get to know prospective advertisers. Then, candidates are reminded to thank the manager and to ask for a business card so that they can follow up. Not surprisingly, one car dealership invited Rachel to make a publicity appearance during a Saturday sale, at which she was featured in its local commercial.

This car dealership example serves as a reminder that pageant candidates should NOT be afraid to go to the big places for ad sales. Initially, Rachel was apprehensive because she figured it would take forever for her information to go up the ranks, or not go up at all. Instead, the car dealers went to the owners within two days! "Remember, car dealerships are big but the people who work inside are *people* too!" [44]

Car dealerships are not the only dealerships interested in sponsoring pageants. Another MAC candidate, who lived in the country where few car dealerships existed, had no difficulty in getting tractor dealerships — *all three of them* — to purchase advertising in MAC's PPB!

Begin target practice by writing an Advertising Sales Letter. As long as candidates direct letters to one particular type of business, the heading can be the same. For instance, they might direct their respective requests to modeling agencies, dance studios, pizza parlors, and dentists.

Circulation Information

Your circulation can comprise of all of the ways you get your Pageant Program Book (PPB) into the hands of your audience before, during, and after your pageant event. It can consist of each age division's PPB respective demographics and any information from the already-noted "Circulation Demographics" material. Additionally, it can note:

- the number of people that typically make up your audience and the percentage of those who purchase PPBs

- the number of PPBs you expect to sell

- the number of PPBs that are given out for free (judges, pageant staff, candidates, businesses that purchase full page advertisements, etc.)

- your uploaded PPB at a digital publisher like *issuu.com* and any other(s) you simultaneously employ, factoring the visitor count from each site

- real website traffic to your uploaded PPB

- quality link partners' traffic to your website PPB

- if your PPB is included in your pageant DVD

---

[44] Miss_Rachel. "Great Day of Finding Sponsors!" *MAC Pageant Forum*, June 3, 2006. http://gocoed.com/simple/index.php?topic=453.0.

- if your PPB is included in a pageant-marketing DVD for future pageant candidates — presented for *free* at your Open Call

- life of your souvenir PPB (and the number of viewers it stands to generate during those years, providing you have an established track record with other PPBs from previous years).

Also note if your PPB will be available before, during, and/or after your pageant event and at what cost. (For example, softcopies — $25; downloadable versions — free; presented to thousands of girls at Open Call — free, etc.)

Miss Brea Scholarship Pageant permits official contestants to pre-sale its PPBs. In addition, the pageant offers advertisers exposure on the pageant website.

Fairytale Pageant Productions reminds official contestants that the,

> Miss Lake Martin USA Pageant Program Books are free, so everyone that comes to the pageant will see your sponsor's advertisement.

Advertising Sales "How To" Guide

Miss Plus America pageant officials created an ideal Advertising Sales Guide. It is chock-full of creative ideas to help official contestants sell advertisements in its Pageant Program Book (PPB). One idea suggests that candidates focus on one group to whom to target their advertising efforts to, for example, collectively selling a full-page advertisement to a softball team and featuring a picture of the entire team congratulating the candidate's pageant participation. Another idea suggests that a candidate's family (parents, brothers, sisters, cousins, and aunts and uncles) pitch in to purchase a full page advertisement. Pageant officials designed a "family tree" and placed family members' names on the various branches.

Miss Plus America pageant officials suggest that candidates make a list of all contacts and/or the advertising manager of every business they *intend* to approach. Candidates can prepare for this strategy by calling the company or organization, in advance, to find out who is in charge of advertising. Then, they should direct their *memorized* presentation to that person. When possible, candidates should be encouraged to meet with that person, *in person*. Moreover, candidates should not attempt to sell PPB ads by phone or by writing letters. A personal visit — accompanied by an Advertising Sales Letter — always works best.

Sales Script

The *Miss Plus America* Advertising Sales Guide also includes a "Making the Sale" script that provides details of its Pageant Program Book (PPB), i.e., a

> [seventy-two] page magazine filled with photos and information concerning the plus size woman, delegates' pages, and articles from plus-sized celebrities who are behind this 100 percent.

Other helpful advice includes:

> Now shut up and wait for him/her to speak! (S/he who speaks first [loses]!); if s/he says s/he doesn't have the money now, tell him/her that you understand and remind him/her [that s/he] would have until May 15 to turn in the money; if s/he says that s/he doesn't advertise in program books, tell him/her that you understand, however, this is so different that you felt sure s/he would like to be included; if s/he's still stalling, come up with an idea for the [advertisement]. Example: "I've got an idea. How about getting your staff together for a group shot? Put that at the top of the ad with 'Good Luck Jane' in the center and your logo on the bottom. What do you think of that? That would work in any ad size."

Other topics include how to successfully "Get the Order" and how to "Turn in the Order." If all of this helpful information isn't enough, *Miss Plus America* Executive Director Melissa Stamper will personally give delegates a crash course in sales!

Miss Plus America isn't the only pageant system telling candidates, in its Advertising Sales Guide, to "shut up." Richard E. Bernico, owner of *Hawaii Profiles*, created an excellent advertising guide *any* pageant system would benefit by: Program Book Ad Page Requirements Including Tips. This pin-pointed, generic guide helps candidates in their quest to sell PPB advertising. Tip number four states:

> Do NOT ask any "Yes" or "No" questions. "Would you like to sponsor me?" "NO, SORRY." Instead, tell them about your pageant, tell them how you will benefit and give back or influence the community should you win, and then give them the sponsorship form, tell them the ways they can sponsor and ask them: "Which way would you like to help?" Then SHUT UP, smile, and wait.

National American Miss Associate State Director Breanne Maples offers similar advice that can be applied to obtaining sponsors *and* advertisers:

> Don't say to your potential sponsor... "Will you sponsor me?" Instead, say "I KNOW you would like to be one of my official sponsors and help make my dreams come true by becoming the next National American Miss!" And don't forget to tell your sponsor that their contribution is tax deductible (you will have to give them the sponsor receipt so they can use it at tax time) AND they get credit as an Official Sponsor in the State Souvenir Program Book![45]

Miss American Coed has a colorful ten-page Advertising Information Booklet that is helpful for official contestants. According to the index, you will find Advertising Awards on page one, FAQs on pages two and three, Everyone Can Win on page four, *Walt Disney World* Trip information on page five, Advertising Information on page six, Advertising Copy on page seven, Layout Samples on page eight, Layout Form on page nine, and a Record Sheet on page ten. Candidates find FAQs extremely helpful.

One FAQ makes note of the first sponsorship installment. At the time official contestants receive the "Advertising Information Booklet," many haven't yet turned in their entire sponsorship fee. *Miss American Coed* warns candidates to *not* confuse advertising and sponsor fees. Sponsors are listed under their roster photo in the first half of the PPB, and advertisers appear in the second half.

---

[45] Maples, Breanne. "Great Ideas on How to get sponsors!!" NAMISS ROCKS BLOG! http://namissrocks.blogspot.com/2009/05/great-ideas-on-how-to-get-sponsors.html.

Candidates are also reminded that if they send in their sponsor fee and advertising money at the same time, they are to make it clear which are sponsors and which are advertisers.

Additional Ideas for Selling Advertisements

Little Miss, Mister & Teen Citrus sells its full page Pageant Program Book (PPB) advertisement for $125. When official contestants are asking prospective advertisers to purchase an advertisement, pageant officials suggest that they might find it easier to break down the advertisement into affordable component sizes: five business cards on a page at $25 each equal $125; two half-page advertisements at $67.50 would make the difference. Candidates can obtain advertisers for *any* dollar amount, as these examples are just guidelines. Candidates are reminded to also approach their sponsors to see if they would *also* like to purchase a PPB advertisement. Many would like an opportunity, for example, to purchase a display advertisement and not just a sponsor listing. Even prospective sponsors who turned down sponsorship might have it in their advertising budget to purchase a PPB advertisement.

America's U.S. Miss offers excellent tips on selling advertising space on page eight of its four-color Final Newsletter. One tip includes:

> Set up a table at your school or church and accept $5 or $10 donations for a signature page.

Alexandra Curtis, *National American Miss All-American Teen 2011*, provides sponsorship tips in her "Help Finding Sponsors for National American Miss" TipClip:

> When I say getting Cover Girl was a lot of hard work, I mean it. This page here was done entirely by my local skin care salon. The owner bought a page on the condition that I come on in for a few weekends and help where it was needed. It was a great trade-off because I got work experience and it was a huge step closer for me to achieve my goal of selling four pages.

Miss American Coed candidate with the username "Princess_kyb" found Pageant Program Book (PPB) advertising buyers in an unlikely place. Princess and her mother went to a nail salon they frequently visit. Her mother started talking about the MAC pageant and how much work they need to do to get the two required PPB advertising pages sold. At the end of the conversation, an older lady, who Princess had been talking to earlier, asked her about the pageant. Then she said to her,

> Honey, if you need to raise money, just ask people. Just ask everyone you talk to. You are a great representation of the state of Maryland!

Princess asked, and the older lady gave her $100! Then the nail lady that was doing her mom's nails reminded her, "Don't forget to ask EVERYBODY." By the time Princess and her mother left the salon, they had $642 for advertising! First page is done! Ironically, Princess wasn't even wearing her crown or sash, but what she learned as a State Queen is that she is always representing *Miss American Coed Pageants*. She also learned that you have to give people a chance to say "yes." You cannot presume that they'll say "no," and therefore, not ask at all!

Camera–Ready Advertisements

Will advertisers need to submit camera-ready advertisements? If so, Pageant Program Book (PPB) advertisements should be ready for print on photo paper or in digital format (specify the dimensions). All typesetting, borders, insets, etc., need to be intact to avoid typesetting fees. Advertisements should be in .jpg or .pdf file format. For a full page advertisement, the size is typically 8.5"x 11" vertical layout; one-half page is 8.5" x 5.5" horizontal layout; one-quarter page is a 5.5" x 4.25" vertical layout; and one-eighth page is a standard business card size. *Photo Retouching by Courtney*, the cover designer of my *Producing Beauty Pageant* series, is an expert at advertising graphics. She is familiar with such advertising layouts and formatting details.

Remind official contestants not to staple business cards to the Advertising Order Form. Even paper-clipping the Advertising Order Form to the camera-ready copy will cause damage. Preferably, candidates should scotch tape the *back* of the business card to the Advertising Order Form. If a business submits a camera-ready advertisement and wants to *add* extra words, or the advertisement is frayed at the corners, then that copy is NOT camera-ready and would be subject to extra typesetting charges.

Let's revisit with Richard E. Bernico, owner of *Hawaii Profiles*. Richard has been involved in pageantry for a number of years, both as a photographer and graphic designer. Richard has extensive experience in layout and design of PPB advertisements, representing a vast number of pageant systems. To view a sample PPB advertisement he created, in 2009, for *Miss Hawaii USA* Aureana Tseu, scroll to the bottom of his Program Book Ad Page Requirements Including Tips guide. Official contestants do not need to live in Hawaii to benefit from Richard's services. Richard can be reached via email at rick@hawaiiprofiles.com or at his website.

Pure American Pageants informs official contestants that it doesn't accept paper advertisements. The advertisements must be sent via email or on a disc. Note if your Pageant Program Book (PPB) will be printed in black and white or color. If your PPB is in black and white, advertisements will reproduce better if copy is also submitted in black and white.

International (Louisiana) Fresh Faces pageant officials note,

> All ad pages must be print ready. We do NO layout or design.

Miss Black Texas Beauty notes,

> Full color business cards and flyers are not permitted. You must create these ads.

Colorado *Cinderella State Pageant* welcomes advertisements that are already laid out. Pageant Program Book (PPB) advertisements sent electronically must be in ".jpg", ".giff", "word", or "pub," and in file format only. Its full page PPB advertisement size is 7.125" x 9.875"; one-half page horizontal is 7.125" x 4.875"; and one-eighth page is 3.5" x 2.0". Candidates are also reminded to include their photos *within* the measurements of the advertisement.

Miss Rodeo New Mexico Pageant composes its Pageant Program Book (PPB) using *Adobe InDesign CS5*. If advertisers want to submit camera-ready advertisements by email or CD, they need to know that the resolution is 300 dpi/Grayscale. The software programs advertisers can use are *Adobe Illustrator, Adobe PhotoShop, Adobe PageMaker 6.0* or higher, *Adobe InDesign*, and .pdf's in *Adobe Acrobat 4.0* or higher. Advertisements in *Microsoft Word* cannot be submitted, as it is incompatible with software used for professional printing. If the PPB advertisement is built in *Publisher*, the advertiser is to follow the advertisement sizes using 300 dpi photos and export as a high quality .pdf. *Publisher* users submitting native *Publisher* files will have its advertisements rebuilt in Illustrator if the size is incorrect. Regarding fonts, clients are to include all fonts used. Otherwise, typefaces not attached will be matched with something similar. If copy is submitted in an *Illustrator* file, all type should be converted to outlines. *MAC* users are requested to use *TrueType* or *OpenType* fonts or convert text to outlines, because the *Miss Rodeo New Mexico Pageant* is PC based, and *MAC* fonts will not work. When generating .pdf files, clients are requested to check that their image files are of a high resolution (300 dpi) and that they are saved as Grayscale. Furthermore, all of the fonts used should be embedded *or* changed to outlines. Regarding photos and images, all electronic image files must be submitted as Jpeg (.jpeg or .jpg), Tiff (.tif), EPS (.eps), or *PhotoShop* (.psd) files. All images are converted to Grayscale and have a resolution of no lower than 300 dpi. Regarding Web graphics, it cannot be used in print media. Adobe Illustrator files must be submitted as EPS files with the type converted to outline, or fonts should be included with the file. Lastly, advertisement sizes must conform to the sizes on the sample advertisement page. Otherwise, it will be adjusted, which could result in distortion of the artwork. For advertisements that are not camera-ready, *Miss Rodeo New Mexico Pageant* requires that photographs be submitted either printed or in hi-res .jpg files.

Advertising Copy and Spec Requirement Guidelines

Advertisements submitted that are not camera-ready are known as Advertising Copy. Also known as a Rough Sketch or Layout Copy, Advertising Copy costs more to typeset because it's not camera-ready. Stipulate your Pageant Program Book (PPB) advertising layout, spec requirements, and the various costs in writing. Will advertisements need to be in black and white or color? A black and white advertisement costs less than one in color. Also note that an Advertising Copy submitted in light ink will NOT reproduce. Advertisements that are not camera-ready will likely be set in standard type — selected by your printer. Moreover, an additional fee for typesetting, per advertisement, is typically charged. If a candidate is *not* submitting camera-ready advertisements, she should submit her Advertising Copy on a disk in one of the following formats: .tif, .pdf, or .eps. She should also attach a hardcopy printout. While most printers will accept Advertising Copy in *MS Publisher* or *Word*, most will NOT accept *PrintShop* or *Excel* files. Remember to note the size of your PPB because not all are the standard 8 ½" x 11". The advertisement size of the *Salem Apple Butter Festival Queen and Teen Queen* PPB full page ad, for example, is 6" x 9".

Will advertisers be able to choose how their advertisement will be laid out and opt out of using a candidate's picture in the copy? Many National pageants permit a picture of the official contestant on a full page advertisement that she sold; however, not all advertisers want to include a candidate's picture in their advertisement. Give advertisers the option to choose. Advertisers should be able to advertise their product or message as they want — which might NOT include a candidate's picture. *Fairytale Pageant Productions* states that advertisements may or may not include a photo of the official contestant.

Submitting Advertisement Material

Will official contestants be expected to submit camera–ready advertisements, or will only Advertising Copy be accepted? Will photographs used in advertisements need to be actual photographs and not scanned copies? Will advertisements need to be in a .pdf format? Program Book Ad Page Requirements Including Tips, compiled by Richard E. Bernico of *Hawaii Profiles*, provides official contestants with continued sound advice about submitting ads:

> It is your responsibility to get the ads to me. Even if you give the ads to the director please follow-up and make sure I got them okay. Ads may be given to me on a flash drive, CD, CF card, or email. If your file sizes are too large to email, then I suggest you start a *You Send It* account (it's free) by going to https://www.yousendit.com/. Through *You Send It*, you can send one file at a time at up to 100 MB. If you need to send more than one, then simply send them separately. *You Send It* [now known as *Hightail*] will send a link to my email and I will retrieve your ad page. When sending an ad through email or *You Send It*, please make sure the contestant's name and ad page [number] is in the [SUBJECT] of the email.

Please don't assume I recognize your email and I will know who the ad is for. Having the info [on the SUBJECT line] helps me tremendously and saves time. You have no idea how many files I receive that are named "Ad page 1" or "Ad page 2"; please name each ad page uniquely and with the last name of the contestant such as "Riley01; Riley02; McDonald01; McDonald02; McDonald03, etc." If you have a certain order, then number them in the order you would like them. If pages need to be next to each other, then identify them as such: "Richards01L; Richards02R." I cannot guarantee where the pages will wind up in the book, but I do my best to keep a contestant's pages together and I definitely keep facing pages together if informed.

Miss ARK–LA–TEX Princess Pageant candidates who submit advertisements as a Word document are to include $20 *per advertisement page* set up fee. Furthermore, if emailing or mailing on a disc, all advertisements must be submitted in a black and white, high-resolution .pdf format of 300 dpi or higher. When mailing a disc, candidates are asked to also mail a hard copy.

America's Heavenly Beauties prefer .jpg images; however, if candidates have no way to send the images, AHB will accept a scannable image that is also printer ready. If official contestants don't know how to send .jpg or scannable images, for a cost of $25 per page, pageant officials will design and create the advertisement page.

All Canadian Pageants reminds official contestants to only send:

> [complete] pages, which means send the fee, the information, and your picture at the same time.

Circle City Classic Beauty Pageants notes,

> Email is the preferred method for ad submission.

Miss Mabry Pageant informs,

> All ads must be on a CD! We are not doing hard copies as in the past. Create your ad page on the computer using *Microsoft Word* and burn it to a CD. Put your name on the disk and put it inside a sleeve. If you do not have the capability to burn your ad onto a CD you may email your complete Word document to [the pageant]. Please be sure to put the

contestant's name and "Pageant Ad" as the subject line in the email.

Miss American Coed advises,

Please use an overnight mail service such as *Federal Express*, so your [advertising] mail may be tracked.

Advertising Deadline

To stay on top of their Pageant Program Book (PPB) advertising, many pageant directors are requesting that candidates email Advertising Copy (or place it on a CD and mail it to pageant headquarters) *as they secure the advertisements*. Otherwise, set a deadline for official contestants to turn in all advertisements and photos for your PPB. Although *Superstarz Pageants* has a deadline for candidates to turn in ad copy, they are encouraged to send in each page *as they are sold*. Speak to printing company managers early to find out how much time they need to include advertisements in your PPB.

Selling Cover Space

Will you have special awards for any candidate who sells any of your Pageant Program Book (PPB) covers? Will you be selling a full page back cover or inside full page front and/or back cover? If so, will it only be available in color (even if the inside is black and white)? *Miss, Teen, & Mrs. Lafayette* awards an entire entry fee along with paid seats [plus two reserved (not paid) seats] to one official contestant who sells the back cover.

Photo Costs in Advertisements

Printing companies usually charge extra for Pageant Program Book (PPB) advertisements containing photos. Pageant directors often pass this cost on to official contestants. Most pageant officials permit candidates to place their picture in every full page PPB advertisement they sell, usually for an extra cost. If you only include pictures on full-page advertisements, allow candidates to piece together quarters, halves, and business card sized ads in a mosaic fashion. Then they can place their pictures in the center. Note the extra charge (if there is one) when a photo is included in the copy. Some pageants allow the first photo to be free. Each additional photo used in other advertisements is subject to a $15 or $20 fee. _Miss American Coed_ permits candidates one photo free of charge for each full page of advertising sold. If candidates want a photo placed on an advertisement that is less than a full page in size, they are charged a $20 photo processing fee.

Photo Specifications

Specify the photo size official contestants can submit with their advertisements. While a large photo can reproduce into a smaller photo, a smaller photo cannot be enlarged into a full-page advertisement. Advertisement Copy that include pictures copied from a photocopier don't reproduce well and shouldn't be accepted. Specify if photos can be glossy, with a matte finish, or if they need to be in high resolution digital. Moreover, do photos need to be black and white or color?

Miss Valley Center Pageant notes to candidates that photos submitted for the Pageant Program Book must be Grayscale. Grayscale is a range of achromatic colors having several, usually ten, equal gradations ranging from white to black.

Little Miss, Mister & Teen Citrus asks official contestants to submit original photos — no laser or inkjet copies. If a candidate wants to submit the same photo as her Pageant Program Book roster photo, she would need to submit two photos.

Pure American Pageants permit official contestants to use photos that aren't "busy" and, when enlarged, don't look blurry. Candidates should submit a variety of photos to be used for different advertising pages sold. If photos are busy, _Photo Retouching by Courtney_ can retouch photos to suit the pageant's natural or glitz needs.

Bleeding Photos

Photos on full page advertisements are usually "bled" from edge to edge of the sheet with an over-burn of advertisement copy. This, of course, is an added expense. _Miss India International_ does not permit bleeds. Therefore, its 8.5" x 11" page would include a 3/16" to 3/8" white edge, no bleeds. _Miss Hawaii USA_ does allow a full page setup with full bleed: 8.75" x 11.25". The design page width of 8.75" would then be trimmed to 8.5"; and the design page height of 11.25" would then be trimmed to 11". Keep all text at least .5" away from the edges with full bleed.

Incentives for Advertising Sales

Pageant officials have come up with some creative incentives to encourage candidates to sell advertisements in their Pageant Program Book. A few incentives are listed below.

Cover Girl Title and Other Awesome Prizes

One of the first incentives ever created to motivate official contestants into selling Pageant Program Book (PPB) advertisements is the Cover Girl award. The Cover Girl award — also known as the Top-Hand Award in the *Miss Rodeo New Mexico Pageant* — was especially designed years ago for the candidate who sold the most number of advertisements in the PPB. As part of her award, she would receive her picture on the PPB cover. If your pageant is structured so that your reigning Queen appears on the cover of your PPB, the Cover Girl winner can appear on the back or inside covers. If you have multiple Cover Girl title winners, note how you will feature their "win" in print or electronically. It's "official" recognition that girls want.

Golden Miss & Mr. Pageant places its top Pageant Program Book advertising winner on the inside front cover. The second place winner appears on the inside back cover.

American Cover Miss awards its top Pageant Program Book (PPB) advertisement sales winner, the National Centerfold title. Her picture is featured in the center of the PPB.

Miss American Coed rewards official contestants for outstanding Pageant Program Book (PPB) advertising participation in a number of ways. Candidates selling a half-page advertisement in the PPB receive a trophy; selling one full page qualifies for a trophy and a featured photo; $800 in advertisements sold receives (in addition to the above mentioned premium prizes) a free hotel room premium prize at the host hotel during pageant weekend or a $100 cash award; cash awards of $100 each — in addition to special prizes — are presented to candidates selling advertisements in varying amounts such as $1,200, $2,400, or $3,000. Sellers of $3,000 in PPB advertisements are awarded an all-expense paid trip to the National pageant in Hawaii. Girls selling over $5,000 in advertisements become "Cover Girls" for the PPB covers. Learn how to barter for FREE hotel rooms to dispense as premium prizes by reading my book *Producing Beauty Pageants: Brokering a Pageant through Barter*, Chapter 7, "Barter Your Prize Package" under "Hotel Rooms as Premium Prizes."

America's U.S. Miss offers impressive gifts to encourage candidates to sell advertisements in its Pageant Program Book. Official contestants who sell two pages earn one free Optionals competition; selling three pages earns a National Ambassador title, plus prize listed above; selling four pages receives one additional free Optionals competition, plus all prizes listed above; selling five pages earns $200 cash, plus all prizes listed above; selling six pages qualifies for the Cover Miss title, plus participating candidates receive one additional free standard hotel night stay during pageant weekend, a $50 novelty table gift certificate, plus all prizes listed above; selling seven pages earns a *Carnival Cruise* to the Bahamas, plus all prizes listed above; selling eight pages earns a $300 travel allowance, plus all prizes listed above; selling nine pages earns a *Dell* Laptop Computer, plus all prizes listed above; and selling ten pages earns a $1,000 savings bond, plus all prizes listed above.

National American Miss allows official contestants participating in the National pageant to include the number of ad pages they sold for the State Pageant Program Book (PPB) into the sum of the National PPB ad sales, for a chance at earning the National Cover Miss award. This certainly is a GREAT incentive for National candidates needing that "push-start!" For example, if a candidate sold two pages at her State pageant, and then twelve pages at the National pageant, that totals to fourteen credited National pages. Although a candidate can apply advertising pages sold at her State pageant towards the National Cover Girl title, and as well to the National Cover Model and National Cover Miss titles, premium prizes that were awarded at the State pageant level are not re-awarded at the National pageant. The winner would receive — among other earned prizes — the opportunity to travel throughout her reign and represent both her National Cover Miss title and the pageant system. (It wasn't clear if NAM would pay her traveling expenses or if it would be the responsibility of the National Cover Miss winner.) Any National Cover Miss contender who sold *twenty* pages (at $600[46] each page) for the National Yearbook (PPB), in 2012, had the option to choose a cruise vacation for two (maximum value $2,300) or their earned prizes. If you're wondering if selling twenty pages at $600 is even possible, let's look at *the top three candidate sales* (from each age division) who participated in the NAM 2012 National PPB ad sales:

- *Princess National Cover Miss*: Baylie H. sold twelve pages; Marysa R. came in second with five pages; JaDore H. came in third with four pages.

- *Jr. Pre-Teen National Cover Miss*: Marisa L. sold nineteen pages; Malayna S. came in second with twelve pages; Jada M. came in third with eleven pages.

- *Pre-Teen National Cover Miss*: Madelyn H. sold eight pages; Tia B. came in second with seven pages; Melissa O. also tied for second with seven pages.

- *Jr. Teen Cover Miss*: Madonna M. sold ten pages; Najee L. came in second with eight pages; and Sarah B. came in third with seven pages.

- *Teen National Cover Miss*: Ashley R. sold twelve pages; Katie F. came in second with eleven pages; and Brittney H. came in third with ten pages.

- *Miss National Cover Miss*: Anna L. sold twelve pages; Amanda C. came in second with seven pages; Amanda S. tied for second with seven pages.

What *is* clear is that these eighteen NAM official contestants *alone* sold 169 full advertising pages (at $600 per page). These girls brought in nearly $102,000 in PPB ad sales, in 2012, at the National pageant — NAM's 10th anniversary event! NAM had nearly 700 official contestants in the National pageant, and although not all candidates participated in PPB ad sales, many did. After all, the five NAM National PPBs — featuring six age divisions and two National pageants: *National American Miss* and *National All-American Miss* — stack up to *over three inches tall*! In the Jr. Pre-Teen National PPB alone, for example, the ads

---

[46] In 2014, $750.

took up more than half of the PPB pages. Those PPB ads begin on page 118 and end at page 288! Nearly 170 full page ads were sold in this one PPB alone, yielding NAM over $100,000 from this *one age division*! And there are six age divisions at National! Each of NAM's nearly forty State pageants usually yield the same candidate numbers — often more — as its National pageant. And, each NAM State pageant's full page PPB ad *also* sells for $600; in 2014, it sold for $750!

But, if Marisa L. only sold nineteen full page ads for the National PPB, and the pages she may have sold for her State PPB only counted "in title," then she was short by one page at National to have the option of choosing the cruise prize. My guess is that Marisa L. and a guest *somehow* set sail on a cruise. Learn how to barter for cruise-for-two prizes by reading my book *Producing Beauty Pageants: Brokering a Pageant through Bartering*, Chapter 7, "Barter Your Prize Package" under "Cruise Prize."

What NAM Gained from One National Pageant PPB Ad Sales

Let's look at *National American Miss*' Pageant Program Book (PPB) ad sales activity. At its 10th Anniversary National pageant, in 2012, NAM's five National PPBs *sold* ads comprised of:

- 57 pages from the Princess division

- 166 pages from the Junior Pre-Teen division

- 118 pages from the Pre-Teen division

- 114 pages from the Junior Teen division

- 115 pages from the combined Teen and Miss divisions

These 570 full page ads, at $600 per page, totaled $342,000. This was the result of *one* of NAM's pageant's combined age divisions PPBs at its National event. Every one of NAM's nearly forty State pageants, in 2012, *also* featured a PPB Advertising Program with similar official contestant numbers and similar $600 page ad sales. At $750 per page, in 2014, and with around 800 National candidates, and if NAM had similar ad sales, the NAM National PPB *alone* would have gained *over a half million dollars*! Multiply that by about forty NAM State pageants and, well, you get the *ad sales* financial picture.

SAG/AFTRA Submissions

In the early years of pageant competition, candidates who won pageants received screen tests with major film companies. However, past experience has been that not all pretty girls are prepared to benefit from a screen test. Even if you cannot secure screen tests for your winners, you *can* send a Pageant Program Book (PPB) to the *Screen Actors Guild* (SAG) and *American Federation of Television and Radio Artists* (AFTRA) offices. Both federations joined forces, in 2012, as SAG-AFTRA.

Knowing that a PPB will be sent to SAG-AFTRA often boosts advertising sales participation. Official contestants usually sell more PPB advertisements knowing that they *might* be seen by a guild executive. After all, candidates want the opportunity to include their headshot on every full page ad they sell in the PPB. Encourage even stronger advertising sales by reminding official contestants that the winning Cover Girl's photo — if it appears on the PPB cover — could be the *only one* seen by SAG-AFTRA if a rep opens his/her mail, glances at the cover, and then tosses it. What you hope is that the rep will, at least, tear off the cover and put it aside before tossing the PPB.

Crown or Tiara

Crowns motivate. *Beautiful Faces Pageant* presents a crown or tiara to every official contestant selling one Pageant Program Book (PPB) ad page; two PPB ad pages earns a crown or tiara and a trophy; three PPB ad pages earns the same plus a $40 entry fee; and so on. Candidates who sell ten PPB ad pages are crowned the Overall Supreme Entrepreneur and receive a 12" crown or tiara, a six-foot trophy, entire paid entry fee for the Supreme Package, and all the best categories *and* free entry to the *Beautiful Faces Pageant* Preliminary. Be calculatingly certain before giving away free income streams. If your pageant budget is tight, give away "free" reserved seat passes and not the admission tickets.

Credit Entry Fee or Offer Prizes

For every full page advertisement sold, allow a portion of each participating candidate's entry fee to be credited. If an official contestant sells a certain number of Pageant Program Book (PPB) ad pages, allow her a free entry, or offer the winner a cash prize equal to twenty percent of her total ad sales. If she has advertisement sales totaling $1,000, she could receive a $200 cash prize. The first alternate could receive fifteen percent of her PPB ad sales; the second alternate, ten percent; and all official contestants with sales over $300, for example, could receive a savings bond. Pageant directors could allow everyone working on PPB advertising sales to deduct $25 off their entry fee, regardless of if they sell the minimum $25 or unlimited maximum. _National American Miss_ awarded any candidate who sold twenty $600 page ads (totaling $12,000), in 2012, a $2,300 cruise for two. Imagine if you secured a cruise line Official Sponsor to donate the cruise. You wouldn't need to pay an out-of-pocket cent for the "20%-in-ad-value prize." Your Cruise Line Official Sponsor covers this expense by donating a cruise for two of the same value. And your pageant system gains $12,000 preservable cash _from one official contestant alone_! Learn how to barter for a cruise for your Queen(s) by reading my book _Producing Pageants: Brokering a Pageant through Barter_, Chapter 6, "Barter Your Prize Package" under "Cruise Prize."

Miss Louisiana Florida Parishes & Louisiana Northshore Pageant official contestants selling a $200 full page advertisement receives $100 towards their entry fee; selling a $100 half page advertisement receives $50 towards their entry fee. The maximum a candidate can earn in entry fee-defraying costs is $200.

Pure American Pageants offers a "Design Your Ad Price" program. Full page advertisements are $50 each. Official contestants can choose to sell each advertisement for $75. The $25 difference will go directly to the candidate's balance.

Little Miss, Mister & Teen Citrus offers a big money making opportunity for official contestants with its full page advertisements, which sell for $125 each. Candidates may secure ten sponsors per advertisement page, at $50 each, bringing in $500 for that full page. The advertising page still costs $125, and the candidate would profit $375. Selling advertising pages is a great way for official contestants to pay for their hotel room, wardrobe, and any other costs associated with the National pageant, and candidates who sell ten or more pages also receive all Optionals categories fees paid. This is a huge income stream to be giving away.

TV and Magazine Promotion

If you have a TV Official Sponsor for your next pageant, arrange for the Cover Girl winner to appear in your pageant promotional commercial. If you promote your next pageant in a major magazine such as *Girls' Life*, *Girl's World Magazine*, *Discovery Girls*, *Teen Vogue*, or *Seventeen*, recognize your Cover Girl winner by including her picture in the magazine promotional advertisement. (Additional teen magazines will keep you current.) *All Canadian Pageants* not only has a written agreement with one of Toronto's well-known agents to present the advertisement sales winner with a one-year representation contract, but the winner appears in a two-page spread within the Pageant Program Book (of the following year's pageant) and on TV to promote the pageant.

Virtual Ads

More and more pageants are selling virtual ads. *My Chance Novice Nationals* sell virtual ads for $50 each. Official contestants who sell seven virtual ads receive the Supreme Package free; selling ten virtual ads receives the same plus a 4' trophy and crown; selling fifteen virtual ads receives the same plus all events listed with the Discounted Package; and selling twenty virtual ads receives all events listed on the entry form, a 10" National crown, a 5' trophy, and a gift. All virtual ad "tickets" then go into a drawing for an LCD TV. To view a sample virtual ad, visit the website and click on "National Paperwork." Once sold, these virtual ads are displayed on TV's located in the pageant ballroom. The virtual ads are also included on the *My Chance Novice* pageant DVD.

Beautiful Me Productions, and likely its sister pageant, *Toy Fest Pageant* (a.k.a. *America's Best Pageants*), also sell virtual ads for $50 each:

> If you make your virtual ads they must be sent in a .jpg format if emailed. Please call [National headquarters] for information on how to make virtual ads. All ads need to be mailed or emailed completed. We can make your virtual ads for $10 each.

Virtual Ads Benefits

Pageant officials can present many benefits to businesses purchasing virtual ads in a variety of tiered package groups. The low-cost advertising can be presented with adjustable online advertising packages (see "Virtual Ads Packaging" below). Pageant officials can offer advertisers an option to purchase more than one year of website visibility, even if they have not been invited by another official contestant to purchase a virtual ad in the next year's pageant. When a quality pageant has a high traffic website, businesses that purchased website virtual ads in the past could, in subsequent years, continue providing the revenue stream for the pageant.

Virtual Ads Packaging

Offer several tiered virtual ads packages for your virtual Pageant Program Book (PPB). To give you an example, here you will find four packages — each graduating into a bigger package and price. You will need to create a Virtual Ads Sales Form that includes headings: PKG 1–4; Company Name; Company Contact; Email; Total Collected. Then, attach costs to each package, for example, PKG 1 – $75; PKG 2 – $125; PKG 3 – $175; PKG 4 – $225:

> Package One: Company listing on pageant website: company name, description of services, contact information for one year, AND a business card size virtual ad in the virtual PPB, $75

> Package Two: Company listing with link to company website: company name, description of services, contact information, clickable link to website for one year, AND a quarter page ad in the virtual PPB, $125

> Package Three: Company listing with company logo and link to company website: company name, description of services, contact information, clickable link to website for one year, AND a half page advertisement in the virtual PPB, $175

> Package Four: Company listing, company logo and interactive map to location: company name, description of services, interactive map showing your location, contact information, clickable link to

website for one year, AND a full page advertisement
in the virtual PPB, $225

Virtual Display Ads

Offer virtual display ads on your website. *Miss Plus America*
provides website advertising opportunities in its ever-growing
trafficked website. Prospective advertisers can view
MISSPLUSAMERICA.COM Website Advertising Opportunities,
and then scroll down to page 4 to gain additional information. To
understand buttons and banner ad dimensions, visit *Designer's
Toolbox*, *Yahoo! Ad Specs*, or *AOL Advertising*. For MPA's button
and banner ad pricing, you are asked to email the National
Director. Examples of ad button banners sizes to place on *Miss
Plus America's* website include:

- 120 x 60 button
- 125 x 125 button
- 120 x 240 button
- 234 x 60 half banner
- 489 x 60 full banner

Virtual Ads Information Form

You will need to create a Virtual Ads Information Form that
includes: Who to Contact (name, phone, and email address),
Website Address (if applicable), Contact Name (if applicable),
Phone Number, email Contact (if applicable), Company Physical
Location (if applicable), Short Description of Services, Package
Purchase (circle one), Purchase Form (candidate's name), and any
other notation from the pageant director:

> Our pageant will contact you in regards to your
> purchase to confirm the information provided, if we
> have any questions. Thanks for your purchase and
> your support of the Miss XYZ Pageant! Our website
> is: (address).

Vinyl Ad Banners

Diamond Dolls Pageants sells Ad Banners as part of a combo pack that includes a Pageant Program Book (PPB) ad and a website ad. The DDP Ad Banners are 3' x 1.6' vinyl banners (weighing ten ounces) and are custom made for each particular advertiser — with their choice of artwork, photos, and/or business logo. DDP displays Ad Banners throughout the pageant ballroom, during pageant week or weekend. Ad Banners become the property of (and are given to) the advertisers following the pageant.

Let's use a hypothetical Ad Banner "selling" combo example here. In order for an advertiser to be able to purchase an Ad Banner, s/he must also purchase a full page advertisement in the PPB. S/he couldn't just purchase the Ad Banner. Basically, Ad Banners provide incentive for prospective advertisers to purchase full-page ads in your PPB.

If your PPB already pulls in _National American Miss_-like PPB advertising numbers, you won't need to encourage advertisers with Ad Banners. Instead, consider using Ad Banners (in larger sizes) only for your Official Sponsors. Promoting Official Sponsors in your pageant ballroom during pageant week, with in-your-face visibility, is what they want. Remember to make use of any Queen and court photo ops next to those Official Sponsors' Ad Banners. Now, you can synergize photos of your pageant Official Sponsor on various social media sites. Such synergy efforts often encourage a long Official Sponsor relationship. An Official Sponsor who continues sponsoring your pageant, year after year, means that you can use the same vinyl banners for every pageant event it is tied to. _BannersInVinyl_ offers full color (logo and graphic) vinyl banners, in a variety of sizes. The vinyl banner is made of 13 oz. heavy duty Scrim Vinyl material, reinforced hems, grommets for easy hanging, and is printed with Grand Format digital printer.

Chapter 14

Judging

Arbiters of beauty need to be wise in selecting the right girls for the crown, barring any girl who expected them to judge, not what she was, but what cosmetic arts could make her seem to be. "Judges should be objective and not be influenced by external factors," says Nanci Wudel, a former _Miss America_ judge. A girl must be personable, intelligent, alert, have the ability to speak clearly, have poise and composure, good eye contact, and possess a well-proportioned figure and pretty face. For the most part, judges should look for the most consistent girl, the one who achieves moderately in all areas of competition — factors other than beauty. Beauty pageants are a big business, so the judges look for a girl who is ready, smart, and can deal with the pressures ahead. Since there is rarely any time to train the winner, she has to be there.

Selecting Judges

A panel of judges has an important responsibility to the director, each pageant contender, and her immediate family. "Serving as a pageant judge is a very important position and should not be taken lightly," says former _Miss America_ judge Nanci Wudel. The judges are in a position to create a new life, not only for the winner, but also for the Runners-Up. Real integrity in being a judge involves honesty and devotion. Furthermore, "A good judge must be fair and look at each contestant with a fresh start." Judging can be an intense experience. They say Grace Kelly broke two pencils in half as she pondered that final crucial ballot in judging the _Miss America_ pageant.

Just about anyone with an excellent reputation can serve as a judge, provided that s/he receives training and instruction from pageant officials. Pageant directors should do their best to select a judging panel that is diverse — culturally and professionally. A judging panel can consist of experienced pageant judges, lawyers, talent representatives, doctors, educators, former titleholders, a boutique owner, a designer, and business owners. The judges and manner of judging differ from pageant to pageant. In order to select the best Queen, judges should be geographically distributed, occupationally different, and scattered in age. *Cinderella Scholarship Pageant* notes,

> The judging panel should be more capable than famous. In selecting judges, you should not be interested in a publicity campaign for celebrities. Your primary interest should be in building your pageant by choosing a panel who will select great winners.

Judges to Avoid

When official contestants pay so much to be professionally judged, it's not professional to have conflict of interest "judges" on a panel. *Miss America* notes,

> You cannot serve on the board of a State or Local pageant OR serve as a judge if you profit from the contestants.

Make it a written rule in your pageant system that states these people will not judge your pageant. Place this information on your Director's Corner page of your pageant newsletter/magazine/handbook. People invest a lot of money in pageants, so they expect judging to be of the utmost quality and fairness. A spouse of a pageant staff, for example, should not be judging at *any* level. Moreover, don't recycle judges — especially for the following year's event. *Miss Icon* notes,

> Judges are not recycled. Once an individual has judged for this system, [he] will never be invited to return as a judge.

Judging Taboos to Consider

A list of judging taboos to consider include, but are not limited to:

- Don't have parents of visiting royalty as judges, especially when they are judging friends of their daughter(s). This makes the pageant director look like s/he will grab anyone to fill in a judge's seat.

- Don't have the parents of the emcee (the person who reads the results) as judges.

- Let the judges form their own opinions of the candidates when they are choosing the Queen and her court. The Head Judge/Judges Coordinator should NOT be the one deciding on who wins the crown. Moreover, a Head Judge/Judges Coordinator should NOT appear before a panel of judges — while judges are judging girls in the final phase (or any phase) of the competition — to "remind" them what the pageant "is looking for." If that's the case, then don't have judges judging. Let pageant officials pick the winners.

- Don't have pageant coaches as judges, particularly if they are well known to the pageant system. Pageant coaches tend to score their own girls higher, and even if they didn't, it just doesn't reflect well on the pageant.

- Don't have a Queen on the panel who actually competed against some of the girls she is now judging.

- Don't have on the panel the mother or father of the Queen who actually competed against some of the girls in the past.

- Don't have two judges who are married to each other on the same (or different) panel.

- Don't have pageant staff or their spouses judging.

- If you are a National system, don't allow your State directors to judge.

- Don't use the same judges time after time, at least not two consecutive years, and certainly not three years! Moreover, place photos of your judges in your Pageant Program Book every year. This proves you're not using the same judges year after year. (People remember photos, not names, and will appreciate new judges' faces.)

- It is best that the same panel of judges judge the same division throughout the competition, in all the main areas of competition, for that one age division. If one judge is sick in the second or third round of the competition, his/her entire row of scores can be deleted to bring balance to the scoring.

- Be careful of having a judge on your panel that is from another major pageant system, a modeling agency, or from a popular pageant coaching company. If you do, have in your Judging Guidelines that those judges will not judge any candidate they know. At the very least, *don't* allow a coaching service to post Good Luck messages to their clients who are competing for the very pageant system they are judging, even if it is a different age division! It's a great way to promote coaching services, but an awful way to promote your pageant.

- If you're going to invite a Queen to judge, and your system is several years old, invite one who was crowned a dozen years ago. She shouldn't know any of the current candidates.

- The official contestant with the highest score SHOULD win the pageant. After all, pageants are like sports, so the person/team with the lead (in points) wins. Period. Sports judges don't give a rank (or place) within a grading system.

- Last, but not least, the pageant director should NEVER step into the judging scene during any judging period to "contribute" to the decision as to who will win. If the director simply wants to make sure the scores are being tabulated correctly, then hire *two* professional auditors to do just that. Stay away from the results. You certainly don't want to appear as if you are tinkering with the scores!

If you *do* want Queens on your judging panel, take note from pageant officials of the _Miss Icon_ Organization. They note to official contestants:

> Our judges are current or past titleholders from other pageant systems because they are the only ones who have truly been in your shoes.

On the other hand, MIO pageant officials *don't* allow any employees, judges, or *current* titleholders to privately coach contestants.

Rotating Judges

If you rotate judges, you may want to reconsider your judging system. When there are approximately seven or eight judges rotated through each phase, and there are different judges for each overall competition phase, the result is that one judge *may only see an official contestant once!* The judges really don't get to know the candidates, and each candidate may end up being scored by fifteen different people. Parents would prefer that their children be judged by the *same panel throughout the pageant*, because they spend a whole lot of money to make sure that their kids are known by the judges. The statistical result of having this large of a rotating panel of judges is likely that the scores come in very close, with many ties, and without a clear group of top Finalists.

Some pageant systems don't rotate judges at the State pageants, but do at the National. _National American Miss_ is one such pageant system. Beth Anne, whose daughter *was* a NAM State Queen, noted,

> [what] happens at National is there are a different set of judges for each phase of competition. About seven or eight are present but rotated, so you may not have the same judges seeing you in gown that see you in interview or Personal Introduction. Most people have no idea this happens but I saw it myself — twice. [Girls] deserve to have a set panel of judges they truly meet and who get to know them, from Interview through Finals, and not these random on-the-spot judge rotations. Most pageants have one set of judges who judge one [age] division and each phase within that division. Then, another set of judges will judge a different [age] division and each phase within that division. But at NAM National, pageant officials rotate the judges for each phase. NAM puts this in tiny print somewhere in the Magazine, but it's interesting because it is totally different from its

State pageants, where there *is* just one panel of judges.[47]

It's the pageant's choice whether or not to rotate judges; however, in my experience as both a pageant participant and as a director, official contestants *and* judges would prefer the same panel of judges from the beginning to the end of a pageant competition.

Head Judge

The Head Judge typically acts as liaison between the other judges, the pageant organizers, and the auditor. The Head Judge has many responsibilities. S/he:

- supplies all the necessary competition sheets and tabulating supplies (computer, calculator, and manual tabulation forms)

- holds a meeting well in advance of the first competition to review the rules with the judges and pageant organizers, constantly referring to the Judges Handbook

- supervises the auditor when handling the scores for Finals calculations

- and last, but not least, presents the judges' outcome to the emcee.

Ideally, a Head Judge would be a certified pageant judge. (Many states offer courses to become a certified pageant judge.) In the *Miss Awoulaba Canada* pageant, a designated Head Judge even *tallies* the scores. Tallying should be left up to a certified auditor, and *preferably two at the same time*!

Judges' Committee Chairperson

If you don't have a Head Judge, appoint a judges' committee chairman to guide your judges through the pageant judging. This

---

[47] Beth Anne. Email written on December 10, 2012.

person can be responsible for the judges' briefing, explain all areas of competition, and answer any questions they may have. Consider letting your chairperson select the judges — subject to your approval.

Pageant Judge Application

The Glass Slipper Natural Beauty Pageant is always on the lookout for quality judges. The pageant system even provides a link on its website, which leads prospective judges to the Judges Information and Application. In addition to a host of other questions, it asks if the applicant has ever been convicted of a crime. Prospective judges will find that, in order to be a judge for the pageant, they will be subject to a background check. Once they fill out the application, prospective judges are required to hit the "submit" button in the application field box for further consideration.

Qualified Judges

Will your pageant feature circuit pageant judges? Circuit pageant judges are individuals who judge for multiple pageant systems throughout the year. While circuit pageant judges are very experienced at judging pageants, there is a good chance that they will have already judged some of the candidates in your pageant. Consider sprinkling your pageant with both seasoned and unseasoned pageant judges if you use circuit pageant judges.

There are a number of resources that can put a pageant director in touch with qualified judges. For example, *Brittany's Beauties* is a Georgia pageant resource center. You can find a list of qualified judges from the Georgia area by clicking on the "Judges List" button. Do an Internet search to find out if other states are offering a similar service. You can also find certified pageant judges via the *Pageant Judges Certification Course & Recertification Course.* Scroll down and click on the Certified Judges link to view two lists of current Certified Judges with rankings of Novice Judge, Level 1 Judge, Level 2 Judge, and Chief Judge — each with their contact information.

Full Panel of Judges

It is disheartening for official contestants to arrive at their pageant and find an empty seat or two at the judges' table. Candidates pay a lot of money to participate in a pageant, so they feel that they should be judged by a full panel of judges. A National pageant should have a minimum of five judges on a panel. They should also have (standing in the wings) two additional backup judges — actual pageant judges, not pageant workers or family members — in the event that a judge or two doesn't show up. If this isn't possible, at least remove the empty seat, mug, and other judging material, because candidates don't need to see that there is a missing judge as they perform their "making eye contact" scan at every judge and spot the empty seat. A quality pageant will have five or seven judges on a panel — an odd number to help prevent a tie. Moreover, a candidate doesn't need to be reminded that not all of the judges she "paid to judge her" were physically present to judge her — as she is reminded every time she views the "empty-seat" in the pageant video!

Inform and Coach Your Judges

Meet with your judges before the pageant to clearly express both the pageant goal and the type of winner that you want. Indicate whether or not the winner advances to another level of competition. If the judges are not using the same criteria to judge the pageant, you may get judges who will give a fair score to a mediocre girl, a high score to a less-than-flattering girl, or a low score to the right girl. If the three judges canceled out each other's favorites by voting as just described, their confusion would enable the mediocre girl to win. When that happens, all the judges (and the audience) wonder how she won! It is important that you give your judges as much information as possible about your official contestants. Prepare a Candidate Fact Sheet (bio) for your judges. If possible, give the judges Candidate Fact Sheets at least a week prior to your pageant. If this is not feasible, give them some quiet time prior to the judges' interviews to review Candidate Fact Sheets. Former pageant coach and judge trainer Barbara Kelley notes,

> You have to read the bio so you have an idea of what the girl is all about. Point your questions toward that

bio so you bring out the contestant's personality and make her think on her feet.

Category descriptions should be provided to the judges in advance of the pageant. An informed Judges Panel will clearly select the best candidates to enter the Finals.

Give Judges Time to Prepare Notes

Do not rush the next official contestant into the interview room or on stage immediately after the last one leaves the area of competition. Instead, give judges time to carefully analyze the last candidate's strengths and weaknesses and make notes. Experienced judges use codes to quickly make notes, so very little note time is necessary. For instance, "WC" stands for weak chin. "H" means heavy. "BB" stands for beauty and brains (not to be confused with "big bottom"). When all the judges raise their heads, it is time for the next candidate to appear for judging.

Inspect Facility Conditions

Give judges a chance to look at the conditions under which official contestants will be competing. Facility conditions vary widely, and this might be helpful in determining a candidate's score, especially for a girl who has slipped while performing her jazz dance. Was it because she was incompetent, or was the floor slippery?

Judges' Dress

Judges should dress appropriately and within the range of each other when in the public view. If judges are not told what to wear, they will arrive in everything from business suits to jeans to fad dresses. Clearly state the judging dress code.

Give Official Contestants Undivided Attention

All candidates should receive the judges' undivided attention in all areas of competition. When an official contestant is performing her Talent and sees two judges talking, she will think that she is performing badly. This also makes the audience think that the judges are bored or don't care. *Miss South Texas Teen* Kelli Lee says,

> I do not like to see the judges' opinions during competition. That is, I do not like for judges to confer while judging, I do not like judges to point during lineups. In general, I do not want to know the outcome of a pageant before it is officially announced.

Judges should clear their minds when preparing to judge the next candidate. It is important for judges to remember that each official contestant they meet is the best they have seen. Judges must use this same thought for each candidate in each category. Judges should not compare girls to each other. Each candidate must be judged as an individual and rated as to how she measures up against the standards of the pageant.

Pageant systems that videotape its pageants could learn from those tapes. Some of the larger pageant systems could be made aware of, upon viewing the videos, that judges are completely ignoring some of the girls while they are on stage, some look bored, and others are constantly looking at their watches. At one National pageant, a male judge could be seen (on the video) as looking almost mad that he was there! (With nearly 300 official contestants in that age division, maybe he was!) Another judge held his head with one hand and the other stretched out on the table, with a miserable look on his face. If judges are expected to judge official contestants in their body language, then they should set an example and have excellent body language. You *can* yawn without opening your mouth! In a consecutive year's video of the same pageant system, a nearly identical judging panel appeared *yet again* disinterested in being there! Study your pageant videos, and make necessary corrections for your next pageant event.

Allow Time to Judge Official Contestants

When a pageant has so many candidates, it's hard for anyone to understand how they can be judged fairly. Allotting thirty or forty seconds for each official contestant to appear on stage and be judged is not only unfair to them, but it truly makes the judges feel as if they are in the midst of a cattle call and need to rush the herd through! Candidates' parents spend lots of money on their daughters' competition outfits, so rushing them on and off the stage is bad business practice for any pageant system. What about personal interviews? Giving candidates thirty or forty seconds to be judged by each judge, in a Round Robin style, or any fashion, is NOT enough time to be fairly judged. How can pageant officials teach candidates how to perform well under rushed conditions? If the pageant cannot give more time to every candidate, in all areas of competition, then cap off pageant entries. Cut corners elsewhere.

Pre-Judging

In some pageants, especially the Finals of a National pageant, there is pre-judging. Preliminary competitions are held prior to the actual pageant stage show, something the audience members usually don't see. Pre-judging for all areas of competition takes place during official contestants' week-long stay, away from family and the press. The bulk of major pageant systems begin its pageant events with an introduction of all official contestants, followed by an immediate announcement of the Semifinalists (Top 15) or Finalists (Top 10). Depending on the pageant system, some pageant officials use the practice of wiping the scores that got the candidates to the Semifinals or Finals, allowing Semifinalists/Finalists to ALL start the next judging stage with a clean slate. Others carry forward some or all of the scores that ALL official contestants earned during the first round.

In the _Miss USA_ pageant, candidates are first seen, but not judged, in their state costumes via a Parade of Beauty. This allows judges to see what the competition is like before critiquing each individual candidate. Most judges find a preview helpful. In most Preliminary and State pageants, personal interviews take place a day or two before the pageant coronation. Other areas of competition are judged on the Finals night, in front of family, friends, and the press.

Judging

Judging procedures vary according to the pageant. The method you choose will depend on the level of your pageant, the number of participating official contestants, and the categories to be judged. To facilitate judging at a State or National level, divide candidates into three groups with a designated number of Semifinalists being selected from each group, or take the highest scoring candidates after all scores are combined. Alternate each group by allowing one-third of the candidates to compete in Evening Gown, one-third in Swimsuit (or Sportswear, Outfit of Choice [OOC], etc.), and the final third in Talent (or whatever is your third area of competition). It's best that judges interview all candidates on the same day.

Tie Breaking Procedure

One procedure every pageant needs in place is a tie-breaker. If you don't have a tie-breaking procedure in place, a coin-flip or run-off is what you'll be doing. This is hardly the best way to select your winner, and certainly NOT fair to candidates. Have tie breaking criteria in place before your pageant begins.

Whatever your tie breaking procedure is, note in your Rules & Regulations how it will be utilized. Make sure you are prepared to handle this scenario on the off chance that it happens, because a three-way tie is even more complicated. Santa Cruz *Toastmasters* had a three-way tie for its speech winner. How did it break the tie? By involving the vote counter. Here's how the tie breaking procedure worked: A vote counter got to record his vote, but put it aside, and didn't count it unless s/he needed to break a tie.

Miss America Organization's tie breaking procedures for the _Miss Kentucky_ pageant can be found at the State pageant's website _Local Pageant Resources_ page. Then, scroll down to "Auditor Forms" and click on "Tie Breaking Procedures." You will find procedures on how to break ties in various areas of competition, including ties for Preliminary awards, ties into or within the Top 5, ties into the Top 10, and so on. It is obvious that this pageant system has thought of every scenario that could possibly happen, at any given time. Moreover, this is where the pageant puts the Tally Sheet Disclaimer, which says that if the pageant is ever in dispute "[an] independent auditor will review the results." Therefore, keep judges scores or tally sheets in a sealed envelope for *at least one year*.

Sick Judge Procedure

How will you handle judges' scores when one of your judges is no longer able to complete his/her judging? Will you continue by having another judge pick up where the other left off? Will you delete all of the departing judge's scores from the tally? If you visit the *Miss Kentucky* website, and then the Local Pageant Resources page, scroll down to "Auditor Forms" to find the "Sick Judge Procedure." Here you will find three case scenarios and procedures for handling each one. Case number one states that there is no change in the number of judges throughout all of the competitions. Case number two features a scenario where a judge does not complete the first phase of the completion and the resulting outcome from that circumstance. Case number three features a scenario where one judge completes at least one competition, but does not complete any others, and the resulting outcome from that occurrence. In addition, *Miss Kentucky* includes three more scenarios regarding 1) if the original panel had five judges (the high and low scores are NOT dropped); 2) if the original panel had six judges (the high and low scores ARE dropped); and 3) if the original panel had seven judges (the high and low scores ARE dropped). Moreover, *Miss Kentucky* includes rules regarding the Final Ballot at the end of the Sick Judge Procedure.

Judges Personally Knowing a Candidate

Pageant directors strive to find judges who have no connection with the candidates. No matter how hard they try, there will come a time when a judge on the panel personally knows a candidate or two. If a judge knows a candidate, *Pristine Pageants* will not allow those scores to be included. The highest score from each of the other judges will be used (if three judges) or the average of all scores (if five judges). This prevents any conflict of interest. *All Canadian Pageants*, in the event that a judge knows a candidate, will not permit that judge to score the official contestant. Instead, for that moment, an alternate judge fills in.

Unbiased Judges

Keep judging unbiased by not telling judges the names or hometown of the official contestants. Only include space on the score sheet for evaluating poise and verbal expression, and maybe a space for noting their appearance. Ask judges to avoid political or religious questions in the interviews. Cynthia Klein, then *Miss Universe* publicity director, gladly stated that no political questions were asked in the 1988 *Miss Universe* pageant:

> It's a way to get a sense of their approach to life, their poise and self-confidence, and to see the types of clothes they choose to present themselves.

Miss India International reminds official contestants:

> [no] political or religious questions [are] allowed unless you bring the subject up yourself.

Judging Personal Interviews

The judges' interview with candidates is the most important phase of a pageant. Judges are to look for natural feedback and mental alertness from candidates. Judges should never look for perfection, but they should look for self-confidence, enthusiasm, and a special aura that radiates from genuine people. A girl should have poise and a command of situations. Strong interview and speaking skills — including a broad vocabulary, good grammar, and a pleasant speaking voice — are a must. Judges should look for someone who does not use slang and who has good diction and enunciation. They need to remember that the girl, after she wins — especially in the *Miss America* system — does not normally have to perform in a swimsuit again. She seldom, if ever, performs her Talent again, but she does have to speak. She must be able to think on her feet and possess the ability to clearly express her opinions without offending anyone.

Interviewing judging formats change from time to time and from pageant to pageant. Prior to 1970, girls in the *Miss America* pageant were judged in trios rather than individually. Since then, the judging panel has interviewed only one official contestant at a time. Conducted over a two-night period, _Miss USA_ judges interview candidates on a one-on-one basis, rather than as a collective panel. The candidates enter a room in groups, the number equaling the number of judges. As each candidate is interviewed by each judge in the allotted time, the candidates rotate until all have been interviewed by all judges.

Most pageants allow each official contestant five to seven minutes to communicate with each judge. The judges consider this small amount of time sufficient to make a fair evaluation of each candidate. Many believe they can see what they need to see in five to seven minutes. In that short period of time, they will find the girl who has the best personality and who makes the strongest impression visually and verbally. If a candidate tries to put on an act, judges will see right through her. Most candidates today try to impress the judges with their intellect by stating their political convictions. Warn your judges to not let them get away with this. Candidates should not discuss heavy topics. They should be natural, relaxed, and keep their answers as short and concise as possible.

Panel Seating Interview/Podium Interview

Will an official contestant face a panel of judges, a.k.a. press conference style, with judges asking her questions in no particular order? Or, will she be required to stand behind a podium during the interview? In either event, will the moderator — the person who tells the official contestants and judges when to begin and end the interview — introduce each candidate and her number as she enters the room? Or, will each candidate be expected to introduce herself and announce her own number? The interview for the _World's Perfect Teen_ National pageant is carried out in a press conference-style, where judges ask a variety of questions from each candidate's Personal History application during her _seven-minute_ interview. For a pageant with younger candidates, _Mid-South Pageants_ pageant officials note,

> This is a "no stress" interview with one child and two judges. This is just fun.

Round-Robin Style Interview

Will official contestants be interviewed in a round-robin style interview, for example, three minutes per judge, and then move on to the next judge to repeat? If so, remind official contestants that they need to introduce themselves to each individual judge as they appear at each judge's station. Each candidate will be expected to say: "Good Morning. I am contestant number three, Jane Smith." The moderator will call time at the end of the three minutes. All candidates in the interview room (five if there are five judges) will stand up and turn around. With each back to their respective judge, judges will score and critique each respective candidate. When the last judge puts his/her pen down, the moderator calls time and the candidates rotate to the next judge, repeating the process until every candidate has met with each judge, in a round-robin fashion.

Should a Judge Ask the Same Question of Each Official Contestant?

Many times one judge on a panel will ask each official contestant the same question. They find that asking the same question is a good way to "see" sincerity. Another may ask a question that they know the candidate cannot answer just to get the reaction. Most questions asked are geared to encourage full, thoughtful responses that paint the attitude of the candidate.

Encourage Judges to Ask Difficult Questions

Judges need not be afraid to ask difficult questions. Difficult questions show the judges have done their homework well. Therefore, the "selling job" that follows is comparatively simple. At one San Diego pageant, a judge asked pageant contender Shari Boone the simple question, "What animal would you describe yourself as and why?" Shari responded, "I apologize if I sound rude, however, if you would like for me to answer the interview questions with some intelligence, could you please ask intelligent questions?" Thinking that the judges will be shocked or angry at her reply, she was surprised and grateful that they agreed with her response. They understood that she was not being rude and degrading the question, but that she was nervous and not able to answer petty questions. Besides, only moments before the pageant, the director told official contestants to answer the questions with confidence and poise. How can judges expect a girl to give confident answers if the questions are simple and meaningless? The judges scanned the uniform list of questions more carefully. They agreed that many were petty questions and talked about how there could have been more difficult questions from which to choose. That year, Shari Boone did go on to win the 1986 *Miss Greater San Diego Teen* pageant.

Judging Poise

Judges define poise as the evidence of good breeding, the way a girl takes care of herself, femininity, it is in her eyes, the ability to handle any situation in good taste, carriage, style and grace, the right amount of confidence, and something inborn that cannot be described. Some judges think that the first place to see poise is in the eyes, while others find it in the way a girl walks or sits and talks. Poise identifies itself in many ways. *Miss America* pageant judge Nanci Wudel says,

> You must look at the feet first, because that is going to determine the bone structure, and if you don't have good bone structure, you cannot walk well, and if you cannot walk well, you cannot possess poise.[48]

Give extra points to someone who glides down the ramp with sophistication and elegance and to someone who feels comfortable on stage. If a candidate makes a mistake on stage, then smiles it off, and goes on to her next scene, that's another point. If a candidate appears to be enjoying herself, that's another point. Reacting with grace when a girl makes a mistake is the true definition of poise. Olivia Culpo, *Miss USA* 2012, must have seen her chances of winning the coveted *Miss Universe* crown slip between her fingers after taking a tumble in front of the judges when she tripped on the fabric of her dress as the rock band *Train* performed. Instead, she gracefully composed herself, rose to her feet, and continued on to capture the 2012 *Miss Universe* title.

---

[48] DeFord, Frank. *The Life and Times of Miss America*, Penguin Books, 1978.

Judging Swimsuit Competition

Female judges are pickier than male judges. Women are more likely to seek defects in parts and mark off in Swimsuit competition, whereas men tend to look for positive factors and judge the body as a whole. Experienced judges look for proportion when judging the swimsuit competition. Technical judges look for well-toned bodies and shoulders that do not slope to one side, or forward, and are not too wide. Necks should not be stiff, or too long, or too short. The most critical areas of all are the bottom and the thighs. Heavy thighs are point stealers, and even if a girl works hard to rid herself of the weight, she can still be penalized for retaining flabby, unconditioned skin. If a girl has entered a pageant, there is no excuse for a bad body in the swimsuit competition. If she has taken the time to enter the pageant, she should take the time to keep her body toned. Just because a girl is slender does not mean her body is toned. Judges will notice flabby thighs and count off for them. Muscles should be firm, not bulging. Beauty should be comparatively small and delicate, with one section melting neatly into the next. Candidates must project a confident image, showing it in their walk and in eye contact with the judges and the audience.

Judging Evening Gown Competition

In the Evening Gown portion of the competition, judges should look for personality projection, poise, and naturalness. A candidate should wear a dress that complements her figure and skin tone, i.e., similar to one of many classic styles offered at *Dazzles Pageant and Prom*. Many pretty girls wear gowns with too many ruffles that look unnatural. Simple, well-cut gowns in solid colors are most flattering. Pageant contenders should always wear dresses appropriate for their age. Furthermore, the dress should be comfortable and easy to walk in.

In the Evening Gown (or Swimsuit) category, each candidate stands in full front position while being judged on the following points:

- An imaginary line through the center of her head must pass through the torso, dividing her legs.

- The neck must be graceful enough to act as a pedestal for her head.

- Shoulders must be wider than hips and slope at a twenty degree angle from the base of her neck.

- Arms must flow as she stands or walks.

- Legs must be elegant when standing and graceful when walking.

Judging Talent

Talent is not an easy exercise to judge. To compare singers, pianists, actresses, dancers, and other performers is nearly impossible. Besides, few judges have expertise in more than one or two talent areas. Unbalanced knowledge can be unfair to official contestants when a diversity of talents are being judged. _Miss America_ judge Nanci Wudel notes,

> [a] judge who is a pianist may be inclined to vote for a contestant who plays the piano. On the other hand, s/he is also capable of being more critical, and will be expressively harsh on a piano performance while giving high marks, say, to a flashy dancer whose presentation is just as flawed, but which s/he has no background to evaluate.[49]

If your pageant does include a Talent competition, and there is a piano that candidates can access, let them know if it is a baby grand or an upright. If there isn't a piano at the pageant location, note that information in your pageant material, as does _Miss Louisiana Plus America_. _Our Little Miss_ not only reminds official contestants that a piano is not available for their Talent, but they are informed that they _can_ bring their own keyboard. _Miss Ireland_ pageant officials state,

> If you choose to do something musical, you MUST provide your own accompaniment, which means making arrangements to use the piano if needed or bringing in any other instrument.

---

[49] Ibid.

A candidate's presentation must be interesting and entertaining. Talent should reveal an aspect of the candidate's personality. Furthermore, a candidate's Talent costume must be flattering and appropriate for her Talent. *Cinderella International Scholarship Pageant* doesn't fail to reward official contestants who are exemplary in Talent. These Superlative Awards include Best Baton Twirler, Best Musician, Best Vocalist, Best Pantomimist, Best Tap Dancer, Best Ballerina, etc.

Rank Scoring Finals

When pageant contenders make it to the Finals, ALL Finalists must be fairly judged into the winning positions, i.e., rank scored. (Documentation supporting the ranked scoring should be saved for future validation, should the need arise.) Therefore, if you have five official contestants in your Finals, each one of the five candidates will be rank scored; if you have ten official contestants in your Finals, all ten candidates will be rank scored, etc. *Don't rank only some of your Finalists.*

This is an actual scenario from one pageant system at its National pageant: Going into the Finals, twenty-five girls (give or take, and depending on the particular age division) made the Finals. From those twenty-five girls, only five girls with the highest averages after their Preliminary judging were predetermined (selected) to be judged for the winning positions. Unbeknownst to the audience and the twenty-five girls who again appear before the judges in the Finals, only the predetermined five girls are actually judged in this round. The other twenty Finalists are essentially just going through the motions for "entertainment value."

Judges are expected to keep an eye on only those five preselected girls during the Finals stage lineup and *only* score those Top 5 girls for Queen to Fourth Runner-Up positions. This could mean that the girl who wins may not actually have the highest scores overall — which would explain how a candidate can finish first in two competitions and not win the title. The parents, official contestants, and audience would understand this if they knew that this sort of judging and rank scoring was occurring. Often, most don't because it's not in writing. Moreover, they are not told of this "entertainment value" procedure.

It isn't fair that pageant officials let the remaining twenty "Finalists" go through the motions of being "judged" for those "winning positions" when they're not. Pageant systems that employ this judging technique mislead the girls who are not being ranked into the Finals. The twenty-five Finalists likely all assume that they *are* competing in the Finals and are eligible for winning, but they are NOT, and they also don't know that they are just part of the pageant's "entertainment value."

This sort of pageant "entertainment value" isn't what those prospective contestants signed up for when they signed the contract (Official Application), and it certainly wasn't one of the pageant's clauses within its Rules & Regulations. Sadly, when the pageant paperwork is vague, at best, prospective contestants don't know what they are signing up for!

If you have twenty-five official contestants going into the Finals, rank score ALL twenty-five candidates. If you only want to rank score five official contestants, have a Top 5 from the start. If you want twenty-five girls on stage for the "entertainment value," then label them Semifinalists and choose five girls from that pool of pageant contenders as your Finalists. Now, there would be less confusion when your judging panel ranks those five Finalists because twenty other candidates aren't crowding the five leading contenders! Moreover, imagine that one judge is mistakenly rank scoring one of the non-Finalists! Several pageant parents I interviewed would not have allowed their daughters to participate in the pageant if they had they been made aware of this score ranking procedure.

Top Candidates Canceling Each Other

In most major pageants, there are multiple candidates slated as favorites to win the title. Having more than one favorite can adversely affect scoring when it comes to Finals voting by the judges. For example, two candidates are in the running for the title. When it comes to the Finals vote, if the judges are split in their decision for both contenders, the winner could end up being a completely different candidate. She could represent the majority of second or third place votes — which would then give her the highest combined score from all the judges — as opposed to the other two candidates who each received only half the votes for the title. The key to an official contestant winning the title is to score consistently high in all components of the competition but not necessarily win all the categories.

Judges' Affidavit

Some pageant officials require that judges sign a Judges' Affidavit before judging their pageants. This affidavit states certain key points that judges will adhere to, serving as a reminder of what they have agreed to in performing as a judge. Miss Kentucky requires pageant judges to sign a Judges' Affidavit. This affidavit can be found at its Local Pageant Resources page. Scroll down to the "Judges Forms," and click on "Judges Affidavit." A Judges Affidavit can also be found in my book *Producing Beauty Pageants: Creating a Synergized National Pageant System*, Chapter 12, "Pageant Paperwork and Forms" under "Judges Affidavit."

Judges Guidelines/Handbook

Judging a beauty pageant is a difficult task. Aid your judges in their decision by presenting a simple method of selecting the right girl. Once you place the score sheets in front of the judges, ask them to set aside their own personal preferences and find the best in each pageant contender.

Miss America makes a Judging Disk available for their Preliminary and State pageants available to its State directors. The disk contains, among other items, score sheets, auditor's instructions, and tie-breaking procedures.

Many pageant officials have developed a Judges' Handbook for judges to follow. It can be extremely helpful to judges, especially considering that anyone can be fallible — in memory or health. A Judges' Handbook should contain important documents that guide judges through successful pageant judging. A Judges' Handbook can include a Judging Ethics Form (a simple form that talks about fair, impartial judging; not conversing with other Judges while judging; not talking to candidates during pageant week, etc.); Judges' Notes Sheets; Judges' Official Contestant Comment Sheets; Scoring Method; Directions on Casting a Ballot (Rank Scoring); and last, but not least, a list of questions that they can use for the Personal Interviews. A Judges' Handbook will help create consistency among judges' scoring. Miss Rodeo North Dakota posted its well-written, well-organized, twenty-page 2015 Official Pageant Rulebook online — which is continuously revised and updated. Both the judges and official contestants have access to the rule book, so there is no question of misunderstanding. *Beauties of America Pageant* *uploaded* *its* *State Judges' Handbook* at *Docstock*.

So that judging will be as fair as possible, you might instruct the judges as follows:

1. Do not consider the section, city, or town of the state where a girl is from.

2. The director, in *no way*, desires to influence your voting.

3. If any judge has any personal or particular knowledge about any official contestant, her relatives, or friends, this should be brought to the attention of the director.

4. Ignore rumors.

5. Candidates are encouraged to bring a large audience to support them. Do not let audience reaction influence you. *Crown Bound Pageants* even promotes this by presenting the Crowd Pleaser Award (and a 4 foot trophy) to the candidate with the most audience support.

6. Do not consider braces on teeth.

7. Do not let an official contestant's winning a separate award influence your voting.

8. Consider a girl on the basis of her total beauty, not just one particular feature.

9. If a candidate becomes upset in her interview, excuse her and recall her at a later time.

10. There may be a tendency to vote for a candidate because she is of the same ethnic or national background. Do not consider this factor.

11. Do not ask questions about religion or politics during personal interviews.

12. The winner should possess some degree of intelligence, personality, and beauty of face, figure, and poise. Her grace, or lack of it, should be noted.

13. Do not consider the expense of the evening gowns, etc.

14. Do consider good bone structure, good body-tone, and good teeth.

15. Judges should not applaud during any part of the competition. If they do applaud, they should do so for all pageant contenders.

16. We desire that each judge vote individually. There should be no official conferring about candidates or consulting between judges.

17. Do not badger the girl in the interview.

18. If any changes in scores are to be made by you, a judge, you should not erase the original score. Instead, a line should be drawn through the original score and next to it the new score indicated, with an initial to complete the alteration.

Request from Your Judges

It is important that each judge know what is expected of him/her. Directors realize emergencies sometimes do arise. Ask each judge to have someone in mind to take his/her place in the event that an emergency should arise. It is a director's nightmare for a judge not to appear. Judges are important people, and many people are depending upon them. Judges should be considerate and arrive on time. Delaying a pageant to wait for a single judge is unfair. Will you expect the judges to tabulate their own votes? A judge should judge, not tabulate. Tabulation should be left for public accountants. To avoid ties, arrange your panel so there are an odd number of judges on the panel, such as five, seven, or nine.

If you want to produce an outstanding pageant, the following should be requested of the judges and can be added to as needed:

1. Be prompt regarding the activities involved with the pageant.

2. Avoid talking, laughing, etc., during competitions. An organized pageant director realizes that official contestants will see the judges at various times during the pageant week/weekend. They are instructed to say a simple "hello" to a judge in passing, but nothing more.

3. Judges should not converse with candidates during the pageant except during official interviews and functions. In the event judges do converse with candidates during non-pageant events, *Social Butterfly Pageants* tell official contestants, "It is okay to speak with the judges if they approach you." It's best that official contestants know this than be paralyzed should a judge speak to them during a non-judging period.

4. Judges should not converse with family or friends of any candidate during the pageant or any of the pageant activities. A simple "hello" is permissible.

5. Make this as positive of an experience as you can for the candidates. Smiling at each candidate puts them at ease and helps them to perform better on stage.

6. Do not hold back on scoring. If the first pageant contender deserves a top score, give it to her. Don't "save" your high score for a candidate who could perform better. The first one might *be* the best one. Do not be concerned with who will be the following candidates.

7. Positive and constructive comments are encouraged for every pageant contender. Such positive comments might include, "Those lovely eyes need to make more eye contact" or "Beautiful hair should not cover that beautiful face." Furthermore, do not reduce a score due to missing teeth, braces, eyeglasses, casts, bandage wraps, etc. *Miss Plus America*, on the other hand, states "Because of time constraints during judging, no comments are provided."

8. Never discriminate against race, nationality, and disabilities.

9. Do not count off for weight, as children often fluctuate in their growth pattern.

10. A candidate in the younger divisions may have a dress that is too tight because, after it was purchased two months ago, she had a growth spurt! Do not reduce her score if the dress doesn't fit one way or the other. It's hard to plan for growth spurts.

Present Judges with an Official Contestants Portfolio

Give each judge a portfolio containing a photograph and biographical information about each candidate. Judges should read the bio so they have an idea of what each girl is all about. They can make notes on each candidate during the events. It is better that a judge rely on her notes at the time of the appearance than on memory at the conclusion of the pageant. Cut pictures from the Pageant Program Book (PPB), and tape a picture of each candidate to her application for the judges. Also, provide them with a copy of the PPB so that they can use it to take notes. *Cinderella International Scholarship Pageant* permits judges to use the PPB as a reference tool during deliberations. While most pageants do provide judges with a copy of the PPB, *Miss/Mr. Edwardsburg Pageant* judges are *not* provided with one (nor are they directly made aware of how much fundraising money any particular candidate has brought into the pageant). The first time they see official contestants is when they compete in the Judges' Interview. Some pageants feel viewing official contestants' photos prior to judging will influence judges' voting; others, not so. Use your own judgment. *Miss Trussville Pageant* organizers remind candidates to include six copies of their Platform Essay; six copies of their résumé; and six copies of their photograph (5" x 7" or 8" x 10", black and white or color) on their paperwork checklist, among other forms, in the judges' Official Contestants Portfolio.

Paying Judges for their Services

Particularly, in today's economy, pageant officials should pay judges for their work. Paying judges a real amount, such as $200 per day, makes them "want to judge, happy to be there, and most importantly, qualified to judge," noted a *volunteer* judge (and a pageant director of her own system) at the *National American Miss* National pageant. [50] *The Glass Slipper Natural Beauty Pageant* pays its judges for their services.

---

[50] "You All Just Seem Dumb..." December 13, 2011. http://www.national-american-miss-scam.com/2011/12/by-jones-you-all-just-seem-dumb/.

Caring for Judges

Judges are not usually paid for their time, but they are treated well. For instance, National judges spend a week at a lovely hotel enjoying the sun and good food. Some judges consider judging a pageant a working vacation — with the emphasis on work. Once you have organized your pageant and judges committee, turn your attention to the caring of your judges. Be prepared to make necessary adjustments concerning locations, number of days, the amount of "free" time, etc. Identify the free-time periods during the judges' stay. Then, develop ways to keep judges busy and/or entertained. Stop short of exhausting them. Judges like to chat with other judges and get to know one another.

Most pageants of more than one day in length house its judges in a local hotel. If your pageant is the main attraction at that time, try to get rooms for judges and pageant staff donated. To become the unofficial headquarters, many hotels will give you several free rooms if there are reservations for fifteen or more rooms. More information on obtaining free hotel rooms can be found in my book *Producing Beauty Pageants: Brokering a Pageant through Barter*, Chapter 5, "Pageant Venue Bartered."

Adequate meals must be provided for your judges. You do not have to supply them with prime rib dinners. There are local restaurants that are "unique" in their selection of entrees and are reasonably priced. Assess your community strengths, and capitalize on them. Most restaurants are happy to host "visiting dignitaries" in exchange for promotional consideration. This information is also provided in my book *Producing Beauty Pageants: Brokering a Pageant through Barter*.

Should Judges Stick Around?

Once the pageant ends, it is best for judges to leave as quickly and quietly as possible. Otherwise, family and friends of participating candidates will hound them with questions as to why their daughters did not win, or what they could do to win. In the *Miss Brazil* pageant, judges are removed from their booths before the winner is announced. This is a common pageant procedure in the *Miss Brazil* pageant. The public is fanatical. If they don't agree with the judges' choice, they throw tomatoes! Often the audience — as a whole — views official contestants differently from the judges. *There She Is: The Life and Times of Miss America* author Frank DeFord noted,

> The audience at a *Miss America* pageant falls in love with a girl it sees on a huge stage, on TV. But the judges share a more personal relationship with a woman they all meet within a small room.

Only judges know official contestants' strengths and weaknesses. This is precisely why *Beautiful Girls Pageant* and *Miss Texas State* encourage its judges to stick around after coronation. They can answer questions candidates may have regarding competition and provide guidance on how they can improve their scores.

Chapter 15

Auditor

When I produced my first pageant, I secured my pageant committee, that is, all except a certified public accountant. Actually, I thought that tabulating would be quick and simple. I had a math-savvy friend tabulate *after* all three areas of competition were completed. Was I ever wrong! After this horrifying first-time experience, I became completely aware of how the tabulation was to be performed and the time needed to do it.

My tabulation problem could have been avoided had I had ongoing tabulation in groups of every five or ten official contestants. For example, for a seventy-candidate age division, deliver score sheets to the tabulator after every five candidates. This way the auditor can be tallying the scores of candidates numbered one to five while the judges are judging candidates numbered six to ten. Tabulators should use a computer. It can be set up to automatically add scores and sort in each category.

Better yet, set up an automated beauty pageant scoring and tabulation system for your pageants. Beauty pageant tabulation system software allows any number of judges to enter their scores on a pageant-provided laptop for varying rounds throughout the pageant. Upon completing each round (and ultimately the pageant), .pdf reports can be generated and printed. The reports have lines for the judges to sign, indicating that their scores are accurate. This ensures a complete paper trail of the Finals pageant results. *Southern Elite Pageants* tabulates all scores via a computer as the pageant progresses.

Often pageant producers hire auditors from accounting firms to tabulate. This gives them peace of mind while keeping people from saying their pageant was rigged. After all, no pageant producer needs scoring mistakes to blemish her event.

Some of the world's biggest pageants take care to find top notch auditors from the best accounting firms: *Miss South Africa* employs *PricewaterhouseCoopers*; *Miss Asia USA* employs accounting firm *KPMG Forensic Department*; and *Miss World* employs *Ernst and Young*. Latest pageant newcomer, *American*

Glamour Pageant, is proud to have former *Fortune 50* (not 500) Lead Accountant Mr. Guy Rosati officiating over scores. Nevertheless, for a smaller scale pageant, a local accounting firm can provide excellent tabulation/auditing services that can certify pageant scores — often retained *pro bono* as does *Essence Pageant.* Learn how you can barter with an accountant by reading my book *Producing Beauty Pageants: Brokering a Pageant through Barter,* Chapter 9, "In-Kind Sponsors" under "Accounting/Audit Services."

Magical Moments USA pageant director makes it clear about her pageant's scoring method:

> I, the director, will not tabulate the scores. I have an accountant to do that for me! I will double check [his] work and make any corrections *with* [him]!

Again, stay out of the tabulation and hire two accountants.

Auditor Briefing

While auditors are briefed of pageant scoring procedures approximately two weeks prior to an event, another mini briefing should occur a few hours before the pageant begins. The mini briefing should include information for all areas of competition — the Semifinals, Finals, and placement of the Runners-Up and Queen. After all, it is the auditor's responsibility to make sure that the Fourth Runner-Up is placed on the Fourth Runner-Up line and not reversed — on the winner's line — as can easily happen. In this event the emcee would announce the Fourth Runner-Up as the winner and the winner as the Fourth Runner-Up!

Such an innocent error had happened at the 1994 <u>Miss Moses Lake</u> pageant, with accounting firm *LeMaster and Daniels* at the helm. That year Iliana Pruneda, 20, was crowned Queen of the pageant, but was dethroned two days later when judges realized that they had reversed her name and number with that of official contestant Stephanie Hill, 19. While the accounting firm tabulated the scores correctly, the error occurred because the names and identification numbers of candidates Iliana Pruneda and Stephanie Hill were reversed on the judges' ballots and the auditor's tally sheet. Therefore, while your auditor is responsible for making sure that each of the Top 5 placements into the winning positions are in order, the Head Judge should ultimately be responsible to see that the names are not accidently reversed.

Every pageant differs in what it expects of its auditors. *Our Little Miss* notes that an auditor's job is also being,

> [responsible] for catching any infractions or violations during competition week; allowed to inform the judges of any violations given to make sure they are aware of which contestants are not eligible for the Top 8 Placements; at every competition and in direct contact with the State/Country directors to inform them of infractions and violations given; and responsible for handling any disqualifications and removal from the competition property.

Auditing Tabulation Errors

It's not just Local pageants that have had accounting difficulties. Human error can occur at any pageant organization level. In a pageant that took place on December 5, 2007, Cristina Silva, of Koreatown, was crowned *Miss California USA*. Four days later she found out that the crown rightfully belonged to *Miss Barstow*, Raquel Beezley, who had been Second Runner-Up. As it turned out, an error in the tabulation of voting by pageant judges (performed by a volunteer accountant who tabulated the votes) was found. Pageant officials offered Cristina a complete refund of her $1,500 entry fee. They also allowed her to keep her crown, sash, and the $4,500 *Miss California USA* necklace, but it was the title that she was asked to relinquish to Raquel Beezley. Cristina chose, instead, to hire an attorney to argue her case.

In another tabulation error incident, after discovering a tabulating error during a tie-breaking Finals placement of the 2011 *Miss Clatsop County's Outstanding Teen* pageant the following day, director Sandy Larson consulted with State pageant officials. A decision was then made to award an additional title to Hannah Garhofer, who was mistakenly given the First Runner-Up position. Both Preliminary winners went on to represent their county at the *Miss Oregon Scholarship Program*, a part of the *Miss America* Organization.

Head Auditor

A pageant should have one head auditor and one assistant auditor to count ballots. The head auditor should be the one to communicate with the moderator. The head auditor is responsible to double-check the ballots. The head auditor and assistant auditor are to sign their initials on each ballot sheet. Judging instructions and score sheets should be given to both auditors at least two weeks before your pageant event. About this time, both auditors would meet with pageant officials to review everything and to be sure that they understand the tabulation procedure.

Head Judge

The Head Judge — also known as Judges' Chair or Coordinator — is the only person who interacts with the judges and the auditor before, during, and after the competition. The Head Judge is responsible for handling the score sheets before, during, and after the pageant. At no time before the final judging should the Head Judge "remind" the judges what pageant officials are looking for in a Queen. She is also responsible for verifying the accuracy of the scores and the placement of the winning positions. However, the head auditor is responsible for stopping the pageant if the pageant emcee announces the winners incorrectly. Therefore, it is essential that the Head Judge and auditor pay attention to the emcee, as the winners are announced, to make sure that the winning positions are announced in the correct order and not reversed.

The Head Judge should meet the pageant auditor during the briefing (if the Head Judge isn't leading the briefing). The Head Judge should provide the auditor with a hardcopy of your Manual Tally Sheet and your Computer Tally Sheet programs for every area of competition in the Preliminaries and Finals.

The Head Judge will instruct the auditor to turn the Judges' score sheets over to him/her after every fifth candidate (best to do when divisions are large). If you have five judges on your panel, the auditor will have a set of five score sheets presented to him/her at the start of the Interview competition. As the auditor begins tabulating the first five candidates' interview scores (times five judges), s/he is manually entering a total of twenty-five numbers into the computer program. That takes time. Moreover, if your pageant scoring is based on a 1–10 scale with decimals (8.9, 9.5, etc.), as opposed to whole numbers (8, 9, etc.), the auditor will be even busier with numbers insertion. It is recommended that judges score with whole numbers. More than one official contestant may earn the same score with whole number scoring. Therefore, to eliminate the need for a tie-breaker, pageant directors should include only *one* judge who scores in decimals.

An efficient Head Judge will bring the next set of candidates' Interview scores to the auditor about the time that the auditor has entered the scores for the first five candidates. This will continue until the end of the Preliminary competition. If you have more than one division competing simultaneously — and particularly if your pageant includes many official contestants — have more than one auditor present. When the last candidate's interview score has been entered into the program, this would be the time that the auditor will discard the high/low scores for every candidate (if this is what your pageant system does). The remaining figures (between the high and low scores) would then be added horizontally and multiplied by the appropriate factor to obtain the total points for that phase of competition for every official contestant.

Breaking Ties/Sick Judge Procedures in Place

The Head Judge is fully prepared to brief the auditor on the pageant's breaking ties/sick judge procedures. The Head Judge will have a copy of both procedures to give to the auditor during the initial auditor's briefing. The auditor will need to understand the mechanics of both procedures in order to be prepared to calculate scores throughout the competition and/or into or within the Top 5 of the pageant. For additional information, visit Chapter 14, "Judging" under "Tie Breaking Procedure" and "Sick Judge Procedure."

Auditor Position during Judging

Auditors are to have a private table and NOT be seated at the judges' table. Auditors are NOT to chat with judges or audience members during the pageant. Make sure that when your auditor uses a laptop to enter scores, s/he minimizes the screen or closes the laptop in between entering scores. Pageant systems don't want someone with binoculars reading the scores on the laptop. Furthermore, someone in the first or second row might have great vision and see all scores being entered. The auditor needs to keep scoring as concealed as possible. S/he is never to leave the document open and the laptop open in plain view.

Proper Handling of Score Sheets

Prior to each phase of judging, the Head Judge is responsible for distributing score sheets to the judges. Right before each Preliminary competition, the Head Judge would distribute each set of competition score sheets. For example, s/he would only present to the judges, prior to the Interview competition, the Interview binder containing *only* the Interview score sheets. The other score sheets (Swimwear, Evening Gown, etc.) remain in his/her possession. At the conclusion of each competition, the Head Judge gathers the judges' signed score sheets and presents them to the auditor. When the next competition is ready to be judged, s/he will hand over the next competition score sheets binder over to each judge. This helps to avoid one competition's scores accidently written on another's score sheets, i.e., Interview scores erroneously written on the Evening Gown score sheet. Therefore, it is wise to NOT have the Head Judge actually judge the pageant, but rather positioned as an overseer between the judges and the auditor.

At no time should a pageant director be in the room as candidates are being judged and/or giving judges judging advice. The time for that has passed, and pageant directors should NEVER handle completed score sheets.

Manual and Computer Tally Sheets

The *Miss America Organization* officials instruct its State and Local pageant directors to provide its auditors with a Manual Tally Sheet hardcopy and Computer Tally Sheet program for each night of competition. Auditors are to continuously maintain and update both a Manual Tally Sheet and a backup file of the Computer Tally Sheet during each pageant night, in the event that the original computer files become corrupted or the computer crashes.

Moreover, the Computer Tally Sheets are designed to automatically create, and then update, a backup file at every "save" operation.

Pageant auditors should continuously maintain and update both a manual and computer tally sheet during pageant judging. The Manual Tally Sheets are a backup for if the computer crashes. The Manual Tally Sheet.xls (Excel Format) is a traditional, long form tally sheet for the Preliminary part of the competition. The auditors manually fill in the scores presented to them by the Head Judge — one auditor verifying the others' manual insertions. (Then they tabulate the scores on their respective computers.) Instructions for printing the Manual Tally Sheet should be included on the computer monitor's image of the tally sheet somewhere at the top. Auditors will need to prepare a separate first round multi-night tally sheet for each division group.

The Computer Tally Sheet.xls (Excel Format) is a self-contained auditors' program for the first rounds of a multi-night competition. If your pageant uses this program, your auditor should become familiar with it prior to your pageant. The auditor needs to obtain official contestants' names and corresponding numbers so that s/he can insert them onto a spreadsheet for every first competition round. Then, all the auditor will need to do is to manually insert each judge's score. Furthermore, having an advance copy of the spreadsheet and candidate data allows an auditor to test the program to see that the built-in formulas work. At the *Texas Choice Pageants,* while scores are tabulated via computer on *Microsoft Excel,* the tabulator only has access to contestant numbers and *not* names.

The Computer Tally Sheet.xls automatically eliminates high and low scores, so if your pageant doesn't eliminate them, inform the auditor so that s/he can make changes in the program. When you have a multi-night competition, prepare a separate first round multi-night tally sheet for each division group. Your auditor can create all of your competition sections to the right of the score sheet that automatically calculate the first round winners for each division group, i.e., Interview, Talent, Sportswear, Evening Gown, etc.

Royal Majesty Pageant notes,

> Tabulation is computerized and entered in a database on an Excel spreadsheet. Contestants may have access to viewing the master spread sheet immediately after crowning.

347

Miss Georgia Girl notes,

> Our scores are entered in a computer program that was designed especially for pageant tabulation. We will provide scores via email as time allows.

Computerized Scoring and Hand Tabulation

Pageant officials across the board are including both computerized scoring and hand tabulation in their pageants. Computerized scoring and hand tabulation is the successful culmination of official contestants being judged. One auditor tabulates scores on a computer while another auditor tabulates manually to verify that they match. *East Coast USA Pageant* offers computerized scoring *and* hand tabulation, along with *carbon copied score sheets* returned (to official contestants) immediately after the pageant. Utilizing software such as *CompetitionSuite* — software that can be customized to work with any pageant scoring system — can make scoring and tabulation easier.

Semifinals/Finals Phase of Competition

The completed Interview scores are inserted in the "Interview" column — usually the day before the stage competitions — providing that you start the pageant competition with Interviews. Repeat the process with the next Preliminary round competition, such as Swimwear/Sportswear. As scores are inserted into each appropriate column (labeled with the competition name), they will be "subtotaled" with the previous Interview scores. At the end of the last Preliminary round competition, such as the Evening Gown competition, the auditor will have the Semifinals results. Now, the Semifinals phase of the competition can begin.

Top 10/Semifinalists

Prior to announcing the Top 10 (Semifinalists) from the Preliminary rounds' combined scores, auditors will have a prearranged Semifinals, Finals, and/or Multi-Night Tally Sheet. This is when the auditor will transfer the ten highest-scored official contestants onto the Semifinals Tally Sheet. When the Top 10 Semifinalists are ready to be announced, their names (in random order) are placed on a Top 10 Semifinalists sheet marked "In Random Order."

If your pageant drops the Preliminary scores after the Top 10 are selected, this would be the time to do so. If Preliminary scores are retained, and then valued at fifty percent to add to the Finals score (or whatever percentage you choose to use), your spreadsheet would need to be set up in advance to accept the Preliminary scores at the applied value. (Candidates generally want to keep some of the value of their Preliminary scores.)

Top 5 Finalists

Once in the Top 10 Semifinals, the Semifinalists will start all over again in competition, if Preliminary scores are wiped clean. They ordinarily re-compete in Swimwear and Evening Gown. While in Evening Gown, they may be presented an Onstage Interview. From those three areas of competition, the five highest-scoring candidates will become the Top 5 Finalists. When the Top 5 Finalists are ready to be announced (in random order), their names are placed on a Top 5 Finalists sheet, also marked "In Random Order."

Concluding Finals

The Top 5 Finalists official contestants' names are presented to the judges. Pageant directors have their own ways of proceeding from here. Some choose to have judges rank score every Finalist by assigning each one points. For example, one judge's first choice position would receive five points; her second choice, four points; third choice, three points; fourth choice, two points; and fifth choice, one point. The second judge would prefer his ranking to be in different order, and so on. With a panel of seven judges, a director lessens the chances that a tie will occur. However, should one occur with any of the positions (Fourth Runner-Up; Third Runner-Up; Second Runner-Up; First Runner-Up; or the Winner), a tie-breaker needs to be in place. For additional tie-breaking information, refer to Chapter 16, "Scoring Procedure" under "Breaking Ties."

Other pageant directors present each Top 5 Finalists with one more stage personality question to answer in order to see how they continue managing under pressure. Instead of rank scoring, Judges score this area in the typical fashion. If a pageant director chooses to keep the weight value of the scores that Semifinalists earned that got them into the Finals, then the auditor will add that score to the stage personality question score. As usual, the auditor will preprogram the scoring in advance, in preparation for calculating the Finals. Moments later, a winner and four Runners-Up are ready to be announced.

Chapter 16

Scoring

The scoring procedure for any pageant system should always be of the highest quality and have an experienced panel of judges. Prospective contestants want to know that a pageant they are considering has a fair scoring system in place. They *want* to understand how the judging (scoring) process works: the weight distribution for each area of competition; how each component is scored; how Semifinalists are scored; and how scoring is done in the Finals. If you have twenty girls step into the Finals, and, unbeknownst to those girls, only rank an already-predetermined five Finalists, inform prospective contestants of your scoring procedure (in your pageant marketing materials) *before* they sign a contract (the Official Application) and become official contestants.

Judging Components

Judging for most pageants consists of three components of equal importance: Interview, Swimsuit, and Evening Gown. But these are not the only components that could be considered in a pageant.

Mickey Stueck, then director of the _Miss Moorpark/Miss Moorpark Teen Queen_ pageant, felt that the emphasis should be placed on a girl as a person and not just beauty, so she not only did away with the Swimsuit component of the pageant, she also instituted a test of written communication skills to be included in the overall evaluation. Candidates could not purchase the answers to this written communication test as they could purchase a "canned" speech (or seek out parental/teacher help when developing Personal Introductions that is valued at about a third of the overall Preliminary score). Official contestants truly earn this score on their own merit. Such a written communication skills test is administered in a private room in front of pageant officials.

Judging Matrix and Weight Percentage

Every pageant system is different when it comes to structuring the weight value of each judging component. Some place equal weight balance in every component, as does U.K.'s _Miss Beauty Queen_. Each component makes up twenty percent of the score: Fun Fashion Wear, Fitness, Evening Gown, Personal Interview, and Personal Interaction. Some pageants weigh heavy on the Interview, less on the Evening Gown, even less on the Swimsuit (or Sportswear) competition, and even less on the Onstage Question. _Miss Southwest County Scholarship Pageant_ candidates are judged on (panel) Interview (40%), Evening Gown (30%), Sportswear (20%), and Onstage Question (10%). Some pageants even change weight value from the Preliminaries to the Semifinals and then again for the Finals.

USA's Pageants use a judging matrix between a one and ten point system; it doesn't compare or rank score. Each component is weighted differently. The _Wee Miss_ division, for example, includes 50% Dress, 25% Personality, and 25% Total Overall Appearance; _Tiny Miss_ & _Junior Miss_ divisions includes 10% for On Time Submission of all required forms and fees, 15% Introduction, 40% Evening Gown, and 35% Total Overall Appearance; _Junior Teen Miss_ is based on 10% for On Time Submission of all required forms and fees, 10% on Introduction, 10% Onstage Question, 30% Interview, 30% Evening Gown, and 10% Overall Appearance; and _Teen_ & _Miss_ divisions include 10% On Time Submission of all required forms and fees, 30% Interview, 10% Onstage Question, 25% Evening Gown, and 25% Swimsuit.

Notice that each of USA's Pageants age divisions has a different weight value placed on the Dress/Gown competition (50%, 40%, 30%, and 25%). An organized pageant director will take care to see that one division's Evening Gown judging percentage isn't traded out with another's by mistake. Double-check your accountant's percentages for every age division to see that they are, in fact, what they are supposed to be.

Miss Michigan Scholarship Pageant's single night State pageant Talent score is weighted at 35%. At the opening night of a multi-night State pageant, the Talent score is also weighted at 35%. However, at the Final night of the multi-night State pageant, the Talent score goes _down_ in weight value to 30%. For the same three nights, the Swimsuit competition is weighted at 15%, 15%, and then goes up to 20%, respectively.

Score Scale

What is your pageant's Score Scale? A general Score Scale reflects like this: Perfect, 10; Above Average, 7–9; Average, 4–6; and Below Average, 1–3. This permits only ten possible scores. *Miss America* uses this Score Scale in its Preliminary, State, and National pageants. *West Georgia's Prettiest Faces* employs the same Score Scale to help prepare candidates for a future in higher pageants, such as the *Miss America* pageant system, and although the average candidate receives a score in the range of 4–6, WGPF believes this IS a good score.

Universal Royalty Beauty Pageant judges are asked to judge official contestants *on a score scale of 9.4 to 10* — with the option of an additional plus point. It is also suggested that they award their pluses *after* the candidates had presented and were in the Final category lineup — should one or two "stick out" from the group. If a candidate earned a 10 on a scale of 9.4 to 10, and is awarded an additional point, she will have scored an 11. *This means one judge can change the entire outcome of the pageant before the Final scores are tabulated.*

But, if a pageant system's judging is on a scale of 9.4–10, and require judges to give a "9. something" to every candidate, the "point something" number is the real score. So, a candidate with a 9.3 is really earning a 3 (out of 10), and a candidate with a 9.9 is really earning a 9 (out of 10). This is fine if prospective contestants are informed that the first 9 (the digit that comes before the point) is really valueless — *before signing the Official Application and becoming official contestants.* Otherwise, the pageant system could be seen as misleading prospective contestants.

Rather than say its pageant scoring is based on a scale of 1 to 10, *She's A Beauty Pageants* makes it clear to prospective contestants that the lowest score they will receive is an 8, and the highest a 10:

> Scoring will be based on a decimal system between 8 and 10. Each judge will be required to score more than a whole number. For example, a candidate could receive scores like 8.7 or 9.4 from each category.

In this method of scoring, there are twenty-one possible scores — a much more granular scale than the previous scoring methods.

Enchanting Dreams Pageants' scoring system is even more granular. All candidates are scored on a scale of 6 to 10. The important thing is that prospective contestants know (before becoming official contestants) that the lowest score they could earn is a 6, and the highest is a 10 — with or without decimals in between.

Bobbie Ward Hinds, owner of *RodeoRoyalty.com*, suggests that pageant judges begin scoring at a Local pageant with the average possible points:

> For instance, if 10 points are available for the speech, an average speech would score a 6 or 7. An outstanding speech would score a 9 or 10. Be cautious when handing out the 10s, though. Few contestants are "perfect" and by rewarding those with such high scores, especially at the Local level, [say] to them that they need no improvement. And this is rarely true. On the other hand, when a judge scores a candidate a zero (0) out of 20 for personality, did the judge think she was dead?

Miss Georgia Girl Pageant knows the true value of judges' scores. The score scale is as follows: 1–3: was not prepared and needs improvement, attire change needed; 4–6: good, but could make minor changes in attire, needs a little more practice, and needs better stage presence; 7–9: very good, great stage presence and personality, little to no improvement needed, well prepared, and appropriate and well-fitting attire; and 10: perfect, no suggestions for changes. It's important for a candidate who *truly* scores a 9 that they truly earned that score, and therefore, is *truly* in the right direction to obtaining a crown. On the other hand, a candidate who is a "9.4," when the "9" part is valueless, is truly a "4," and according to the *Miss Georgia Girl Pageant* score scale, would require "minor changes in attire, a little more practice, and a better stage presence."

Let's revisit the *Universal Royalty Beauty Pageant* score scale. An average candidate who would ordinarily earn a 3 or 4 in another similar pageant system (a week before or after the *Universal Royalty* pageant) will come home with a 9.3 or 9.4 from *Universal Royalty*, and there is nothing wrong with this score scale *if parents and prospective contestants understand that the 9.4 is really a bottom-of-the-barrel score* before they sign up and then are invited to become alumnae candidates. If, on the other hand, a parent (or candidate) doesn't understand the scoring and assumes (or is led to believe) that scoring is based on a 1–10 scale, or doesn't understand the true value of a "9.4," the parent will think that her child performs better in the UR system. Then, when the scores are mailed out a month or two after the pageant, and the parent sees that Suzie scored "high" — a 9.4 — both mother and daughter are happy. Once again, the parent will allow Suzie to participate in that pageant system *still without knowing what Suzie did wrong.*[51]

Moreover, comments by the judges also need to be truthful. When judges are instructed to state only positive comments, it doesn't do candidates any justice if they want to hone their pageant skills. *Buttons and Beaus Pageant* notes in its Judges Guidelines, "Please write a *positive* comment about each child. Parents LOVE to read the comments!" Nowhere in the guidelines does it say to write constructive comments. On a positive note, a BBP pageant official noted, "[we] have to have our top winners, and your scores have got to be scattered." It's not fair when a candidate and her family spend hundreds (and often thousands) of dollars to participate, yet walk away from the pageant clueless as to what they did wrong. A judge doesn't need to point out only negatives; mix constructive negatives with positives critiques.

Pageant contenders deserve a clear understanding of a pageant's score scale. Better yet, include a Score Scale Rubric on your website. If the lowest score is 9, and the highest a 10 (with "point" something in between), *and* with a possible added bonus point, this means "the best of the best will be scored on a scale of 9–11." State this in your pageant literature, being sure to include the ".4 to .9" part — which would now mean that two simultaneous scores are given out: one that counts and one that doesn't. This scoring disclosure would be extremely helpful to prospective contestants who want to pursue pageantry on a bigger scale and, in the process, learn from and improve upon their mistakes.

---

[51] Juzwiak, Rich. "I judged a child beauty pageant." http://fourfour.typepad.com/fourfour/2011/11/i-judged-a-child-beauty-pageant.html.

Scoring System for Different Age Divisions

Will you feature different judging components for your different age divisions? *America's U.S. Miss* features two sets of scoring. Official contestants in the Tween, Teen, Junior Miss, and Miss divisions are judged on Interview, Evening Gown, Personality Wear, Academics, Community Service, and Résumé & Accomplishments. Official contestants in the Princess and Junior Tween divisions are judged on Interview, Fun Fashion Wear/Casual Wear, and Evening Gown.

Scoring Rubric

One beauty pageant isn't like another, so it's important that prospective contestants understand how one pageant differs from another. Pageant systems featuring scoring rubrics help prospective contestants to understand what their pageant is about. Prospective contestants often wonder what pageant judges look for in a winner. *MakeWorksheets.com* includes a custom rubric maker (to create a custom rubric or a four-point instant rubric) that can be downloaded in a .pdf format.

The *Miss Eau Claire* pageant already has a judging rubric in place. It notes that the Swimsuit competition is meant to show official contestants as everything from meeting good physical health to maintaining good physical health. The Evening Gown competition assesses beauty, stage presence, poise, and grace. Regarding the Interview competition, if candidates gracefully admit they don't know the answer to a question, they can still earn credit if they show poise and grace when giving even that response.

Cumulative Scoring

Judging for many pageants is based on a Total Point Accumulation System, a.k.a. Cumulative Scoring. Dropping the high and low scores typically doesn't occur in Cumulative Scoring. *Royal International Miss Florida* allows for the highest Cumulative Score, within in each age division, to be crowned.

(Each judge enters a score from 1–15 for each of the four required competitions.)

Olympic Scoring

The _Miss America_ judging system uses a form of Olympic scoring where each candidate ONLY competes against herself, and it only uses whole numbers. In the Preliminary competition, auditors drop the high and low scores in each category of competition and add the remaining points. In the Final Ballot competition, however, the High and Low scores are not eliminated. _Miss Earth_ judges use an Olympic style scoring system — albeit modified by including half points (example 7.5). A better explanation of the _Miss America's Outstanding Teen_ Olympic scoring can be found in the eight-page Instructions for Auditors for Local Pageants.

Dropping High/Low Scores

The jury is out regarding keeping high/low scores or dropping them. Many pageants drop the high and low scores (as is done in Olympic scoring) from Preliminary competitions. Whether or not you choose to drop them, indicate this in writing at an introductory time. In the _Miss North Carolina Entertainer of the Year_ pageant, "[high] and low scores _may_ be dropped at the discretion of the promoter." If the pageant promoter doesn't like the outcome without dropping high/low scores, s/he could change it by dropping high/low scores. This would only be fair to official contestants if they were informed of this potential scoring procedure, in writing, when they were prospective contestants — before signing the Official Application (contract) and paying the (non-refundable) sponsorship fee. Then, those prospective contestants can determine if they want to partake in the pageant or seek another that doesn't drop high/low scores.

There are other score-dropping variations. _America's Model Miss_ only drops the _lowest_ score in every event. _Rumble in the Jungle Open State Pageant_ notes, "You do not have to compete in both OOC and Jungle wear; the lowest of the two will be dropped."

Adjudicated Scoring

Tutu Glitz Pageants appears to be the first pageant system to incorporate adjudicated scoring. In adjudicated scoring, official contestants do not compete again each other in any age division. Instead, they are evaluated according to a total range of points scored. For example, there may be *two or more* High Queen, Queen, High Princess, or Princess winners in the same age division: High Queen (98.5–100); Queen (97–98.4); High Princess (95–96); Princess (90–94) and Rising Star (89 and below). *Tutu Glitz Pageants* notes, "[each] contestant will receive a beautiful tiara and sash based on her adjudicated score."

Scoring with Weights

The *Miss Deaf Utah Pageant* scoring for each category is as follows: 0–poor; 7.5–below average; 15–average; 22.5–above average; and 30–outstanding. Using the Interview and Modeling competitions as an example, each judge will circle numbers on the ballot sheet according to how s/he rates each official contestant in each category. Let's say that for the first candidate, the four judges circle the numbers 15, 15, 22.5, and 22.5 on their ballots for Interview and 7.5, 15, 22.5, and 15 for Evening Gown. This gives a total score of 15 + 15 + 22.5 + 22.5 = 75.0 for the first candidate's Interview and 7.5 + 15 + 22.5 + 15 = 60.0 for the first candidate's Evening Gown.

The assistant auditor adds the ballots together and places the total score on an official ballot, initials it, and hands it over to the head auditor. The head auditor now has the official ballot sheet with the total scores for the respective categories of 75.0 and 60.0. The head auditor then multiplies the total scores by the appropriate "weights" for the Interview competition and the Evening Gown competition. Then, the head auditor will place the new total on the official score sheet. For example purposes, say that the weight for the Interview portion of the *Miss Deaf Utah Pageant* was predetermined by pageant officials to be thirty percent, and the weight for the Evening Gown portion to be seventy percent. This means that the head auditor will multiply the weight of 30% (for the Interview competition) by the initial total score of 75.0. Now, the weighted Interview score comes out to 75.0 x 0.30 = 22.5. Performing a similar computation for the Evening Gown portion gives a weighted score of 60 x 0.70 = 42.0. Since the weights 30 and 70 total to 100%, we can determine the final score by adding the individual weighted scores, i.e., 22.5 + 42.0 = 64.5.

How to Calculate a Weighted Average Score can provide guidance in calculating your own weight number(s). If you do score with weights, be sure to inform prospective contestants before they register for the pageant, not after they become official contestants and are judged. Moreover, don't change your rules in the middle of the game, i.e., say that you'll score a particular division with weights and then not do that. You'll unfairly change the pageant winners' outcome. A Certified Public Accountant (CPA) can help pageant officials create weighted numbers for any pageant judging component. Additionally, s/he can explain the advantages and disadvantages through various possible outcomes from different input percentages. Moreover, s/he can explain the pros and cons of scoring with weights.

Factors Affect Scoring

There are many factors that can affect pageant scoring, and consequently, the Finals' results. There has been speculation on whether pageants are fixed, especially when an audience favorite does not win. This can all be explained by evaluating the total circumstances of how the judges' scores for Preliminary, Semifinals, and Finals competitions were applied — along with how the Finals vote was scored — when determining the winner of the pageant. In the _Cinderella Scholarship Program_, judges are instructed to look for wholesomeness. The Talent winner, Tot Personality winner, and Cinderella Beauty winner are selected from the Preliminary rounds of competition and will not necessarily be one of the Top 5 Finalists. The judges do, however, select a Top 5 from each age division to re-compete in the Finals night show for the Overall winners. Arming your audience and official contestants with this information can help them to practice good sportsmanship.

Extra Points/No Extra Points Policy

Tiny Miss Tennessee includes Optionals event scores in the overall total and notes this in its pageant marketing materials. Although Optionals events are typically considered optional, they are factored into the overall score of TMT's title. This pageant, therefore, is an Extra Points competition because the Optionals event score that is used for various titles aren't really "optional." In my opinion, candidates are pressured into entering these Optionals events because those points count towards the crown IF they are not forewarned prior to entering (it is my understanding that TMT [and its parent pageant *Tiny Miss Pageants*] does forewarn):

> The contestant with the highest combined mandatory event total, highest Optionals event score, AND Talent score will be crowned our first ever *Outstanding Miss Tennessee*. Your highest Optionals Event score will be used to add to your Total score for the Outstanding and Highpoint titles.

Learn how to ethically and lucratively design your Optionals by reading my book *Producing Beauty Pageants: Optionals*.

Glamour Girls Pageants, on the other hand, has a "No Extra Points" policy. It doesn't pressure official contestants into entering Optionals events by adding points to their total score. *Glamour Girls Pageants* also doesn't require that judges give an extra point to "standouts."

Breaking Ties

At the *Miss USA* pageant, in 2002, in an exciting twist of fate after two weeks of preparation and competition, the judge's panel ballots were returned from the auditor with a tie that would produce not a Top 10, but a Top 12 group of young women who would vie for the honor of being chosen *Miss USA* and the opportunity to represent her country in the upcoming *Miss Universe* pageant. But, only seasoned Florida presidential ballot auditors and a few long-shot casino odds makers would have understood the rarity of a Top 12 competition tie-breaker, and so the pageant featured a Top 12 that year, not employing any of its tie-breaking procedures to break such a rarity.

Create a guide on how to break a tie within your pageant. Find the category of the tie you need to split. If your pageant weighs heavy on the Interview (private or onstage), look to see which candidate has the higher Interview score and use that competition to break the tie. If the tie still exists, move to the second tie-breaking phase of competition, and, if one candidate has a higher score in that phase, she receives higher placement. If all phases are considered, and a tie *still* exists, the names of each of the tied candidates are written down on a sheet of paper for each of the judges, titled "Tied for Top 5." Then, each judge would circle his choice for placement. In the event of a tie, *Mr. & Miss Unlimited Newcomer*, which weighs heavy on Talent, will allow the candidate with the highest Talent score to be declared the tiebreaking winner. If a tie *still* exists, then the interview score will be used and, if necessary, the Creative Formal Wear/Evening Gown. If yet a tie *still* exists, the Board of Directors chooses who wins the pageant.

When breaking a tie, do not introduce any other phase of competition to split a tie. This would be unfair to the tied candidates. Ideally, a tie will be broken from within the first phase comparison. If, for example, all phases are considered and a tie still remains, the only new phase acceptable is that of allowing the judges to re-rank the tied candidates to separate them from the tie. This can happen with the Winner's position, two First Runner-Ups, two Second Runners-Ups, and two Third Runners-Ups. If you have a Winner, First Runner-Up, Second Runner-Up, and two candidates tied for Third Runner-Up, a tie-breaker will occur from the latter two candidates to come up with a Fourth Runner-Up.

Some pageants plan in advance for ties and include an "extra" judge on the panel — an Honorary Judge — from the start. An Honorary Judge scores official contestants just like the other judges; however, those scores are only used in breaking a tie. Avoid a tie altogether, as does *USA Pageants*, by having one judge on the panel that *only* scores in decimals.

Michigan Galaxy Pageants uses the following procedure to break ties: Each judge will assign the Top 5 a ranking from 1 to 5. A ranking of first place would then equal = 5 points; second place = 4 points; third place = 3 points; fourth place = 2 points; and fifth place = 1 point. Points earned from rank scoring are *added* to the delegates' scores. If, at this time, the rankings do not resolve the tie(s), the higher individual competition score will determine the higher placement in this order: Interview, On-Stage Question, Photogenic, Evening Gown, Fashion, and then Swimsuit. In the absence of ties, judges are not asked to provide rankings.

Although scoring is based on a scale of 1–10, due to subjectivity in scoring, *Crowned Price & Princess Charm Pageants* simultaneously includes a ballot component. This is where a judge lists the candidate's name and number who did the overall best in each age division. In the event there is a tie, this ballot component is readily available and is used as an alternative to the cumulative score.

Miss Southern California Cities and *Miss Long Beach* pageants note, "Approximately [five to eight] Finalists are expected to be announced in each [division.]"

Emerald Pageant Productions allows judges to use up to three plus (+) marks, which are used in its pageant to break ties.

Miss Bright Star of America, in the event of a tie, will add admission ticket sales *and* sponsor advertisements.

Little Miss Imagination Pageants asks official contestants to send in one natural headshot — one that will be used in the event of a tie-breaker.

American Royal Beauties will not re-rank official contestants at the finale unless there is a tie.

Standard Scoring System

Just as there are many pageants, there are also many methods of scoring. Most pageants create their own method of scoring, distributing points according to the areas of competition.

Primary Competition

The Preliminary competition is generally comprised of three ballots: Interview, Swimsuit, and Evening Gown. After each official contestant appears in front of a judging panel, judges are to assign points (typically) on a scale of one to ten. Candidates with the highest number of points comprise of the Semifinalists.

Some pageant systems include other components, along with its cumulative score value, to the mix. *Miss Hardee County* pageant includes a component where candidates are judged on meeting deadlines for forms and clothing, as well as Cooperation, Attendance, and Participation (in pageant functions). The five components in the Primary Competition of the *Miss Teen Achieve Pageant* include: Application/Participation Score, Judges Interview, Sportswear/Physical Fitness, Arts Presentation, and

Formal Wear. The six components in the Primary Competition of the *Miss Fayetteville State University Scholarship Pageant* include Interview (thirty percent); Talent (twenty-five percent); Evening Gown (fifteen percent); On Stage Knowledge (ten percent); Fitness & Athletic Wear (ten percent); and Student Vote (ten percent).

Semifinal Competition

The Semifinal competition (typically) comprises of two ballots: Stage Presence and Stage Interview Question. Judges give each Semifinalist a score on Stage Presence and a score for the Stage Interview Question. The five candidates with the highest number of points make up the Finalists.

Finals Competition

The Finals competition generally comprises of one ballot: the Judges' Choice. Judges individually rate every official contestant to determine the winner and alternates. This would be the first (and only) time when a variation of points is assigned for the order of preference. Points assigned can be as follows:

Winner	5 points
First Runner-Up	2 points
Second Runner-Up	1 point
Third Runner-Up	½ point
Fourth Runner-Up	0 point

Supreme Scoring System

Do you ever wonder how scores are determined in pageants that feature Supreme titles? *Glass Slipper Natural Beauty Pageant* shares this information on its website. Listed are the categories the pageant offers. Next to each category is the scoring format for that particular component. While the categories are not necessarily the same as other pageants', the idea is for every pageant to clearly define how the scores are determined for every judging competition, in writing, within the pageant system. Various Grand Supreme scoring examples are noted below.

Grand Supreme Queen

This is the highest total (excluding elective events) of the following scores for *Glass Slipper Natural Beauty Pageant*: Beauty, Eyes, Personality, Beautiful, and Theme wear. All scores are added together. Then, the candidate with the highest score in the entire pageant — from all age divisions combined — is crowned Grand Supreme Queen. This gives the pageant an opportunity to separate candidates who score high and give others a greater advantage to ensure that competition is equitable. Often, for any Supreme title, a candidate must be entered into a "Supreme Package" if she wants the chance to be pulled for the higher title. Learn more about being "pulled" (and "Ultimate Grand Supreme" or "Mega Ultimate Supreme" not included here) by reading my FREE e-book *Producing Beauty Pageants: A Guide to Pageant Terminology*.

Mini Supreme Queen

This is *Glass Slipper Natural Beauty Pageant*'s second highest total (excluding elective events) of the following scores: Beauty, Eyes, Personality, Beautiful, and Theme Wear. All of these scores are added together. Then, the candidate with the second highest score — from all age divisions combined — becomes the Mini Supreme Queen.

Divisional Supreme Princess

This is the highest total of the following scores: Beauty, Eyes, Personality, Beautiful, and Theme Wear. All of these scores are added together. Then, the candidate with the highest score in each Division I, II, and III, is the Divisional I, II, or III Supreme Princess. (The Grand Supreme and Mini Supreme Queens are excluded from this since they were pulled to win a higher title.)

Age Group Beauty

This is the highest Beauty score (only) in each age group. The other categories are NOT added to get the age group Beauty Princess as with the above Supremes. A candidate is not eligible for this title if she won a Grand, Mini, or Division Supreme title.

Age Group Category Winners

Most Beautiful, Best Personality, Best Hair, Best Eyes, Best Smile, Best Dressed, and Best Theme Wear — Superlative Awards — go to the official contestant that scored the highest in each of these categories. These categories go to the highest score in each age group, and as a result, are NOT a crowned category. Therefore, one official contestant is eligible for more than one winning. If an official contestant entered any one of the Overall Electives and won one, the next highest score in her respective age group would win for the age group. *The Glass Slipper Natural Beauty Pageant* has a system of judging for its elective categories, as do all pageant systems with Optionals. Learn how to judge and score Optionals by reading my book *Producing Beauty Pageants: Optionals.*

Balloting

To make every scoring phase simpler, *Miss Louisiana/Miss Louisiana's Outstanding Teen* requires judges to score every component of competition in a different color of paper. This makes it easier for the auditors to tabulate the scores. It also keeps the Head Judge from having to open a folded score sheet (to see which division score sheet it is) when trying to group them together to hand to auditors.

Color also plays a part in the *Licking PRCA Rodeo Pageant*. Regarding judges' signatures, *Licking PRCA Rodeo Pageant* does not have the judges sign their names to score sheets. Instead, each judge is assigned a book number and is given a different color pen. Pageant officials can identify the score sheets by the color of ink.

Preliminary Ballots

Judges generally cast a total of three ballots during the first round of pageant competition: one for Personal Interview, one for Swimsuit or Outfit of Choice (OOC), and one for Evening Gown. At the end of the competitions, the ten highest scoring official contestants make up the Semifinalists.

Semifinalists Ballots

Once the auditor has tabulated the Preliminary scores, and the selection of the ten Semifinalists is announced, the emcee generally interviews each Semifinalist on stage. Each chooses (or is given) a question at random. The judges then assign each Semifinalist a score as each Semifinalist answers her on-stage interview question.

Finalists Ballots

From the ten Semifinalists, only five compete as Finalists. Each Finalist typically receives, but not always, an identical personality question to answer. Some pageants don't ask a personality question. Instead, they rank Finalists. Others employ both. Pageant officials, who do include the personality question in the Finals, do so as an opportunity to aid judges in their final decision. At this time, Finalists are compared closely with one another. In the event of a tie, each judge receives a tie-breaker ballot and the names of the Finalists who are tied. In this case, the names of the Finalists who are tied are on the ballots, but not with the combined tying scores that landed them there. Each judge writes his/her order of preference (or employs another tie-breaking method) and returns the ballot to the auditor. As an early-entry motivating tool, pageant officials may want to present the tied candidate with the earliest postmarked entry, the title. (Such postmarked information should be presented to the auditor before Finals judging begins.) When tabulation is completed, signed, and audited, the Finals decision is ready for the emcee. No one in the audience, on the staff, or on the judging panel knows the outcome of the tabulation until it is announced from the stage.

Mentions Ballots

In a Mentions Balloting, no numeric score is given by the judges. Instead, they circle the names of the official contestants they believe have the winning qualities the pageant represents. Each time a candidate's name is circled, she is given a point by the auditor. For example, say there are fifty candidates vying for the title. The Head Judge asks the judges to circle a total of ten to fifteen names on their ballot. (A judge can circle a candidate's name only once.) The more often a candidate's name is circled, the greater her chances of making it to the Top 10. The ten candidates with the most points make up the Top 10. Once the Top 10 are selected, judges are then asked to circle their favorite three candidates' names. Finally, judges are to circle the one candidate's name that they believe should be the titleholder. _Miss Illinois USA_ State Preliminary pageants currently use the mentions-system of judging. After the Top 5 Finalists are in final presentation, each judge ranks them in the order s/he believes each Finalist should place, assessing point values for each ranking. The Finalist with the most points wins.

Consensus Ballots

This type of judging often occurs at festival pageants. The judges will only take notes throughout the competition. After the pageant, the judges go into a closed room and talk about the competition. Then, they must all agree on who will be the Queen and her court. More often than not, there is a lot of negotiation with this form of balloting.

Score Sheets

Some pageant systems will have all Preliminary competitions for each candidate printed on one page. At the conclusion of the first area of competition, the Interview, the score sheets are collected for the auditor. Then, at the beginning of the second area of competition — for example, Swimsuit — the same score sheets are returned to the judges table for every judge to see before claiming their own ballots at the start of the next round of judging. These score sheets (are in a mixed batch) and contain not only the various judges' scores, they also include the comments judges made for every candidate — meant only for candidates to read. This method of balloting exposes the judges to each other's comments and scores even before the next phase of competition. Instead, produce clean ballots for every area of competition.

Main Components Score Sheets

Enchanting Dreams Pageants score sheets for Interview, Beauty, Fashion, and Talent are provided below. Each score sheet would have a heading that includes the judge's name, the judge's judging number, and the official contestant's name and placement number.

Interview
Personality (6–10)
Confidence (6–10)
Overall Appearance (6–10)
Responsiveness to Questions (6–10)
Eye Contact (6–10)
Total (30–50)

Beauty
Personality and Stage Presence (6–10)
Stage Presentation and Modeling (6–10)
Overall Appearance (6–10)
Age Appropriateness (6–10)
Total (24–40)

Fashion
Personality and Stage Presence (6–10)
Stage Presentation and Modeling (6–10)
Overall Appearance (6–10)
Creativity (6–10)
Total (24–40)

Talent
Personality and Stage Presence (6–10)
Entertainment Value (6–10)
Totality of Elements (6–10)
Technical Skill Level Based on Age (6–10)
Total (24–40)

Photogenic Score Sheets

All-Natural Miss Bootiful Inner-Beauty photogenic score sheet is provided below. Each area judged in photogenic is already weighted by the percentage of the score. The maximum number of points an official contestant can earn is fifty. The candidate closest to fifty points is the winner — unless there is a tie that needs to be broken. Having pre-printed numbers means you won't need to struggle to read a judge's handwriting, trying to figure out if s/he wrote a 7 or a 9. Remind judges to carefully circle their choice score so as not to accidently circle two or three numbers. This way the auditor won't be wondering if the center number was his choice or the number to the left or right! Provide ample spacing between each number to help ensure that judges don't accidently circle more than one.

Judge's name and number:_____

Official contestant name and photo number:_____

Facial Beauty: 1 2 3 4 5 6 7 8 9 10 11 12 13 14 15

Smile: 1 2 3 4 5

Modeling: 1 2 3 4 5 6 7 8 9 10

Photo Quality: 1 2 3 4 5

Overall Package: 1 2 3 4 5 6 7 8 9 10 11 12 13 14 15

Total _____ / 50 Points

Enchanting Dreams Pageants photogenic score sheet:

Judge's Name and Number:_____

Official contestant Name and Photo Number:_____

Overall Photogenic Quality (1–60):

Creativity of Photograph (1–10):

Photo Composition and Photography Ability (1–20):

First Impression (1–10):

Total (1–100):

Score Sheet Tips

Tips on preparing pageant score sheets, *How to Monitor Beauty Pageant Scoring*, can be found on *eHow*. *Miss Kentucky Scholarship Pageant* score sheets can be found at its website under Local Pageant Forms: Auditor Forms and Score Sheets at http://www.misskentuckypageant.com/resources.html. A sample youth pageant score sheet can easily be created. *Beautiful*

Pageantry of New England provides score sheets for Evening Gown with Platform, Interview Competition, "My Own Style" Competition, Semifinalist Question, Talent Competition, and Swimsuit Competition (scroll down to see all). *Arizona Little Miss* official contestants are judged on Beauty, Personality, Attire, and Overall Appearance; they are given two scores from each judge.

Computers for Judges Scoring

A computer system for judges to enter their scores makes tabulating competition rounds much easier than manually inserting them. Invest in five computers (or in as many judges as you plan on having), so that each judge will be able to enter candidate scores into their respective laptops. Moreover, your computer scoring system can prompt judges when it is time to enter a score. This helps judges to save scores as they go and then make changes — up until they're locked in at the end of each round. Include a notes field so that judges can type in their comments. Make sure the automatic updating/refreshing mechanism is working. Remember to include signature pages for each judge to sign. Then, as a new round of judging occurs, all that the judges would need to do is rename the round, because the contestants' names and their numbers are automatically displayed exactly the same way as they were in the previous round. Finally, make sure the score grid is displayed smaller so that people behind the judges can't (easily) read it over the judges' shoulders.

If your pageant system does not feature computers for judges, your emcee will need to prompt judges when it is time to enter a score and comment. This should not be when the candidate leaves the stage but rather, when she is at a certain point on the stage. Judges need to focus on the candidate *and* quickly write her scores and comments before she leaves the stage. Then, cue your emcee to look for a "finished" sign from all the judges, such as a collective fist under the chin or a tap on the head, before proceeding to introduce the next candidate on stage.

Score Sheets in Front of Audience

Help ease the audience's mind by keeping all on-stage score sheets in front of the audience. For example, *All Canadian Pageants* takes pride in being a fair pageant system, particularly when it comes down to the score sheets. Judges pass their score sheets down to the tabulator where they are then transferred to the official result sheet. A hostess delivers the score sheets to the emcee where they are then read to the audience. The judges' sheets are never taken out of the room. They are always on the judges table until they are announced to the audience. Obviously, you cannot do this for the Interview scores; however, having judges initial any changes, AND including a Certified Public Accountant as your tabulator, can alleviate that issue with concerned parents and candidates.

All tabulation at for *Essence Pageants* is conducted by a state licensed Certified Public Accountant. Pageant founder Sue Drakeford noted, "If a CPA miscalculates, it's his/her responsibility. S/he could lose his license!" Even if CPAs work *pro bono*, if they miscalculate pageant scores, it can be serious for their accounting firm, but it would fall under their responsibility and not the pageant director's. Sue continues, "That's why we *always* use a CPA." _Porcelain Dolls Nationals_ also employs a CPA. Director Kathy Raese notes, "Your child will have solid fair judging and checks and balances in tabulations." Learn how to enlist a CPA, *pro bono*, by reading my book *Producing Beauty Pageants: Brokering a Pageant through Barter*, Chapter 9, "In-Kind Sponsors" under "Accounting/Audit Services."

Destroying Score Sheets

Do NOT immediately destroy score sheets at the pageant's conclusion. Ask your auditor to place them in a sealed, dated, and identifiable envelope for safe keeping, at a predetermined location established by the pageant board, for a *minimum* of one year. A pageant director never knows when the outcome of a pageant will be in dispute and an independent auditor will have to review the results. If directors plan on destroying score sheets, state in writing when that will happen, i.e., one year after the pageant. It is best that pageants keep score sheets for at least one year, as does _Miss America_. After all, what's the rush to destroy score sheets? It might look as if a pageant system has something to hide when it's in a rush to destroy score sheets.

Southern Royalty Pageants makes it mandatory that candidates pick up their score sheets at the tabulator's table immediately after crowning, ONLY on the day of the pageant. If they don't pick up the score sheets, they are immediately discarded. Why the rush to discard score sheets?

Crown Bound Pageants shreds all scores three business days after the pageant. Again, why the rush to shred score sheets?

Score Report

Right after the pageant, *National American Miss* mails every State Finalist (official contestant) an Official Score Report. This letter tells her what a great job she did, how she is an OUTSTANDING young lady, and how proud NAM is of her. NAM reiterates the four categories of judging that occurred at the NAM State pageant. Next, NAM includes an algorithm chart that not only tells the official contestant her overall score, it also compares her score range to girls of "Below Average," "Average," "Above Average," and "Exemplary." Right next to that, NAM notes the "Highest Score of any Girl" in its pageant." Now the recipient of the Official Score Report sees that she wasn't far off and WILL want to try out again! This display seems to work for girls with *any* score they received.

National American Miss patterns its Official Score Report after the national standardized tests that students typically receive at school — *including a bell curve distribution of scores for each and every category of judging*. NAM includes scoring for all the main areas of the pageant (Formal Wear, Introduction, and Interview) in addition to any Optionals divisions an official contestant might have purchased (Actress, Talent, Photogenic [up to four photos], Casual Wear, etc.).

Additionally, the second page of the Official Score Report includes generic descriptions for each Optionals competition a candidate had entered. Then, in the next column (and on the same row of the first page), the candidate's total (average) score is placed on the right side (of each judged Optionals component).

To provide an example, next to Formal Wear: 7.7; Introduction: 8.2; and Optionals Casual Wear: 8.4. Then, in a box next to the candidate's actual scores, is a "Score Ranges for Completed Competition" that shows a range of scores that would fall under "Below Average," "Average," "Above Average," and "Exemplary." A column next to that notes the "Highest Average Score of any Girl" — which reflects the actual candidate in the pageant's same age division scoring the highest for that particular competition. View Cassidy's NAM Official Score Report on *Instagram.*

NAM pageant officials used to deliver Official Score Reports over the phone; however, outraged parents complained because people were calling and pretending to be a different NAM candidate and get "their" daughters' scores. They did this just so they could see why the other girl made the top cut and their daughters didn't. Now, NAM pageant officials only mails scores — accompanied by a discounted alumnae invitation to enter the next NAM State pageant. Learn how to incorporate a successful Optionals program within your pageant by reading my book *Producing Beauty Pageants: Optionals.*

Scores Given to Official Contestants

After the pageant event, candidates should be able to leave the event with a copy of each judge's score sheets, or expect one in the mail. If you do provide the master scores on your website, make sure that it is only accessible to official contestants — and not to just anyone who visits your website.

- Miss Utopia provides its "Master Score Sheets" link on the left side of its website. It lists the current and past years' master score sheets. It's best to create a veiling for all candidates except for the one who is accessing her own personal scores.

- *Heartbreaker Productions* does make score sheets available at the end of crowning. Nevertheless, if candidates have concerns with the scores, it must be submitted in writing and sent at a later date. The letter won't be accepted on pageant day.

- *Miss Arkansas FFI* provides contestants' scanned score and comment sheets on Finals night. Additionally, the *Miss Arkansas FFI* pageant master score sheet, including Preliminary scores, is presented to each candidate at the end of the pageant. Moreover, *Miss Arkansas FFI* makes it available online.

- America's Prestigious Miss distributes score sheets after the pageant. Candidates are reminded to examine them away from the ballroom, so that hurt feelings are not in view of other candidates and pageant officials. To respect other candidates' privacy, *America's Prestigious Miss* pageant does not permit viewing of the master score sheet.

- Judges' comments and scoring for any *Shining Crowns Productions* pageant is available to official contestants; however, it must be requested during pageant registration. Once available, and *if* requested on time, the information will be emailed or mailed to respective contestants.

- *East Coast USA Pageant* features computerized scoring and tabulation, making it easier to provide carbon copied score sheets to official contestants immediately after the pageant.

- *Beautiful Me Productions* doesn't give out score sheets. Instead, candidates are asked to call a couple of weeks following the pageant to receive scores and comments over the phone.

- *Virginia State American Royalty* pageant dispenses scores to official contestants only by phone or email.

- *USA's Pageants* will give official contestants scores by mail if they include a self-addressed stamped envelope (S.A.S.E.) prior to the pageant's finale.

- *Miss Southern Beauty USA* asks that the S.A.S.E. accompany the application if an official contestant wants a returned score sheet.

- *Crowned Princess Charm Pageant* notes,

    For a $15 processing fee official contestants may request that their scores and judges' comments to be received no less than three weeks after the competition. Rushed scores (one week) are available for a $25 fee.

- *Parade of Hearts Pageant* does not give out judges' scores, only critique sheets.

- *Miss Maud Pageant* notes that score sheets will be included in the photo packets. If photo packets were not purchased, then official contestants will be given their scores in a sealed envelope. This effort takes about two weeks.

- *Crown Bound Pageants* states, "No scores will be texted or sent via FB [*Facebook*]. They will only be sent [by] mail or email."

- U.S. United States Pageant System makes the scores available 30 minutes after the final night of the pageant. Candidates must pick up their scores, as they are not mailed.

- America's Talented Beauties & Cuties reminds, "No score sheets will be given until all winners' pictures are taken!"

- America's Gorgeous Girls not only hands out score sheets at the end of crowning, but judges ARE available to answer any questions official contestants might have after crowning.

- Miss Denton County United America gives copies of pageant scores if requested, but, if official contestants want to receive ranking information and judges' comments, there is a $5 fee.

- Miss Patton Pageant does NOT give out score sheets or critiques.

- Midwest Dreams MN Pageant notes,

    You will always leave a *Midwest Dreams MN Pageant* with your score sheets in hand!

Chapter 17

Voting Options

Miss USA and *Miss Universe* successfully implemented a digital brand strategy, in 2011, one designed by brand consultant Pablo Ulpiano of <u>*Singular Brand*</u>. It targeted young females between the ages of eighteen and thirty-four who would want to interact and vote while watching the *Miss USA Pageant* on television. The objective was to generate relevant buzz and create interest around the *Miss USA* candidates by using digital elements like blogs, *YouTube*, *Facebook*, and *Twitter* (along with traditional advertising). The goal was to multiply its *Facebook* Likes! and increase followers, which would lift the pageant system out of the stuck growth pattern that it was in. In harnessing followers and potential viewers, *Miss USA* and *Miss Universe* would increase digital engagement before, during, and after the televised pageant via *Twitter*, *Facebook*, *YouTube*, and Mainstream Media (MSM) over the Miss USA Live Web page and *Facebook* page. The summation of all digital elements and traditional advertising would leverage brand equity — create value — for the pageant system and for sponsors and advertisers.

Digital Marketing Campaign to Generate Online Voting

To begin a digital marketing campaign, one that would resemble a political one, *Miss USA* started a digital advertisement program based on the use of digital elements like *Facebook*, *Twitter*, and *YouTube*. The goal was to blend in with, and support, the traditional marketing efforts as *Miss USA* candidates were being promoted. Using the banner campaign, the *educated* target audience would be told precisely how they were to connect with *Miss USA* candidates *before* the pageant and precisely how they were to interact with them *during* the pageant. This would be accomplished *while* encouraging viewers to get up and vote for the new *Miss USA* on its Web page or via <u>SMS</u> (Short Message Service) from their cell phone or smartphone.

This could be done — judging by the "Simultaneous Media Usage Based on Demographics: Profiles of the U.S. Simultaneous Media User" report data that *Singular Brand* used in designing this digital marketing campaign. It had discovered, among other findings, that people with a college education (across all races) are more likely than the less educated to go online, use their smartphone, and read while also watching TV. The *Miss USA* and *Miss Universe* marketing team could teach this highly targeted audience how to interact digitally with the pageant while simultaneously guiding them to vote during the *Miss USA* telecast.

Teach Target Audiences How to Participate

The *Miss USA* and *Miss Universe* marketing team began the campaign by placing advertisements on *YouTube* to encourage people to vote *and* to explain to them what would happen if they didn't. The tonality was inviting, which generated a demand call of action that made each viewer ask herself, "What would happen if I didn't vote?" *Miss USA's* message was clear: Vote for *Miss USA*!

Miss USA and *Miss Universe* pageant officials reasoned that they could succeed with their intended target because, for one, from the media usage demographics report, they learned that seventy-seven percent of smartphone owners *have* used their cell phones simultaneously while watching TV, and another, women are more likely than men to go online, read a magazine, or use their smartphone *while* watching TV. They concurred that their demographic market — these eighteen to thirty-four year old educated women of all races — would <u>SMS</u> vote while they watched the *Miss USA* telecast, and so they developed voting and engaging tools that would be used mainly on mobile devices, but also on home TV screens and home computers for the 2011 *Miss USA Pageant*.

Increase Facebook Likes! to Reach Objectives

Miss USA and *Miss Universe* had several objectives: to generate buzz about the pageant, generate candidate interest, increase followers to its *Facebook* page, increase digital engagement —

before, during, and after the *Miss USA* pageant telecast, grow visits to its *Miss USA* webpage and *YouTube* page, and ultimately, influence the *Miss USA* franchise brand value while creating the same worth for sponsors and advertisers. In order for this synergy to happen, the "Likes!" on its *Facebook* page needed to be increased. This would provide pageant officials with measurement: it would give them a human ranking relevancy from its *Facebook*-engaging efforts. This, in turn, would allow them to reach their ultimate goal. After all, an engaged network is the best type of network for marketing *any* product.

Candidates to Synergize Participation

Miss USA candidates were required to create a blog, a *Twitter* account, a *Facebook* page, *Flickr*, and a *YouTube* account, where they posted relevant information about themselves. They were expected to blog about their lives, interests, opinions and values, and more importantly, why their fans should vote for them. On *Twitter*, they had to post their everyday thoughts, retweet what they found important, and tweet about their social lives and everyday experiences in order to synergistically connect *emotionally* with followers. (Followers were invited to tweet questions they would like to ask the candidates during the pageant.) *Miss USA* official contestants were required to upload their own promotional videos on *YouTube* — which encouraged fans to vote for them. On *Flickr*, candidates uploaded pictures of themselves that displayed their style. On their *Facebook* account, they were measured by the "Likes" they received — all this in an attempt for each candidate to generate media buzz through hidden RSS Feeds. Pageant officials even anticipated that TMZ (the people who put out celebrity entertainment news) would likely generate gossiping content both on its cool website and in the popular celebrity magazines that they're connected to — which would attract *yet more* followers and potential viewers. Guide your official contestants into positive synergy territory by reading my book *Producing Beauty Pageants: Creating a Synergized National Pageant System*, Chapter 1, "Becoming an Innovative Pageant Producer" under "Promotion Synergy Chain" — subheading "Official Contestants."

Synergized Media Buzz Equals Huge Revenues

This synergized media buzz — dished up in three stages: pre, during, and post broadcasting — primarily added up to a *single vital motion*: to get target viewers to SMS vote for their favorite candidates BEFORE the pageant ended. Why? This voting action would generate *huge* revenues for *Miss USA* and *Miss Universe*! To encourage voters to participate in SMS voting, a drawing for a prize was given to the lucky winner!

The "after" part — post — was designed to: 1) focus on making the *Miss USA Pageant* relevant to the media for as long as possible; 2) post all content generated in the gala on its *Miss USA* Web pageant — with links to *YouTube* videos and relevant tweets; 3) have TMZ cover the event and generate "after buzz" stories; and 4) put out blogs that would encourage viewers to give their opinion about the 2011 *Miss USA Pageant*. Then, a database was generated with information about all digital followers and participants (likely mostly generated through RSS Feeds), to 1) market promotions for the following year's pageant; 2) keep them informed with continued activities where *Miss USA* is involved during her reign — communicated to respective followers by the medium they chose to originally engage with the *Miss USA Pageant*; and 3) weigh and shape further actions and decisions by pageant officials to improve the following year's event. [52]

Online Internet Voting

Online Internet voting has become a new platform for many pageants. Online voting appears to increase website traffic and projects an illusion of audience participation. As in Text/SMS Message Voting (see below for description), if someone campaigns enough with their social media connections, that attempt takes away the "popularity" part of the online Internet voting — which is what it was intended for.

---

[52] Ulpiano, Pablo. *The Miss USA & Miss Universe Pageant 2011 Digital Marketing.* http://issuu.com/pablou./docs/miss-usa#.

Miss World recently teamed up with *AOL* for online voting. Doing so allowed viewers, for the first time, to fast track *Miss World* official contestants. In December, 2008, the competition launched a social network of all 127 candidates, enabling them to rally online support and get them into the Finals lineup. The network was featured within the *Miss World* portal and co-branded channels on *AOL* and *Bebo* in Great Britain. These networks featured each candidate's profile, photographs, blog, and information on their country and charity work. Additional information about fast tracking in pageantry can be found in my FREE e-book *Producing Beauty Pageants: A Guide to Pageant Terminology.*

Online Internet voting is a popularity vote. *Miss Brazil USA* solely uses online Internet voting to select the winner by a popularity vote. Each voter is only permitted one vote for his/her favorite candidate. To vote, visit the website, and click on "voting by the Internet." At the *Miss Brazil USA* pageant, in 2010, voting began on November 15th and continued until November 19th, when the live contest was held. The online voting system was developed for the pageant by *VejaTV.com*.

Voting Guidelines

Miss Universe announced on its *Facebook* page, on August 17, 2011, that, for the first time in the history of the pageant, it was incorporating a global fan vote that might automatically advance a candidate to the Semifinals. Fans who resided in represented countries would be able to vote online at *Miss Universe's* website or at *NBC.com*. View *Miss Universe's* Online Voting Guidelines. These guidelines include: Fan Vote FAQs, how they can vote, how many times they can vote, how the votes are tabulated, how much it costs to vote, why a voter's information is collected, how that information is stored, how they can find out the results, Voting Rules, and Disclaimers.

New Zealand's *Miss Auckland* voting guidelines include:

> Only ONE vote per IP address is allowed to help keep the results as accurate as possible. This means one vote per computer. If you are voting from an office, your computers likely share an IP address. If someone else at your office voted, you cannot vote from there anymore. In this case we recommend

voting from your home computer and mobile phones.

Some pageant officials allow voters unlimited votes while others only allow one. *Miss USA* permits a total voting amount of ten times per e-mail address per day, and up to ten times per originating phone number via text message per day. Any additional votes attempted to cast above these limits (or votes cast outside of the voting window) would NOT be counted as valid.

Therefore, producers reserve the right to disqualify, block, or remove any votes for any reason, including those votes from individuals who vote by any electronic, mechanical, or automated means, or otherwise tamper with the vote process. In fact, voters receive a confirmation text for each valid text vote; therefore, only votes received in a valid voting window are counted. *In Search of the World's Most Beautiful Woman* includes a cheating disclaimer regarding text votes. Furthermore, the Contest Rules states that official contestants are prohibited from creating Judge Accounts, and they are forbidden to create duplicate Contestant Accounts. Only one Contestant Account per person is permitted.

Online Voting Works in Different Ways

To take part in the online voting for Russia's *Miss Atom International Beauty Contest*, a voter must enter his/her personal email address in the special field on the right side of the screen. An e-message with a link for entering the system would instantly be delivered to this address. Online voting will occur as follows: The voter makes his/her own Rating List of five contestants. Each official contestant will score one point if put on each individual Rating List. The voter can, at any point of time and for an unlimited number of instances, change his/her individual Rating List by adding or removing candidates. A total number of points scored by the selected candidates will change accordingly.

Contest Administration reserves the right to warn and withdraw a candidate from the voting process in the following cases: 1) attempts of forced adding of points (by placing links to the Questionnaire in chats and webcasts; by voting with the use of software and computer technologies; and by creating fake, one-time mail-boxes, including corporate/group ones, etc.); 2) calls to vote for a particular candidate or links to the Questionnaire placed in social networks, dating websites, live journals, blogs, etc.; and 3) posting, through contact lists of social networks, web-messengers, links to the Questionnaire, or calls to vote for a particular candidate.

Miss Teen Australia includes Internet Voting Judging for its *People's Choice* award. This is an opportunity for the general public to voice their opinion on who should be in the Top 10 National Finals. The People's Choice winner receives a Wildcard and becomes an automatic Finalist. Learn more about the Wildcard by reading my FREE e-book *Producing Beauty Pageants: A Guide to Pageant Terminology.*

Online Voting Tips

Pageant information site *PageantsUK.com* provides a great tip for official contestants to aid them with online voting (winning) chances regarding their online photo submissions. It notes that:

> [you] may not be able to change your photo submission once it is done, so choose wisely. Make sure your image is clear and recent. Make sure you are the only person in the photo so the organizers know who you are.

Online Votes Costs

Some pageant systems include free online voting; other systems charge. *Mrs. Wisconsin United States Pageant* has online voting set up for its photogenic contest. Each vote costs $10, and voters are asked to click on "Pay Online" to vote.

Arkansas International Pageants has a Vote for Your Favorite Mrs. Contestant online voting page. To vote, click on the "Add to Cart" button, and you will be taken to its secure *PayPal* Payment Page. There is a $5 minimum vote. The quantity is the number of votes a voter wants to make, for example, a quantity of ten votes equals $10. This means that a voter can vote ten times for his/her favorite candidate. If the voter scrolls down to the bottom of the page, s/he can click on "Miss Contestants" and "Teen Contestants" and vote for them as well.

Miss Jamaica World, a Preliminary to *Miss World*, notes of its free online voting,

> Voting is free, simple, and transparent! Simply register your name and email address and verification token will be emailed to you. You must

use this voting token in order to vote. Tokens automatically expire after one hour, allowing you to cast another vote with the same email address. Multiple votes will be accepted but are limited to one vote per contestant per hour.

Interlinc Communications sponsors *Miss Jamaica World's* online voting, "The People's Choice Competition." It's online voting system enables fans to cast their votes by clicking on a button provided at the website under the link, "Online Voting." Furthermore, *Interlinc Communications* also offered a $10,000 gift voucher to a random voter after the pageant. It was valid towards any services at *Interlinc Communications* — a full service advertising and communications agency, and the Official Technology Sponsor, since 2000, of the *Miss Jamaica World Pageant*.

Text/SMS Message Voting

A pageant system can build an additional income stream into its business model by including Text/SMS message voting into its pageant event. Popularized in the U.S. by shows like *American Idol* and *Dancing with the Stars*, Text/SMS voting is spreading among pageants. In such voting, the audience can telephone (televote) their vote in. With such a system in place, televoting can also extend to voting by SMS text message via a cell phone. *CommerceTel*, a provider of proprietary mobile marketing technologies and solutions, in 2011, teamed up with the *Miss Universe Organization* to facilitate voting aggregation through mobile and online channels to pick a fan favorite Semifinalist for the *Miss USA* pageant while pioneering fan engagement to the event. Understand voting aggregation by visiting Vote Aggregation Methods. *Votenet Solutions*, *eBallot*, and *Scytl* are other providers of mobile marketing technologies and solutions. (*Trumpia.com*, *ipipi.com*, *openmarket.com*, *involvemobile.com*, *eztexting.com*, *bulletin.net*, *txtwire.com*, *innovativemobile.com*, *clubtexting.com*, and *qwasi.com* are other companies that may provide text voting services to fit most pageant systems' needs, including pay-per-text or toll-free text voting.)

Text Voting and Online Voting Differences

The design of text voting is different from online voting. First, both are different in terms of open/close times. Secondly, both differ in who can vote. For online voting in the *Miss USA* pageant, for example, the voter must be at least thirteen years of age, located in, and a legal citizen of, the fifty United States, the District of Columbia, or Puerto Rico. For text voting, any wireless subscriber who has access to a wireless device capable of two-way messaging and is located in, and a legal resident of, the fifty United States, the District of Columbia, or Puerto Rico, may vote. View *Miss USA's* 2011 Fan Vote FAQs, 2011 Voting Rules, and *Miss Universe's* 2012 voting instructions.

Miss Africa Belguim gives the general audience an opportunity to send SMS to a short code that is unique to individual candidates. This means that a person can vote via SMS to have their say in who should be crowned *Miss Africa Belgium!* The telecommunication service providers that *Miss Africa Belgium Beauty Pageant* uses include BASE, Mobistar, and Proximus.

Many pageants are including text voting into their event. *Miss Teen Bermuda* is one of the latest to introduce text voting into its pageant — at least for two components. Bermudians can send a text message to vote for their favorite candidate in her quest to win the photogenic title. *Miss Teen Bermuda* features candidates from twelve countries, so it's smart to include text voting for its photogenic component. The candidate receiving the most number of text messages with the code P441 is awarded the Miss Photogenic title. The candidate receiving the most number of text messages with the code W441 is awarded the title of "Most Likely to Win the Competition." The remaining portion of the pageant is voted by a panel of judges.

The popular online beauty pageant *Face of Zimbabwe* partnered with *Enerco, Ltd.* to introduce text voting for the Finals. The move was expected to provide a second and alternative voting platform for the pageant. According to one of the pageant organizers,

> Voting by text will supplement online votes, especially for voters with no access to the Internet. We have partnered with a Value Added Services (VAS) company, *Enerco*, based in Zimbabwe, to launch and manage our mobile/cell phone/SMS

voting and content download services. Initially, this will be launched in the UK, USA, and South Africa, with the hope of bringing the service to Zimbabwe in the near future.

Voters had the option of voting online on the website or by text voting. But in order to safeguard against multiple votes, voters were required to register to cast their votes. Voting by text was open to voters in South Africa, UK, and USA. Voters could vote for their choice by texting FOZ followed by the name of the person they were voting for. For example, to vote for *Miss January* Kaya Chipungu, a voter needed to text "FOZ KAYA" to the following numbers: United Kingdom, text vote 68899; USA, text vote 23333; and South Africa, text vote 38355. Negotiations were under way to acquire voting shortcodes for several other countries.

To take part in the SMS voting for Russia's *Miss Atom International Beauty Contest*, each voter could add extra points to the candidates by sending a SMS with a candidate's sequential number to a short phone number. For Russian Federation-based voters, the message to number 1320 should start with the prefix atom followed by a sequential number (without space) of the candidate (which could be found on the right side of the pink patch on its voting page). For example, to support the candidate number 999, a voter should send a message like this: atom999. In this case, the candidate would score one point. The voter had the right to send several SMS messages with sequential numbers of different candidates; however, one voter could not vote for the same candidate more than once. Repeated SMS messages voting for the same candidate was not scored. On the left side of the screen, the "Contest Leaders" listed twenty candidates who were leading as a result of the summation of individual ratings won and SMS voting, showing their current points scored. The "Contest Leaders" were updated every twenty minutes. The three candidates who scored the highest number of points resulting from the sum of the online and SMS voting after eighteen hours (Moscow time), on June 9, 2011, were declared the winners of the *Miss Atom 2011 Beauty Contest*. The first place winner was awarded a one-week vacation to the fabulous beaches of Rio de Janeiro; second place received an exotic vacation to a Vietnamese resort; and third place won a luxurious week vacation at Anatolia seaside.

Open/Close Dates and Times

State, in writing, the days and times text voting will begin and end. _Teen Queen UK_ started its February 2012, pageant text voting at 12 p.m. on February 11th, and ended it at 11:30 p.m. on February 29th. For the month of March, votes started at 12:00 p.m. on March 1st, and ended 11:30 p.m. on March 15th. Any votes that were placed before or after these times "may still be charged but will NOT be counted." The pageant provided a voting help desk telephone number. The two winners for this heat were announced online and competed in the live 2012 Finals in London.

So, how often does _Teen Queen UK_ run these online Heats? Each month 100 girls — many scouted by pageant Contestant Recruiters — appear on the pageant website during that month, where they participate in a public text vote. People wanting to vote are requested to text the abbreviation TP or TQ followed by the two digit number of the candidate they want to vote for to 81319. To vote for candidate number one in the _Teen Princess_ category, text TP01; for candidate number one in the _Teen Queen_ category, text TQ01. As of this writing, text votes were charged 75p plus standard network charge. Additional information regarding UK heats can be found in my FREE e-book _Producing Beauty Pageants: A Guide to Pageant Terminology._

UK's _Miss Fresh Teen Model_ runs its public online voting in four-week intervals for every heat they run. From that one online heat and public vote, the pageant will shortlist six girls with the highest number of votes into the Finals judging round. (That one online heat was winnowed from a longer list that has been deemed suitable for the Finals. Other heats' shortlisted winners follow suit.) Text votes cost 50p plus standard network rate. From the six shortlisted contestants, _Miss Fresh Teen Model_ judges will select one winner from each online heat who will go forward to the _Miss Fresh Teen_ Photo Finals at the _Fresh Academy._ Additional information about shortlisting can be found in my FREE e-book _Producing Beauty Pageants: A Guide to Pageant Terminology._

If the public vote winner doesn't win the Photo Finals heat, she will then go through the Miss Popularity round of _Miss Fresh Teen._ This is an exclusive online competition for the winners of each photo heat. It basically gives a girl another chance at the _Miss Fresh Teen_ Finals, should she not be chosen as the winner. The pageant organizers will also choose Wildcards from the heat to go through to the Wildcard Round — another opportunity for a contestant who pageant organizers think has modeling potential.

More information on Wildcard Rounds can be found in my FREE e-book, *Producing Beauty Pageants: A Guide to Pageant Terminology*.

How Official Contestants Find Text Voters

When Abigail was scouted to participate in the *Teen Queen UK* pageant, little did she know that she'd be in a heat that required text votes if she had any chance at securing her place in the London Finals. Up against forty-nine other girls in her division, only two girls with the most text votes would go to the Finals. So, Abigail placed a press release about her plight in this issue of the *Tamworth Herald*. Sisters who competed in the *Mini Miss UK Beauty Pageant* had their text-voting plight featured in the *Lancashire Evening Post*. At the very end of the release, readers learned they were able to text vote for the sisters and were given the text codes to do so.

Text/SMS Message Votes Costs

Miss USA Top Model charges .99 cents per text vote. Pageant organizers remind official contestants to inform their voters of this charge. They also place a disclaimer in its marketing material stating, "*Miss USA Top Model* or [its] Affiliates will not refund or be responsible for any vote charges. No exceptions." *Miss Teen Queen UK* texts are 75p plus the caller's standard network charge (calls from mobiles may vary). Each text vote for the *Miss London* pageant is 60p plus the standard network rate. A landline vote for *Miss Universe Wales* cost £ 1.02; via SMS/text, £1 plus standard network charge. *Liverpool ECHO Baby of the Year* charges 25p per text vote plus standard message rate. Five pence from each call and text goes to the ECHO's charity Liverpool Unites. UK's *Miss Earth* charges 60p plus standard network charge, per text. *Miss Atom International Beauty Contest* SMS message cost for the Russian Federation was 25.00 RUR, VAT included.

Ticket Voting by Audience

Miss Africa Belgium permits the audience to partake in pageant voting in a unique way. A VVIP ticket purchased will be entitled to two votes of the ticket bearer's choice. The cost of a VVIP ticket is

€100 (a VVIP ticket holder enjoys the comfort of prestigious seating, a bottle of wine or champagne, and a chopped meat).

A VIP ticket purchased entitled a single vote of the bearer's choice. The cost of a VIP ticket is €60 (a VIP ticket holder also enjoys the comfort of prestigious seating, a bottle of wine or champagne, and a chopped meat).

A normal ticket entitled a purchaser to a single vote of the ticket bearer's choice. The cost of a normal ticket is €20 (a normal ticket holder enjoys the comfort of a good seat.)

Public Online Voting

More and more pageant officials are incorporating public voting into their pageant systems. _Miss Kentucky_ introduced _Kentucky's Choice_, in 2012, a chance for two of the Top 12 Semifinalists in the _Miss Kentucky's Outstanding Teen_ pageant to be determined by public voting. Anyone wanting to vote could visit _Kentucky's Choice_. Votes cost $1 each, and people could vote as many times as they wanted to. The two candidates with the most votes were named as _Kentucky's Choice_ winners. They would compete among the Top 12 Semifinalists on the final night of the _Miss Kentucky Outstanding Teen_ pageant. Public voting created a huge income stream for the pageant while offering the public a chance to participate at a reasonable cost.

Chapter 18

Pageant Boutique

Are you a pageant with big numbers? Do you have large candidate entries and an even bigger audience? If so, you have the potential for a major income stream by selling pageant paraphernalia at your pageant boutique or bling table. When candidates and their families are at a pageant event for a week (or weekend), they want to shop in a pageant boutique — *everyday*.

Huge Income Stream Potential

What if you had around 800 official contestants in your National pageant and nearly 6,000 attendees, as did <u>National American Miss</u>, in 2014, at its National event? What if you had those same numbers in most of your State pageants, as often does NAM, at its nearly forty NAM State pageants? You have the potential for having thousands upon thousands of people visiting your pageant boutique — in *each of your State and National pageants* — and each spending about one hundred dollars, and often more! A great number of those people want to purchase pageant paraphernalia, emblazoned with your pageant logo, for their pageant girls, siblings, and/or granddaughters. This would represent a HUGE income stream for you — not to mention FREE advertising for your pageant when recipients wear your pageant-logoed products!

But also be forewarned: Many people find it tacky to see a bling table filled with *extremely overpriced* sashes, tiaras, t-shirts, sweats, costume jewelry, etc. Be smart when pricing pageant paraphernalia. No pageant is *Disneyland*! And, of course, have fun naming your pageant boutique. <u>Miss Colorado</u> named its pageant boutique *Bippidi Boppidi Boutique*! It didn't, however, feature *Disneyland* prices!

Manufacturers for Your Pageant Products

You can take advantage of a huge profit margin if you find the right suppliers for your pageant boutique products. Say you want products to sell pageant paraphernalia at your pageant boutique and online store. You can begin by finding manufactures in the U.S. 4imprint USA sells a vast line of wholesale products that can feature a pageant's logo. Product ideas include, but are not limited to, Chi Chi Mini Tote, emery boards, nail file on a key tag, flavored lip balm, cosmetic bag, travel bag, microfiber cosmetic bag, vanity case, Cosmo Bag, stress ball (that releases spa-like scents), manicure set, diva mirror, *Charlotte Cosmetic Case*, compact silicone mirror, and a jewelry organizer. View these logo-imprintable items for your own product ideas. Be sure to visit all five pages to see the complete line of products. If you request to see samples before placing an order, some will be sent to you. Simply click on "request a free sample" on any product page. Moreover, you will receive free logo prep and design help on every item *4imprint* sells. *4imprint* can also be found in Canada, Ireland, and the UK.

You can also contact manufacturers in China. Beijing Ting Dance Co., Ltd. goes beyond dance products: backpacks, tote bags, and yoga pants. Imagine the free advertising your pageant company would get with your pageant logo emblazoned on the back of candidates' yoga pants? Shenzhen City Da Rong Xing Technology Co., Ltd. makes silicone cell phone cases, silicone handbags, slap watches and bracelets. Guangzhou Diqi Clothes Co., Ltd. makes t-shirts, sweatshirts, and more; and last, but not least, Pimpa (Fujian) Shoes & Clothing Co., Ltd. makes bags, clothes, and adornment. All of these companies are suppliers for top U.S. pageant companies. While these are only some product examples that these companies produce, most will customize your order. If you want to find a supplier from China, Alibaba's Industry Sourcing Specialists can help you find your match.

Pageant Jewelry Wholesalers

Glamour Goddess Jewelry, a U.S. based rhinestone costume jewelry manufacturer at super low prices, is located in Boca Raton, Florida. GGJ features a line of pageant jewelry, pageant pins, and pageant tiaras that you can sell in your pageant boutique. If you want a stash of quality crown rings to market in your pageant boutique, visit Queen's Choice. You will find crown rings for all ages and pageant systems. While Queen's Choice might not be a wholesaler, a discount might be given for large quantities. Check out its "There She Is" ring featuring Aurora Borealis (AB) stones, worn by candidates in the Miss America and Miss America's Outstanding Teen programs. Its classic beautiful Crown silver ring that replicates the look and feel of the Miss USA State crowns are popular with official contestants competing in any state or national pageant. If you need further assistance on your order, email Queen's Choice at queenschoice@hotmail.com, or call (304) 296-3294. Rhinestone Jewelry Corporation wholesales crown pins, stars, and hearts — and a whole lot more. CB Flowers & Crafts sell mini rhinestone tiaras. They measure approximately 1 ¼" to 1 ¾" tall and 2 ¾" wide. Perfectly small and delicate, mini tiaras are great for decorations, young girls, pageant party favors, or doll play. Available in 50 different styles, these mini rhinestone tiaras come in a pack of 12, each selling for $25.20. Wholesale crown rings sold by piece or lot can be found at AliExpress.

Income Stream from T-Shirts

National American Miss has the pageant t-shirt market cornered. Not only are official contestants required to purchase a t-shirt as part of the State pageants' Opening (Production) Number for a "nominal" $40, NAM also introduced a Spirit Competition, in 2011, in which it was optional for official contestants to purchase yet another NAM t-shirt. Noted a NAM pageant parent, seemingly referring to a NAM State pageant:

> [Girls] are divided into teams and encouraged to buy another NAM t-shirt (for $10) to show their team unity, by wearing a specific color t-shirt representing their team. [53]

Imagine the profit generated by having nearly every one of your 500+ official contestants purchase a $10 t-shirt for a Spirit Competition (generating about a $5,000 income stream), at each

---

[53] "Cha-Ching $$ or the Real Thing—You Decide." National American Miss—Scam? December 6, 2011. http://www.national-american-miss-scam.com.

of your State and National pageants! If you have about forty State pageants, that would be about a $200,000 combined income stream! (It's not clear if National official contestants were/are "encouraged" to also purchase a $10 t-shirt to show team spirit.)

This doesn't even factor NAM t-shirts sold during pageant week or weekend at its various State and National pageants' NAM Boutiques, NAM t-shirts sold at the online NAM *Prep Sportswear* store, NAM t-shirts sold for the State pageants' Opening Number, and a SECOND $40 "Opening Number outfit" t-shirt sold to the *same* girls because the first one became sweaty and smelly during rehearsals at the candidates' respective State pageant! After all, NAM State candidates are *also* required to wear their Opening Number t-shirt in the Acting Optional, so many candidates purchase a second $40 Opening Number t-shirt because, after all, they want to make their best impression in the Acting Optional competition. Multiply this by about forty State pageants, and top it with one huge National pageant, and you've about *doubled* the Opening Number "outfit" repeat sales within the same competition year.

Let's not stop at t-shirts. The nearly 700 National official contestants at the NAM National pageant, in 2012, were required to purchase an $80 Opening Number outfit (shirt with black Polyester and Spandex pants). This income stream was a cool $48,000 from (let's just factor) 600 National contestants ($52,000 if you factor closer to the actual number [650+] of National contestants for that year). View one of NAM's Opening Number outfits. The price of the Opening Number outfit NAM charges, for all age divisions at the time of this writing, was the same — $80. A supplier like *Beijing Ting Dance Co., Ltd.,* who produces stretchy dancewear products on the cheap, can help increase a pageant's profit margin.

Change the t-shirt color or style every year (as NAM seems to do for its State Opening Number outfit), and now, *alumnae* will need to purchase a new Opening Number outfit (that consists primarily of a T shirt) every year! NAM's T shirt income stream *alone* generates more money than most pageants' total official contestant entry fee intake!

Market Pageant Products

National American Miss knows how to move its merchandise out of its NAM Boutique doors. In 2011, NAM introduced a Pajama

Party at the two New York State pageants (North and South, directed by National directors Steve and Kathleen Mayes). New York NAM official contestant Chrystle noted,

> If you don't have awesome pajamas to go to the Pajama Party, [NAM sells] them at the NAM Boutique and you can purchase some there!

Moreover, NAM, in 2012, presented a fashion show at its National pageant Orientation. It featured NAM Queens modeling various products that were available for sale — a partial preview of what was to be sold in its NAM Boutique — onstage at the *Anaheim Marriott*.

What wasn't displayed at NAM's fashion show, or in its NAM Boutique, was its popular online *FREE FLY First Design Pink Crown Letter National American Miss Throw Pillow*. Young girls treasure housing such a throw pillow in their bedrooms and also having it accompany them on travel. Take every opportunity to imprint your logo on such treasured, popular products, and stock them in your pageant boutique! A U.S. company like *Zazzle* can create a customized pillow to sell in your pageant boutique.

The *International Junior Miss* crown ring, as of this writing, was marketed on its website as "Coming Soon." The *IJM Crown Ring* would be available for special order as early as 2016. Moreover, IJM featured the lovely crown ring on its website's landing page. When you click on the link, you are brought to The IJM Store. If a customer has any questions, IJM provides a Live Chat line available to answer questions during normal business hours. If the Live Chat line is closed, it is denoted "Offline." A girl doesn't need to participate in the IJM pageant to purchase this lovely ring.

Featuring unusual pageant products at your pageant boutique for parents who want to splurge is another option. *Culver Cutie* tutu bag is an upscale product to feature in a pageant boutique. Retail price is $150. The wholesaler typically earns about 40% from the retail price, which makes the wholesale price $90 per unit. Wholesale prices in large quantities can be had.

Think you need new products for your pageant boutique? *Treasured Heart Pageants* features new *and* used items in its pageant boutique. A pageant boutique provides a great opportunity to sell gently-used pageant items on consignment. Simply inform official contestants about this business opportunity, and split the profit with them!

Inform Candidates of Your Pageant Boutique

Let official contestants know at least a week prior your event, via newsletter or email, that you will feature a pageant boutique. Also, let them know what you will sell, the price, and what form(s) of payment will be accepted. This allows official contestants (and their families) an opportunity to prepare a budget and know how to pay for it. _Miss American Coed_ pageant officials remind official contestants, in a newsletter _before_ they arrive at a State or National pageant,

> [In our pageant gift shop] items, including jackets, book bags, tiaras, rings, jewelry, stickers, state finalist ribbons, banners, and bears will be available. If you wish to purchase any of these items, you must pay in cash. Prices range from $1 to $50 for these items.

Why cut impulse purchases by not accepting credit cards? Very few people plan cash purchases.

Create Demand for Pageant Products

Typical pageant bling sells. But why not layer that same old, same old by promoting, for example, a Pajama Party? Now, you have the perfect opportunity to bring in a manufacturer to create PJs and place your pageant logo right on the merchandise. PJs are a sensible buy, and even if a candidate brought her own to the pageant, by the end of the week she will likely NEED fresh PJs. This affords you a perfect opportunity to sell loads of PJs at your State and National pageant. After all, look at _National American Miss_' numbers — from every direction! But remember to have royalty model them in a fashion show during your pageant Orientation. Now, candidates are aware of your PJs merchandise. And _they_ likely have their own credit cards.

Pageant Boutique Location

Plant your pageant boutique in a high traffic area. This could be inside a hotel salon; in a meeting room off the foyer of a town theater; or even inside of the main pageant ballroom. _Universal Royalty_ featured a bling table, in 2012, inside the ballroom of its National pageant (at the _Holiday Inn Midtown_ in Austin, Texas). Pageant merchandise was sold in the same room while the pageant was being presented. Housing a pageant boutique in a spacious salon, as did _National American Miss_ at its National pageant (at the _Marriott Anaheim in Anaheim_, California), in 2012, enabled pageant officials to design an IKEA-like labyrinth. To exit the NAM Boutique, customers needed to go through the entire maze — intertwining and connecting rows of 4' x 8' tables featuring white cloths with black pleated skirts — before seeing an exit sign (near the checkout station). Moreover, the intense display of NAM merchandise warranted pageant officials to place security cameras inside the salon. (These security cameras might already have been the hotel's equipment.) Several NAM staffers manned the checkout table — equipped with a mobile merchant account attached directly onto their _iPads_!

Point-of-Sale Square Stand

If you do use an _iPad_ for mobile payments, purchase a swiveling _Square Stand_ — a special piece of hardware that transforms an _iPad_ tablet using the _Square Register_ app into a digital point-of-sale system — to replace a traditional cash register. _Square Register_ is a mobile app that turns an _Apple iOS_ or _Google Android_ device into a mobile payment system when paired with a credit card reader. The _Square Stand_ features a built-in card reader that connects to accessories such as receipt printers or bar-code scanners hardware will work on second- and third-generation _iPads_.)

Payment Options

A mobile merchant account is your solution to accepting credit cards at your pageant boutique. A credit card terminal, also known as a payment terminal or EFTPOS (electronic funds transfer at point of sale) terminal, allows a merchant to perform a transaction. With _BluePay_'s mobile merchant account services, pageant staff can accept credit cards with their cell phone, _smartphone_, or _iPhone_. If you don't want to accept credit card payments using a cell phone or _smartphone_, there are other payment acceptance solutions. _Square_, for example, will mail you a free _Mobile Card Reader_ once you sign up. With _SwitchPay_, once you are approved, your card reader will be mailed to you. Download the free _SwitchPay_ app, available in the iOS App Store, _BlackBerry_, and _Android Market_, and you can begin processing immediately through key-entered transactions. Visit the Internet to find a host of credit card terminals, _WiFi Laptop_ and _Swiper_, and accessories to prepare yourself for accepting credit cards and debit cards at your pageant boutique. If you do accept checks, _Mobilescape 5000_, available for purchase or lease, is one of many wireless terminals and printers that accept Visa/MC/AMEX/Discover/Checks Online.

Pageant Online Store

Pageant online stores can serve as headquarters for pageant directors to sell various pageant fees, early release of Pageant Program Books (PPBs), last year's PPB edition, pageant DVDs, admission tickets, pageant logoed bling, promotional sashes, and last, but not least, _used_ pageant gear. Why wait for a pageant event to sell your pageant logoed bling when you can sell it _now_ and _immediately promote your pageant_? Moreover, official contestants have an opportunity to view pageant merchandise _before_ they arrive for pageant week/weekend. Statistics show that prospective customers will view a product/ad seven times before purchasing it — "The Seven Times Factor." This presents pageant officials with an opportunity to pre-sell pageant merchandise to official contestants _before_ they sell the same products at their physical pageant boutique. Why miss a pre-sale opportunity? Even if candidates don't purchase pageant bling online, those that viewed the item (that they are contemplating on buying) six times before their pageant event arrival, are primed to purchase when they physically see the merchandise on your seventh "attempt" to put that product out in front of them — if it hasn't already been sold to them online! Besides, the more merchandise you can move through the U.S. mail, the less of it you will need to tote to your pageant event. This opens a door to bringing in yet "NEW," unadvertised merchandise to your pageant boutique. Now you are ready for impulse shoppers equipped with a credit card!

Another bonus to pre-selling at your online store is that candidates pay for the shipping. And the best perk? Those same candidates who visited your online store will inevitably purchase yet more pageant bling at your physical pageant boutique — especially any "NEW" and exciting merchandise that just became available. Put something aside for this "NEW" and exciting moment. Don't think that _National American Miss_ doesn't! Various pageant systems use online pageant stores in a variety of ways:

- _Sterling Miss Productions_ sells SMP logoed overnight bags, checkbook wallets, and cosmetic cases at its Sterling Girl Boutique.

- _Pure American Pageant_ sells PAP logoed rhinestone ornaments matching its National Queen's crown, all-rhinestones t-shirts, and glittered sweat pants at its _Zebra Boutique_.

- _Distinguished Young Women_ sells DYW logoed coffee mugs with built-in spoons, umbrellas, and Jump Drive Bracelets at its DYW online store. Be sure to visit both pages of its online store to view all of its pageant bling.

- _USA National Miss_ sells UNM logoed laptop decals, car vinyl decals, popular crown fleece headbands, embroidered towels, fleece scarfs, custom autograph cards, custom car magnets — even _koozies_! Be sure to visit both pages of its online store.

- _America's National Teenager_ sells ANT logoed stainless steel travel mugs, tote bags, and mousepads at its online store, powered by _cafepress_.

- _Arkansas International Pageants_ sell pageant fees, admission tickets, and some logoed pageant bling at its online store.

- _Mrs. America_ sells only two items at its online store: pageant DVDs and PPBs. This would be the perfect opportunity for pageant officials to be prepared to harvest the synergy that, say, logoed drink coasters could generate — both as an income stream and a promotional vehicle. Why miss that ride?

- _American Royal Beauties_ sell various items at its online store, including People's Choice Award votes, various Optionals fees, and Vendors' Booth Rental fee. Moreover, it reminds official contestants that its pageant store will be on site, during pageant weekend, with lots of fabulous logoed pageant merchandise to purchase!

- *Face of the Globe* sells at its online store FOTG logo adult onesies, promotional sashes, and Annabelle's Wigs (in a large selection of hair pieces from ¾ and full wings to clip-in extensions and ponytails). You don't need me to tell you that hair extensions are one of pageantry's best kept secrets! Be sure to click on "Visit Site" to view its entire wig and hair extensions collection.

- *The Glass Slipper Natural Beauty Pageant*'s Pageant Resale Shop sells lightly used pageant gowns, cocktail dresses, Talent outfits, interview dresses, jewelry, Check-In outfits, purses, shoes, swimsuits, etc. *The Glass Slipper Natural Beauty Pageant* officials provides this service not only to its pageant girls, but to anyone wanting to list pageant merchandise for FREE at its Glass Slipper Pageant Resale Boutique. To learn about posting new and pre-owned pageant items, visit the boutique's FAQ, and then its "How to List Tutorial."

Pageant Online Stores are Not Just for Bling Products

Visit *Miss American Coed* pageant's online store for a unique take on an online pageant store. Then, click on "Index." You will find three pages of pageant business products, listed alphabetically, for sale. For $10 you can purchase "Eveningwear, Interview, and Interview Comments" from page one's offering; for $99 you can purchase "National Pageant Rapid Release Upgrade" from page two's offering; and for $5 you can "Send a Text Shout Out to the Stream!" from page three's offering. Family and friends who are unable to attend the National pageant can purchase a "Shout-Out" — a twenty-word, custom message announced by the pageant emcee while the candidate is on stage. MAC National candidates can also purchase their own National pageant Shout-Out to thank their personal sponsors.

Also available for sale are "Stream Text Shout-Outs." For a Thursday Stream Text Shout-Out, it costs $10; for a Friday Stream Text Shout-Out, $15; and for a Saturday Stream Text Shout-Out, $20. These Stream Text Shout-Outs are "pre-recorded" and displayed on MAC's *UStream* live video during its National pageant. With over 400 National candidates in the *Miss American Coed* National pageant, in 2012, if 400 official contestants purchased Stream Text Shout-Outs for all three *UStream* days, the pageant gained an additional $18,000 income stream. MAC has been realizing this income stream, since 2006, when it introduced Stream Text Shout-Outs. This is entirely possible, if you suggest and factor grandparents booking day one; parents booking day two; and candidates booking day three (to thank personal sponsors). MAC's Thursday Stream Text Shout-Outs are announced during Eveningwear Preliminaries for each candidate's age division; Friday Stream Text Shout-Outs are announced during its Optionals contests; and Saturday Stream Text Shout-Outs are announced during the Finals. Learn how you can turn your Optionals into one of your biggest income streams by reading my book *Producing Beauty Pageants: Optionals*.

One of many smart items offered on MAC's online store include its fifteen "State Pageant Sponsor Payment" options, ranging in price from $25 to $375. If a sponsor wanted to pay for the National sponsorship fee, for example, all that s/he would need to do is bypass the Index and click on "National Queen Sponsor Fees." S/he is offered various National sponsor payment options in amounts ranging between $10 and $600. If a sponsor wanted to pay only $75 of the $375 State sponsorship fee, s/he would click on "State Pageant Sponsor Payment $75." This motion takes him/her to a Checkout page, or s/he can click on "PayPal" if s/he prefers that method of payment. If a sponsor wanted to pay the full $375 State sponsorship fee, a payment option is available for that purchase, so is the one for MAC's parallel $600 Victory National pageant. In fact, the price of everything related to the MAC State and National pageant is listed at this online pageant shop — including a variety of State and National Pageant Program Book (PPB) advertising payment options. You can even purchase PPBs, for $25, from previous years' pageants (for any of MAC's six age divisions) remaining inventory.

Additionally, *Miss American Coed* also arranged with *CafePress* to sell their "Personalized Contestant Logo Gear Setup" item at MAC's website online store. Once purchased, official contestants were able to customize products that they purchase at *CafePress* — hoodies, mugs, stuffed bears, jackets, totes, magnets, stickers, and throw pillows — to include the pageant's company name and logo. To activate this service, MAC candidates would visit this link. Then, click on "Index." Next, visit page three and click on "Personalized Contestant Logo Gear Setup." Candidates would need to pay a $15 setup fee. This enables them to begin customizing pageant MAC paraphernalia at the *CafePress* online store.

Fulfillment Pageant Online Stores

Prep Sportswear is the leading online retailer for team markets. They exclusively produce and fulfill orders. If you visit National American Miss' online store at *Prep Sportswear*, you will find the National American Miss Pageant Women's ¾-Sleeve T-Shirt (3577) for $27.99. It is available in nine color choices with forty-four design choices (each at an additional $1.99). You will also find t-shirts in short and long sleeves, Polo shirts, outerwear, warm-ups, sweaters, flannel pajamas, eco-Heather pants, bathrobes, backpacks, duffel bags, towels, hand towels with grommets, scarves, blankets, and baby products, just to name a few. Discounts are offered on bulk orders. Visit *Prep Sportswear* to find out how you can feature your pageant logo on such products.

Cash Boxes

You will need a cash box at every point-of-purchase location. An array of cash boxes can be found online with a Google search. Once set up with cash boxes, make change in each. Be sure to include plenty of one's, five's, and a few ten's — at least to start. If you have a pageant boutique, include various rolls of coins to make coin change.

Cash Bags

You will need cash bags to transport your cash. Visit BankSupplies to view various options. Since a key can be lost, purchase cash bags featuring combination locks.

Cash Management Procedure

Have a *secure* cash management procedure in place so you won't experience what the late George Scarborough, producer of Miss American Coed, experienced at one of his mid-'80s National pageants. George shared his story with me about the time that it happened. I include his never-been-told story in my book *Producing Beauty Pageants: Sponsorship Entry Fee*. For suggestions on cash management procedures, visit All About Financial Management in Business. Take every measure to insure your safety — and that of your money — during your cash-heavy pageant event so that you won't experience what happened to the late George Scarborough!

Vendor Booths

Girls participating in National pageants expect to find vendor booths, if not pageant boutiques. Before you commit to any vendor, find out your pageant venue's sublease policy. You will need to know what can and cannot be sold at your pageant venue *before* you commit to subleasing to any vendor. Prepared foods, i.e., a bakery vendor booth, might *not* be permitted. Will electricity be available for booth vendors? If so, will there be an additional charge?

Finding Vendors

Begin by obtaining a copy of *Pageantry Magazine*, *Glitzy Girl Magazine*, and *Pageant Girl Magazine* and sending your booth information to all the pageant vendors listed in the magazines. Next, approach hair and nail companies in the area that your pageant will take place. Offer them rental booth space to sell to official contestants wanting to use its services. Announce your vendor booths on Facebook, as did the *Little Miss Capital City* pageant. *Little Miss Capital City* pageant secured purse, jewelry, hat, beauty, health, and even household vendors! *Regal Princess Pageant* invited vendors to add their names to its pageant vendor list (at the bottom of its homepage). There were twenty-eight vendors at the *Universal Miss and Master International* pageant, in 2007, who signed up on its website page! However you find vendors, never duplicate them *unless* you have a huge number of official contestants who require you, then, to secure additional hair, nail, makeup, and tanning vendors. And, if you are securing duplicates, let them know in advance which duplicate vendors will be at the pageant. Do this *before* prospective vendors apply.

Pricing Vendor Booths

Southern Elite Pageants booth prices include one rectangular table for full pageant day, $100; two rectangular tables for full pageant day, $175; and three rectangular tables for full pageant day, $250. They charge a flat fee of $100 for hair, makeup, and tanning vendors. Furthermore, vendor links are listed on the pageant website. All vendor fees are to be paid prior to pageant day. Hair, makeup, and tanning vendors need to pay well in advance if they want to have their links included on the pageant website. Payment for official vendor booths can be made via *PayPal*, through the pageant website under "Payments," or by making a check payable to *Southern Elite Pageants* and mailing it to the pageant organization. *Universal Royalty National Pageant* sells booth space for $500.

Getting a Cut of the Vendor Booth Action

Will you charge for booth space at your pageant? Will you charge a percentage of sales? Or, will it be a combination of both? Maybe you have an option to, say, bring in a pageant photographer to your event. This photographer could be bartered for other areas of your pageant business as well, in exchange for him/her being the "Official Pageant Photographer." Understand how this works by reading my book *Producing Beauty Pageants: Brokering a Pageant through Barter*, Chapter 9, "In-Kind Sponsors" under "Photographer." Anyone who runs a booth at your pageant could be disposed to paying a pageant producer a percentage of his/her sales, if you know how it works.

Vendor Application

You will need to supply a Vendor Application registration form to prospective vendors. This should include your pageant contact information, a cell number of a pageant official who will be working the pageant, the location of the event, and the phone number of the location event. Then, on the application part, the vendor will include his/her business/organization name, detailed description of vendor type/products, Informational: Type of information that will be displayed, primary (and secondary) contact name, his/her position within the company, seller's permit number, Tax ID number, physical address, email (and another email repeat, to make sure that both match), website, cell and office phone number, the number of tables s/he requires, and if s/he requires electricity.

Be sure to include a Limited Liability Waiver and signature line. Include a "Vendor Rules and Regulations Information Form" with the Vendor Application. Information you would have on this form include setup and arrival time, a notation that vendors are required to pay a cleaning fee (if applicable), a notation that it is the vendor's responsibility to collect and report sales tax, a notation that vendors managing a booth need to be over the age of eighteen, and so on.

What will you charge for booth rentals? *Miss Plus America* charges, for its week-long pageant, $50/day each for Tuesday, Wednesday, and Thursday; $75/day on Friday; and $100/day on Saturday. Vendors can choose any or all days. Note how you will accept payment and your Refund Policy.

Miss Southeast U.S. of America Pageant Expo Contractual Vendor Agreement indicates a vendor's level of participation: $200 for booth rental only; $125 for half page Pageant Program Book (PPB) advertisement (black and white); $200 for full page PPB advertisement (black and white); $275 for booth rental and half page PPB advertisement (black and white).

PCI Pageant Expo's five-page Vendor Packet includes an introductory letter; Vendor Guidelines; Vendor Agreement; and a page of sponsors, partners, supporters, and participants' logos.

Miss Plus America's Vendor Application can be found here, on its Sponsor Page. Here is the direct link for its 2015 Vendor Application. The application asks vendors if they would like to purchase an advertisement in the PPB, and if so, in what size and cost. Moreover, vendors are asked if they want to become an Official Sponsor by donating marketing items they would like to donate to the delegate gift bags. If they require electricity, they are to provide a detailed explanation of the equipment they will use. Last, but not least, vendors are to write a detailed description of the items they will be selling at the booth.

Pageant Resources

The hyperlinks in this print version can be accessed at the e-book version of the same title within the *Producing Beauty Pageants* series.

Beauty Pageant News

Pageantry Magazine

Tiara Magazine

Glitzy Girls Magazine

Pageant Pages

Pageant Girl Magazine

Pageant Girl (UK)

Miss Pageant (UK)

Quinceañera Magazine

Pageant Examiner

American Model Magazine

Beauty Pageant News

MISScellanea

Missosology.Org

PageantCast

Pageant Talk Radio

Multi-Resource Center

The Glitzy Crown Pageant Pages

Pageant Center

The Great Pageant Community

PageantsUK.com

The Pageant Planet

Pageant Junkies

Pageant Junkies (Twitter)

Turn for the Judges

Pageant Emporium Digest

Pageant Authority

Model and Talent Zone: Pageant Resources

Ask the Crown

Chinese Pageant Page

Wholesale Crown Companies

Rhinestone Jewelry Corporation

Wholesale Crowns

PeacockStar

Wholesale Pageant Crowns

Jingling Crown

YiWu Home of Crowns Co., Ltd

Spirit Mall

Tiara Connection

Retail Crown/Scepter Companies

Dina, Inc.

Shindigz

Queen's Choice

Anderson's

Holly Hardwick Crowns

The Best Crowns

Secret Sparkles **(UK)**

Diva Designs USA

Ejools.com

Crown Masters

Allens Crown & Trophy

Premier Crowns & Trophies (available by email at any time for emergencies)

Crystal Crown, Inc.

Tiara Town

Rainbow's End

The Glitzy Crown

Alabama Crowns

Pageant Photography

Robert Goold Photography (*Producing Beauty Pageants* series cover photographer)

togally (a place to find ratings, reviews, and portfolios before hiring a photographer)

Sash Manufacturers

From Wishes to Stitches Embroidery (cinderellagrammy@swbell.net) (plush sash featured on the cover of my *Producing Beauty Pageant* series)

Royalty Sash Company

KD Creations

Banners Plus

The Glitzy Crown

LadyBug Designers

Rainbow's End Sashes

Holly Hardwick Crowns & Custom Sashes

The Sash Out

Sash Me

Graphic Designers

Photo Retouching by Courtney (cover designer of the *Producing Beauty Pageant* series)

Paper Patina Design Studio

Kelly Johnson Designs

Gratzer Graphics

PostcardMania

Atlanta Glitter Girls Graphics

Vive Designs (UK)

Pageant Graphics by Sharon

Pageant Ready Glitz N' Glitter Graphics

Crowning Glory Graphic Designs

Pageant Program Books — Design Your Way... to the Crown

99designs

PR Inc.

Social Media Expert
My Business Presence

Everything for Competition

Dazzles Pageant & Prom (original red gown featured on the cover of the *Producing Beauty Pageants* series; all other colors were manipulated by *Photo Retouching by Courtney*)

Everything for Pageants

Pageant Resale

TexasPageantScene

*Ashley Rene's Prom * Pageant * Bridal*

Joyce's Boutique—The Pageant Room

The Ritz

The Pageant Boutique—UK's Prom and Pageant Specialists

Pageant Calendars
Brittanys Beauties

Pageant Center—Pageant Calendars

Illinois Pageant Calendar

Texas Pageant Scene

Pageant Blogs

Pageant Stars USA

Ask the Crown

Pageant Pages

Normannorman.com

Amanda Beagle Blog

Clap for the Crown: The New Pageant Blog

Love That Max Special Needs Blog

Pageant Stars USA Blogspot

The Sisterhood of the Crown

Pageant Consultants and Coaches

The Pageant King—Bill Alverson

Pageants 2 Go

Pageant Coaching—The Pageant Planet

Pageant Page Consultants

PR Pageant Coaches

Sashes and Crowns Pageant Coaching

Pageant Prep

Pageant Professors

Heather Noelle Davis—Pageant Coach PhD

Haggerty & Associates—We Produce Winners

Professional Pageant Preparation, LLC

Image & Pageant Consulting—Wendi Russo

Jodi's Voice & Pageant Coaching

Pageant Coaching and Consulting

Hailey Best Pageant Coaching

Crown Me Pageant Coaching

Palm Beach Etiquette Pageant Coaching

Amanda Beagle Pageant Coaching

Moore Image Consulting

Be Beauty Marked

Pageant Coaching with Shiemicka LaShanne

Lauren Parkes—Speaker & Pageant Coach

Integrity Pageant Coaching

Elaine Swann Lifestyle & Etiquette Expert

Capture the Crown by Kayla Wharton

Allure Coaching by Christine

Michelle Jones Pageant Coaching

Faith Schway Pageant Coaching

Pageantry by Chris

Carolina Reyes—Pageant Life Coach

The Pageant Place—Kim Gravel

Tiffany Ogle—Pageant & Entertainment Coaching

Shelly the Pageant Coach

Michelle Field—Expert Pageant Coach

Cheri Kennedy Pageant Coach

Heather Habura Studio

Be Victorious Pageant Coaching

Professional Pageant Development

Everything for Pageants

Image Impressions Consulting

Etiquette School of Ohio

Seattle Pageant Coach

Abbie's AcroBabes Pageant Coaching

Crowned, Inc.

ALUP International

Pageant Coach—Kim of Queens

Pageant Academy

Center Stage Elite

Pageant Perfect by Raven

CrownHeadz—Choreography and Consulting

Interview Image Associates

Sarah's Winning Edge

Nicole Erwin Vocalist & Voiceover Artist Pageant Coaching

Miss Allie J Pageant Consultant

Etiquette Now!

Winning Wand Pageant Consulting

Sing Like a Star Pageant Coaching

Time for the Tiara—Pageant Consulting

B. Youneek Pageant Coaching

Rita Verreos Pageant Consultant

Feminia Miss India Pageant Coaching

Kaya Shereen Pageant Coach

Wendi Russo Image Consultant and Pageant Coach

Jolie-Noelle Beauty Pageant Coaching

Grace Fontecha Pageant Coach

The Crown Coach

Pageant Ready

Critical Beauty—Pageant & Image Consulting Services

Triple Crown Pageant Coaching

Triple Crown Trainers

Kaitlyn Bruce Pageant Coaching

True Beauty Pageant Coaching

To Coach a Queen

Dreams Unlimited Pageant & Beauty Consulting

Dawn Rochelle Pageant Coaching

Grace, Style and Etiquette Pageant Coach

Lisa Quast Pageant Coaching

Pageant Smart—From the Interview Room to the Stage!

Winning Edge Pageant Coaching

LaVogue Pageant Coaching with Krisann Lakewood

Donna's Studio—Struttin' Across the USA!

Crystals and Crowns Pageantry

Pageant Preparation by Terri Bloen

Pageant Pros—If the Crown Fits...

Fit for the Crown

Pageant Training

Legacy Group Pageant Consulting

Sparkle! With Holly Ernst

Crowning Moment—Self Enhancement Coaching

The Rhinestoned Magznolia Pageant Coaching

Megan's Team Pageant Coaching

LaTosha Maynard Dance & Pageant Coach/Choreographer

Winner Views

Talking Points

Fierce Pageant Coaching with Miss Candice

The Art of Pageantry—Comprehensive Pageant Coach

Distinct Impressions—Pageant and Image Consulting

PageantPrep

Quest for the Crown Consulting—Be Transformed into the "Total Package!"

Index

Made in the USA
Middletown, DE
15 November 2020